Cognitive Remediation Therapy for Schizophrenia

Cognitive Remediation Therapy for Schizophrenia describes the background and development of this new psychological therapy and demonstrates how it provides the first structured help to overcome the thinking problems associated with schizophrenia.

In three sections, the book covers the theoretical and empirical underpinning of cognitive remediation therapy and explores its application. Part one, 'The Development of Therapy', provides the historical context and theoretical background to the therapy and emphasises the value of the rehabilitation of cognitive deficits. In Part two, 'Improving Cognitive Processes', the process and effects of changing cognition are examined. Finally, in Part three, 'The Process of Therapy', the authors provide a clinical guide to the delivery of cognitive remediation therapy and use case examples to support its efficacy.

This book is the first to describe an individual cognitive remediation therapy programme based on a clear model of the relationship between thinking and behaviour. It will be of both academic and clinical value to all those health professionals and clinical academics who want not only to understand the relationships between thought and action but also to intervene to improve therapy.

Til Wykes is Professor of Clinical Psychology and Rehabilitation at Institute of Psychiatry, Kings College, London

Clare Reeder is a Clinical Psychologist at Oxleas NHS Trust and Honorary Lecturer at Institute of Psychiatry, Kings College, London

Cognitive Remediation Therapy for Schizophrenia

Theory and Practice

Til Wykes and Clare Reeder

 Routledge
Taylor & Francis Group

LONDON AND NEW YORK

First published 2005 by Routledge
27 Church Road, Hove, East Sussex BN3 2FA

Simultaneously published in the USA and Canada
by Taylor and Francis Inc
270 Madison Avenue, New York, NY 10016

Routledge is an imprint of the Taylor and Francis Group

© 2005 Til Wykes and Clare Reeder

Typeset in Times by RefineCatch Ltd, Bungay, Suffolk
Printed and bound in Great Britain by
Biddles Ltd, King's Lynn, Norfolk
Paperback cover design Sandra Heath

British Library Cataloguing in Publication Data
A catalogue record for this book is available from the British Library

Library of Congress Cataloging in Publication Data
Wykes, Til.
    Cognitive remediation therapy for schizophrenia : an
introduction / Til Wykes and Clare Reeder.
        p. cm.
    Includes bibliographical references and index.
    ISBN 1-58391-970-8 (hbk : alk. paper) – ISBN 1-58391-971-6
(pbk : alk. paper)   1. Schizophrenics – Rehabilitation.   2. Cognition
disorders – Treatment.   3. Cognition disorders – Patients –
Rehabilitation.   I. Reeder, Clare.   II. Title.
    RC514.W95 2005
    616.89′806 – dc22   2004027214

ISBN 1-58391-970-8 (hbk)
ISBN 1-58391-971-6 (pbk)

Contents

Figures

Tables

Acknowledgements

We have been stimulated to write this book following conversations with Alan Bellack, Will Spaulding and Morris Bell. These conversations have continued throughout the writing and we are grateful for their comments and criticisms, as well as those from Kathy Greenwood and Tony David. But putting fingers to the keyboard would not have been as easy without the aid of Geraldine Davis and Elizabeth Hutt who understand word processing more than we do and have got us out of some sticky situations.

Finally, without the forbearance of our families and their support, particularly from Bryn and Johan, we would never have made it past Chapter 1.

Part I

The development of therapy

The historical context of cognitive remediation therapy (CRT) for schizophrenia

Cognitive problems are the most obvious sign of a diagnosis of schizophrenia, but for a considerable time following the genesis of the diagnosis little attention was paid to the alleviation of these problems. The prime targets for treatments were the positive symptoms and cognitive difficulties were considered to be reduced by medication. It is only recently that both the pharmacological and psychological research communities have identified improving thinking skills as an important target. This is, in part, because several studies have now suggested that cognitive problems rather than symptoms are associated with later functional outcome.

As treatment moved from relatively supportive institutions to care within the community, the effects of functional disabilities became more prominent, particularly as these disabilities were chronic. This encouraged health services to focus attention on rehabilitation potential, which was not, of course, a new focus, but a renaissance of ideas from the eighteenth century. There have been a number of research drivers resulting from this change of focus. Increased social inclusion for people with mental health problems has now become a policy issue for mental health services all over the globe, fuelling research into the technology for achieving this goal. In order to justify expenditure on rehabilitation programmes, outcome data for an evidence base, particularly randomised control trials, are needed. This in turn illuminates the lack of clear theoretical underpinnings for these programmes.

Investigations into functional outcome have highlighted the role of cognition not only in concurrent functioning but also in the prediction of future outcome and this led to the recent concentration of efforts to enhance cognition. Two primary strategies have been adopted to provide (a) pharmacotherapy and (b) psychological therapy. For the first – medication – the effectiveness was initially seen as solely for hallucinations and delusions, but lately the additional effects of these same medications on cognition have been investigated. As yet, no specific pharmacological intervention has been advocated exclusively for the cognitive problems, but this is clearly an important avenue for future research. This process of the development of cognition-specific medication has been hindered in part by controversies over trial design and how to assess whether medication has an effect on cognition. These are currently under investigation in the MATRICS project in the USA (www.matrics.ucla.edu).

Recent advances in psychological interventions have produced a new rehabilitation technology which we will call Cognitive Remediation Therapy (CRT). The theory behind this technology is based on broad empirical findings concerning the relationships between cognition and functioning and is supported by some clinical outcome data. CRT is an umbrella expression under which there are a number of different sorts of intervention. These are mainly defined by their surface characteristics, such as use of a therapist and the types of training task used. It is harder to differentiate them on the basis of their theoretical model, as few describe one. Models that do appear tend to describe the relationships between cognition and performance (Brenner *et al.*, 1994; McGurk and Mueser, 2003) but do not indicate what the technology for changing the relationship would look like. The modelling process and the rehabilitation approaches have been influenced by approaches to the rehabilitation of traumatic brain injury. For instance, the Spaulding *et al.* (2003) model of cognitive recovery is a relatively bottom-up model with basic cognitive functions being the prime target. This is akin to some of the models of brain plasticity. This is one of the few models that could drive the technology for rehabilitation.

The aim of this book is to describe the current context for CRT, to introduce our own model that we believe can aid the future development of more effective CRT therapies and finally to describe one way of implementing the model into treatment. The model is based not only on changing specific cognitive processes but is predicated on the importance of metacognition. Metacognition here refers to the ability to reflect on your own cognitive abilities and adjust cognitive processing accordingly. So when people are aware of memory difficulties they can make adjustments, for example, use a cueing system in their diary to remind them, or try to encode information more deeply so that they are more likely to retrieve it. The main emphasis in our model is on changes in performance based not only on the development of new schemas to guide thinking behaviours such as rehearsing to-be-remembered information, but also the use of such schemas in new situations, i.e. a transfer of training. This transfer is vital if these cognitive interventions are to have a more widespread effect on behaviour than merely increasing the scores on neuropsychological tests.

Cognitive remediation is a therapy which was subject to little investigation until the 1990s, and even then it was introduced to support the hypothesis that it is impossible to teach certain cognitive operations to people with schizophrenia. The research zeitgeist at that time was that cognitive problems were a trait factor in schizophrenia related to biological changes which could not be reversed. While not yet arguing for recovery using this sort of therapy, it seems to us that undoubted improvements can be made in thinking skills with treatment. Although some have argued that simply finding improvements in thinking should be the sole outcome measure of such a rehabilitation technology, we are of the view that interventions should attempt to have an impact on functioning, particularly that which relates to social inclusion, such as employment.

All new therapies need to be justified from a theoretical and practical standpoint. This book will present evidence on the criteria for successful therapy with practical examples to aid the introduction of therapy into services. But, in addition to scientific criteria on which to judge the efficacy and effectiveness of therapy, we must also consider a new set of criteria – those fixed by consumers. Both the therapeutic target and the measurement of outcomes need their endorsement. If consumers are not included at an early stage then the likelihood of therapy being translated into practice in mental health services is seriously in jeopardy. These consumer views have also been given a high priority in guiding the development of our form of cognitive remediation therapy.

This book is designed to provide an introduction to psychologists, nurses, psychiatrists, social workers and occupational therapists to this new form of cognitive therapy, but it will also provide a guide to researchers on issues that need to be further investigated to stimulate therapy development.

Should we use syndromes, symptoms or diagnosis?

In order to design a therapy we need to define who we are talking about, and in the field of schizophrenia there are several different views of who should be included. For instance, we could take a broad view and design a therapy for anyone who experiences a single symptom of the disorder, or we could confine our therapy for those who have a specific set of characteristics (termed syndromes or diagnoses). This is an important question because it will affect not only which studies we should use as evidence but also the final scope of a health service to provide such therapy.

If we consider using the loosest definition, we must turn to epidemiological data from which it is possible to estimate how many people experience some of the symptoms of schizophrenia at some time during their life. The lifetime estimates of the occurrence of hallucinations in the community lie between 10 and 39 per cent (Johns and van Os, 2001). Although it is clear that there are different rates between different cultural groups (Johns et al., 2002), we also know that the majority of people who experience individual symptoms lead ordinary lives and do not come into contact with the psychiatric services.

Psychological researchers have often advocated the investigation of these individual symptoms rather than collections of symptoms (syndromes) or diagnostic categories because they do exist outside diagnostic categories and there is also an overlap of symptoms between different diagnostic groups (e.g. Bentall, 2003). But although agreeing with the principle of this research paradigm, it is clear that a diagnosis of schizophrenia not only picks out those people from the community whose symptoms are distressing, but there is also evidence that it confers a higher likelihood of reductions in functioning over a lifetime (van Os *et al.*, 1997). If cognitive technologies are to have the maximum impact, we feel that they should concentrate on the most disabled group of people. The majority of data on general treatment and outcome as well as cognition also relate to diagnoses. We have therefore chosen to concentrate on a categorical diagnosis of schizophrenia throughout this book. However, we will also make reference to the relationship of cognition to individual symptoms and will discuss the direct and indirect effects of CRT on these symptoms in the context of a diagnosis of schizophrenia.

The course of schizophrenia

Schizophrenia affects around 1 per cent of the population. For many of these people the effects of the abnormal perceptions and changes in beliefs are not only distressing but are also disabling. The symptoms can be episodic and disappear between episodes and some people with the diagnosis undoubtedly making a good recovery from the disorder. Follow-up studies suggest that between 27 per cent and 46 per cent never have a subsequent episode or show a good recovery between episodes (Ciompi, 1980; Shepherd *et al.*, 1989). However, since the changes in the diagnostic criteria with many countries adopting those published in the fourth edition of the American Psychiatric Association's *Diagnostic and Statistical Manual*, the probable outcomes of people with the disorder have been reduced, as briefer psychotic reactions which are associated with better outcomes are excluded. DSMIV includes criteria for the persistence of symptoms and reduction in social or work functioning of at least six months. Some argue that this has led to more pessimistic views of the outcome of the disorder.

There are different forms of a more chronic course where social functioning is reduced and interspersed with unremitting, acute or residual symptoms. These forms are estimated to occur in about 24 per cent of people with the diagnosis (Salokangas, 1983). It is this group of people who have a need for rehabilitation and support that have been the target for cognitive remediation. However, poor levels of functioning mean that a large number of people with schizophrenia need help with their living conditions in the form of specific residential care, or supportive housing and so may also find CRT beneficial. Few people are financially independent. Although estimates vary with the economic climate, and particularly the background rate of unemployment, the proportion of people with jobs who have a psychiatric diagnosis is always much lower than in the general population. The rate of employment rarely gets above 10 per cent and people with severe mental illnesses, when working, work fewer hours and generally earn less than the national average hourly wage (Cook and Razzano, 2000; Huxley and

Thornicroft, 2003). In addition, the rate of marriage or stable partnerships is lower than the general population and people with schizophrenia also report fewer close friends and supportive relationships outside the psychiatric services (Becker *et al.*, 1998)

Mapping the problem

What are the key factors to be considered if the aim is to improve cognition and its impact on the quality of life of people with schizophrenia? The first issue to map out is the actual extent of the outcome problems. Clearly, if the outcomes are uniformly poor, with little change over the lifespan, then any therapy probably needs a considerable effect size to have any consequences for functioning. The outcome data do appear pessimistic with a cursory look and this view is generally taught in psychiatric texts and was accepted in the psychiatric care community for many years. Schizophrenia was viewed as a disorder that showed a decline in functioning, particularly over the early years. But there are now data to suggest that even when the disorder is chronic, there is still room for change. For instance, Harding and colleagues have shown that good outcomes can be achieved with positive changes in aspects of functioning taking place at different times in the life course, even in a chronically disabled sample (Harding *et al.*, 1987a, 1987b). This had led to some optimism about overall outcome and more enthusiasm for recovery models and the results of rehabilitation programmes.

One could argue that if it is functioning that is to be improved then there should be a concentration on efforts to change this directly and this has been the approach to improving life skills in the past. However, it is now clear that there are a number of different factors that impede skills learning. These include cognitive difficulties which are apparent in a proportion of people with schizophrenia. As well as cognitive intervention programmes affecting cognition, they could also have a knock-on or a boosting effect on the results of life skills programmes. We will also argue that a comprehensive approach in which cognitive difficulties are taken into account in the design of the life skills programmes is the most adaptive way forward.

The model of schizophrenia that is most widely accepted is the biopsychosocial model which consists of interactions between social, biological and psychological factors. These factors may be either the vulnerability or protective factors and affect the onset, recovery and subsequent episodes of illness. Identified protections include, for example, social support, and vulnerabilities include stressful environments particularly where there is a high level of personal criticism (see Figure 1.1). John Wing (1978) suggests that primary impairments, which consist of the basic processes, secondary impairments (the personal reactions to these impairments) and society's responses, combine to produce the level of handicap. Although rehabilitation should be comprehensive and try to consider factors that lead to good or poor results, the development of this comprehensive system is likely to necessitate the identification of individual efficacious therapies that combat only one or two vulnerability factors or enhance only one or two protective factors.

The beneficial effect of any intervention is governed by traditional methodology in randomised control trials (RCTs) that emphasises a single simple outcome measure even for complex interventions. This single outcome is linked directly to the focus of therapy such as improvements in social skills following psychosocial therapy. The identification of more distal outcomes, like employment or friendships from a focused therapy often requires much larger studies for adequate statistical power. Few trials in psychosocial treatments for schizophrenia include more than 60 people in a group (Thornley *et al.*, 1998). In addition for any analysis of the mediating variables the statistical analysis will be more complex.

There is evidence that therapies affect this biopsychosocial model and do have distal effects; for example, therapy to decrease the effects of stressful family environments has an effect on admissions to hospital (Pilling *et al.*, 2002a). The psychiatric community also provides advocacy for people with psychiatric problems to reduce the effects of life events and chronic difficulties through its enhanced support. This reduces the effects of stressful experiences which occur relatively often for people who have reduced finances irrespective of any symptoms that might interfere with coping. This advocacy is clearly laid out in some of the Assertive Outreach models of care and has been shown to have effects on admissions to hospital. But what is clear from the stress-vulnerability model is that there are a variety of stress and coping responses that are dependent on the personal resources of the individual concerned. One such personal resource is thinking skill. No one in the psychiatric community would argue that this is not a basic difficulty or primary impairment associated with a diagnosis of schizophrenia. However, researchers and health professionals, although noting the importance of these cognitive difficulties, have spent little time developing therapies that could directly affect these problems.

The model shown in Figure 1.1 illustrates the development of symptoms through a complex interaction with vulnerability, resilience and stressor factors. It is clear that an intervention for cognitive skills might have an impact at several different points. It could increase processing capacity, reduce information processing overload, change reasoning biases and affect appraisals of information, given that our model of CRT aims to change metacognition. Social and occupational functioning in this symptom-focused model are affected by intrusive experiences, as well as the full blown psychotic symptoms.

We have added another point at which cognitive skills can affect social and work functioning. Cognitive skills can also have a direct link to outcome, in addition to the effects of symptoms on functioning outcomes. The cognitive

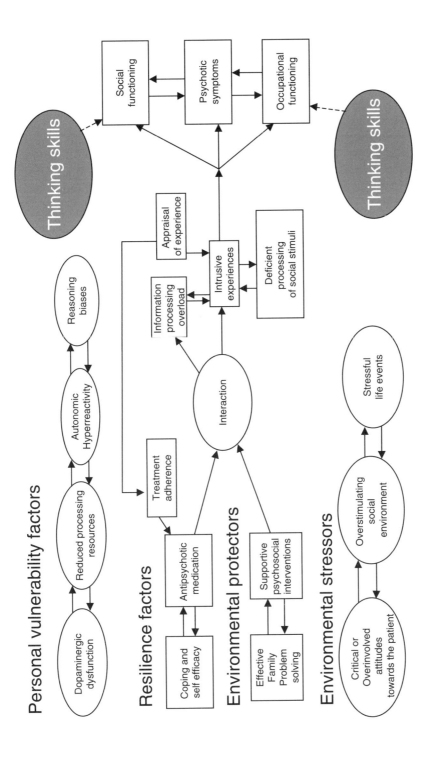

Figure 1.1 A vulnerability stress model for schizophrenia

intervention we will develop has been designed to have an impact on this direct factor as well as on the other parts of the vulnerability-stress model.

Cognition: What's in a name?

Throughout this book we have referred to cognition which differs from the term neurocognition that has been used, mainly in the USA, for the past decade. The term arose from the original thinking by Weinberger and others (e.g. Weinberger, 1988) that impaired performance on neuropsychological tests in people with schizophrenia was the result of specific lesions in the brain. Performance was relatively stable over time and did not change even after training. Therefore a very pessimistic view of rehabilitation arose for this group.

While we acknowledge that thinking processes are inextricably linked to brain functioning, we feel that the use of the term neurocognitive must imply a concentration on the biological substrate of thought and a reductionist model. We do not consider that the use of the word cognitive carries all this baggage. The change of the term is not just contrariness; we feel that its use may lead us to narrowly define the influences on thinking skills and to forget some of the advances in cognitive psychology over the past 30 years.

It is clear that cognitive skills may be influenced by a vast number of psychological factors such as motivation, personality, and affective states as well as the context in which the thinking takes place. For instance, mathematical thinking is defined by the number system in which the problem operates. Chinese has a simple syntax for numbers and only 13 different words to learn, whereas in English the same numbers require 29 number words which are longer and the syntax more irregular. It is therefore unsurprising that Chinese children learn mathematical concepts earlier, do calculations faster and remember longer lists of numbers than in English (Dehaene, 1998).

It is also clear that brain activation for a single cognitive task is influenced by many factors and can also differ depending on the way in which the task is carried out. For instance in a SPECT scan study of performance on a verbal fluency task where the object is to say as many words beginning with the same letter, different patterns of brain activation were observed depending on the thinking strategy adopted. For the person who spoke as many words as possible and made errors, the temporal lobe was highly activated, whereas for a different person who limited his output and reduced his errors then the anterior cingulate was highly activated (Wykes, 1998). Furthermore, brain activation can differ on the same task at two different times following instruction. Using fMRI, Wykes and colleagues (2002) showed differential activation in a working memory task over time in both people with schizophrenia and normal control participants.

In addition, the use of the term cognitive also has a more positive effect of allowing us to draw on the relevant cognitive psychology literature and that from educationalists. We agree with MacDonald and Carter (2002) that this is a paradigm shift. Neuropsychological assessments are useful in clinical practice but are limited for the investigation of specific cognitive processes. It is these cognitive processes that are essential to the understanding of how cognition affects outcome and how we might develop a model to improve cognition.

What are cognitive functions?

Cognitive functioning here means cognitive and metacognitive processing involved in perception, attention, memory, problem solving and planning. These thinking skills underlie all routine personal and social activities. For example, successful shopping involves a whole series of cognitive functions. First the task has to be planned, including such subtasks as writing a list, ensuring you have the money and choosing a suitable shop. Choosing items requires the perception of the item, matching it to the memory of the item on the list and, as each subgoal is attained, monitoring it for errors so that the next subtask can be engaged. Even watching a TV programme, particularly one of the soaps, requires the engagement of sophisticated thought processes. In order to understand the plot, it is essential to be able to put oneself in the other person's shoes and to understand what they may be thinking and their misunderstandings that are fundamental to an interesting storyline. These sorts of thought processes are known as social cognition and, together with other cognitive processes, affect our understanding of the social world. Metacognition, the ability to reflect on our own thoughts, also clearly has an overarching effect on the selection, use and efficiency of these information processes as well as the control of behaviours that have a direct effect on the environment and supplement or substitute for impaired information processing.

How important are cognitive difficulties?

Even though positive symptoms (hearing voices, delusions, etc.) are the most obvious indicators of the diagnosis of schizophrenia, impairments in cognition have always been at the core of the disorder. When Kraepelin first described his simplified scheme for the psychoses he identified intellectual deterioration as a key feature of dementia praecox, the forerunner of schizophrenia (Kraepelin *et al.*, 1971). Bleuler later refined this definition in terms of the positive symptoms but he too placed cognitive problems, particularly attention, as a cardinal defining criterion (Bleuler, 1950). These two authorities on schizophrenia, although not disagreeing on its key importance, did disagree on whether the cognitive problems were stable (as proposed by Bleuler) or were increasing over time (as proposed by Kraepelin).

The current evidence, provided in detail in Chapter 2, is that there is clearly a deterioration of functioning just prior to and immediately after the first episode of schizophrenia. Some of the functions seem to recover (e.g. set response shifting; Nopolous *et al.*, 1994) but other aspects of cognition remain at a lower than expected level, particularly memory function. There is a deterioration of some cognitive functions with each episode of illness, again with improvements as symptoms wane. Over the next five or six years cognitive functioning seems a little unstable but stability does emerge (Hoff *et al.*, 1999), and there are few changes over the next 20 years. Many of the inferences about stability have been based on comparing cohorts of people from different age groups. This procedure obviously has inherent difficulties because treatments and types of care have changed over the last 30 years and so cognitive outcomes may also be affected. But despite possible treatment confounds, few cognitive differences have emerged between studies of recent onset and more chronic conditions.

Difficulties in cognition are not just the result of the onset of symptoms but are evident even earlier. Indications from childhood records of children at risk who contacted the psychiatric services in childhood suggest that people who later develop schizophrenia are cognitively different even in childhood and that these cognitive difficulties do not change much over time (Russell *et al.*, 1997). An alternative approach, which essentially produces the same data, is to investigate putative cognitive precursors in a whole population of people and later compare those who developed schizophrenia to those who do not. One such birth cohort study, based in Dunedin, has shown that people diagnosed as having schizophrenia in their early twenties had cognitive development problems at each assessment stage from age 3 to 11 (Cannon *et al.*, 2001, 2002). A further study of young conscripts in Sweden investigated the later development of schizophrenia and its association with IQ. They found that even after adjusting for confounders, intellectual performance was lower for those who later developed schizophrenia and that this was particularly marked in their verbal ability (David *et al.*, 1997). A similar result was found for conscripts in Israel (Caspi, *et al.*, 2003)

But it is not just evidence from experimental studies that has suggested the importance of cognition in schizophrenia, people with the disorder also give it emphasis. They complain about memory problems and attention difficulties associated with the disorder and in a seminal paper by McGhie and Chapman (1961), patients described their own cognitive experiences of having schizophrenia. One patient's disturbance of attention was described as:

> My concentration is very poor. I jump from one thing to another. If I am talking to someone they only need to cross their legs or scratch their head and I am distracted and forget what I was saying. (p. 104)

Perception also changes with people reporting: 'Colours seem to be brighter now, almost as if they were luminous' (p. 105). There is a marked change in the process of thinking:

> My thoughts get all jumbled up. I start thinking or talking about something but I never get there . . . People listening to me get more lost than I do. (p. 108)

More recently, in a television programme (*Inside my Head*, June 2002, UK Channel 4), an adolescent called Mike, who had already had two episodes of psychosis, described his thinking difficulties. He had been studying for his examinations at age 16 and although he 'was looking at As and Bs for my exams now I'm looking at Cs and Ds'. In fact he did get reduced grades. He says, 'My concentration is a real problem' and reports on his memory difficulties. Overall he has some insight into his problem and says, 'I'm just getting used to have a learning disability.' People who have the disorder may be aware of some of their difficulties as shown above, but are unaware of others.

Even though many people do show deficits in some key areas, it does not mean that everyone with a diagnosis of schizophrenia performs below average. In the birth cohort studies even though the people who developed schizophrenia did have reduced IQs, they still overlapped with the normal population. There are also instances of people who have performed in the normal range when they have been asked to complete formal neuro-psychological testing. Palmer and colleagues (1997) showed that 27 per cent of their 171 patients performed in the normal range. There are also examples of individuals who despite having a diagnosis of schizophrenia were able to contribute significantly to society. For instance, John Forbes Nash was given the Nobel Prize for economics and even though the work was carried out prior to his first onset of psychosis he was clearly an innovative thinker. Even earlier, Dr William Chester Minor in the nineteenth century was a prolific contributor to an early version of the *Oxford English Dictionary* while being incarcerated in Broadmoor Asylum for the Criminally Insane.

Cognition therefore is a key factor in the understanding of the problems associated with schizophrenia. Given that it has been highlighted by people with the diagnosis and by clinicians, it is surprising that treatment programmes have ignored this problem area for many years. Below is a description of the historical context for the investigation of schizophrenia that might show why cognitive interventions have been so underdeveloped.

Cognition and schizophrenia during the twentieth century

The twentieth century saw a dramatic rise in the interest in cognition with a concentration on individual thinking skills such as attention, memory and problem solving. In fact in our survey of the literature on cognition up to the

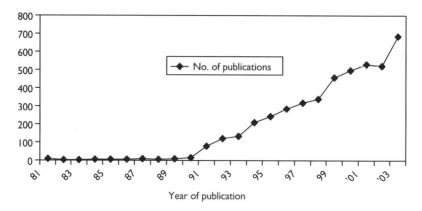

Figure 1.2 Number of studies of cognition and schizophrenia over 20 years

end of 2003 (see Figure 1.2) we found that the proportion of papers on schizophrenia in 1981 was less than 1 per cent but in 20 years the proportion had risen to 7 per cent. Although the numbers of papers on schizophrenia has increased over time, mirroring the overall interest in cognition, the types of papers have changed and various themes have emerged, sunk and then re-emerged.

Initially there was a concentration on the reasoning processes in schizophrenia that were thought to be abnormal. For instance, Arieti (1955) suggested that the concrete thinking often found in people with schizophrenia is due to their reasoning process regressing to a former childlike state. The process by which this happens was based on the psychodynamic theories of the time. As the evidence accumulated for genetic and other biological factors in schizophrenia, any theory which did not encompass these biological processes fell out of favour. In addition, there was a lack of any evidence to support the specific psychodynamic processes that were a key to Arieti's thesis. But Arieti's theory was essentially that the reasoning processes themselves were deficient and this view – but not the cause – has since been rehabilitated by some authors, notably Hogarty and Flesher (1999a) who suggest that the development of social cognition has slowed down in schizophrenia. They propose that cognition is stuck at a prepubertal level which may only become apparent when the person is required to take part in normal social roles, such as in education, marriage and work. The developmentally later forms of cognition they suggest are 'gists'. 'Social gists include the personally meaningful and abstract relational schemata, attributions and inferences, and rules and principles that underlie perspective taking and context appraisal' (p. 686). It is this last descriptive formulation which seems similar to Arieti's (1955) thesis. Arieti's theory was hampered by the lack of sophisticated experimental paradigms in which to test his hypotheses.

Although there is little evidence that the processes described in Arieti's model could be reversed or changed, Hogarty and Flesher (1999a, 1999b) do suggest the way in which therapies may have an impact (see also Chapter 7).

An alternative view of thinking processes that depends on the experience of perceptual or sensory abnormalities was emphasised by experimental cognitive psychologists. This work suggested that reasoning processes are intact. For instance, Maher (1974) proposed that a delusional individual suffers from primary perceptual anomalies that are biological in nature and an individual who is prone to experiencing these anomalies seeks an explanation through normal cognitive mechanisms. Frith (1979, 1987) elaborates on the process of abnormal percepts coming to conscious awareness which he argues triggers the attempt to explain and understand this unnatural occurrence in a similar way to Maher's approach. However, the underlying mechanism is more sophisticated. For instance, Frith suggests that feelings of alienation occur as a result of a failure to monitor internal plans (willed intentions) and the actions that are carried out. The person is unaware that an action was carried out under their own volition and therefore assumes that it was under the control of another person or force. Here again there is an emphasis on basic underlying difficulties rather than faulty logic or inferential processes.

Chapman and Chapman (1978) argue against this approach from the evidence that even when people are presented with abnormal sensations not everyone produces delusional ideas to explain them and so there must be other factors to consider. Further advocates of this view (e.g. Kaney and Bentall, 1992 and Garety and Hemsley, 1994) suggest that attributional style and other biases in thinking, such as jumping to conclusions, contribute to the formation and maintenance of delusions and both sets of authors consider that these processes might, in the absence of abnormal perceptions, produce delusional beliefs. It is this later type of model which led to the development of a new therapy for thinking – cognitive behaviour therapy or CBT. This therapy concentrates on aiding people with schizophrenia to reconsider their thoughts through hypothesis testing and guided discovery. This produces reductions in symptoms, particularly delusions, but little effect on hallucinations or more general functioning (Pilling *et al.*, 2002a; Wykes *et al.*, 2004).

Regardless of the research on cognition, there was a brake on activity in the field of psychological therapy. This can be accounted for, in part, by the emphasis on drug therapies with their clear success in reducing symptoms. The industrial backing was also a clear boost to pharmacotherapy and no similar levels of support were available to psychological therapies. But this is not the whole explanation; some of this brake comes from the early research on cognition that concentrated on the description of deficient cognitive processes. These assessments failed to distinguish patients with brain injury from those with schizophrenia; i.e. there were no specific differences in cognitive profiles. In fact diagnoses might well have been chosen based on flipping a coin (Heaton *et al.*, 1978). The lack of usefulness of cognition for diagnostic clarity made it less of a target for consideration at that time, as the clinical psychologist's role mainly extended to providing diagnostic information. The focus was therefore on other possible psychological assessments that might be helpful. It was also suggested that cognitive deficits were static or possibly got worse over time although rarely were these longitudinal measures of the same patient group. A similar conclusion was reached for the prognosis of deficits resulting from traumatic brain injury. The lack of any improvements suggested an immutable deficit and with, at that time, only pessimistic outcomes for rehabilitation programmes for people with brain injury. Without an efficacious cognitive technology at the time and with the pressures from the moves to care in the community, the focus on rehabilitation efforts was placed on the development of global skills such as work or daily living abilities. But it became clear that when cognitive impairments were present this limited the outcomes from these programmes.

At this point in recent history, the similarities with people with brain injury became a specific focus of research and theory development, and so interest in the patterns of cognitive deficits came back into fashion. Schizophrenia became a disorder of frontal lobe functioning and research then concentrated on describing the similarities and differences in cognitive processes between people with brain injuries or lesions and those with schizophrenia. The field also expanded with the use of brain imaging techniques.

In this biological era the development of psychological therapies was further restrained through the emerging theories about the underlying problem. One hint about the reasons for this comes from the work by both Gray, Hemsley and colleagues (Gray *et al.*, 1995a) and more recently by Kapur (2003). They indicate that the underlying problem in schizophrenia is a biological one in which perceptual phenomena are given their inappropriately high levels of salience through the action of dopamine. The symptoms of schizophrenia result from the person trying to make sense of this high level of salience, in a similar fashion to the models suggested by Maher and colleagues. Following this model it is suggested that the sole way of reducing this salience is to reduce the overactivity in the hyperdopaminergic system so that there can be a psychological readjustment (i.e. a change in beliefs). In this model the concentration is on the dysregulated neurochemistry with the only therapeutic input being medication with little role for psychological therapy.

However, with the realisation that skill training – essential in a post-institutionalisation era – was hampered by the cognitive deficits of the patients, there was a new impetus for the development of novel therapies. Atypical antipsychotic medication had not yet been fully exploited so there was room for newer psychological therapy. But there was still much scepticism about its likelihood of success. One issue of *Schizophrenia Bulletin* at the time had titles for papers such as 'Cognitive rehabilitation for schizophrenia: Is it possible? Is it necessary?' (Bellack, 1992) and 'Cognitive remediation in schizophrenia: Proceed . . . with caution!' (Hogarty and Flesher, 1992). But these authors have since carried out empirical work and are more convinced about the likely benefits of therapy to improve cognitive skills, although both have adopted a different approach to the identification of cognitive targets and therapies. We are therefore in a new era when therapies for cognitive difficulties do seem possible even if they are not yet clearly delineated.

What is cognitive remediation therapy?

Although the term cognitive remediation has been used here, the literature suggests a number of different names including cognitive rehabilitation and cognitive training. The term remediation suggests that it is the correction of a fault or deficiency whereas rehabilitation refers to restoring a function back to normal by training (*Oxford Dictionary*, 1999). We have therefore chosen remediation because it does not suggest such recovery, nor does it imply how the fault or impairment is remedied. However, we do assume that the process or the therapy is by instruction or training. We will draw a model of CRT that could equally well be applied to other rehabilitation programmes. The use of the term also does not imply that the process of therapy is either restorative or compensatory.

CRT has concentrated on the form rather than the content of thought and the main outcome of the therapy is, of course, to improve thinking skill itself. We consider that the distinction between form and content begins to fade as we take into account another process, metacognition. We also highlight the role of cognitive schemas in defining the cognitive processing necessary for carrying out tasks. Cognitive schemas have generally been thought to be manipulated in the domain of cognitive behaviour therapy (CBT) but we will argue that they should also be central to CRT.

Improved cognitive skills are what many people with schizophrenia say is one of their goals. They want to be able to remember more and be able to learn new skills. This is in addition to any other ambitions for their quality of life. Because of the demand for cognitive improvements to have a bearing on overall functioning, the emphasis in outcome measurement includes both proximal (cognition) and distal (work) outcomes even at the time the therapy is developing. This does seem a little unfair given that the sole measure of medication is the reduction in symptoms rather than an increase in functioning. However, it may be that a consideration of distal outcomes may change the type of therapy offered. We have used this distal outcome to develop our top down approach to cognitive remediation. The transfer of cognitive skill necessary for cognition to have an effect on distal outcomes we consider to be the key to determining the rehabilitation technology.

The relationship between improved cognition and improvements in general functioning has not yet been determined. There may be multiple routes as are suggested for brain injury. For instance, it may be that functioning improvement directly follows improved cognition or, and this maybe the more likely, when cognition is improved this leads to fewer limitations on skill acquisition and increased confidence. This latter route would require that further rehabilitation programmes build on to the gains made in the CRT programme. Therapy, particularly within our own model, may also affect secondary impairments – the reactions to the primary cognitive impairments or self efficacy – as well as having a knock-on effect on quality of life and skills.

In summary, cognitive difficulties have been acknowledged as important since the identification of schizophrenia more than a hundred years ago. However, therapies to change these basic difficulties have only just begun to be developed and tested. As well as providing background material for the development of therapy in this field, this book will also provide a guide to the different types of therapy that fall under the description of cognitive remediation therapy. We also want to put some order into what is now a more expansive but variable literature. The main tenet of CRT is that a concentration on cognitive processing is essential to functioning improvement. But although it is possible to improve cognitive processing skills, only on occasion do they seem to have effects on functioning. In our view the effects are understandable within a specific model of CRT. Models to guide the process of therapy delivery have been absent in this field with pragmatic and empirical benefits substituting for theory testing. It is only through testing hypotheses that are clearly grounded in an overall model of CRT that we will be better able to design efficient and effective therapies to increase our service users' happiness and reduce the limitations on their aspirations.

Chapter 2

An overview of cognitive function in schizophrenia

The importance of cognitive dysfunction in schizophrenia, highlighted by Kraepelin and Bleuler at the turn of the century, was largely ignored until the late 1950s, when the study of animal and human cognition began to flourish. This new line of research by experimental psychopathologists was marked by the publication of a book called *Perception and Communication* (Broadbent, 1958). Using work relating to vigilance, selective listening and shifting attention, Broadbent postulated a central control mechanism for filtering out irrelevant information. It was later proposed that a defective 'filtering' mechanism may underlie the psychological dysfunction in schizophrenia. McGhie and Chapman (1961) also concluded that the primary deficit in schizophrenia was in the control and direction of attention. This broad conclusion was accepted with general consensus amongst schizophrenia researchers in the 1960s. Since then, experimental cognitive paradigms have been used to identify specifically impaired cognitive processes in schizophrenia, and theories have emerged which aim not only to provide a unifying cognitive framework, but also to link them to symptoms (e.g. Hemsley, 1977, 1993; Frith, 1979; Frith and Done, 1988; Frith, 1992).

An alternative line of investigation developed as neuropsychological methods were applied to people suffering from schizophrenia. The beginnings of modern neuropsychology stem from the work of Hebb (1949), Teuber (1950), for example, who were interested in examining the behavioural correlates of brain disorders. As evidence has accumulated to suggest a neurobiological basis for schizophrenia, neuropsychological tests have increasingly been used to hypothesise about underlying neuropathology. This development has emphasised the importance in its own right of cognitive dysfunction in schizophrenia.

The neurodevelopmental model of schizophrenia

A further shift in the development of the understanding of schizophrenia which was highly influential in promoting research into cognitive dysfunction occurred in the 1980s, when schizophrenia was no longer viewed as a neurodegenerative disease, but as a neurodevelopmental disorder. The neuro-developmental model suggests that subtle brain abnormalities acquired in utero (e.g. due to genetic vulnerability or maternal illness during pregnancy) or perinatally (e.g. due to insults at birth or later genetic effects) result in abnormal neurodevelopment (Murray *et al.*, 1992). The onset of symptoms may subsequently occur when brain maturation reaches a critical stage at which neurologically abnormal regions are required for normal development. The presence of stressors (e.g. life events, cannabis use) and an absence of protective factors (e.g. living within a calm and uncritical family) may interact with the psychological and cognitive consequences of this neurodevelopmental abnormality to promote or protect against the emergence of psychotic symptoms. The greater the vulnerability, the fewer subsequent risk factors may be required to trigger the onset of symptoms. The neurodevelopmental model refines a traditional vulnerability-stress model (described in Chapter 1), specifying the nature of the vulnerability and accounting for the interplay between genes and environment in the aetiology of schizophrenia (Nuechterlein and Dawson, 1984; Tienari, 1991).

Global deficits in cognitive function

The neurodevelopmental model predicts that people with schizophrenia will have cognitive deficits, and group studies have consistently shown that they do perform significantly worse than healthy controls on a wide variety of cognitive or neuropsychological tasks. Global cognitive deficits or anomalies are apparent across sensory modalities, but the variability of intellectual abilities is wide and follows a normal distribution which mirrors that of the healthy general public. However, as a whole, the intellectual curve can be considered to be shifted downwards by approximately ten IQ points (Aylward *et al.*, 1984). For a significant proportion of people with schizophrenia (approximately a quarter), who lie at the upper end of the spectrum, cognitive functioning falls within the normal range (Palmer *et al.*, 1997; Kremen *et al.*, 2000a; Weickert *et al.*, 2000). However, most people with schizophrenia have lower IQs than would be predicted by their own family and environmental background (Aylward *et al.*, 1984; Crawford *et al.*, 1992), and those with intact cognitive performance are likely to have a higher premorbid IQ than control subjects with similar current intelligence, indicating a decline in functioning (Kremen *et al.*, 2000a; Holthausen *et al.*, 2002).

We have chosen to review the vast literature on cognition in schizophrenia in two ways. The first, in this chapter, provides an overview of cognitive processing in schizophrenia within a simple framework of normal cognitive function. A basic understanding of healthy cognitive processing and the interrelationships between cognitive functions is vital for researchers and clinicians who aim to develop cognitive remediation programmes. The second approach in the following chapter uses the outline of impairments identified but investigates these problems in more detail in order to specify impaired component cognitive processes.

The term 'impairment' has been used in differing ways in the literature on cognitive dysfunction in schizophrenia. The neuropsychological tradition defines it as a level of performance which is at least two standard deviations below the normative mean, but higher levels of function have frequently been considered indicative of impairment in the cognitive literature on schizophrenia. Our review relies primarily on group studies and so 'impairment' will refer to levels of performance which are significantly worse than those of healthy controls.

Cognitive function in schizophrenia

Cognitive deficits associated with schizophrenia may best be understood with reference to a model of normal cognitive functioning. However, there is no current consensus regarding either a model of normal information processing as a whole, or models of the subcomponents of the information processing system.

We have drawn together a number of key concepts and models within the literature including Baddeley's working memory, Shallice's executive function and Cowan's information processing, to provide a simple framework of information processing within which we will examine the deficits associated with schizophrenia (see Figure 2.1). Our model suggests that the information

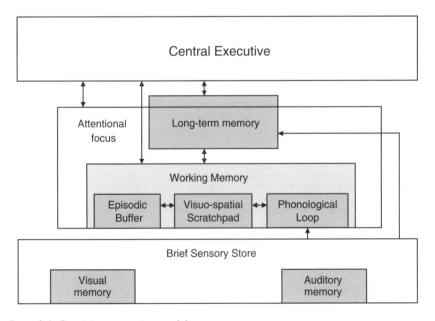

Figure 2.1 Cognitive processing model

processing system is composed of five main interacting multicomponent systems:

- a brief sensory store
- working memory slave systems
- an episodic buffer
- long-term memory
- a central executive.

In addition, attentional processes, controlled by the central executive, allow processing resources to be differentially focused upon the working memory slave systems, the episodic buffer or long-term memory.

The working memory slave systems, the episodic buffer, and the central executive are taken from Baddeley's well-established model of working memory (Baddeley and Hitch, 1974; Baddeley, 2000) in which working memory is conceptualised as a 'system for the temporary holding and manipulation of information during the performance of a range of cognitive tasks' (Baddeley, 1986). It is proposed that working memory comprises at least two slave systems responsible for the temporary storage of information, the articulatory or phonological loop and the visuo-spatial sketchpad. These are governed by a central executive modelled on Shallice's 'supervisory attentional system' (Shallice, 1982; Norman and Shallice, 1986; Shallice and Burgess, 1996). More recently, a fourth component of working memory, the 'episodic buffer', was proposed to account for the ability to retain chunks of information that clearly exceed the capacity of either the phonological loop or the visuo-spatial sketchpad and to form representations which combine both visual and verbal information (Baddeley, 2000).

Cognitive processes which fall within the social domain are generally referred to as 'social cognition'. Social cognition has not been included in the current cognitive processing framework, since basic cognitive processes form the necessary building blocks for adequate social cognition (Penn *et al.*, 1997a). Therefore, data relating to social cognition in schizophrenia will be summarised separately.

The brief sensory store

Perceptual information first enters the cognitive system via the brief sensory store (Cowan, 1988), comprising at least two modality-specific pre-attentional stores, a visual memory store (sometimes referred to as 'iconic memory') and an auditory memory store, lasting only a few hundred milliseconds (Efron, 1970a, 1970b). The memory traces held in these stores are then transferred to more permanent stores. It is proposed that transfer may occur not only to short-term memory stores (which are responsible for the immediate processing of presented stimuli) but also to long-term memory stores, since a number of patients have been identified who show severe damage to short-term memory stores, in the absence of long-term memory difficulties (Shallice and Warrington, 1970; Vallar and Papagno, 2002).

Iconic memory in schizophrenia has been targeted in two paradigms, Span of Apprehension (Estes and Taylor, 1964) and Visual Backward Masking (Miller et al., 1979). The Span of Apprehension test is designed to assess the ability to detect a target from an array of visual items, presented for no more than a few hundred milliseconds. People with schizophrenia generally detect significantly fewer target stimuli than healthy controls (Asarnow and Mac-Crimmon, 1981; Nuechterlein et al., 1992). Even though this task relies in part on working memory, deficits have been interpreted as evidence for rapid decay or impaired pre-attentional scan processes in iconic memory.

The Visual Backward Masking paradigm consists of the brief presentation of a simple target stimulus (usually a letter) followed by the presentation of a 'masking' stimulus (e.g. overlapping Xs). When the two stimuli are presented in rapid succession, most people are unable to identify the target stimulus – it has been 'masked' by the second stimulus. As the time between the presentation of the target stimuli and the mask increases, the target stimulus is more easily identified. People with schizophrenia seem to require a longer time interval between the presentations of the two stimuli in order to identify the target than normal controls (Butler et al., 2003; Green et al., 2003; McClure, 2001).

Suggested mechanisms of masking include 'integration' and 'interruption'. The 'integration hypothesis' (e.g. Kahneman, 1968) proposes that the rapid succession in which the two stimuli are presented leads them effectively to occur simultaneously in the mind, as if the masking representation (or 'icon') has been superimposed over the target representation. Integration is thought to occur most markedly when the mask has high 'energy' or intensity, occupies a similar spatial location to the target stimulus, and when the interval between the target and mask presentations is short.

The 'interruption hypothesis' (e.g. Turvey, 1973) suggests that the mask interferes with the visual processing of the target stimulus and thus although the target iconic image is clearly formed, it fails to be transferred to a more permanent store. Several investigators have recently found evidence for deficits in masking by interruption using low energy masks in patients with schizophrenia (Cadenhead et al., 1998; Green et al., 1999). Currently there is no consistent evidence in favour of one theory of backward masking over another. However, there is consistent evidence of failure with almost any paradigm in early visual processing in people with schizophrenia.

Auditory and verbal pre-attentional processing has been assessed using measures of priming. Semantic priming refers to the phenomenon in which the speed with which a word can be pronounced or recognised as a word is decreased if preceded by a semantically related word or prime (e.g. 'orange' would be recognised more easily if preceded by 'apple' than by 'piano'). This is assumed to be due to spreading activation through the semantic memory system. It can be influenced by both automatic and controlled processes, with automatic processes prominent under brief presentation rates and low proportions of associated word pairs (Neely, 1991). Automatic processing is likely to rely on an interaction between functioning of the brief sensory store and long-term memory. People with schizophrenia show variable semantic priming effects under automatic processing conditions primarily during acute phases of illness, indicating enhanced, normal and impaired spreading activation (Minzenberg et al., 2002; Gouzoulis-Mayfrank et al., 2003).

Negative priming consists of the normal increase in reaction time seen when participants are required to respond to a target which has previously been actively ignored. People with schizophrenia generally fail to show negative priming effects (Beech et al., 1989).

Other paradigms which rely on the generation of pre-attentional associations within memory are latent inhibition, Kamin's Blocking Effect and pre-pulse inhibition. Latent inhibition refers to the increased time it takes for healthy participants to learn an association between a stimulus and a reinforcer when the stimulus has previously been repeatedly presented without reinforcement. This effect has been found to be absent in people with acute or untreated schizophrenia, who appear to show no slowed learning of the new association (Lubow et al., 1987; Baruch et al., 1988).

A second paradigm, Kamin's Blocking Effect (Kamin, 1968), involves participants first learning an association between two stimuli. They are then presented with a new association. Normal participants demonstrate reduced learning of the new relationship. As with Latent Inhibition tasks, people in the acute phase of schizophrenia often fail to show this effect (Jones et al., 1992; Oades et al., 2000).

Finally, a similar attentional disturbance has been demonstrated in studies involving the inhibition of the startle reflex by a weak pre-stimulus at an inter-stimulus interval of between 50–500 milliseconds. This is referred to as pre-pulse inhibition. Pre-pulse inhibition appears to be reduced in people with schizophrenia (Braff, 1993).

These paradigms all take place at pre-attentional levels, suggesting the brief sensory store is activated. Consistent impairments are apparent in people with schizophrenia but primarily in the acute and untreated phases of illness.

Working memory slave systems

Memory traces from the brief sensory store are transferred to short-term memory stores where they decay over a period of a few seconds unless refreshed. These memories may be accessible to conscious awareness. The phonological loop holds verbal and auditory information, and comprises a temporary phonological store and an articulatory rehearsal component, which is used to refresh memory traces. Information may be held within the phonological loop in a sequential form (e.g. a series of digits) and its capacity (usually about seven items or chunks of information) is limited by the time taken to refresh the memory trace using subvocal rehearsal (about two seconds). The phonological loop is thought to facilitate the acquisition of language (Baddeley, 1998) and in this respect it acts as an intermediary between the brief sensory store and long-term memory. Information held within the visuo-spatial sketchpad may be separable into visual, spatial and possibly kinaesthetic components, and tends to form a single complex pattern, such as a visual image. Its capacity is about three or four objects. Logie (1995) suggests that the visuo-spatial sketchpad may comprise two components: a visuo-spatial store and a retrieval and rehearsal process. The visuo-spatial sketchpad may be used in the acquisition of semantic knowledge about the appearance and use of objects, spatial orientation and geographical knowledge (Baddeley, 2003), again providing an interface between the short-term store and long-term memory.

An alternative, widely used model of working memory within the schizophrenia literature is that of Goldman-Rakic (1987, 1991, 1999) who emphasises the maintenance or holding online of information over a period of seconds, but does not refer to its manipulation. One of the difficulties in assessing the literature on working memory is that whilst many researchers use Baddeley's model to guide their selection of working memory tasks, others use tasks in which participants are prevented from refreshing the memory over long delays (e.g. 30 seconds). These tasks would exceed the capacity of Baddeley's working memory slave systems, and are more consistent with Goldman-Rakic's model.

The phonological loop

The capacity of the phonological store is usually assessed using immediate serial recall of digits, letters or unrelated words. Evidence from studies of serial recall with people with schizophrenia is mixed. Whilst some studies suggest that most people suffering from schizophrenia have a forwards digit span within the normal range (e.g. Salamé et al., 1998; Kiefer et al., 2002), others report that the mean digit span may be mildly impaired (e.g. Perry et al., 2001b; Silver et al., 2003). Impairment on digit span tasks appears to be more marked when a delay, filled with a distraction task designed to prevent rehearsal, is included (Fleming et al., 1995).

The visuo-spatial sketchpad

Studies of the capacity of the visuo-spatial sketchpad in schizophrenia have tended to focus upon the spatial (rather than visual) span. Again, a mixed picture emerges with some studies showing impairment and others showing intact performance (Hutton *et al.*, 1998; Salamé *et al.*, 1998; Pantelis *et al.*, 2001).

The classic delayed response task is also frequently used to assess short-term storage of spatial information. These tasks assess the recall of the location of a target item presented after a delay of at least five seconds filled by a distractor task designed to prevent rehearsal. People with schizophrenia have consistently shown marked deficits relative to controls (Park and Holzman, 1992; Ross *et al.*, 2000; Stratta *et al.*, 2001; Pukrop *et al.*, 2003).

The delayed response task is crucially different from classic serial span tasks in the inclusion of a delay and distractor condition, which disrupts rehearsal. It may be argued that the central executive is required to protect information in short-term storage systems from interfering material (Barch, 2003). The distractor tasks have typically involved arithmetic calculations, which rely upon executive functions (Furst and Hitch, 2000), or identifying words which were not exemplars of a particular category, which requires abstraction, a specific executive function. Executive function may therefore be the key in poor responding instead of, or in addition to, short-term storage. Another possibility is that the delay is sometimes sufficient for long-term, rather than working memory to be required for the recall of the spatial information. Therefore, we suggest that delayed response tasks may not solely assess visuo-spatial working memory.

The episodic buffer

Incoming information from the working memory stores and long-term memory is integrated to form multimodal representations within the episodic buffer. The capacity is limited but exceeds that of the slave systems. It is controlled by the central executive, which may retrieve information from the buffer which forms conscious awareness, and the central executive may then reflect upon, manipulate and modify that information. Representations within the episodic buffer can be fed forward into long-term memory.

The immediate recall of short passages of prose is considered to be a function of the episodic buffer (Baddeley, 2000). People with schizophrenia have been consistently found to show impaired immediate prose recall relative to healthy controls (Gold *et al.*, 1992; Clare *et al.*, 1993; Toulopoulou *et al.*, 2003).

Long-term memory

Long-term memory is a multimodal long-term store of infinite capacity, which receives input from the episodic buffer, the working memory stores and the brief sensory store. Its function is the storage and retrieval of information across the lifespan from less than a minute after encoding. It is a multicomponent system whose constituent parts are dissociable and may thus be differentially impaired.

Explicit memory

Explicit memory involves the active conscious recollection of previously learnt information. A distinction has been proposed between episodic memory (for personally experienced events) and semantic memory (for general knowledge) (Tulving and Markowitsch, 1998), but Cirillo and Seidman (2003) suggest that the two explicit memory processes are not clearly distinguishable in studies of verbal long-term memory in schizophrenia.

Recent meta-analyses have shown that the mean performance of people with schizophrenia on tasks of both verbal and non-verbal explicit memory falls more than one standard deviation below the normative mean (Heinrich and Zakzanis, 1998; Aleman *et al.*, 1999; Cirillo and Seidman, 2003). Whilst a number of studies have found greater deficits with verbal than nonverbal materials (Saykin *et al.*, 1994; Barch *et al.*, 2002), Aleman *et al.* (1999) concluded that there was no diffierence between impairment in verbal and non-verbal memory.

Episodic memory impairment is seen in a wide variety of tests, including free and cued recall of word lists or designs (Goldberg *et al.*, 1989; Paulsen *et al.*, 1995; Tracy *et al.*, 2001), verbal, spatial and visual paired associate learning (Gruzelier *et al.*, 1988; Goldberg *et al.*, 1993) and word, spatial and face recognition.

The assessment of episodic memory for remote events in schizophrenia has methodological problems, as failure may be due to a lack of awareness of events at the time of their occurrence rather than poor memory. Despite these difficulties, a number of studies have found that people with schizophrenia have poorer knowledge of famous events and personalities of the past (e.g. Squire and Cohen, 1979). Autobiographical memory assessment has also been found to be impaired (Tamlyn *et al.*, 1992). People with schizophrenia have performed consistently poorly on tests of semantic memory, including vocabulary or sentence processing tests (Clare *et al.*, 1992; Duffy and O'Carroll, 1994) and categorisation tasks (Chen *et al.*, 1994).

Implicit memory

Implicit memory involves the unconscious acquisition, storage and use of knowledge to govern behaviour which is unavailable to conscious reflection (Schacter, 1987). Evidence for preserved implicit memory in the classical amnesic syndrome was first demonstrated by Warrington and Weiskrantz (1974) who showed that amnesic patients were likely to complete word stems with words previously encountered in a learning trial, despite being unable to recall their presentation. Normal performance on stem-completion tasks has also been demonstrated in people suffering from schizophrenia (Brebion *et al.*, 1997b; Kazes *et al.*, 1999).

Another frequently used paradigm to investigate implicit learning is an artificial grammar-learning task (Reber, 1967). In a learning phase, participants are presented with rule-based strings of letters. Normal participants generally fail to extract explicitly the rules and are unaware of the acquisition of these rules, yet are able to identify those letter strings which are 'grammatical' (i.e. follow similar rules to those presented in the learning phase) at a rate well above chance (Mathews *et al.*, 1989). Artificial grammar learning is intact in patients with schizophrenia despite them being significantly impaired on tests of explicit and working memory (Danion *et al.*, 2001b).

Repetition priming becomes apparent when previously encountered words, faces or objects invoke a more accurate or quicker response than novel items and is another test of implicit memory. This phenomenon appears not only to be preserved in schizophrenia, but some studies have shown enhanced repetition priming (Bavin *et al.*, 2001; Moritz *et al.*, 2001; Surguladze *et al.*, 2002).

Implicit memory in the form of skill learning is usually assessed by the rate of learning to perform a task over a series of trials. Performance on the Pursuit Rotor Test, in which participants aim to track a rotating target with a hand-held pointer shows normal rates of improvement (e.g. Huston and Shakow, 1949; Kern *et al.*, 1997). Clare *et al.* (1992) tested speed of repeated assembly of a jigsaw puzzle and rate of improvement in reading words presented as their mirror image, and found their rate of learning in people with schizophrenia to be comparable with that of control subjects. Other researchers have argued that performance on the Tower of Hanoi task requires implicit memory and a number of studies have shown that people with schizophrenia improve at the same rate as controls (Schmand *et al.*, 1992; Goldberg *et al.*, 1993; Gras-Vincendon *et al.*, 1994). The evidence is therefore overwhelmingly in favour of intact implicit memory in schizophrenia despite problems in other memory systems.

Semantic organisation

Information is organised within memory according to schemas, scripts or mental models (Bartlett, 1932; Schank 1977; Johnson-Laird, 1983), which are generic knowledge structures or templates. For example, a 'writing schema' will include a writer, implements, a surface on which the writing occurs and the writing itself, but the particular nature of each of these elements is not specified by the schema. A person having a writing schema is able to use this generic information to make sense of a writing situation even if some of the elements of the schema are omitted. The schema provides the slots that can be filled either by perceptions or which can be extrapolated or inferred from the context. The more closely an event matches an existing schema, the more likely is the person to remember the event (De Soto, 1960). The recall of events is influenced not only by the actual event, but also the schema by which the memory was organised. Thus, mistakes in recall are likely to be systematic, predictable and consistent with pre-existing schemas (Freeman *et al.*, 1987).

There is evidence to suggest that the semantic organisation of material in long-term memory is aberrant in people with schizophrenia. Evidence comes from impaired verbal fluency (Allen and Frith, 1983; Goldberg *et al.*, 1998), with schizophrenia patients producing few words within each semantic cluster. Studies of automatic processes within semantic priming also suggest that some people with schizophrenia may have enhanced spreading of activation within semantic memory, although for some, spreading activation is normal or even slowed (Minzenberg *et al.*, 2002). These all suggest that the connections between related concepts may be abnormal.

Central executive

This is a fractionated system for the control and regulation of voluntary behaviour to achieve internally generated goals. More specifically, it controls and regulates the working memory slave systems, the episodic buffer, long-term memory and attentional focus. A highly influential model for this central executive was developed by Norman and Shallice (1986) and Shallice and Burgess (1996), in the form of the Supervisory Attentional System (SAS).

The SAS comprises the higher order component of a two-tiered information processing system by which different sequences of responses are selected. The lower level component, which operates automatically and is modulated by the SAS, is the Contention Scheduling System (CSS). The role of the CSS is to carry out routine activities, consisting of subroutines (or thought or action 'schemas'), which are selected from a large but finite set of discrete and goal-directed cognitive and motor programmes located in long-term memory, and which are automatically triggered by well-learned perceptual or cognitive cues.

The SAS is required for novel or less routine tasks which are not specified by the environment or by automatic cues, or when there are several competing possible responses. It is under deliberate and conscious control and may alter the priorities of the CSS by activating or inhibiting particular programmes. Specifically, Shallice and Burgess (1996) suggest that to cope with a novel situation, a temporary new schema is constructed and implemented, and this takes the place of schemas triggered by the environment, and controls lower level schemas to achieve internally produced goals. This temporary schema may be an existing schema which is not triggered by the environment, or a modification of an existing schema or schemas. This active temporary representation is presumably formed and held online within the episodic buffer and forms the focus of awareness. The functioning of the SAS is said to operate over at least three stages:

- constructing a temporary new schema
- maintaining the schema in working memory and implementing it
- monitoring and subsequently rejecting or modifying the temporary schema when necessary, and inhibiting automatic responses which are not consistent with the temporary schema or current goal.

Each stage requires a number of component executive processes. These components are generally believed to be dissociable and thus can be differentially impaired.

The Wisconsin Card Sort Test (WCST) has emerged as the most commonly used measure of executive functioning in schizophrenia research. For this task, participants are required to match a pack of cards to one of four key cards, according to changing conceptual categories (colour, shape or number). Participants are not told how to match the cards, but are told whether or not the match they have made is correct. After a number of correct responses, the rule is changed and the participant must determine the new rule. Performance on the WCST depends on abstraction of the matching rule, maintenance of this concept, and then suppression of this habitual response and initiation of a novel response (i.e. set shifting). Evidence from numerous studies suggests that people with schizophrenia have difficulty in attaining concepts and perseverate on incorrect responses (e.g. Goldberg et al., 1987; Koren et al., 1998; Gold et al., 1999; Nieuwenstein et al., 2001).

Other neuropsychological tests frequently aim to provide more specific evidence of component executive processes. We will examine the evidence for impairment in these processes in schizophrenia in relation to the three stages of processing proposed in Shallice and Burgess's (1996) model.

Stage 1: Constructing a temporary new schema

The construction of a temporary schema is proposed to include a number of component processes:

- spontaneous strategy generation (i.e. when a strategy comes to mind without an explicit attempt to solve the problem)
- problem solving/planning
- forming and realising intentions
- setting goals
- retrieving relevant material from long-term memory.

Response initiation skills have been assessed using fluency tasks, in which participants are asked to generate as many items as possible of a particular type within a certain time limit. This involves retrieving information from long-term memory, spontaneous strategy generation or more deliberate generation of strategies/planning. People with schizophrenia demonstrate impairments in verbal fluency, in tests of both letter fluency and category (i.e. semantic) fluency (Joyce *et al.*, 1996; Elvevag *et al.*, 2001; Moelter *et al.*, 2001) and in design fluency (Beatty *et al.*, 1993; Johnson-Selfridge and Zalewski, 2001). These tasks also tap monitoring skills and the ability to inhibit competing inappropriate responses, which form part of the third stage of executive processing.

Poor planning and problem solving have been assessed on a number of tasks. The Modified Six Elements Test (BADS, Wilson *et al.*, 1996) requires the participant to carry out a number of simple tasks without breaking a certain rule within a time limit. This can be most effectively achieved by generating a plan of action before beginning. The Tower of London task (Shallice, 1982) requires participants to plan and sequence a number of moves of coloured discs to match a static array of discs in increasingly difficult pre-arranged formations. The Tower of Hanoi was the forerunner to the Tower of London tasks and is similar in requiring participants to move a set of discs one at a time to match a target arrangement. Impairments have been demonstrated on both of these tasks (Modified Six Elements: Carstairs *et al.* 1995; Morris *et al.*, 1995; Tower of Hanoi: Hanes *et al.*, 1996; Tower of London: Pantelis *et al.*, 1997; Rushe *et al.*, 1999). Schizophrenia participants also seem to have impaired strategy use (for example, in semantic priming, under experimental conditions favouring controlled processing), although this may reflect in deficits in maintaining rather than constructing a schema (Iddon *et al.*, 1998; Minzenberg *et al.*, 2002; Greenwood *et al.*, 2003).

Stage 2: Maintaining and implementing the schema

Stage two covers the implementation and operation of the temporary schema which requires a special purpose working memory. Baddeley (2000) suggests that the episodic buffer forms the storage component of the central executive and so we may expect the use of the episodic buffer as well as the working memory slave systems to fall within this stage of processing.

Studies which require the manipulation and updating of information within working memory, such as the spatial working memory task from the Cambridge Neuropsychological Test Automated Battery (CANTAB) show consistent impairment in people with schizophrenia (Pantelis *et al.*, 1997, 2001; Hutton *et al.*, 1998), although this is frequently attributable to impaired strategy use (a stage one function) (Iddon *et al.*, 1998; Joyce *et al.*, 2002). Impairments are also apparent on verbal tasks which require manipulating and updating information within working memory, such as the Letter–Number Span (Gold *et al.*, 1997; Pukrop *et al.*, 2003).

Stage 3: Monitoring the schema and inhibiting inappropriate responses

This stage involves:

- monitoring the success of the temporary mental representation
- modifying or rejecting the active temporary mental representation when necessary
- monitoring output
- inhibiting inappropriate responses.

Impaired monitoring has been shown on tasks assessing error correction (Malenka *et al.*, 1982; Frith and Done, 1989; Turken *et al.*, 2003) and source monitoring (i.e. the ability to identify the source of uncertain experiences such as one's own previously recorded thoughts) (Heilbrun, 1980; Bentall and Slade, 1985; Harvey, 1985).

The ability to shift between cognitive sets, which relies on self-monitoring and inhibition of automatic responses, has been measured using the Trail-Making Test (Reitan, 1958), although this is frequently labelled a test of divided attention and of visuo-motor processing speed. Participants are required first to join consecutive letters of the alphabet and in the second part, to link numbers so that they must alternately shift between two sets of information. Impaired performance is consistently found in people with schizophrenia (Goldberg *et al.*, 1989; Heinrichs and Zakazanis, 1998; Nopoulos *et al.*, 1994). This test also relies on stage two processing, since it requires the online maintenance and updating of cognitive sets.

The classic Stroop paradigm (Trenerry *et al.*, 1989) has also been conceptualised as a test of focused attention. Participants are asked to name colour words or the colour of the ink in which they are printed. When the word and the ink do not match, they are required not only to shift to an alternative cognitive set (the ink colour), but also to inhibit the automatic response (the word itself) and to monitor their output. In normal participants, this leads to an increased response latency: this is known as the Stroop interference effect. The majority of studies have demonstrated an enhanced interference effect for people with schizophrenia (Wapner and Krus, 1960; Vendrell *et al.*, 1995; Hepp *et al.*, 1996).

The ability to inhibit habitual responses in favour of an alternative response set has also been assessed using the Hayling Sentence Completion Task (Burgess and Shallice, 1996). In the first part, participants are asked to complete a sentence with a single word which has been strongly primed by the context. In the second part, participants are asked to inhibit the strongly primed word, and to provide an alternative word to complete the sentence that doesn't make sense. People with schizophrenia show both increased errors in the second part (i.e. they provide words which are compatible with the sentence) and increased response latencies (Nathaniel-James and Frith, 1996; Greenwood *et al.*, 2000). Impairments are also apparent on a spatial response inhibition task (Wykes *et al.*, 1992, 2000).

Attention

Attention can be viewed as a pool of nonspecific resources which are allocated deliberately (by the central executive) or automatically (in response to environmental input) to information processing tasks (Kahneman, 1973). Attention acts like a selective filter, which may dampen processing of some stimuli to preferentially process alternative stimuli and the focus of attention may comprise the most highly activated representations in memory. For the purposes of the current framework, it is presumed that the attentional focus falls primarily on representations within the episodic buffer, but it may also be directed towards the phonological loop, visuo-spatial sketchpad or long-term memory. This is consistent with Baddeley's (2000) suggestion that highly activated contents of the episodic buffer form conscious awareness.

Attention is proposed primarily to be under the control of the central executive. In the absence of input from the central executive, attentional focus is automatically directed towards novel stimuli within the environment. As habituation occurs, attentional focus is recaptured by alternative stimuli which are sufficiently discrepant from the habituated stimuli to cause distraction (Cowan, 1988).

A number of specific modes of action may be attributed to attention, although it can be argued that these are in fact a subset of specific functions of the central executive (Shallice and Burgess, 1996). These may include maintenance of an alert state, orienting to novel stimuli, selectively filtering relevant information, shifting from one set to another and rapidly discriminating or scanning stimuli (Posner and Boies, 1971; Keitzman, 1991).

Attentional deficits in schizophrenia have most frequently been inferred from slowing of performance on timed tasks, such as the WAIS digit symbol subtest (Shapiro and Nelson, 1955; Shallice *et al.*, 1991), letter and number cancellation tasks (Babcock, 1933; Nelson *et al.*, 1990), the Trail-Making Test, parts A and B (Watson *et al.*, 1968; Heaton *et al.*, 1994), and simple and complex reaction time test (Zubin, 1975; Hemsley, 1982).

Selective and divided attention

Consistent with clinical observations, evidence from laboratory studies suggests that people with schizophrenia are more easily distractible than healthy controls, suggesting an impaired ability to attend selectively to target stimuli. Impaired performance on dichotic listening tasks (Harvey and Pedley, 1989), and immediate serial recall tests (both with and without a distractor condition) have usually been assumed to indicate increased vulnerability to distraction (Weiss *et al.*, 1988).

The ability to monitor two concurrent tasks is considered to assess the function of the central executive by working memory theorists, but may be regarded as a test of divided attention. People with schizophrenia perform significantly worse than healthy controls on dual-task paradigms which employ a variety of auditory, visual and verbal tasks (Salamé *et al.*, 1998; Granholm *et al.*, 1996; Pukrop *et al.*, 2003).

Sustained attention

Sustained attention or vigilance may be defined as 'a state of readiness to detect and respond to certain small changes occurring at random intervals in the environment' (Mackworth, 1948). The most widely used measure of sustained attention in clinical research is the Continuous Performance Test. In this task, stimuli (usually a random series of letters or numbers) are briefly presented one at a time over a period of several minutes and the participant is required to respond to target stimuli and to avoid responding to distracting stimuli. People with schizophrenia make a greater number of errors in the form of both target omissions and false positive responses than normal controls (Mirsky, 1988; Servan Schreiber *et al.*, 1996; Elvevag *et al.*, 2000b).

Social cognition

Cognition that is used for interpersonal functioning is called social cognition. These cognitive processes underlie social interactions and include the ability to recognise emotions and understand discourse. Social cognitive deficits in perception, problem solving, knowledge and theory of mind have been identified in schizophrenia.

Emotion recognition has been investigated in the visual and auditory modalities, via facial affect recognition and affective prosody recognition. Numerous studies have shown that people with schizophrenia show impaired performance on tasks of facial affect perception (Edwards *et al.*, 2002; Mandal *et al.*, 1998; Morrison *et al.*, 1988). A much smaller literature exists on affective prosody recognition, but people with schizophrenia do consistently perform worse than normal controls on these tasks (Murphy and Cutting, 1990; Hooker and Park, 2002). More generally, there is evidence to suggest that people with schizophrenia show impaired social-cue perception (Corrigan and Toomey, 1995; Ihnen *et al.*, 1998; Corrigan and Nelson, 1998), although some studies have failed to identify a deficit (Morrison *et al.*, 1988; Bellack *et al.*, 1996; Joseph *et al.*, 1992).

Other areas of social cognitive impairment in schizophrenia are in social problem solving (Addington *et al.*, 1998; Sayers *et al.*, 1995; Grant *et al.*, 2001) and in theory of mind. The latter refers to the metacognitive ability to represent mental states. People with schizophrenia consistently perform at a lower level than healthy controls on measures of theory of mind (Frith and Corcoran, 1996; Pickup and Frith, 2001; Langdon *et al.*, 2002; Tenyi *et al.*, 2002; Greig *et al.*, 2004).

Identified cognitive processing problems

Table 2.1 summarises the cognitive deficits that have emerged from the literature described above. There are clear impairments on nearly all elements of cognitive processing. The only component which seems to escape major difficulties is implicit memory.

The course of cognitive function

In order to place CRT in some context and to identify targets for intervention we need to understand the durability and stability of cognitive impairments. The neurodevelopmental model of schizophrenia is consistent with the finding that neuropsychological impairments are apparent well before the onset of symptoms. Thereafter, cognitive function remains relatively stable throughout the course of the disorder, although there do appear to be discrete periods in the lifetime of sufferers of schizophrenia in which cognitive

Table 2.1 Cognitive processing in schizophrenia

Cognitive processing system	Process	Level of functioning
Brief sensory store	Iconic memory	Impaired
	Auditory memory	Unknown
Working memory slave systems	Phonological loop storage	Unclear/mildly impaired
	Phonological loop rehearsal	Unknown
	Visuo-spatial sketchpad storage	Unclear/impaired
	Visuo-spatial sketchpad rehearsal	Unknown
Episodic buffer	Short-term storage	Impaired
Long-term memory	Explicit memory	Impaired
	Implicit memory	Intact
	Semantic organisation	Impaired
Central executive	Response initiation	Impaired
	Strategy generation	Impaired
	Planning/problem solving	Impaired
	Self-monitoring	Impaired
	Set shifting	Impaired
	Response inhibition	Impaired
Attention	Selective/divided attention	Impaired
	Sustained attention	Impaired

function is vulnerable to significant decline. In general, the cognitive profile of first episode patients closely matches that of people with chronic schizophrenia, although the extent of impairment may be greater in people with more chronic forms of the disorder (Bilder et al., 2000; Kravariti et al., 2003; Saykin et al., 1994).

Early cognitive deficits

A number of recent birth cohort studies have shown that children who go on to develop schizophrenia perform more poorly on both verbal and non-verbal neuropsychological tests at the ages of four and seven (Cannon et al., 2000), have lower IQs at age seven, and show poorer educational achievements than those with emotional problems or healthy controls (Cannon et al., 1999). Other population-based cohort studies have examined associations between IQ and the subsequent development of schizophrenia in teenage conscripts. Low intellectual ability has also been identified in studies of conscripts as a significant risk factor for developing schizophrenia (David et al., 1997; Caspi et al., 2003) and in prospective high-risk studies (Cornblatt and Obuchowski, 1997; Cosway et al., 2000).

Around the time of the onset of symptoms, and possibly within the prodromal phase of the illness, cognitive function generally appears to undergo a period of significant decline (Kremen et al., 1998; Bilder et al., 2000; Cosway et al., 2000). Some aspects of cognitive function (e.g. executive functions) appear to improve and stabilise in the first few months after the first acute episode but following this period of stabilisation, people with schizophrenia continue to show significant levels of global cognitive impairment relative to healthy controls (Hoff et al., 1992; Haas et al., 2003; Kravariti et al., 2003; Saykin et al., 1994).

The stability of specific cognitive impairments

Cognitive function then appears to remain stable throughout the course of the disorder, although specific cognitive functions show some fluctuation, usually in relation to psychotic episodes (Rund, 1998; Fucetola et al., 2000; Heaton et al., 2001; Hijman et al., 2003; Kurtz, 2005). Some have argued that these cognitive functions make good targets for CRT because they already show some natural recovery.

Nuechterlein et al. (1994) propose three classes of cognitive deficits in schizophrenia: stable vulnerability indicators, mediating vulnerability factors and episode or symptom indicators. They argue that evidence that cognitive abnormalities may act as stable vulnerability indicators for the disorder comes from studies showing information processing difficulties in first-degree relatives of people with schizophrenia (e.g. Green et al., 1997), and people with schizoptypal personality disorder (e.g. Balogh and Merritt, 1985;

Lenzenweger *et al.*, 1991), all of whom may share a genetic vulnerability to schizophrenia, but who do not have the disorder. However, it is not clear that the common deficits are indicative of vulnerability, since they are apparent in people who do *not* show symptoms of schizophrenia. For the purposes of this review then, we will refer to 'stable deficits'. Nuechterlein *et al.* (1994) propose that mediating vulnerability factors ('chronic fluctuating deficits' in this book) are similar to stable factors in showing impairment in schizophrenia across the course of the disorder and in people with a genetic risk of developing schizophrenia, but are also to some extent related to symptoms, and worsen shortly before or during a psychotic episode. Episode indicators are cognitive functions which only show impairment just before or during an acute episode.

Stable deficits

The Continuous Performance Test has frequently been used to detect cognitive abnormalities in high-risk groups. Deficits have been identified in children of people with schizophrenia (Nuechterlein, 1983; Rutschmann *et al.*, 1986) and among siblings and parents of people with schizophrenia (Steinhauer *et al.*, 1991; Mirsky *et al.*, 1992; Chen *et al.*, 1998; Chen and Faraone, 2000; Egan *et al.*, 2000), although impairment tends only to be apparent on more complex versions of the task with higher perceptual loads. CPT abnormalities are also apparent in both chronic symptomatic schizophrenia patients and remitted schizophrenia patients (Wohlberg and Kornetsky, 1973). Thus sustained attention appears to act as a stable factor which is independent of symptoms.

Other highly stable cognitive skills include verbal skills (word meaning, word association and verbal fluency), long-term and short-term visual and verbal memory and pre-attentional information processing (backward masking) (see Rund, 1998 for a review). Studies of first-degree relatives of people with schizophrenia also suggest that long-term explicit verbal memory (Ismail *et al.*, 2000; Staal *et al.*, 2000; Faraone *et al.*, 2001) and verbal fluency (Chen and Faraone, 2000; Ismail *et al.*, 2000; Laurent *et al.*, 2000) may constitute stable factors for the disorder (see Kremen *et al.*, 1994 for a review).

Chronic fluctuating deficits

Using a version of the CPT which included a high verbal working memory load, Nuechterlein and Green (1991) showed that a persistent working memory deficit worsened in a schizophrenia sample during psychotic episodes. In a review of longitudinal studies, Rund (1998) also found that sustained attention, attentional span, and executive function (as assessed by the WCST) were also variable across the course of the disorder. Similarly, working memory and executive deficits have been found in relatives of people with schizo-phrenia implicating a role for genes (Conklin *et al.*, 2000; Staal *et al.*, 2000; Egan *et al.*, 2001a, 2001b).

Episode indicators

A number of associative learning paradigms, such as latent inhibition and Kamin's Blocking Effect show specific impairment only during the acute and untreated phases of illness (Lubow *et al.*, 1987; Baruch *et al.*, 1988; Jones *et al.*, 1992; Oades *et al.*, 2000). Table 2.2 shows a summary of the stability of deficits associated with schizophrenia which have well-validated empirical support.

Table 2.2 Stability of cognitive deficits

Stable deficits	Chronic fluctuating deficits	Episode indicators
Early visual processing	Working memory	Latent inhibition
Long-term memory	Executive function	Kamin's blocking effect
Sustained attention	Attention	

The course of deficits in old age

Recently, evidence has emerged to suggest that a neurodegenerative process may take place in a subsample of people with schizophrenia over the age of 65. Elderly patients who have a history of poor outcome characterised by lifelong institutionalisation show very substantial cognitive impairments, suggestive of cognitive decline (Arnold *et al.*, 1994; Davidson *et al.*, 1995; Harvey *et al.*, 1998; Harvey *et al.*, 1997). But more compelling is evidence from a series of longitudinal studies which have shown that a small propor-tion of elderly schizophrenia patients experience significant global cognitive decline which exceeds that which may be expected as a result of normal ageing (Friedman *et al.*, 2002; Harvey *et al.*, 2003). This decline is associated with advanced age, lower levels of education and more severe positive symptoms of schizophrenia. Like with dementia, cognitive remediation may be a protection against this rapid decline.

Differential cognitive deficits

Different groups of people might respond differently to CRT so we need to try to identify possible patterns of deficits that can help us to classify people and then to investigate any differential benefits. Differences in the severity of cognitive dysfunction in schizophrenia emerge not only with respect to particular individuals and the current phase of the disorder, but also in relation to specific cognitive processes, since people with schizophrenia do not perform equally poorly on all tests of cognitive function. However, differential deficits have been notoriously difficult to establish due to variations in the power of psychometric tests to discriminate between groups (Chapman and Chapman, 1973, 1978). Differential discriminating power depends upon the variance and reliability of measures, and varies widely between tests such that while one may be highly sensitive in detecting impairment in a schizophrenia sample relative to a control group, another test of the same function may barely register the deficit.

There must be differential deficits because cognitive dysfunction is not wholly explicable in terms either of a single cognitive factor or of a generalised impairment in schizophrenia:

- The level of performance of people with schizophrenia may differ across tests that have been carefully matched on difficulty (e.g. Calev, 1984a, 1984b; Calev et al., 1991).
- Within a schizophrenia sample deficits may not be correlated (Hill et al., 2002).
- Deficits associated with schizophrenia often continue to be apparent even when IQ is normal (Kremen et al., 2001).
- The performance of people with schizophrenia on some cognitive tests surpasses that of the general population (e.g. Lubow et al., 1987; Baruch et al., 1988).

A specific profile of deficits has not been identified, but there are areas of stable cognitive impairment, most notably in early visual processing, attention, memory and executive functioning, which have been consistently found in studies of schizophrenia.

Variation in cognitive profiles

Although a number of domains of cognitive impairment have been clearly identified in schizophrenia, deficits are highly heterogeneous and there is considerable within-group variation in cognitive profiles and the extent of impairment. Furthermore, about a quarter of people with schizophrenia appear to be cognitively intact (Palmer et al., 1997; Kremen et al., 2000b; Weickert et al., 2000; Allen et al., 2003). This variation may affect the provision of specific types of CRT. It is possible that if specific subgroups could be identified then the method of CRT may be tailored to the needs of each group. Four methodologies have been used to identify subgroups on the basis of cognitive performance:

1 Cluster analyses.
2 A priori division into subgroups.
3 Rating individual cognitive profiles.
4 Division according to symptoms.

Cluster analyses of performance on batteries of neuropsychological tests for schizophrenia samples have tended to identify a functionally normal subgroup, a severely globally impaired subgroup as well as one or more intermediate groups with moderate deficits, which are frequently differentially dominated by either executive or memory impairment (Heinrichs *et al.*, 1997; Goldstein *et al.*, 1998; Hill *et al.*, 2002). While many of these researchers have argued that the clusters represent distinct subgroups, they may in fact reflect artificial divisions along a continuum of severity.

Others have attempted to define subgroups according to a priori principles, generally on the basis of premorbid or current IQ. Weickert *et al.* (2000) divided 117 participants on a clinical basis into groups who showed: (a) a general intellectual decline of 10 or more points; (b) consistently low premorbid and current IQ with no evidence of decline; and (c) average estimated premorbid IQ with no decline. The group demonstrating intellectual decline also exhibited deficits in executive function, memory and attention. The group with poor intellectual functioning showed language and visual processing deficits in addition to those shown by the former group. The remaining group of average IQ exhibited a mostly normal cognitive profile with some executive and attentional impairment. These clinically defined subgroups were validated using cluster analytic techniques.

In studies which have divided schizophrenia samples into relatively high and low ability groups, there have been either few differences across a wide range of cognitive functions (Kremen *et al.*, 2001) or, in a first episode sample, relatively few executive problems in the high ability group, despite impairments in memory in both groups (Bilder *et al.*, 2000).

Other researchers have specifically examined groups of schizophrenia patients whose neuropsychological function falls within the normal range (Kremen *et al.*, 2000; Holthausen *et al.*, 2002; MacCabe *et al.*, 2002). These studies have generally aimed to establish whether this group of patients constitutes an aetiologically different subgroup. Cognitively 'normal' patients tend to have higher premorbid IQs than control participants with similar current intellectual functioning (Kremen *et al.*, 2000; Holthausen *et al.*, 2002), suggesting a decline in function. They also tend to show subclinical deficits similar in profile to those with cognitive impairments. These findings have led some researchers to argue that this is not an aetiologically different subgroup (Holthausen *et al.*, 2002; Kremen *et al.*, 2000). So, in summary, the evidence from a priori separation of the groups is mixed, although those with poorer functioning seem to have a wider range of information processing problems.

A third method by which researchers have investigated within-group differences has been to individually rate cognitive profiles, which may then be used either in a case study or group design. Kremen *et al.* (2000) individually rated neuropsychological profiles of people with schizophrenia according to traditional clinical neuropsychological syndromes from lesion studies. Six subgroups emerged: (a) left temporal; (b) frontal; (c) widespread dysfunction; (d) within normal limits; (e) schizophrenia average; and (f) other. Allen *et al.* (2001) also attempted to classify participants as having either temporal or frontal lobe dysfunction and found that about a fifth of participants fell specifically into each category. Using a case study approach of five participants, Shallice *et al.* (1991) suggested that whilst the patients showed varying levels of general impairment, all five demonstrated executive deficits. By contrast, in a series of ten case studies with people with schizophrenia, Laws *et al.* (1996) showed that a majority had severely impaired verbal recall and familiar face naming, and that while memory and executive functions were independent in some patients, memory appeared to be the core deficit.

Finally, cognitive profiles of people with schizophrenia with different syndromes, characterised primarily by negative, disorganised or positive symptoms have been investigated. Groups defined by a predominance of negative symptoms have been associated with impairments executive functions (Cuesta and Peralta, 1995; Bryson *et al.*, 2001; Brazo *et al.*, 2002, Greenwood *et al.*, 2003); episodic memory (Brazo *et al.*, 2002), and working memory (Mahurin *et al.*, 1998).

Executive function (Greenwood *et al.*, 2003), working memory (Daban *et al.*, 2002), long-term memory (Brazo *et al.*, 2002) and attention (Ngan and Liddle, 2000) have also been associated with the disorganisation syndrome. The reality distortion syndrome has generally not been found to be correlated with cognitive deficits (Liddle and Morris, 1991; Basso *et al.*, 1998).

The data suffer from adopted methodologies which are bound to produce different subgroups given the different sampling criteria. If enough groups are defined or the criteria for groups are wide enough, then it is possible to classify everyone in a sample. However, this sometimes produces unusual groups labelled, for instance, 'other'. Consistent subgroups have not been found and the divisions made probably reflect level of severity as well as wider variations in the cognitive profiles. Even people who are cognitively normal have discrepancies in the level of cognitive functioning across different tasks, which suggests that CRT would be applicable across the severity range, although the empirical evidence for its worth has still to be produced.

The story so far

People with schizophrenia generally suffer cognitive dysfunction or inefficiency relative to levels which may be expected on the basis of family or environmental factors. This is apparent even before the onset of the symptoms of the disorder. Cognition function may undergo some decline at the first onset of symptoms, but then appears to remain relatively stable throughout the course of the disorder, with some fluctuations in relation to psychotic episodes. Some attentional impairments appear only to present during periods of psychosis. A subgroup of people who suffer a particularly poor outcome may be vulnerable to marked cognitive decline in later life.

Against the background of global deficits, people with schizophrenia frequently show differential impairment in pre-attentional processing, working and long-term explicit memory, executive functions, attention and social cognition. The extent and profile of these impairments varies widely between people. These particular cognitive processing components may make appropriate targets for intervention if the improvement of cognition was the sole objective of CRT. Alternatively, it may be possible to identify common underlying deficient cognitive processes which account for impaired performance on a range of tasks, and which could therefore provide a narrower focus for cognitive intervention. We will explore this possibility in the next chapter.

Chapter 3

Explaining cognitive dysfunction

So far, we have given an overview of cognitive function in schizophrenia and identified a broad range of cognitive deficits. If we are to develop cognitive remediation programmes, we need a clear and detailed understanding of the nature of deficits in each area of cognitive processing and of the links between various deficits. This may help us to develop a more parsimonious account of cognitive dysfunction in schizophrenia.

Much of the data we have already reviewed are ambiguous for two main reasons. First, the majority of studies that assess cognitive function in schizophrenia have used clinical neuropsychological measures, which were designed to identify brain regions which may not be functioning adequately. The availability of a large body of normative data for comparison makes their use advantageous, but they are generally complex and rarely measure specific cognitive functions. Second, even experimental cognitive tests which are more precise do not always allow the fractionation of gross abilities. Simpler subprocesses such as encoding, storage and retrieval in memory may be differentially impaired and may be influenced by other independent, but interacting cognitive processes (e.g. attention). Thus, impaired performance on any test may occur as a result of a variety of deficits. Furthermore, these deficits may not always be cognitive but may relate to motivational or affective factors.

Making sense of neuropsychological test performance

To overcome some of these problems, researchers have attempted to specify the cognitive processes involved in particular neuropsychological tests. Their approaches are exemplified by the study of one of the most frequently used tests, the Wisconsin Card Sorting Test (WCST, Grant and Berg, 1948). Performance on this test is notoriously difficult to interpret since it relies on a wide range of executive functions. For example, someone may achieve few categories because they are unable to:

- abstract new categories (abstraction)
- inhibit reinforced responses relating to a previous category (inhibition)
- attend well enough to maintain the current matching rule (sustained attention)
- remember the current matching rule (working memory).

Numerous studies have attempted to deconstruct the component executive functions required for the successful completion of the WCST. The main three methods are summarised below.

First, the structure of performance on the WCST has been investigated using exploratory factor analyses. Two or three factors have generally been extracted. Three-factor solutions tend to be composed of perseverative errors, non-perseverative errors and failure to maintain set (Greve et al., 1998; Koren et al., 1998). Two-factor solutions also identify a failure to maintain set factor, in addition to a factor which combines perseverative and non-perseverative errors (Greve et al., 1998). This latter factor appears to be associated with problem-solving ability (Greve et al., 1996, 1998), abstraction and sustained attention (Greve et al., 1995; Koren et al., 1998), and verbal long-term memory (Greve et al., 1998), but few associations between the failure to maintain set factor and performance on other neuropsychological tests have been found. The inconsistent results of these factor analyses in part may be accounted for by the varying samples used, which generally include both healthy controls and mixed clinical samples.

A second alternative is to investigate the correlations between WCST performance and performance on other neuropsychological tests, based on the assumption that high correlations should emerge when two measures assess similar underlying cognitive processes. Significant correlations have been found between WCST scores and measures of working memory, set shifting, verbal fluency, abstraction and attention (Gold et al., 1997; Glahn et al., 2000) but others have failed to find significant associations with working memory (Stratta et al., 1997a; Perry et al., 2001b).

Third, modifying the test instructions of the WCST, to place demands on different cognitive functions, has been used to investigate their influence on performance. Hartman et al. (2003) showed that differences between schizophrenia and control samples were largest when working memory demands were high. Providing visual cues to aid working memory did not lead to a significant reduction in impairment, but performance was normalised after controlling for speed of encoding information in working memory. Rossell and David (1997) showed that modifications which promoted planning, working memory and self-monitoring were the most successful in improving WCST scores for people with schizophrenia. Attempts to reduce motor demands had no effect. Pantelis et al. (1999) employed a similar strategy with a task closely related to the WCST, and showed that many people with chronic schizophrenia failed to 'learn set' and were impaired at both set shifting and concept formation.

The inconsistency of the findings using these various strategies to explain impaired performance on the WCST is marked. Some have emphasised sustained attention and executive functions such as problem solving, abstraction, planning and set shifting, but there is mixed evidence for verbal working memory and verbal long-term memory. It is possible that variations result from differences in the samples used across studies, but alternatively, significant within-group differences may influence the results. If performance relies on individual strengths and weaknesses, some people may fail due to working memory deficits, whilst others may have difficulty due to deficits in abstraction or attention and so on. Therefore, a clear understanding of the cognitive processes involved in WCST performance may never be established using group studies.

Experimental cognitive psychology

CRT needs to be designed so that it hits specified component processes but the literature so far has not allowed this precision. An alternative, more helpful approach comes from the experimental cognitive psychology tradition. While lacking extensive normative data, these tests tend to assess specific cognitive processes, and the performance of people with schizophrenia on these tests can be compared with that of healthy controls.

Making sense of the cognitive deficits in schizophrenia

Brief sensory store

Deficits in early information processing may result from a variety of cognitive impairments, for example, in attention, perception or speed of processing. The Span of Apprehension paradigm (Estes and Taylor, 1964; described in detail in Chapter 2) provides evidence for these alternative possibilities. This test asks participants to search an array of briefly presented visual items for a particular target. People with schizophrenia generally detect significantly fewer target stimuli than healthy controls. A number of cognitive processes appear to underlie this test. First, the representation of the array appears to be sorted in an iconic memory system, which stores the visual display in the form of visual representations, including information about the location, colour and size of the images (Neisser, 1968). This information is then transferred from iconic memory to working memory, both in a visual form and in an auditory form, as the items are rehearsed subvocally (Sperling, 1960). The stored stimuli are then scanned in iconic and/or working memory to detect the target stimuli (Estes and Taylor, 1964).

Since people with schizophrenia perform poorly on the Span of Apprehension task when they are required to report on only a small portion of the array (thus minimising the requirements of working memory), it seems likely that the crucial deficit occurs at the stage of iconic memory processing. A number of specific impairments have been proposed. First, people with schizophrenia may be impaired in visual search, in particular, in engaging, moving, or disengaging attentional focus. Second, less information may be processed each time attention is refocused and fixed on the array, and have a 'narrower attentional spotlight', so more shifts of attention would be required to encompass the same number of stimuli. Third, slowed response initiation may lead to generalised slowing in the task. At present, there is little evidence to distinguish between these hypotheses (summarised in Table 3.1). However, each of these may be attributable to impairments in the central executive.

Table 3.1 Impairments in the brief sensory store

Function	Level of functioning	Likely explanatory factors
Early visual processing	Impaired	Inefficient visual search (attentional control) Narrowed attentional focus Slow response initiation

Working memory slave systems

These form the maintenance components of working memory. Deficits may arise from the transfer of degraded or weak initial iconic representations from the brief memory store, which may thus be more susceptible to decay. Upon entry to the slave systems, deficits may occur in one or a combination of three stages of processing: encoding, storage and retrieval. Encoding refers to the initial phase in which memory traces are laid down (which may involve attending to stimuli, and creating an internal representation in working memory). Storage is reflected by the rate at which memories decay from the store and how well stored representations are refreshed by rehearsal. Executive deficits may lead to insufficient rehearsal or increased susceptibility to interference (distractibility) if attention is poorly controlled. Retrieval refers to the access of encoded memories.

Encoding

Encoding has been inferred from immediate recall on delayed response tasks. Significant impairment on spatial tasks at no delay has been found in most studies (Carter et al., 1996; Keefe et al., 1995; Fleming et al., 1997; Hartman et al., 2003). Those that have found no impairment suffer from ceiling effects

(Javitt *et al.*, 1997; Snitz *et al.*, 1999; Tek *et al.*, 2002), but it does seem likely that the impaired encoding in spatial short-term memory is relatively mild. Deficits are also apparent for visual information (Rabinowicz *et al.*, 1996; Lencz *et al.*, 2003) verbal and auditory information (Javitt *et al.*, 1997; Rabinowicz *et al.*, 2000) and proprioceptive information (Javitt *et al.*, 1999).

Slowed processing speed may account for encoding deficits in working memory. For instance, Hartman *et al.* (2003) found that when task difficulty was equated in the no-delay condition of a delayed response task, schizophrenia participants required longer presentations of the task stimuli.

An alternative hypothesis may be that impaired selective attention leads to working memory deficits, by hindering encoding or by reducing rehearsal which contribute to the maintenance of working memories (Oltmanns *et al.*, 1978). Selective attention refers to the ability to inhibit irrelevant material in order to focus on relevant stimuli. An impairment may be apparent by increased distractibility which has been found in schizophrenia (Goldberg *et al.*, 1998; Harvey and Serper, 1990). Brébion *et al.* (2000b) also showed that performance on a test of selective attention (the Stroop test) was predictive of performance on Digit Span tests. Similarly, Barch and Carter (1998) showed that reaction time facilitation on the Stroop test was strongly associated with poor performance on the Speaking Span test (a working memory test). It is not possible to differentiate between selective attention impairments contributing to encoding or to maintenance problems from these studies.

Maintenance

Maintenance is generally assessed using the discrepancy between responses at differing delays. Intact maintenance functions could be inferred from changes in responses over delay periods, despite an overall lower level of performance, if these occur in parallel to those of healthy controls. This pattern of responses has been shown in a number of studies using spatial, visual, auditory and proprioceptive modalities (Keefe *et al.*, 1995; McDowell and Clementz, 1996; Javitt *et al.*, 1997, 1999; Hartman *et al.*, 2003). A number of studies have produced conflicting findings, which may reflect a mild impairment which is only apparent with large working memory loads (Snitz *et al.*, 1999; Tek *et al.*, 2002; Lencz *et al.*, 2003).

Reduced rehearsal, resulting from slowed processing may account for maintenance impairments, particularly with large loads. Salamé *et al.* (1998) classified schizophrenia participants as 'slow' or 'fast' according to their reading rate. Only 'slow' participants showed significant impairments on a range of working memory tasks, including serial recall, digit span, and Corsi and pattern spans, relative to normal controls. Studies (cited above) showing associations between impaired selective attention and poor working memory may also indicate inefficient rehearsal which may have the greatest impact at high memory loads. Finally, poor executive control may result in limited rehearsal, although there is some evidence that limited rehearsal cannot account in full for short-term maintenance problems (Goldberg *et al.*, 1998).

The findings relating to impairments in the working memory slave systems are summarised in Table 3.2. There seem to be a number of likely contenders with respect to impaired component cognitive processes which can explain deficits in working memory, including slower processing speed, selective attention and executive control. Again, as with the brief sensory store, executive control (which may be associated with both of the other two processes) emerges as an explanatory factor.

Table 3.2 Impairments in the working memory slave systems

Function	Level of functioning	Likely explanatory factors
Encoding		
Spatial	(Mild) impairments/unclear	Slow processing speed
Visual	Impaired	Selective attention
Verbal	Impaired	
Auditory	Impaired	
Proprioceptive	Impaired	
Maintenance	Mixed findings	Slow processing speed
		Selective attention
		Executive control

Episodic buffer

The episodic buffer receives input from the working memory slave systems and long-term memory and is regulated by executive control. Therefore, we hypothesise that poor functioning of the episodic buffer arises from impairments in any one of these alternative subsystems. However, the episodic buffer is a relatively new concept (Baddeley, 2000) and its function has not been tested directly in schizophrenia.

The episodic buffer is a likely vehicle for context processing which was proposed by Cohen and Servan-Schreiber (1992) to account for inhibition, working memory and sustained attention deficits. In their model context information refers to representations of the local environment that must be actively held in mind to mediate task appropriate behaviour. These context representations will be maintained in the episodic buffer, since they comprise multidimensional short-term representations, potentially incorporating information both from the working memory slave systems and long-term memory. Therefore impairment in the episodic buffer may result in problems in context representation. Evidence of context processing deficits in schizophrenia will be reviewed later in this chapter, but overall, this evidence is not unequivocal or wholly consistent (Servan-Schreiber *et al.*, 1996; Cohen *et al.*, 1999; Elvevag *et al.*, 2000a, 2000b; Barch *et al.*, 2001).

An alternative perspective is that context processing relies on a number of subprocesses to allow the creation, storage and manipulation of context representations which may be differentially impaired. Information should be selectively attended to, accurately and robustly encoded within the episodic buffer, adequately maintained, and actively controlled and manipulated by the central executive. Deficits in these areas may all be explicable by impairments in the central executive (see Table 3.3).

Table 3.3 Impairments in the episodic buffer

Function	Level of functioning	Likely explanatory factors
Context processing	Probably impaired	Single mechanism for representation and maintenance of context Executive control

Long-term memory

The evidence we reviewed in Chapter 2 suggested that implicit long-term memory is intact in schizophrenia. The focus will therefore be on explicit long-term memory, which is impaired.

Explicit long-term memory is composed of three stages of processing: encoding, storage and retrieval. Failure on explicit memory tasks can result from difficulties at any one (or more) of these stages.

Encoding

Encoding is generally assessed by the immediate recall of learned material from one or more learning trials on memory tasks, although potential difficulties with retrieval need to be taken into account. Immediate recall is at least one standard deviation below the normative mean in schizophrenia samples, suggesting modest difficulties (Saykin *et al.*, 1991; Gold *et al.*, 1992; Paulsen *et al.*, 1995; Albus *et al.*, 1996; Tracy *et al.*, 2001).

Non-mnestic cognitive factors which may impact encoding have been assessed using three types of study: (a) correlational studies assessing the relationship between measures of memory and other cognitive functions thought to be influential; (b) studies in which the other non-mnestic variable is controlled; and (c) samples are matched according to the other non-mnestic variables.

The impact of attention

No significant correlations have been found in schizophrenia between measures of verbal or visual explicit memory and sustained attention (Chen *et al.*, 1997; Binder *et al.*, 1998) or more global attentional measures (Gold *et al.*, 1992). Similarly, people with schizophrenia perform worse on measures of explicit memory even when attentional processes are taken into account by matching samples (Rushe *et al.*, 1999) or controlling for attentional task performance (Saykin *et al.*, 1994; Gold *et al.*, 1995). Therefore, attentional impairments, assessed by a variety of measures, appear to contribute little to explicit encoding deficits.

The impact of processing speed

Slower processing speed in a schizophrenia sample relative to normal controls has been shown to be associated with both poorer superficial encoding and reduced efficiency of deep encoding, suggesting that faster participants had time to rehearse the material more often at encoding, strengthening the memory trace (Brebion *et al.*, 1998, 2001; Holthausen *et al.*, 2003).

The impact of executive functioning

Deep (i.e. semantic) encoding ensures better memory than shallow (i.e. perceptual) encoding. It is well established that people with schizophrenia tend not to use semantic features to organise verbal information, and this will lead to shallow encoding (Koh *et al.*, 1973; Gold *et al.*, 1992; Brebion *et al.*, 2001; Iddon *et al.*, 1998; Holthausen *et al.*, 2003). This problem has been proposed to account for their episodic memory deficit in schizophrenia.

Theories to account for the reduced use of semantic organisation in encoding highlight impaired strategy use or semantic processing deficits. People with schizophrenia show significant impairments in their ability to generate or implement effective mnemonic strategies on both visuo-spatial and verbal tasks (Iddon *et al.*, 1998; Seidman *et al.*, 2003). However, attempts to provide support for strategy use have not always led to normalised performance (Cutting, 1985; Iddon *et al.*, 1998), suggesting that general strategy use deficits cannot fully explain the failure to use semantic strategies in encoding.

The impact of semantic processing

Impaired verbal fluency supports the idea that semantic processing may explain problems in deep encoding in schizophrenia (Allen and Frith, 1983; Goldberg *et al.*, 1998). Studies showing reduced semantic priming in schizophrenia also show that categories may not be as highly organised as for normal controls (e.g. Spitzer *et al.*, 1993). Overall, reduced strategy use is highly likely to contribute to encoding deficits in long-term memory but these will be exacerbated by a general semantic processing impairment.

Storage

Storage is assessed using rates of forgetting of previously encoded material. In a recent meta-analysis of verbal episodic memory tasks, Cirillo and Seidman (2003) showed that while normal controls retained 85 to 93 per cent of initially recalled information of word lists or stories over time, people with schizophrenia retained only 74 per cent. They concluded that there is 'a mild but significantly impaired rate of forgetting in patients with schizophrenia'. Similar findings are apparent in studies using nonverbal material (Goldberg et al., 1993; Gold et al., 2000). However, Gold et al. (2000) showed that schizophrenia patients and healthy controls individually matched on level of initial recall (for stories and visual figures) had nearly identical delayed recall performance. Thus, forgetting may depend on the initial amount encoded.

Retrieval

Retrieval is usually assessed by comparing performance across tasks in which retrieval processes are supported to differing extents. Free recall is assumed to offer the least retrieval support, with cued recall and recognition requiring less effortful retrieval. Therefore, impaired retrieval may be inferred from a pattern of performance in which impairment in free recall is combined with normal recognition memory or cued recall. It should be noted, however, that supported retrieval may actually compensate for degraded or poorly consolidated memory traces, attributable to storage rather than retrieval deficits.

Findings in relation to recognition memory in schizophrenia have been mixed, with some studies showing no impairment in recognition memory (Calev, 1984a, 1984b; Goldberg et al., 1989; Nathaniel-James et al., 1996; Ragland et al., 2003) while others find mild to moderate impairment (Paulsen et al., 1995; Danion et al., 1999). In a meta-analysis of memory studies, Aleman et al. (1999) concluded that recognition memory is impaired in schizophrenia, but that the effect size for recognition memory is significantly smaller than that for recall (mean weighted effect size: recognition = 0.64; recall = 1.21). However, most studies have failed to match recall and recognition tasks for difficulty. Where tasks have been matched, people with chronic schizophrenia showed greater impairment in recall, whereas those with a less chronic form of the disorder showed no discrepancy between recall and recognition (Calev, 1984a, 1984b).

We have argued that the failure of people with schizophrenia spontaneously to use effective mnemonic strategies has a detrimental impact on encoding. These deficits are also likely to have a negative effect on retrieval processes. Retrieval relies upon effective searching through the long-term memory stores, and this is facilitated by strategic processes. Aberrations in the organisation of material within long-term memory are also likely to hinder identification of appropriate information for retrieval. Impaired processes which may explain long-term memory deficits in schizophrenia are summarised in Table 3.4. Impaired executive functions again emerge as strong contenders.

Table 3.4 Impairments in long-term memory

Function	Level of functioning	Likely explanatory factors
Encoding	Impaired	Slow processing speed Impaired strategy use Impaired semantic processing
Storage	Unclear/mild impairments	
Retrieval	Unclear/mild impairments	Impaired strategy use Impaired semantic processing

Executive function

The central executive is generally agreed to be a fractionated system, within which component processes may be differentially impaired. There have been few attempts to isolate specific executive component processes and deficits in others areas of cognition, particularly working memory, have been suggested to account for a large proportion of the performance on executive tasks (Goldman-Rakic, 1991).

For example, impaired performance on executive tasks, such as the WCST, could be attributable to deficiencies in the representations stored within each of the memory systems. Without this incoming material, the central executive is redundant as the effectiveness of executive processing depends upon the quality and quantity of material available for manipulation (in the form of stored representations). For instance, performance on the Hayling test, which is considered to be a test of executive function, may actually also rely on working and long-term memory storage. The first part of the test (A) requires participants to complete sentences with a word which makes sense in the context. The second part (B) requires participants to complete sentences with a word that *does not* make sense within the context. Therefore, the prepotent sensible completion word must be inhibited, an alternative word selected, and then a check made that the word does not in fact sensibly complete the sentence. The most efficient and strategic means by which this second part can be carried out, is to select a word from a category of objects (e.g. which are semantically related, or which can be found within the room). The high level of activation of this new category or schema may then automatically inhibit the prepotent responses and provide retrieval cues to facilitate the generation of words unrelated to the sentence. This process relies on a number of executive processes, including strategy generation and implementation, response inhibition, self-monitoring, selective attention and so on. In addition, for semantically related words, the category should be activated from long-term memory (whose internal structure may be poorly organised or subject to rapid decay) and used in combination with task instructions to create a context representation within the episodic buffer. Alternatively, the category may be maintained within working memory. The selection and use of this category of words then relies on executive functions, but the storage must rely on the capacity and efficiency of the episodic buffer or working memory. Therefore, the use of a strategy in the Hayling task may rely not only on executive functions, but also on the working memory slave systems, the episodic buffer and long-term memory.

Shallice and Burgess (1996) showed that a number of component processes used to complete the Hayling task were dissociable in patients with frontal lobe damage by correlating different outcome measures. First, the correlation between performance on parts A and B was close to zero. They suggested that this reflects the use of the contention scheduling system for part A and the supervisory attentional system for part B. Second, two types of correct response on part B were distinguished: those for which a strategy was used, and those for which a strategy was not. Whilst both types of correct response correlated negatively with the number of completion errors, they seemed to reflect separate processes. It was hypothesised that the strategy-related correct responses reflected the ability to generate and maintain a strategy in working memory, and that the non-strategy-related correct responses reflected monitoring and error correction.

In line with the example given above, Goldman-Rakic (1991) has argued that impaired performance in schizophrenia on so-called tests of executive functioning is explicable solely in terms of working memory dysfunction. But findings are mixed and studies of executive tasks other than the WCST are not always supportive of the working memory hypothesis. For example, Rushe et al. (1999) showed that whilst a schizophrenia sample showed significant impairment on the Tower of Hanoi task (a test of planning), they showed no significant impairment on a spatial working memory task.

Fluency tasks have been argued to rely on both executive functions (to initiate and implement efficient and strategic retrieval from memory) (Allen and Frith, 1983; Allen et al., 1993) and the semantic organisation of long-term memory (Goldberg et al., 1998). They may also be influenced by processing speed. Verbal fluency tasks require participants to rapidly generate words based on particular criteria. People with schizophrenia show greater impairment on category fluency tasks than on letter fluency tasks (Gourovitch et al., 1996; Bokat and Goldberg, 2003), which suggests that failure on fluency tasks cannot be explained only in terms of a retrieval (or executive) deficit, since this would have led to equally impaired category and letter fluency. Differential impairment in category fluency suggests that semantic processing impairments may contribute to fluency deficits. Consistent with these findings, Vinogradov *et al.* (2003) showed that for people with schizophrenia (but not normal controls) both lexical decision reaction time and semantic networks were significantly and independently related to category fluency. Therefore, category fluency deficits are likely to arise as a result of impairment in both retrieval processes and the semantic organisation of memory.

In summary, performance on executive tasks may be exacerbated by deficits in other areas of the information processing system (see Table 3.5). But it is clear that working memory problems cannot account for all the decreased performance in executive tasks and there is no doubt that a diagnosis of schizophrenia is associated with impairments in the central executive.

Table 3.5 Impairments in executive function

Function	Level of functioning	Likely explanatory factors
Strategy use and maintenance	Impaired	Long-term memory deficits Working memory deficits
Response inhibition	Impaired	Impaired self-monitoring
Fluency	Impaired	Response initiation Strategic retrieval Semantic processing deficits Slow speed of processing

Attention

Cowan's model (Cowan, 1988) suggests that the focus of attention comprises the most highly activated representations within memory. Attentional capacity can therefore be inferred from span tasks, such as Span of Apprehension, forward digit span or dual span tasks and within our model, these have been assumed to reflect temporary memory storage (see Table 3.6). Both attentional capacity and executive control of attention are reviewed in

Table 3.6 Impairments in attention

Function	Level of functioning	Likely explanatory factors
Capacity	Impaired	Capacity of working memory slave systems and episodic buffer
Control	Impaired	Executive deficits

Chapter 2, where it is reported that both are impaired in people with schizophrenia.

Executive function impairment as an explanatory factor for lower level cognitive impairments

Executive function deficits feature prominently and consistently in explanations for impaired performance, not only on tasks of executive function, but also of early visual processing, working memory, long-term memory, the episodic buffer and attention. Executive function is closely allied to meta-cognitive processes, or the ability to maintain conscious cognitive control of cognitive processing. These processes are therefore likely to make ideal targets for cognitive intervention.

Relationship of social cognitive impairments to deficits in other cognitive domains

Whilst social cognition is clearly related to cognition in non-social domains, non-social cognition seems to be a necessary but not sufficient condition for adequate social cognition (Penn et al., 1997a). The two are seen as different levels of analyses, such that social cognition is thought to represent a specialised domain of general cognition. In support of this view are findings that whilst cognition and social cognition are correlated, the match between performance on measures of the two is far from perfect. For example, 'social intelligence' is not strongly correlated with verbal IQ, performance IQ or other cognitive tasks (Sternberg et al., 1995) and only about 25 per cent of the variance in social functioning in schizophrenia can be accounted for by cognitive test performance (e.g. Wykes et al., 1990, 1992; Bellack et al., 1994).

The relationship between social and non-social cognition is poorly understood and numerous studies have investigated associations between them to more precisely elucidate the nature of social cognitive deficits.

Most affect perception studies have attempted to distinguish between hypotheses that impaired performance reflects an emotion-specific deficit or a face perceptual deficit by controlling for the affective component of the task. In general, people with schizophrenia show facial perceptual processing deficits rather than affective perception impairment per se (Morrison et al., 1988; Mandal et al., 1998; Edwards et al., 2002), but not all findings have been consistent with this (Novic et al., 1984). Furthermore, studies which evaluate schizophrenia participants' own facial expressions of emotions indicate that they are less accurate and responsive in their facial and vocal affective expressions than healthy controls (Borod et al., 1989; Schneider et al., 1990). In a recent review, Mandal et al. (1998) conclude that despite a general impairment in perception or expression of facial emotions, schizophrenia patients are highly sensitive to negative emotions, particularly fear and anger.

Studies that use only facial material cannot distinguish between theories which suggest that the deficit is specifically one of social cognition or which suggest that it can be explained with reference to non-social cognitive deficits. Emotion perception has been frequently found to be associated with early visual processing (Addington and Addington, 1998; Kee et al., 1998), but also sustained visual attention (Addington and Addington, 1998; Bryson et al., 1997), semantic retrieval (Whittaker et al., 2001) and executive functioning (Bryson et al., 1997; Whittaker et al., 2001).

Social cue perception has also been associated with early visual processing (Corrigan et al., 1994; Sergi and Green, 2003), verbal long-term memory (Corrigan et al., 1994; Lancaster et al., 2003), performance on the WCST (Lancaster et al., 2003) and context processing (Penn et al., 2002).

Theory of mind is a metacognitive ability and has frequently been associated with executive functioning. Unsurprisingly, theory of mind deficits have been identified in schizophrenia (Greig et al., 2004) and associations have been found with executive function (measured by the WCST and Trails B), verbal long-term memory (Pickup and Frith, 2001; Greig et al., 2004) and IQ (Pickup and Frith, 2001; Greig et al., 2004) but these latter problems have not been able to account for all of the theory of mind deficit. Associations between social cognitive impairments and other cognitive deficits are shown in Table 3.7.

Table 3.7 Impairments in social cognition

Social cognitive function	Associated explanatory general cognitive processes
Affect perception	Face perception Early visual processing Sustained visual attention Semantic retrieval Executive function
Social cue perception	Early visual processing Verbal long-term memory Executive function Context processing
Theory of mind	Verbal long-term memory Executive function IQ

Non-cognitive influences on cognitive influences on cognitive test performance

It is clear from the above summary that cognitive test performance can rarely be used as a straightforward indication of specific impaired cognitive processes. Cognitive subsystems are highly interactive and impaired test performance is frequently explicable by a breakdown in any number of the parts of the system. In addition, cognitive performance can be influenced by non-cognitive factors, including treatment (particularly medication), mood and motivation (see Table 3.8 for a summary).

Table 3.8 Non-cognitive factors influencing cognitive performance

Influential non-cognitive factor	Impact on cognitive function
Treatment	Marginal inconsistent effects
Depression	Impaired verbal long-term memory Impaired verbal working memory Slow speed of processing
Motivation (negative symptoms)	Impaired executive function Slow speed of processing Impaired sustained attention Impaired working memory Impaired long-term memory

Treatment

It has been suggested that some of the cognitive difficulties experienced by people with schizophrenia may be a result of the treatments rather than of the disorder. Several different approaches have been used, from invasive treatments such as leucotomy and ECT, through to the typical and the newer atypical neuroleptic medications. We have argued that cognitive difficulties exist even before the disorder becomes apparent and that these difficulties can be observed regardless of whether symptoms are present or medication is used (e.g. Saykin et al., 1994). So it seems unlikely that all of the cognitive difficulties are the result of treatment.

The evidence from studies of the most invasive treatments carried out in the past does not show major effects on cognition (Harvey, 2004). Some side effects, such as tardive dyskinesia, are associated with cognitive difficulties not just between groups with and without the side effect, but in relation to the severity of the side effect too (Paulsen et al., 1994). Of course, this could just mean that cognitive difficulties are a risk factor for the development of tardive dyskinesia rather than the medication being a joint cause. A further difficulty in assessing the direct effects of medication on cognition is that medication has an effect on symptoms which then may directly or indirectly result in changes in cognitive performance. However, the evidence suggests that current medication treatment does seem to help cognition and there is inconclusive evidence for any detrimental effects. Further detail on the helpful effects will be reviewed later in Chapter 5.

Depression

People suffering from depression generally perform significantly worse than healthy controls on tests of psychomotor speed, attention, memory and executive function but in general, these deficits disappear on remission of the depressive symptoms (Lemelin and Baruch, 1998; Nebes *et al.*, 2000; Austin *et al.*, 2001). Depression is common in people with schizophrenia (Birchwood *et al.*, 2000) and thus cognitive deficits in schizophrenia may, at least in part, be accounted for by depressive symptoms. Depression has been linked primarily with encoding impairment in both verbal long-term memory, verbal working memory and speed of processing in schizophrenia (Brébion *et al.*, 1997b, 2000b, 2001; Holthausen *et al.*, 1999a). However, this is unlikely to provide a sufficient cause for memory impairments in schizophrenia.

Motivation

Studies which offer monetary incentives for good performance on the WCST have not shown that poor motivation contributes significantly to poor performance in people with schizophrenia. This will be discussed in greater detail in Chapter 5. There is, however, significant evidence to suggest that negative symptoms (which include apathy and amotivation) are associated with impairments in executive function, speed of processing, sustained attention, working memory and long-term memory (Bryson *et al.*, 2001; Nieuwenstein *et al.*, 2001; Donohoe and Robertson, 2003; Heydebrand *et al.*, 2004).

Integrative cognitive theories of schizophrenia

Cognitive deficits in people with schizophrenia may result from a wide range of diverse and complex interacting factors. This panoply of impairments is problematic for designing a parsimonious model of CRT. Without a clear framework for the difficulties then CRT will inevitably have to be designed for specific individual deficits which may result in a multitude of methods. Earlier in the chapter, we suggested that deficits in a range of cognitive domains could be accounted for by impairments in executive control. In the next sections, we will describe the ways in which psychological theorists of schizophrenia have sought to integrate findings and to identify a unifying specific deficit which can explain more specifically the signs and symptoms of schizophrenia.

Metarepresentation

Frith (1987, 1992) and Frith and Done (1989) proposed that the fundamental cognitive deficit in schizophrenia is one of metarepresentation (i.e. second order representation). This is the ability to represent (e.g. think about) a primary representation (e.g. a thought or image of the world) or to reflect upon our perceptions or thoughts about the world. A deficit in metarepresentation is proposed to encompass three crucial specific abnormalities in schizophrenia: in (a) willed action; (b) self-monitoring; and (c) inferring the mental states of others. This theory relies heavily on Shallice and Burgess's (1996) model of executive functioning.

Abnormalities in willed action

'Willed action' refers to internally driven, controlled behaviours which are under the control of the central executive (i.e. actions carried out by Shallice and Burgess's Supervisory Attentional System). A deficit in generating willed actions may have a number of consequences. First, it may result in a failure to act according to internal cues; in other words, goals, intentions or non-routine responses are not successfully initiated. This may account for impaired performance on fluency or planning tasks. Second, since willed actions are no longer available to temper or override stimulus-driven responses (i.e. Shallice and Burgess's contention schedules), these automatic responses can now proceed unchecked. This may lead to behaviour which is inappropriate (i.e. distractibility or disorganisation) or repetitive (i.e. perseveration). Such behaviour is apparent in the performance on a wide range of executive and attentional tasks in people with schizophrenia.

Abnormalities in self-monitoring

In order to be aware of the causes of our actions, Frith postulated a self-monitoring system in the form of a 'corollary discharge' which provides automatic feedback regarding our actions and intentions. This would correspond to the experience of 'will' and would enable us to distinguish between our own actions and those which have external causes, and between our own automatic actions and our own willed actions. Frith suggests that for people with schizophrenia, a failure in the self-monitoring corollary discharge system leads to the misattribution of their own willed actions to external agents. Whilst Frith suggests that the corollary discharge functions automatically, there is evidence to suggest that people with schizophrenia have deficits in self-monitoring, although this has frequently been attributed to the functioning of the central executive.

Abnormalities in inferring the mental states of others

Frith suggests that this equates to an acquired 'theory of mind' deficit or the ability to represent the mental states of other people. Theory of mind is under the control of the central executive and has been shown to be impaired in people with schizophrenia. Metarepresentation (including the ability to infer the mental states of others), generating willed actions and self-monitoring are all functions of the central executive (although Frith suggests that there may be an additional automatic component to self-monitoring in the form of the corollary discharge). Consistent with his theory are clear findings of impaired executive functioning in people with schizophrenia. Furthermore, deficits in other areas of information processing have frequently been attributed to executive impairments: deficits in attentional control may result from impaired executive control; long-term memory deficits may reflect impaired strategy use; the functioning of the episodic buffer relies on executive control processes; working memory storage appears to be due in part, to deficits in selective attention; and deficits in early visual processing have been attributed to problems in visual search (or attentional control) or slow response initiation. While Frith's theory is generally consistent with the data, direct tests of the theory have generally only investigated the relationship between cognitive functions and symptoms. There are therefore a number of interesting hypotheses that are yet to be tested.

The use of context

According to Hemsley (1987, 1993, 1994, 1996, 2005), a weakening of the inhibitory influence of stored schematic information within memory on current perception constitutes the basic deficit in schizophrenia. In normal cognitive function, contextual information is said to trigger the activation of schemas within long-term memory which results in the generation of predictions, 'expectancies' and 'response biases' regarding subsequent sensory input. A breakdown in this system which operates on a moment by moment basis to integrate stored material with current sensory input, leads to the intrusion into conscious awareness of contextually irrelevant or redundant sensory input and long-term memories. This may disrupt the control of speech or action, leading to disorganisation and bizarre behaviour. In addition, the abnormal experience of the covariation of events is said to lead to a faulty reasoning style, by which conclusions are formed on the basis of insufficient or anomalous evidence. For example, some people with schizophrenia require less information to reach a decision on a probabilistic reasoning task than healthy controls (Garety and Freeman, 1999). This finding is consistent with the suggestion of a greater influence of immediate environmental stimuli in people with schizophrenia relative to the effects of prior learning: thus, they may 'jump to conclusions' about the meaning of events.

A lack of spontaneous behaviour is said to reflect 'avoidant' coping strategies employed to minimise the effects of the overwhelming and disordered perception and thought. Furthermore, the cognitive abnormality or 'information overload' may become sufficiently severe to make it difficult for goal-directed activities to be carried out at all.

Evidence in support of the model has come from the performance of people with schizophrenia on a number of experimental paradigms which assess the pre-attentional formation of associations between stimuli. These include tests of Latent Inhibition, Kamin's Blocking Effect, negative priming and pre-pulse inhibition of the startle response, and studies with people with schizophrenia suggest that, particularly in the acute phase, new learning fails to be influenced by previously learnt responses.

Whilst there is significant supporting evidence for Hemsley's theory, this tends to come from studies with people in the acute phases of schizophrenia. Furthermore, latent inhibition appears to normalise as the duration of illness exceeds 12 months (Gray *et al.*, 1995b). However, evidence regarding stable information processing deficits is consistent with the model. First, impairments in the response inhibition, attentional control, semantic organisation in memory and context processing are consistent with the suggestion that people with schizophrenia suffer from intrusions of contextually inappropriate material. Second, disorganised behaviour and poor response initiation is consistent with the hypothesis that an information overload leads to a shutdown of processing or difficulties in initiating goal-directed behaviour.

Cohen and Servan-Schreiber (1992) and Cohen *et al.* (1996, 1999) hypothesise that people with schizophrenia have a deficit in 'the representation and maintenance of context information needed to select task-appropriate action' and that a disturbance in this single mechanism may account for a range of cognitive difficulties associated with schizophrenia. Context representations are used to specify and support task-relevant information against sources of interference. They are composed of different types of information, such as specific prior stimuli, the result of processing a sequence of prior stimuli (e.g. a sentence), or more abstract information such as task instructions.

Initial support for this theory came from an unusual source, computational models, in which context processing is degraded and performance on a variety of tasks (e.g. the Stroop task, the CPT and a lexical disambiguation task) was found to closely simulate that of people with schizophrenia (Cohen and Servan-Schreiber, 1992). We suggested earlier that an association between the Stroop test and working memory performance measured by the Speaking Span test (Barch and Carter, 1998) could indicate that impaired selective attention accounts for encoding deficits in the working memory slave systems. However, this association may be explained in terms of a context processing deficit. According to Cohen and Servan-Schreiber's (1992) model, context representations provide support for task-relevant processes (e.g. colour naming) allowing these to be dominant over irrelevant processes (e.g. word naming). For the Speaking Span test, a series of words are presented one at a time to participants. Participants are asked to recall and use each of the words within a sentence. This procedure is repeated for series of words of increasing length. Context representations support the generation of new sentences, so a deficit in context processing may lead to impairment on both tasks.

Other studies have compared context processing of people with schizophrenia and healthy controls directly. Servan-Schreiber *et al.* (1996) used the A-X version of the CPT to test context processing in both unmedicated first-episode patients and people with more chronic forms of schizophrenia. In this version of the task, letters of the alphabet are presented one at a time on a screen and the participant is asked to respond to the letter X whenever it is preceded by the letter A. The letter A therefore provides a contextual cue for the target X. Two modifications were made to this task. In the first case, the A-X sequence occurred for the majority of the time. The high frequency of cue-target sequences (A-X) was hypothesised to lead to an increased tendency to respond to X. People with schizophrenia made significantly more false alarms following B-X which suggests that they had difficulty taking account of the context in which the X appeared. The second modification tested participants' ability to maintain context information over time by using two different inter-stimulus intervals. Schizophrenia participants demonstrated significantly increased B-X errors with the longer interval, indicating difficulties in maintaining context representations. Similar results have been found in other studies (Cohen and Servan-Schreiber, 1992; Barch *et al.*, 2001).

There are, as always, some inconsistent findings in this area. Elvevag *et al.* (2000a, 2000b) manipulated the length of time that contextual information needed to be held in mind, as well as the consistency of contextual cues for the CPT, the Stroop test and a cued spatial location task. They found that schizophrenia participants showed no specific deficits attributable to context processing in a number of the measures.

Working memory

According to Goldman-Rakic (1987, 1991), the fundamental problem in schizophrenia is a deficit in working memory. Her definition of working memory is different to that of Baddeley and Hitch (1974) in its emphasis on the short-term storage but not the manipulation of information held in mind over a period of seconds. Like Cohen and Servan-Schreiber's context representations, working memories are presumed to be used to guide behaviour, but working memories are only very recent representations of the outside world, and do not include other abstract information or representations held within long-term memory.

Goldman-Rakic argues that the deficits of people with schizophrenia on many tests of executive function can be explained by the impaired ability to maintain representations online to guide behaviour (i.e. working memory). For example, for accurate performance on the WCST, the sorting principle must be maintained in working memory to guide behaviour, as no information about the correct response is available within the environment. In the Stroop task, the participant must retain the task instructions to report the colour of the word in memory and use this to override the prepotent tendency to read the word. The Tower of London task is argued to rely on representations of future events (i.e. goals) or of past events (i.e. previous moves) to guide behaviour and thus a working memory deficit may account for impaired performance. Finally, impaired verbal or design fluency is argued to arise from impairments in the ability to guide behaviour on the basis of representations.

This theory is able to account for a wide range of deficits in working memory and executive functioning, as well as in long-term memory, if deficits are assumed to result from impaired strategy use (which requires the temporary storage and online maintenance of a strategy). However, findings that performance on tests of executive function are not always associated with working memory impairments (e.g. Rushe *et al.*, 1999, see earlier) are difficult for the model to explain.

Processing resources

Nuechterlein and Dawson (1984) have proposed that a wide range of deficits in schizophrenia can be viewed in terms of reduced availability of attentional or processing resources (Nuechterlein and Dawson, 1984). This is consistent with evidence that deficits associated with schizophrenia tend to relate to controlled, effortful, capacity-demanding processing (e.g. sustained and selective attention, working memory and long-term explicit memory) and not to passive, automatic processing (e.g. implicit memory). The reduced availability of processing capacity may be caused by:

• poor executive responses to task demands, despite normal capacity processing resources
• inefficient use of processing capacity which is directed to task-irrelevant stimuli
• controlled processing resources being needed for cognitive operations that usually rely on automatic processes
• reduced total processing capacity.

These theories are insufficiently detailed to account for more recent findings of specific deficits in executive processes such as self-monitoring or strategy use. According to the theories above, we may expect people with schizophrenia to show less efficient but qualitatively similar processing in these respects to healthy controls.

Top-down or bottom-up?

Information processing takes place within a complex and highly interactive system, and impairments in any cognitive task may be accounted for by a variety of cognitive processes or non-cognitive factors such as mood or medication. Cognitive theories of schizophrenia have attempted to identify unifying deficits by which to explain the plethora of cognitive impairments in schizophrenia, but they have differed in crucial ways. For example, Hemsley's theory differs from that of Frith in suggesting that cognitive impairments arise from abnormalities in bottom-up or automatic processing, rather than in top-down, regulatory control, which may be attributable to the central executive. Hemsley is concerned with the boundary between conscious and unconscious processes whilst Frith deals primarily with conscious control. However, a reduced influence of past learning on current behaviour may limit improvements in executive functioning over time, as cognitive skills are unlikely to benefit from past experience.

The models we have reviewed were developed mainly to account either for symptoms or for the variation in cognitive deficits. None provide a clear understanding of their relationship to social functioning and it is not clear to us how any of the models would help in the development of CRT. We have emphasised the consistency with which executive impairments appear to emerge as explanatory factors to account for lower level cognitive impairments. It is also agreed amongst theorists that people with schizophrenia have some difficulty in maintaining a temporary schema to guide behaviour whether this forms a context representation, a metarepresentation or a working memory. We will argue that executive and particularly metacognitive control should form the primary targets for cognitive intervention and that we should teach people broad generic schemas which are applicable in a wide range of situations. We will use these cognitive elements in a model for the relationship between cognition and social functioning.

Throughout this and the preceding chapter we have commented on the discrepant findings from group studies that can be accounted for by the differences between individuals, particularly in people with schizophrenia. It is well known that their performance is highly variable and the explanation for the deficits might then be based on individual cognitive strengths and weaknesses. Clinicians and researchers interested in cognitive remediation should be mindful of the range of explanations for performance on any one cognitive task, and cautious in generating and testing hypotheses about individual cognitive strengths and weaknesses which will be used to guide treatment programmes. Without a clear formulation of the underlying impaired component processes, it will be easy to offer solutions for cognitive difficulties which are inappropriate or ineffective. We also need to capitalise on strengths such as implicit memory in designing training techniques. Later in this book we will begin to develop a model of the relationship of cognition and outcome which we think has heuristic value for the development of cognitive remediation and will suggest targets for intervention which might be most effective in promoting change.

Chapter 4

Why rehabilitate cognitive deficits in schizophrenia?

So far we have identified the key cognitive deficits that are associated with a diagnosis of schizophrenia. The main impairments, pre-attention, attention, working and long-term memory, and executive functioning, by their very nature must interfere with everyday functioning. For instance, problems of sustained attention make it very difficult to follow a television programme or a conversation, with memory problems you forget what you need from the shops and when to take your medication, and executive functioning difficulties mean that large amounts of effort are needed to resolve every new situation. People with a diagnosis of schizophrenia and cognitive difficulties now emphasise that cognition should be a target for rehabilitation. They hope that successful intervention will help them to improve their current quality of life.

We will argue that, in addition to their effects on current functioning, cognitive difficulties should be a target for rehabilitation because of their widespread effect on other aspects of the disorder. There is evidence that this is true of both overall outcome and the factors that make up the bio-psycho-social model and which impact on outcome. Cognition will also be compared to other putative predictors of outcome since to be a key target it should account for a significant proportion of the variance relative to other predictors. So in order to be a key target for intervention we would have to establish not only that there is a relationship between cognition and functioning but also some suggestion that there is a causal link between the two. We can then assume that a change in cognition might have an impact on functioning. Our investigation of the evidence for link has therefore been guided by the following questions:

Question 1: Are cognitive indicators related to outcomes cross-sectionally and longitudinally?

Question 2: Are cognitive indicators related to outcomes following rehabilitation?

Question 3: Do cognitive indicators have a significant weight compared to other factors such as symptoms?

Key cognitive targets could be related to outcome in general or to specific domains of functioning. Targets might also not be directly related to outcome but might limit the rate of rehabilitation by interfering with therapy; for example, interfering with vocational rehabilitation or the learning of social skills. Figure 4.1 shows a model of these possible relationships.

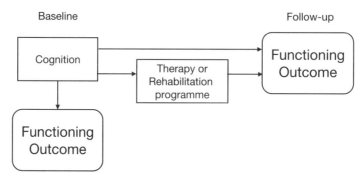

Figure 4.1 Possible relationships of a key cognitive target to functioning outcome

In considering outcomes we make the distinction between functional capacity (the ability of the person to produce a behaviour), functional performance (the actual production of the behaviour in the natural setting) and functional outcome, which is the result of capacity and performance and society's and the person's responses to reductions in ability. This latter effect is known in John Wing's terminology as handicap (Wing, 1978). For people with a diagnosis of schizophrenia, outcome has often been measured in terms of the remission of symptoms – the hallucinations and delusions that make up positive symptoms. This is termed clinical outcome and is important, as it is associated with distress and interferes with everyday life. Overall functional outcome can be additionally divided into a further set of specific domains such as work, independent living skills (shopping, budgeting, etc.) and a social life. A further area that is not often considered but is essential to overall recovery is the person's satisfaction with life (usually termed quality of life) and their feelings of self-efficacy and self-esteem. This outcome has been designated as subjective experience.

The life and clinical course of people with schizophrenia

In order to distinguish clear domains of outcome and the range of functioning within them we must first investigate what course might be expected. We must also know whether changes in services and treatments have had an impact on the natural course. For instance, it may be that a particular treatment has a detrimental effect on long-term outcome or that particular service structures, for example, institutionalised care, are associated with poor outcome. The natural course would then have been affected and unless we take this into account we may under- or over-estimate potential outcome. It will then be possible to set realistic goals for improvement in functioning that should be affected by any new treatment for schizophrenia. This natural course is often thought to be uniformly poor but in fact a number of different and distinct outcomes have been identified including:

- those having a single episode
- those with an episodic course in which the acute symptoms resolve although functioning is less than might have been expected from prognostic factors
- a chronic course in which symptoms may fluctuate against a background of general poor functioning.

In a meta-analysis of studies on outcome since 1895, Hegarty *et al.* (1994) showed varying medical interventions had not dramatically improved the overall outcome of patients with schizophrenia. Outcome is notoriously difficult to define but Hegarty and colleagues described three main domains: symptomatic (recovered, in remission, well without residual symptoms), social functioning (socially recovered or not) and levels of independence. Across the century 40.2 per cent of people with the diagnosis of schizophrenia showed a favourable outcome in any or all of their outcome domains. Hegarty and colleagues concluded that the decade by decade fluctuation in this recovery rate was due to variations in the strictness of the definition of schizophrenia. But even when this factor had been taken into account, the addition of anti-psychotic medication raised the percentage of patients with a moderate to good social outcome from 25 per cent at the beginning of the twentieth century to about 35 per cent in the mid-1990s. So there is some evidence that new treatments have improved outcome but that there is still much room for further improvements.

Similarly both Dick Warner (2004) and Glynn Harrison and colleagues (2001) conclude that just under half the people with schizophrenia have a good global outcome. But even when symptoms or disability were persistent, Harrison and colleagues found about one-fifth were able to sustain employment. In a further set of studies, variability in outcome was again found, but this time in people who at baseline had an established severe and chronic disorder. Harding *et al.* (1987a) in a 32-year follow-up study of patients in Vermont showed that one-half to two-thirds of the sample achieved considerable improvement or recovery. Similarly in two separate studies of the closure of long-stay hospitals in the UK (Wykes and Dunn, 1992; Leff and Trieman, 2000), decreases in dependence on psychiatric care were found in many patients and improvements in the number of friends, although formal measures of social behaviour and clinical symptoms had changed little over the intervening six and five years respectively. Wykes (1994) reported that

16 per cent of her chronic sample were now in open employment and 38 per cent were living in their own homes despite high levels of dependence on psychiatric care at baseline.

Outcome across these studies is therefore variable with people showing some further recovery even after many years of the disorder. This variability may be affected by the presence of a responsive psychiatric service and certainly the Wykes and Dunn (1992) study was carried out in a service which was deemed a centre of excellence in rehabilitation. Recent comparisons of long-term outcome between the Vermont group in Harding's studies and a matched group from Maine also support this conclusion. The good outcome of the Vermont patients may have been due to the availability of a pioneering rehabilitation programme that emphasised engagement with the community. Vermont patients were also provided with a variety of residential, work and social opportunities. These opportunities resulted in a more diverse and favourable course compared to the group from Maine who only received traditional care (DeSisto *et al.*, 1995, 1999). So if appropriate medication (Hegarty *et al.*, 1994) and comprehensive rehabilitation services (Harding *et al.*, 1987a, 1987b) are provided, outcomes can improve even for those people who have chronic disorders.

The results of studies on the course of schizophrenia have been influenced by the use of different sampling methods, types of analysis, diagnostic criteria and historical treatments. It is therefore surprising that different studies over time do contain similar findings of a good outcome in a proportion of people. These data contradict the pessimistic outcome assumed in the early descriptions of the disorder and suggest the need for continued therapeutic optimism and for supporting rehabilitation and recovery services throughout the progress of the disorder even if there has been failure earlier.

Consumers' views of course, outcome and recovery

In measuring good outcome or good functioning there are a variety of possible definitions accepted by epidemiologists, health care professionals and service providers. But in this book we have been emphasising the need also to consult consumers on such measures. What would they consider to be the elements of a good recovery? When we consulted them the list includes the suggestions listed in Table 4.1.

These sorts of recovery elements map onto those described by academics

Table 4.1 Consumer views of recovery

- I want to be able to do things that other people do, like have a boyfriend and a job.
- I want to have friends.
- I want to be able to cook and eat when I want.
- I want to live in my own place not a hostel.

and clinicians as work functioning, social functioning, living skills (being able to cook and clean) and dependence on psychiatric services. These are the aspirations of people who use psychiatric services, but consumers have also written eloquently on the way that these aspirations are achieved, not through rehabilitation but by a process called the recovery paradigm. In recovery, people who are disabled are acknowledged to take an active part in their own rehabilitation and hope is the key to success. Deegan (1997) describes three stages in the recovery process: denial of the illness, despair and finally hope which is born out of small personal successes, such as going to the shops. This view is of people who are not passive recipients but are active and responsible. It contrasts with the historical view of rehabilitation which is something done to an essentially passive person. The modern view is to provide the environment in which these recovery processes can be nurtured. In this formulation a further outcome follows from interaction of the individual with the rehabilitation services – their empowerment, that is their ability to take part in their own, individual recovery.

Predicting recovery

Although outcome can be variable depending on the rehabilitation efforts and recovery opportunities that are available, it may be possible to improve the low level or low rate of recovery. In order to do so it would be helpful to identify what factors are associated with good outcomes. Knowledge of these associated factors may help to identify interventions that can enhance outcome either by providing compensating support or rehabilitation. In this book the focus is on cognition but any intervention to improve aspects of cognition needs also to take into account other factors that may hamper or enhance the effect of any treatment. It may be that treatment needs to be confined to specific groups or specific periods in the course of the disorder and some indication may be provided by work carried out to identify those factors that impede it. It would certainly fit with a recovery paradigm if the rehabilitation intervention was provided in the most hopeful climate.

First, it is essential to have some theoretical model to provide a frame of reference for assessing factors that affect recovery. The most ubiquitous for schizophrenia is one that includes both vulnerability and stress and that links several types of factor together to allow the prediction of a symptomatic episode of psychosis. Genes and other biological factors may predispose (but not determine) the likelihood of developing behaviours and experiences that are described within the schizophrenia diagnostic framework. Environmental factors will influence the expression of the predisposition. This type of model was first proposed by Zubin and Spring (1977) and has been modified many times (e.g. Nuechterlein and Dawson, 1984). The subsequent models now contain three main elements: vulnerability (or liability) factors, resilience factors and stressors which interact with vulnerability and resilience.

Vulnerability factors are usually divided into biological (such as biochemical dysfunctions) and personal (such as low self-esteem). Resilience factors can be social (e.g. supportive family), biological (e.g. appropriate medication) and personal (e.g. coping strategies for abnormal perceptions). Stressors are generally environmental factors such as expressed emotion, life events and an over-stimulating environment. The likelihood of an episode of psychosis is dependent on an interaction between all three factors.

A simple model of the processes involved was provided in Chapter 1 and in Table 4.2 there is a list of the factors involved. We have also included metacognition as a resilience factor as this is involved in our own model of CRT. Metacognition might be useful in recognising the cognitive difficulties and identifying changes in behaviour that overcome or compensate for these problems.

These sorts of models were developed to deal with symptomatic outcome and so cognitive factors have been further divided. They are: (a) those linked to episodes (episode linked factors) which are not noticeably different from normal between episodes; (b) chronic fluctuating factors which are observably impaired from the time of the first episode and possibly before, but which markedly worsen during episodes of illness; (c) stable factors which do not change with episodes of acute symptoms and the course of the illness but are markedly worse than normal levels at all stages of the disorder. Chapter 2 described these in detail. This differentiation may also be relevant for other outcomes. The following overview describes the different factors in relationship to cognition in order to identify its role in the vulnerability-stress

Table 4.2   Factors involved in the onset and relapse in schizophrenia

	Vulnerability factors	Stressors	Resilience factors
Biological	Genetic (e.g. COMT gene) Physiological reactivity	Antenatal (e.g. maternal influenza, starvation) Perinatal (e.g. anoxia) Cannabis use	Medication
Psychological	Poor cognitive processing	Life events and daily hassles	Coping strategies
		High levels of cognitive processing required (e.g. in some social environments)	Metacognition
Social	Poor social skills	Family or staff criticism or overinvolvement	Social supports (e.g. friends, family and health services)
		Chronic difficulties (e.g. poverty, poor housing)	

model. We are particularly interested in the interactions or effects on other variables.

Biological factors

Although genetic factors have been implicated in schizophrenia, it is only recently that these genetic markers have been replicated in samples from around the world (Bray *et al.*, 2003). These genetic markers have also been associated with poorer cognitive functioning, such as executive and memory functions (Egan *et al.*, 2001a; Bilder *et al.*, 2002b). What is not clear is whether the presence of a gene that confers poorer cognition would, in the context of schizophrenia, confer the poorest outcome and whether these markers would have an effect on the efficacy of treatment in the same way that some genes may affect the helpfulness and side effects of drug treatment for other disorders. But genetic influence can be viewed as the upper limit to potential and it is clear that there is still some variation that can be affected by the environmental influences, including treatments or education for the cognitive system.

Demographic and clinical history factors

The onset of schizophrenia is often in late adolescence to early adulthood which is the key period in which new roles in education, work and social life are being experienced and novel ways of responding are learnt. The fact that onset is early will affect functioning in different ways. At this age the person is not only adapting to the odd perceptions which generally accompany the onset of schizophrenia, but because acute episodes often mean spending time in hospital and away from family and friends, they also miss out on the widening of social roles. There will also be effects on cognition solely due to early onset, as the development of memory systems, social cognition and executive functioning can continue into late adolescence. The cognitive system is therefore less of an expert system and the development of cognitive schemas is delayed or disrupted.

Cognitive systems also change with age. They show benefits in social cognition, including theory of mind, and more crystallised processes compared to those in younger people who are more adept (relatively) at dealing with novel problems. Furthermore, effects on short-term memory are noticeable in the elderly with reductions in its efficiency. The effect of this ageing process has been suggested to be more potent in some institutionalised groups with schizophrenia. However, ageing does not seem to have a major impact on functional outcome in the majority of people with schizophrenia as in a recent study, Palmer *et al.* (2002) report that 73 per cent of older people with schizophrenia were living independently and catering for their own personal needs and 43 per cent were current drivers. So whatever the age effect on cognition, this does not seem to be a complete bar to attaining reasonable functioning.

Could we intervene at the level of biological factors? There is little immediate possibility of changing factors that would delay an early or a sudden onset. Interventions will rely on the identification of specific risk factors which is a long way from being plausible (Warner, 2003). Accuracy in the assessment of risk will depend on a description of the genotype, the environmental circumstances under which the genotype will be expressed, and the identification of social or psychological protective and vulnerability factors that are involved in the process of onset of the disorder. It is, however, known that schizophrenia is associated with developmental delays in maturation that are apparent even before the disorder manifests itself for the first time. Cognitive difficulties, for instance, were mentioned previously as being present in those people who later develop schizophrenia (Cannon et al., 2002). These developmental problems are likely to interact with the early onset, and subsequent breaks in education and work roles, to magnify problems in functioning. However, the concentration on treatment has been on the effects on functioning within and between episodes rather than on any underlying vulnerability factor.

Environmental factors

Environmental influences include the stress experienced at home, and several meta-analyses have shown that negative expressed emotion in families has a detrimental effect on illness course, irrespective of the medication adherence of the patient (e.g. Bebbington and Kuipers 1994). Expressed emotion or EE is related to higher levels of admissions to hospital and higher rates of symptom exacerbations. Subsequent studies have shown that EE in staff also has a deleterious effect (Oliver and Kuipers, 1996). A role for cognitive dysfunction has now been identified as a mediating factor in the relationship of staff to patients (e.g. Heresco-Levy et al., 1999).

Life stresses are also known to be related to the occurrence of episodes (Hirsch et al., 1996) and cognitive impairment has an effect on this association by affecting sensitivity to life events. In this case it is the least rather than the most impaired who are the most sensitive (Myin-Germeys et al., 2002).

Interventions at this level would include studies of advocacy services to reduce the level of stress due to life events, hassles and chronic difficulties as well as interventions for the family or staff group. The latter do produce reductions in levels of admission (Pilling et al., 2002a). However, these effects seem likely to be affected by thinking skills. There has been an interest in how cognition interacts with the sensitivity to environmental and social stressors recently but the results of these novel studies have not yet had an impact on the design of interventions.

Personal factors

Personal factors include the level of skills achieved prior to the onset of illness which will affect the baseline level of functioning, and therefore the likely level to be achieved through rehabilitation. Thinking skills will be affected by education which may have been curtailed with an early onset. This will influence occupational outcomes directly. As well as these direct effects, cognitive skills will interact with attitudes to disability. For instance, although there is evidence of a direct relationship between cognition and medication management (Jeste *et al.*, 2003), cognition also has an indirect effect on levels of insight which in turn affect attitudes to medication treatments and treatment adherence.

The reduction of cognitive skills following the onset of the disorder also has detrimental effects on self-esteem. In recovery stories, people with a diagnosis of schizophrenia report the effects on their feelings of self-worth, in addition to the effect of receiving a diagnosis. These consumers also emphasise the role of hope in their own recovery and this has been shown empirically (e.g. Hoffmann *et al.*, 2000). Cognition is related to hope but seems to have its effect in conjunction with coping (Lysaker *et al.*, 2001).

Personal factors, such as self-esteem, self-efficacy and hope might be described not only as factors affecting recovery but also as outcomes in their own right. Interventions to improve these factors have sometimes been successful but usually there is little durability of their effects. It may be that cognitive rehabilitation will add to the level of benefit of other interventions and increases their durability.

Does cognition have an impact on functional outcome?

There is evidence that cognitive impairments tend to precede role functioning impairments (Hafner *et al.*, 2003). We have also seen that outcome might be affected by cognition through its effects on vulnerability, but a review of the evidence for the direct effects of cognition on outcome is disappointing. The relationship between putative predictor variables and outcomes is most often measured cross-sectionally with the outcomes being identified by exploratory regression analyses in a single cohort of patients, and rarely is the model derived from one study tested on another cohort in a confirmatory analysis. However, several studies that replicate the same results would indicate some consistency. Studies which collect data longitudinally obviously provide more information on the predictive power of the variables but these are relatively scarce. In reviews of both longitudinal and cross-sectional studies, Green and colleagues have found strong relationships between laboratory assessments of cognition and functioning (Green, 1996; Green *et al.*, 2000). The effect sizes for the 37 studies were moderate with only immediate verbal memory showing a medium to large effect. Composite scores across different tests tended to give higher effect sizes. Since these reviews, and perhaps because of them, investigators have widened the scope of both the putative cognitive markers and the definitions of functioning outcome.

In order to take advantage of new studies investigating different functional areas we will tease apart some of their categories. We have divided up outcome first into general domains of functioning: social outcome, symptoms, vocational functioning, life skills, dependence on psychiatric care and the subjective experience highlighted by service users. Within these categories we will try to review those studies that provide evidence for a direct association and also evidence for cognitive factors affecting skill learning in that area. There is little real acceptance within the scientific community of how these outcome domains should be measured, so a brief description of the specific domain is given in each section which tries to reflect the current view.

Social functioning outcome

Social functioning is often poor in people with schizophrenia and may even be a hallmark of the disorder in some diagnostic systems, e.g. DSMIV-TR (APA, 2000). Although poor social function is associated with other psychoses it is often more pronounced in schizophrenia in both cross-sectional and longitudinal studies (see Harrison *et al.*, 2001). Social functioning difficulties are also present at the onset of the disorder and frequently between episodes. Although they can fluctuate with episodes of exacerbation of symptoms, there is also a consistent decrease in functioning over time. Like intellectual functioning there is some evidence that poor social functioning is present even before the first onset of acute illness (Davidson *et al.*, 1999) and is present in people whose biological parents have a diagnosis of schizophrenia (Hans *et al.*, 2000). So even when schizophrenia is not yet manifest there is a noticeable developmental delay suggesting that social functioning performance may be an early sign and even possibly a vulnerability factor for schizophrenia. As well as being a target set by consumers, it would appear that any intervention that can change the course of social functioning may also impact on overall outcome, including quality of life.

Social functioning can be defined in a number of different ways. For example, some assessment systems use the numbers of friends you have, whether you have contact with a person you can confide in, or whether you have a life partner. These have been termed macro-social domains and were further subdivided by Wykes and Hurry (1991) into:

- *social attainments* – those roles expected by the norms of the culture such as spouse, child carer, being financially independent, which are usually measured by checklists as demographic characteristics
- *social role performance* – the performance in each role as spouse or

child carer, usually measured over lengthy periods of time, i.e. 1 to 3 months
- *instrumental behaviour* – specific behaviours in real life that contribute to role performance such as the ability to take the initiative in conversations and general socially acceptable behaviour, usually measured over a week to a month.

These global measures are often assessed on questionnaires that add together the amount of social behaviour the person takes part in, as well as the types of individual social behaviours that are generally thought to be appropriate. They are affected by other factors such as motivation, psychiatric symptoms and the context in which the behaviours are expected to occur. They are also rated over long periods of time within the real world, e.g. over a week or month or lifetime. Macro-social skills are related to performance in micro-social domains, which are the building blocks for effective social functioning, and include social problem solving skills (e.g. social cue perception, etc.). These are usually measured over short periods of time by individual tasks or role plays rather than by real life functioning. The predictor variables for these two distinct domains of social functioning may differ and so have been reviewed separately.

In terms of macro-social domains, people with diagnoses of schizophrenia are less likely to be married and less likely to be employed than the general population. Not only are the levels of social attainments lower, but there is also evidence that the quality of performance in such roles is worse than for the general population. Quality of life is also poorer in this group. Evidence from the Social Behaviour Schedule (Wykes and Sturt, 1986) suggests that people with chronic disorders have poor social behaviour and that people who require more support from psychiatric services have the most social behaviour problems.

There is evidence that a number of micro-social domains are also deficient in schizophrenia. In a thorough review, Pinkham *et al.* (2003) provide evidence of deficient processing in social cue perception, facial affect recognition and theory of mind (ToM). These skills are essential to understanding complex social situations including sarcasm, jokes and irony, in addition to simpler issues such as guessing what someone knows in a social situation. There is some evidence that these skills are state rather than trait factors, in other words are worse in the acute phase of the illness and may be subtle or non-existent between episodes of illness (Pickup and Frith, 2001). Pinkham *et al.* (2003) also provide evidence of specific relationships between these micro-social domains of functioning and general outcome domains of functioning such as that measured by the Global Assessment of Functioning Scale.

Problems in micro-social domains of functioning can be relatively independent of some cognitive functions. For example, there is evidence of dissociations in specific clinical conditions such as prosopagnosia (Kanwisher, 2000;

Fine *et al.*, 2001), research on frontal lobe injuries, and from syndromes where the definition contains such a dissociation of social and cognitive abilities such as autism, Asperger's and Williams syndrome (Jones *et al.*, 2000; Klin 2000; Beadle-Brown *et al.*, 2002). Because cognitive abilities and micro-social abilities can be relatively independent, it is worthwhile investigating their possible independence in schizophrenia and to identify if there are any cognitive predictor variables. These are not the only variables, however, that are likely to affect micro-social behaviours. Levels of symptoms which affect basic attentional processing not only in schizophrenia but also in other disorders such as depression also affect social functioning (Deldin *et al.*, 2000; Goddard *et al.*, 2001).

Predicting micro-social domains

Question 1: Is cognition related to levels of micro-social difficulties?

In the previous chapter we showed how social cognitive functions were associated with specific cognitive functions in the non-social domain, including early visual processing, verbal long-term memory and executive functions. Here we will look at the relations between social behaviours and non-social cognitive functions although in practice, social behaviour and social cognition overlap.

The majority of studies that investigate the relationship between cognitive and micro-social abilities assess whether the performance decrements are due to general processing failures or to a specific deficit. Of course, finding a correlation between the two does not actually provide evidence for a specific deficit because they may co-occur or because a differential deficit may not always be readily detectable. The majority of studies have been cross-sectional, and investigate a single domain and few measures of cognitive performance, in a single group of participants with schizophrenia. In other words, there is little investigation of whether there are specific relationships between patterns of cognitive measures and individual micro-social domains in schizophrenia compared to other disorders, and little investigation of the predictive power of cognitive variables in prospective studies. Nevertheless the evidence is relatively consistent, with the majority of studies suggesting that micro-social domains of social perception, social problem solving and general social skill are related to cognitive performance and in many instances cognitive performance was a better predictor than measures of symptoms.

Receiving skills (identification of interpersonal information), processing skills (generation of alternative responses) and sending skills (performance of problem-solving behaviour) which are measured as part of the Assessment of Interpersonal Problem Solving Skills (AIPSS) measure have been shown to be related to attentional processing, in particular sustained attention, verbal memory performance and executive functioning (Bowen *et al.*, 1994; Corrigan and Toomey, 1995; Addington and Addington, 1999). Non-verbal skills are also related to response inhibition factors (Ikebuchi *et al.*, 1999) and executive functioning (Penn *et al.*, 1995). Stratta and colleagues (2000) showed that the ability to use context in order to inhibit responses was related to social outcome and symptoms.

Questions 2 and 3: Do cognitive indicators predict outcome and do they have a significant weight compared to other factors such as symptoms?

One series of studies carried out by Jean Addington exemplifies the sorts of investigations that are necessary in this area. Addington and Addington (1999) showed that measures of memory, verbal ability and cognitive flexibility were related to social problem-solving skills. In a follow-up study of the same participants, the authors found a consistent relationship between initial cognitive performance and social problem solving after two and a half years, even when they had controlled for the possible contribution of negative symptoms (Addington and Addington, 2000). In a further comparative study between people with a diagnosis of schizophrenia and people with other psychiatric diagnoses, the relationship between social problem solving and functioning was found to be specific to people with schizophrenia (Addington *et al.*, 2001). The main consistent cognitive variable was verbal long-term memory.

Predicting macro-social functioning

Question 1: Is cognition related to levels of macro-social difficulties?

Macro-social functioning, as described above, includes the social roles that people are able to carry out as well as the quality of the performance in such roles. Verbal memory, vigilance and executive functioning have been shown to strongly predict social outcome (Green, 1996; Penn *et al.*, 1997a; Green *et al.*, 2000). The main strong predictor was verbal memory, and executive functioning as measured by the Wisconsin Card Sorting Test (WCST) was only a moderate predictor. However, Poole *et al.* (1999) showed that WCST performance was associated with poorer pre-morbid functioning, a smaller probability of having being married and poorer interactive skills. This study is interesting for two reasons. First, participants were unmedicated, thus eliminating the effects of medication on the actual cognitive measures. Second, the interaction between different cognitive impairments was also investigated. When both WCST impairment and motor skills impairments were present in the same individual, the likelihood of an unfavourable outcome was not merely additive but was magnified.

Questions 2 and 3: Are cognitive indicators related to outcomes
following rehabilitation and how does this compare to symptoms?

Many of these associations between cognition and macro-social factors, like the ones assessed for the micro-social domain, were cross-sectional. Several studies also implicate negative symptoms in the predictive equation. However, the importance of these relationships is sometimes difficult to assess, as negative symptoms and social function seemed to be measuring the same concept. If cognition is going to be a target for rehabilitation, then longitudinal studies are required where initial social functioning can be controlled in the analyses and cognitive variables are identified as predictors of outcome. These data come from a series of studies of the closure of a large UK mental hospital with a good reputation for rehabilitation. The importance of symptoms and cognition on social outcome over a six-year period was assessed and patients who had a deficit in their ability to select correct responses and inhibit alternatives were more likely to remain in services which provided high levels of psychiatric care (Wykes *et al.*, 1990; Wykes, 1994). In these studies, neither symptoms nor initial social behaviour added much to the predictive value of cognition which was not confounded by initial functioning levels.

In a similar short-term study, Smith *et al.* (2002) followed people from their discharge from hospital and carried out assessments of symptoms and cognition at three-month intervals for one year. Figure 4.2 shows that working memory function at discharge was predictive of the amount of improvement in social behaviour during recovery. Although the social behaviour scores were similar at recruitment, for those with good working memory there was a 20 per cent improvement over the year of the study, whereas for those with poor working memory there was no improvement. In their random regression models, the two variables that predicted the most variance in outcome were disorganisation and working memory but not positive symptoms. Further investigations of their data suggested that disorganisation and working memory were closely related, and in their final analyses only the relationship over time with working memory was significant. The meta-analyses have not identified symptoms, such as delusions and hallucinations, as having high predictive value for social outcome (e.g. Green *et al.*, 2000).

Symptoms do also predict macro-social outcome. For instance, when patient groups were divided into deficit and non-deficit groups this was predictive of social outcome five years later (Tek *et al.*, 2001). Patients in the deficit group had poorer quality of life, poorer social and occupational function, and more severe negative symptoms. Certainly symptoms, such as thought disorder, are predictive of social skills training output in that the effects of any improvements in social skills are lost for those with the highest levels (Mueser *et al.*, 1992). But in the differential prediction of social outcome by symptoms or cognition, Lysaker *et al.* (1995) support the notion that cognitive impairment and not negative symptoms predicts social skills.

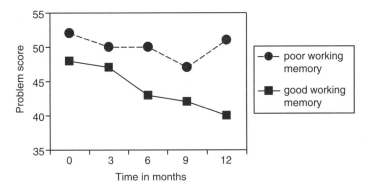

Figure 4.2 Cognitive effects on social behaviour during recovery (adapted from Smith *et al.*, 2002)

There are clear direct effects of cognition on social behaviour outcomes, but perhaps a more interesting issue is whether cognitive difficulties also have an impact on the outcome from treatment programmes specifically designed to improve these skills. The results of several studies suggest that verbal memory is particularly important. This seems to limit the rate at which people can learn skills. It is not that there is no improvement for people who have poor verbal memory but that the level of improvement is less than for those without such difficulties (Mueser *et al.*, 1991). There is also evidence that in the prediction of social skills within work rehabilitation programmes, executive functioning is a potent predictor (Kurtz *et al.*, 2004). Table 4.3 summarises the relationships found in the data between social outcome and cognition.

Until recently there were few prospective studies of the prediction of social domains. There are still many unanswered questions, such as the relationship of cognition to social outcome at different phases of the disorder (Wiersma *et al.*, 2000; Harrison *et al.*, 2001). Differences in participants and in the

Table 4.3 Relationships between social outcomes and cognition

Social outcome domain	Cognitive predictor variable
Micro-social abilities	Sustained attention
Macro-social skills	Spatial working memory Verbal working memory Sustained attention Response inhibition
Acquisition of social skills	Verbal long-term memory Verbal working memory

assessment measures may lead to slightly differing results. Overall there does appear to be a direct relationship between cognition and social outcomes. Negative symptoms may contribute to this association with studies reporting an interaction, independent contributions or no association. Less (or no) influence of positive symptoms has been found, at least for the prediction of outcome over the long term and from rehabilitation programmes. However, there are probably complicated interactions between cognitive and symptomatic behaviours that have not yet been explored in the data.

Symptoms

Cognitive impairments were thought to share only a small common variance with the symptoms that characterise a diagnosis of schizophrenia, even the most spectacular symptoms like delusions and hallucinations (Frith, 1992; Cuesta and Peralta, 1995; O'Leary et al., 2000). Where a relationship was hypothesised to exist, it was mainly between cognitive impairment and negative symptoms. But it seems clear that thinking skills which underlie performance on cognitive tests must also be important in determining the interpretation of abnormal events resulting in delusional beliefs.

Failure to identify relationships may be due to a number of difficulties with current designs. The first is the lack of subtlety in the measures of symptoms currently used, where individual items confuse both frequency and severity (interference with everyday life) as well as giving equal or different weights to different symptoms. Relationships between cognitive measures and total positive or negative symptoms tend to abound where the total score aggregates disparate symptoms, such as hallucinations, delusions and passivity phenomena. This method conceals variability between individuals, particularly in smaller studies which may have been relevant to particular thinking skills. More refined psychological measures, such as the psychotic symptom rating scales (PSYRATS, Haddock et al., 1999) or Beliefs about Voices Questionnaire (BAVQ, Chadwick et al., 2000) may allow more subtle relationships to be determined. The limitations of the assessment system are exemplified by a meta-analysis reported by Johnson-Selfridge and Zalewski (2001). They found significant correlations for both positive and negative symptom scores and the 171 cognitive performance effect sizes (using a range of tests), with poorer executive functioning being associated with higher levels of symptoms when measured by the Positive and Negative Symptom Scale (PANSS). However, no significant correlation was found with the Brief Psychiatric Rating Scale (BPRS), which measures symptoms across a number of domains, including positive symptoms, negative symptoms and general psychopathology.

Subtle relationships may only be identified with more refined symptom measures. But it is possible that thinking skills play a causal role in the development of symptoms, and so a lack of relationship could be due to the concentration on current experience. If thinking skills have a causal effect on the development of symptoms, then it will not be possible to distinguish within the diagnostic group, as most people with a diagnosis of schizophrenia will have experienced the same set of symptoms. Study designs therefore need to take this into account and compare both state and trait measures of symptoms (e.g. Johns and McGuire, 1999) and collect data longitudinally.

Finally, the impact of thinking skill on symptom experience may only be as a vulnerability factor, where small decrements in thinking skill in normal circumstances can be compensated for, and only when the system is stressed does it break down. Investigations of this sort of relationship would be longitudinal or at least investigated over a period of time when environmental stress had been changed.

Positive and disorganisation symptoms

Questions 1 and 2: Are cognitive indicators related to outcomes cross-sectionally and longitudinally and following treatment?

All the data we review here are in the context of medication treatment. Johnson-Selfridge and Zalewski (2001), in their meta-analysis of executive functioning, used 172 effects sizes from 71 studies and showed significant correlations with overall severity of positive symptoms. Kerns and Berenbaum (2002) also in a meta-analysis, using a single symptom approach, identified specific relationships between cognition and one symptom, formal thought disorder, which overlaps with the disorganisation syndrome. The effect size for the 26 studies that investigated executive functioning (measured on various tasks and in various ways) and thought disorder ranged from 0.26 to 0.36 and this moderate association did not appear to be due to the effect of a generalised performance decrement. Other difficulties notably in response inhibition and/or context memory increased the relationship between executive functioning and thought disorder. Most of these studies included patients who had a chronic disorder. Early onset patients also show some relationships between levels of positive symptoms and processing speed (Rund *et al.*, 2004), and Hoff *et al.* (1999) found that improvements in positive symptoms were related to improvements in cognition. Another positive symptom, auditory hallucinations, has also been found to be related to difficulties in inhibition. Waters *et al.* (2003) found significant correlations between the severity of auditory hallucinations and performance on two tasks of inhibition. Task performance was only related to this specific symptom and not to overall levels of negative symptoms or positive symptom (without auditory hallucinations) scores.

The more general category of disorganisation is when a person finds it difficult to carry on with their intentions and they are distracted by each new stimulus. It has been linked to a number of cognitive difficulties, particularly planning, the selection of appropriate responses and the inhibition of a prepotent response (Cuesta and Peralta, 1995; Van der Does *et al.*, 1996).

Most studies are cross-sectional and therefore can say little about whether cognitive difficulties underlie the preponderance of positive and disorganisation symptoms. In one of the few longitudinal studies, Wykes (1994) has shown this positive longer term relationship. In this study, response processing (inhibition and novel responding) was predictive of symptoms after an interval of six years, and accounted for 23 per cent of the variance even after initial symptoms levels had been controlled in the analysis. The symptom measures, however, did not allow for a subtle appraisal of relationships between this cognitive skill and specific symptoms.

In summary, there are mixed results for the relationship between positive symptoms and cognition. Most studies are small, cross-sectional, use different cognitive measures even for the same construct and include a mixture of inpatients and outpatients. All these factors are likely to lead to variable results, although meta-analyses such as that of Johnson-Selfridge and Zalewski (2001) do show some positive relationships to executive functioning because of the aggregation of scores.

Question 3: Do cognitive indicators have a significant weight compared to other factors in the prediction of symptoms?

The relationships between cognitive difficulties and symptoms can be interpreted in a number of different ways. They may be mere markers of symptoms having no specific causal relationship, or they could predispose the person to experience symptoms. If they predispose the person or make them vulnerable, then the cognitive factors may be difficult to isolate, as they may be subtle and only show their effects in the presence of other factors, which in the vulnerability-stress model are termed stressors. If cognitive variables do act in this way, then it would be important to provide some direct intervention, as they would be clearly in the causal pathway to symptoms. Figure 4.3 shows how these relationships might work.

Few data to distinguish vulnerability from markers are available, as designing a study that increases environmental stress has major ethical implications, particularly when the effect is to increase distressing symptoms. However, some studies have relied on naturally occurring stressors, although the number of cognitive domains investigated has been small. The first is a study by Wykes (1994) where patients were followed up for six years after the closure of a large psychiatric hospital. The environmental stressor here was the change from a relatively supported hospital environment to community settings where the opportunities to make personal decisions increased. Wykes and colleagues assessed a response processing measure which required the initiation of novel responses and the inhibition of a prepotent response. They

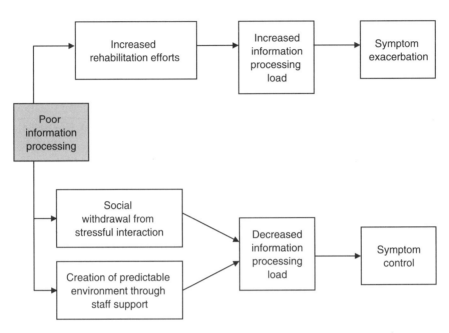

Figure 4.3 Mode of action of cognitive processing problems on symptoms

found that this ability was stable over time (Wykes *et al.*, 2000). However, when people who had little difficulty in processing responses were moved into the community they were able to take advantage of the new opportunities offered and had a decrease in their symptoms. But the group who were impaired on response processing showed the opposite, an increase in positive and negative symptoms. There was no relationship between symptoms and response processing at baseline but after the environmental stressor had been introduced there was a significant relationship, suggesting that response processing was causal in the development of more symptoms, but that this was through an interaction with other environmental conditions.

In a separate study, the interaction between poor working memory and another environmental stressor, expressed emotion by family members, was investigated (Rosenfarb *et al.*, 2000). Again cognitive performance (working memory) and unusual thinking were not related at baseline as all participants were in a remitted state. However, when unusual thinking was measured during an interaction with a family member who showed high expressed emotion (the stressor), then people with the poorest working memory produced the most increase in symptoms, but there was no effect for those with the better cognitive performance. A further cognitive indicator – early visual processing – had no such relationship to unusual thinking.

Some data therefore do suggest that cognitive skills are important for the emergence of symptoms, but only in combination with a stressed system. But of course one clear effect of cognition is on treatment adherence, which may in turn affect the levels of symptoms. This indirect effect was investigated by Vauth *et al.* (2004) who found a relationship between cognitive functions and factors affecting medication adherence. Higher levels of conceptual flexibility were related to attributing adherence to the support of others, whereas better attention was related to the perception of the benefits of medication. These relationships suggest differing therapeutic approaches to improve adherence.

Negative symptoms

Question 1: Are cognitive indicators related to negative symptoms?

Current data do link cognitive deficits to negative symptoms, although the common variance is only about 15 per cent (Addington and Addington, 1993; O'Leary *et al.*, 2000). Many of these relationships are between speeded responses and negative symptoms. Johnson-Selfridge and Zalewski (2001) showed significant correlations between overall severity of negative symptoms and executive functioning as measured by the Wisconsin Card Sorting Test, and more recently, Heydebrand *et al.* (2004) found relationships with executive functioning, psychomotor speed, memory and verbal fluency. Significant associations have been found for recent onset patients who have been followed up after treatment (Censits *et al.*, 1997; Hoff *et al.*, 1999; Schuepbach *et al.*, 2002) but not in chronic patients (Hughes *et al.*, 2003).

Questions 2 and 3: Are cognitive indicators related to outcomes following intervention and are any other factors involved?

There are few direct investigations of these questions. When negative symptoms decrease, cognitive impairments also decrease (Censits *et al.*, 1997; Gold *et al.*, 1999). One study has reported that in a subgroup of early onset patients who showed marked improvements in negative symptoms over a six-month period, cognitive performance measures were close to those of healthy controls at follow-up (Schuepbach *et al.*, 2002). This suggests an association between treatment responsive, negative symptoms and severity of impairment in attention and verbal fluency.

Vocational functioning

Work functioning is a particularly difficult area to measure, as the social security benefits systems that exist around the world tend to place financial barriers to full-time employment. When people with schizophrenia decide to take the plunge into full-time work, they can find themselves disenfranchised from some benefits if the job proves to be problematic. This can clearly be a disincentive. Employment is of course related to the background economy, and recovery as measured by employment is highly correlated with the number of opportunities for employment (Warner, 2004). However, despite all these difficulties, researchers have tended to use the most simple scale for measuring employment outcomes (i.e. unemployed, employed part time, employed full time). The situation is further complicated by the presence of supported employment schemes and vocational rehabilitation schemes that skew the opportunities for paid work. The latest studies have measured work quality rather than quantity, as this can be assessed as part of a work rehabilitation programme where the local economy has less effect on its measurement and where it is possible to differentiate between aspects of work which may be related to different variables.

There is no reason to suppose that the cognitive predictors of success in vocational rehabilitation programmes, supported employment, competitive work or job tenure would be the same. The selection of clients for these programmes in naturalistic studies may also attenuate the effects of cognition on outcome. Despite all these factors, a review of the literature highlights the importance of cognition for work outcomes. There is no evidence that the association can be explained by work affecting cognition as cognition remains relatively stable even after involvement in work programmes or competitive work (McGurk et al., 2003). Also, as McGurk and Mueser (2004) point out, although it is reported often that work has direct effects on a person's sense of purpose there are no self-reports of work having an effect on cognition.

Question 1: Is work outcome related to cognition?

For outcomes of people not in vocational rehabilitation programmes, cognition was related to current or recent work status in all nine of the studies reviewed by McGurk and Mueser (2004). These were generally cross-sectional, but even in studies which were prospective, cognitive functioning was a potent predictor of outcome. One study that differentiated presence at work from performance at work showed that higher levels of thought disorder and poorer performance on the WCST were associated with poorer task orientation in the first week of work (Lysaker et al., 1995). A relationship between good WCST performance and higher attainment scores was also found but the obverse was not true. Those with poor WCST performance were as likely to be at work as not.

Question 2: Are rehabilitation programmes affected by cognition?

Studies of vocational rehabilitation, especially when they are of people who do not drop out of the programme, are likely to identify different cognitive variables to other individual functioning domains. In order to enter the vocational rehabilitation programmes, participants must have certain basic functions, for example, motivation, lower levels of negative symptoms and probably lower levels of positive symptoms such as paranoid delusions. The samples identified for these schemes are therefore likely to differ from unselected populations. So it is not surprising that the results are mixed. In an area with low unemployment, McGurk and Meltzer (2000) found that executive functioning (performance on the WCST), working memory and vigilance but not positive symptoms differentiated people who were fully employed from those who were employed part time. In a further study, McGurk and Mueser (2003) found that processing speed and executive function were the key cognitive predictors. However, there have been some studies suggesting negative results (e.g. Mueser *et al.*, 1997).

Prospective studies of vocational rehabilitation also show the same mixed results. The speculation from several authors is that there was some compensation of cognitive impairments at work. Most recently Gold and colleagues (2001) have investigated the cognitive indicators associated with successful work performance, which was defined as at least six months in employment over half the week. A comprehensive battery of tests was used to identify markers and the results suggested that processing speed was the main predictor of cognitive functioning. Verbal memory was related but was only a modest predictor. In their data, the person with the best memory score was out of work and two people with the worst memory had a job. Again this may be because people with poor memory were able to compensate for their difficulties with a supportive work environment and judicious choice of job.

A further question is whether cognition affects the rate of change within a vocational rehabilitation programme. Bell and Bryson (2001) identified cognition as a rate limiting factor for four out of the five domains of work functioning (see Figure 4.4). Bryson and Bell (2001) also showed that cognitive factors differentiated those who improved to a clinically significant level (25 per cent improvement). However, different cognitive measures were related to different work domains. The cognitive measures identified were somewhat different to those that might be expected from other studies. The main overall predictor was Digit Symbol performance from the WAISr, which is referred to as a speed of processing measure, followed by non-perseverative error rate on WCST. Verbal memory contributed only a small amount to the prediction.

Finally, Bryson and Bell (2003) investigated the learning curves associated with the vocational rehabilitation programme and showed that 28 per cent of the variance in the first half of the programme was accounted for by cognitive variables and 19 per cent in the second half of the programme. They found no effect of symptoms. The main contributors for the initial improvements were sustained attention, response inhibition and idiosyncratic thinking and for the second slope were attention, verbal memory and psychomotor speed. This last study highlights the time-dependent nature of the assessment.

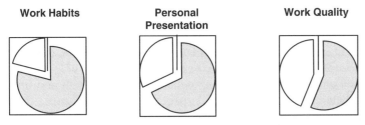

**Work Habits   Personal   Work Quality
                    Presentation**

Grey shading indicates the amount of variance accounted for by cognitive variables

Figure 4.4 How much cognitive variables account for work outcome (adapted from Bell and Bryson, 2001)

Cognitive predictors may change with the task demands and familiarity of the task. A similar approach used time series analyses to define subgroups in vocational rehabilitation. Kupper and Hoffmann (2000) identified five sub-groups within their weekly assessment data. The group that had a high level of stable functioning throughout the programme generally had few negative or positive symptoms at baseline and had good cognitive performance. However, the poorest group had the worst cognitive performance as well as the highest level of psychopathology. In a follow-up study, Hoffmann and Kup-per (2003) showed that the best predictors of outcome in competitive employment were cognitive impairment and the sense of locus of control which the authors suggest is a proxy for self-concept. Their measures of cognitive impairment were sustained attention and a visual memory test.

Question 3: Do cognitive factors have significant weight compared to other factors, e.g. symptoms in predicting work outcome?

There are several studies that show relationships between positive and nega-tive symptoms, and employment with the prospective studies showing weaker associations than the cross-sectional studies (McGurk and Mueser, 2004). For instance, in a series of studies by Bell and Lysaker (1995), the symptom relationship was only apparent when symptoms and outcome were measured concurrently. In recent studies that identify the prediction of symptoms and cognition within the same study, cognitive predictors seem to account for the most variance (e.g. Bryson and Bell, 2003; Bell and Bryson, 2001).

In summary, there is ample evidence that cognition does relate to work outcome and specific job functioning. The relationships seem more muted in vocational programmes which might be accounted for by a system of compen-sation for cognitive difficulties. There is also evidence that the predictive power of cognitive variables outweighs many other factors. The identification of specific cognitive indicators is hampered by the lack of comprehensive assess-ments as this domain of functioning has only recently begun to be explored.

Independence from psychiatric care

Question 1: Are cognitive indicators related to dependence on care?

Cognitive difficulties are predictive of a high use of services. The earliest studies used reaction time as a predictor and Cancro *et al.* (1971) showed that simple reaction time, measured when patients were acutely ill and unmedicated, predicted the number of nights spent in mental institutions during a three-year follow-up. Reaction time (RT) was correlated with length of hospitalisation ($r = 0.50$) and although the degree of thought disorder was the best predictor of amount of time in hospitals, simple RT accounted for an additional 17 per cent of the variance. A further study by Zahn and Carpenter (1978) used a more sophisticated measure of reaction time and also showed that it was related to time spent in hospital. In chronic groups both Spaulding *et al.* (1984) and White *et al.* (1987) have shown relationships between reaction time variables and prognostic variables. Cognitive impairment has also been associated with the cost of care (Wykes *et al.*, 2003) with higher costs being associated with higher levels of impairment (Patel *et al.*, 2004).

There have also been some indications that executive functioning may differentiate between those who go on to a poorer course. Reed *et al.* (2002), in a cross-sectional study using the Wisconsin Card Sorting Test, showed that those with the poorest course had more problems with this test. However, the presence of a chronic course over 15 years did not add to this relationship. Fuji and Wylie (2003) in a longitudinal study with a wider cognitive assessment found that logical memory was the lone predictor of community outcome and Trails B was the lone predictor of length of hospitalisation over 15 years.

Questions 2 and 3: Are cognitive indicators related to dependence on care following rehabilitation and what is their relationship to other factors?

In a series of studies of rehabilitation following a hospital closure, Wykes and colleagues (1990, 1992) showed that response processing was related not only to the services used cross-sectionally, but was also predictive of the use of services in a prospective longitudinal follow-up study. In this series cognition added to clinical history variables, that is previous skills and length of illness, but symptoms (positive and negative) did not contribute to the prediction equations.

It is obvious that exacerbations of symptoms and particular symptoms, such as command hallucinations, must be predictive of continued involvement of the psychiatric services. But when used as predictors, symptom measures, probably because of the crude nature of their measurement, do not account for much of the variance in outcome, whereas there are clear relationships with cognitive variables.

Relationship between Life Skills and cognitive variables

Questions 1, 2 and 3: Are cognitive indicators related to life skills and their rehabilitation?

Life skills such as cooking, shopping and budgeting clearly have a relationship to dependence on psychiatric care. It is still possible to live in your own home but the quality of care for yourself to be poor. This category of outcome has therefore been investigated separately for the effects of cognition on the prediction of outcome. The main problem with measurement here is that many of the instruments assess the capacity to carry out skills in contrived situations and not actual performance in daily life, where initiation skills may interfere with successful functioning. Measures that rely on observer rated behaviours in real life also have problems as they are dependent on the opportunities available to individuals during the measurement period.

Again in this area there are both associations and predictive longitudinal relationships with aspects of cognitive functioning. For instance, Dawn Velligan and colleagues (1997) investigated the relationship between cognition, symptoms and daily living skills outcome in two cross-sectional studies and found that cognition predicted about 40 per cent of daily living skills and that symptoms added nothing to this correlation. In a longitudinal study, Velligan *et al.* (2000) established that executive functioning and verbal memory were related to community functioning and accounted for 25 per cent of the variance.

Most studies use measures of life skills which have some ecological validity, but as discussed above they mostly use a task which is isolated from everyday life. One other approach to measurement is to have a task that is practised in the real world and for which it is possible to have observers rate scores which are clearly anchored. The test which provides all this is the Grocery Skills Shopping Test (Hamera and Brown, 2000). Rempfer *et al.* (2003) using a large neuropsychological battery of tests identified specific measures of association between cognitive measures and different aspects of the shopping task. For her group of mainly outpatients, shopping accuracy was related to processing speed. Redundancy (e.g. going up the same aisle in the super-market more than once) was related to executive functioning and response inhibition. Even though this is a cross-sectional study and the correlations were low to modest, it is an important study in linking specific measures to specific aspects of the task.

The majority of studies in this area are based on groups of patients with an average age of between 30 and 40 years. One study that has moved up the age span to groups of people over the age of 50 was carried out by Twamley *et al.* (2002). They showed that, unlike previous studies where specific cognitive measures were related to life skills, all their measures of cognitive ability were positively related to their skills assessment score even after a stringent Bonferroni correction. These data follow in the same direction as that produced in other studies which investigated less well differentiated aspects of cognition (e.g. Patterson *et al.*, 1998).

There were no independent relationships with depressive symptoms. There were also no relationships with psychotic symptoms, levels of medication or length of illness. Although this is a cross-sectional study, it is supported by other studies and does suggest that the sensitivity of cognition to predict outcome actually increases with older age. It is not clear why this should be the case until there is a comparison with the normal elderly, but it does suggest that studies that can intervene appropriately may also improve the functional capacity of older people with psychosis.

Relationship of cognition to subjective experience (insight and self-efficacy)

Questions 1, 2 and 3: Are cognitive functions related to subjective experience and do changes in cognition impact on subjective experience?

Whilst numerous cross-sectional and longitudinal studies have shown associations primarily between insight and executive function (and less frequently with attention, memory and current IQ), a similar number have failed to identify significant relationships (for a review see David, 1999). It seems likely that there is a significant but small independent contribution of cognitive deficits in predicting insight, but this may depend on the type of sample (with greater associations apparent in chronic samples) and the specific tests of insight used. A further suggestion is that insight might not have a linear association with cognition. Startup (1996) suggested that a curvilinear relationship might exist with the poorest insight being experienced by people with both poor and excellent cognitive skills. Recently, a number of researchers have also suggested that self-monitoring or metacognitive abilities affects insight (Drake and Lewis, 2003; Koren *et al.*, 2004).

Quantitative cross-sectional studies provide again mixed evidence on the relationship between self-esteem and self-efficacy, and cognition. Qualitative reports suggest that self-efficacy and self-esteem are indeed related to cognitive deficits as cited at the beginning of this chapter and by Davidson (2003) and Dykstra (1997), although this does not mean they are the sole contributors.

A number of studies have also supported a longitudinal causal model for cognitive deficits and insight impairment, showing that good cognitive function predicts subsequent good or improved insight following treatment (David *et al.*, 1995; Lysaker and Bell, 1994, 1995) and that improved executive function is associated with improved insight (Chen *et al.*, 2001). However, other studies have reported non-significant relationships between changes in both cognition and insight (Kemp and David, 1996; Carroll *et al.*, 1999).

Is cognition related to functioning?

It seems clear from this review that cognition is not only related concurrently to a number of different domains of outcome, but that when these have been investigated in longitudinal studies they still have predictive validity. In the few studies that have investigated the effects on treatment outcome over time, this is also affected by cognition although the mode of operation is still unclear.

Table 4.4 gives a brief list of the sorts of cognitive processes that have been identified as having a relationship to functioning outcome. Many of the thinking skills are common to several domains although it is not clear whether these contribute the same amount to the variance in scores. The list is long and what would be helpful is to distinguish those cognitive factors that have not been found to be related to functional outcomes, but unfortunately these are likely to be those bottom drawer studies that have failed to get into print. These sorts of studies would be helpful to put into perspective the positive relationships reported, as many studies are small and it would therefore require few non-significant results to affect the interpretation of effect sizes.

Symptoms, particularly positive symptoms, still seem rarely to contribute to outcome, but more sophisticated assessment might increase the number of relationships that are evident in the data. In the majority of studies reviewed here positive symptoms were anyway relatively controlled by medication. The symptomatic variance in the data is therefore small, and it is in this situation that cognitive variables begin to have the most predictive power within the population of people with a diagnosis of schizophrenia.

Table 4.4 Cognitive variables that have been related to functional outcome

Cognitive domain		
Attention	Sustained attention	Directed attention
Long-term memory	Long-term visual memory	Long-term verbal memory
Working memory	Spatial working memory	Verbal working memory
Psychomotor speed	Response inhibition speed	
Executive functioning	Conceptual learning	Inhibition of prepotent responses
Metacognition	Self-monitoring	Metacognitive control

For negative symptoms the relationship is more complicated. This is, in part, due to the overlap between the definition of negative symptoms and the definition of the outcome under study, such that some measures of social outcome are in fact also behavioural measures of negative symptoms. It has also not been possible to differentiate interactive relationships between symptoms and cognition because so few studies have investigated them. One example is Greenwood *et al.* (2004) who suggested that it is in those people who have high levels of negative symptoms where cognitive difficulties have their main effect. In her study, shopping skills were related to verbal working memory difficulties specifically in the group with negative symptoms. These two variables seem to act synergistically rather than just additively.

As people grow older the relationship between cognition and skills seems to increase. It is not clear whether this is a relationship with chronicity of the illness or to do with the pattern of symptoms exhibited by particular groups of more chronic patients. Different thinking skills are also important at different stages of rehabilitation treatments with one pattern of thinking skills being important at the outset for engagement in rehabilitation programmes and others being important for specific learning. So far studies have often failed to distinguish these time dependent cognitive relationships.

Cognition has therefore fulfilled the three criteria to be a target for rehabilitation programmes. Perhaps what is most disappointing in this literature has been the use of gross measures of cognition in many studies. This has meant that although cognition in general clearly lies in the pathway to outcome, it is still not possible to identify specific cognitive processes. For instance, when memory is identified as a predictor it may be storage, encoding or retrieval processes that underlie this relationship. Alternatively it may be that the ability to devise temporary schemas is problematic or that metacognitive regulation is the difficulty. Until there are more specific experimental approaches to cognitive processes, then we cannot identify cognitive targets. This is the same distinction made in Chapters 2 and 3. In Chapter 2 most impairments were identified using complex tasks which is what have been used in the search for relationships to functioning. We would advocate the approach in Chapter 3 where specific cognitive components are identified.

In different functioning domains, different cognitive targets need to be addressed even though we do not know the specific components of the cognitive process so far identified. The relationships investigated here have been interpreted by most of their authors as direct. If they are direct then it can be assumed that if you change cognition then outcome should change. But there are few research strategies that can investigate this possibility unless some treatment programme is introduced to change one of the factors. The relationship may also not be a straight line. For instance, it may be that cognition must change to above a specific level in order to achieve change. For instance, Smith *et al.* (2002) showed that there was improvement over time in social behaviour only for those whose level of impairment was least. Specific thresholds, however, can only be identified once it is clear whether cognition can change at all with whatever research strategy is adopted. Alternatively improved cognition might have an impact on a third factor which in turn has a positive impact on outcome. In order to detect any causal relationship the next step is therefore clear – treatments to change cognition need to be devised.

Part II

Improving cognitive processes

Chapter 5

Changing cognition in the laboratory

Cognition is an important factor in functioning, but as we have already discussed there was little optimism that cognition might change. This was true even though there was considerable enthusiasm within the general public to improve thinking skills. For instance, Tony Buzan is now a best selling author for his series of books showing how 'mind maps' can improve learning and memory (Buzan and Buzan, 1996) and most railway station bookshops contain at least one book on how to improve your memory for names and figures. Techniques for the improvement of cognitive skills are also established in the field of traumatic brain injury and stroke where recommendations for clinical practice contain reference to different evidence-based cognitive rehabilitation methods (e.g. Cicerone *et al.*, 2000).

Techniques in psychiatric settings have been much slower to become accepted. The first psychological approaches were aimed at the content of thought rather than its form. Beck (1952) and Shapiro and Ravenette (1959) both attempted to change the delusional beliefs that were not only distressing but interfered with everyday life. These attempts were not followed up systematically for many years. Until the advent of cognitive behaviour therapy for psychosis, these techniques fell into the category of psychodynamic approaches that waned in the psychiatric community, especially in the USA, as psychiatry concentrated on biological explanations of the disorder. The technique for changing the form of thought for people with a diagnosis of schizophrenia, what we term cognitive remediation therapy (CRT), also started over 30 years ago. Meichenbaum and Cameron (1973) began by engaging clients who were disabled by negative symptoms, thinking problems and a lack of behavioural control with their environment. Their technique took the form of several steps and was based on the notion that people can learn by guiding their behaviour with overt and then subvocal speech until the behaviour is relatively automatic. This followed from theories in developmental psychology of the way in which children learn to guide their own behaviour. Meichenbaum and Cameron first encouraged behaviour to be under the control of the therapist who spoke instructions out loud. Second, the patient took control of the instructions and spoke them aloud, and finally said these same instructions in their mind. The result was that patients who had been very socially withdrawn became more active and showed more initiative. These positive outcomes were then placed in a behavioural rather than a developmental framework as rehabilitation psychologists used social and monetary rewards to improve social behaviour in rehabilitation settings and little specific use was made of this technique to guide other behaviours such as cognitive skills.

Subsequently other cognitive processes were targeted. Monetary reward and verbal encouragement were shown to be effective in improving reaction time (Steffy and Galbraith, 1980) and improved memory was achieved when patients with schizophrenia were provided with an encoding strategy (Koh *et al.*, 1976). However, these studies were mainly used to develop and test theories about the underlying cognitive problems in schizophrenia and were not used to develop treatment strategies. One technique, graduated distraction training (Adams *et al.*, 1981) showed promise in a single case study and was clearly the basis for a novel treatment but the potential of these results too was ignored for many years. Figure 5.1 shows the available literature for studies in cognitive remediation therapy compared to those for family treatments and cognitive behaviour therapy. It is obvious that the cognitive techniques have lagged a long way behind.

The interest in CRT really began in the mid to late 1990s as a technique that could improve cognitive skills for people with schizophrenia. There has been a considerable increase in the publication of articles that are likely to improve cognition in the last decade and these have been fuelled by the need both to support therapy and theory.

There has been considerable therapeutic pessimism about cognitive impairments in schizophrenia. Cross-sectional studies suggested that people early in the course of the disorder had impairments similar to those found in chronic populations. Longitudinal studies also showed little change, and a few even suggested deterioration for some cognitive skills. The static nature of cognitive impairments (see Chapters 2 and 3) led to the assumption that

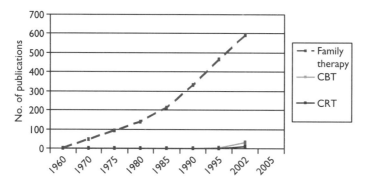

Figure 5.1 Rate of accumulation of information on therapies

there was little likelihood of improvement and this was further fuelled by the theories of the cognitive impairments in schizophrenia being similar to those produced following lesions of the frontal lobe (Weinberger, 1988). At that time the outcome for people with brain injury was not hopeful in terms of recovery of previous thinking skill and a further paper by Goldberg *et al.* (1987) suggested even further therapeutic pessimism for people with schizophrenia. In their study they tried to teach inpatients with schizophrenia to correctly complete the Wisconsin Card Sorting Test. Figure 5.2 shows the results of their study. They found that different training techniques had no effect on performance of the task except when the participants were given explicit instructions and feedback (Block 4 in Figure 5.2). However, they did not generalise from these explicit instructions and so performance returned to baseline in the next block of trials and remained at this low level. This was considered to be yet more evidence that people with schizophrenia were similar to those who had frontal lobe deficits.

However, the move towards care in the community during the 1970s, 1980s and 1990s had highlighted difficulties in providing suitable accommodation and activity for people with schizophrenia. It was clear that there was a limit to success in rehabilitation programmes and this barrier seems to result from cognitive deficits in the schizophrenia population (see Chapter 4 for a review). This provided a further therapeutic impetus to the investigation of change in cognition with the hope that this would then release further rehabilitation potential.

These two threads, the move to the community and theory development, together produced a whole series of studies. Some tried to show that cognition could change in people with schizophrenia and therefore disprove the frontal lobe theory. These we call laboratory studies and they generally concentrate on single tests in highly controlled settings. The remaining studies were more clinically oriented and were designed to remove the rate limiter on rehabilitation. The two sets of studies ran parallel to each other but there was little

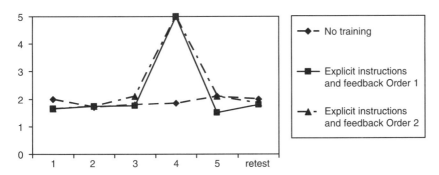

Figure 5.2 Card sort performance with and without training (adapted from Goldberg *et al.*, 1987)

cross referencing between the separate strands. However, they do provide complementary evidence on the development of a successful programme and will be reviewed separately in the following chapters.

Historical issues in the assessment of CRT

The studies described here contribute not only to our view of schizophrenia but also to the design of cognitive remediation programmes. The most obvious question to ask is: What is a successful training technique? Successful programmes often get privileged access to publication even when the study sample is small and the analyses exploratory. On the other hand negative studies tend to be put into the experimenter's notional 'bottom drawer'. Interestingly in the area of cognitive remediation in schizophrenia, this has not generally been a problem. The zeitgeist was that negative results (i.e. those showing no improvement) would support theory and so editors were willing to publish such results and the bottom drawer could be forgotten. Cognitive remediation therefore has the benefit of studies that illustrate failure as well as success. Many likely participants in these programmes have all previously experienced failure in the transfer to less supportive environments (Wykes and Dunn, 1992), in achieving a job (Jaeger *et al.*, 1992), and in developing social skills (Mueser *et al.*, 1991). Failure leads to reduced self-efficacy and self-esteem, both of which are known to contribute to quality of life and both of which affect motivation to agree to take part and engage in further skills training. Reducing failure, not just increasing success, are the two keys to the most effective outcomes. However, publication of negative findings does affect meta-analyses that assess the efficacy of treatment, particularly in its early development. So unlike other new cognitive treatments in schizophrenia (e.g. cognitive behaviour therapy) cognitive remediation has to produce large effect sizes to counter the negative findings from these initial studies.

Laboratory studies of cognitive remediation

The studies reviewed in this chapter were not initially designed to investigate remediation techniques themselves but to investigate and delineate the underlying cognitive deficits. For instance, studies in memory improvement were to define which aspects of poor memory were due to poor capacity and which were the result of a lack of initiation of strategic processing. Cognitive outcomes were also investigated in isolation from other aspects of the participants' lives and were never integrated into rehabilitation programmes. Most studies were designed to test whether there could be any improvement in performance and therefore they tended to carry out remediation over a very short period of time and assess improvement on the same task. It is rare to find examples of a test for generalisation and even rarer to see tests on more than one task.

Cognitive flexibility

The first study to have an impact was by Goldberg and colleagues (1987) of 44 chronic inpatients and this set the trend to concentrate on a specific neuropsychological test – the Wisconsin Card Sorting Test (WCST; Berg, 1948). This test has been pivotal in first producing evidence in favour of a frontal lobe difficulty underlying cognitive impairments in schizophrenia, and also increasing therapeutic optimism that these cognitive impairments could be changed. If Esta Berg had known in 1948 what an impact on schizophrenia research her test would have we are sure she would have called it the Berg Card Sorting Test.

In the WCST, cards are sorted into different categories according to a changing set of rules. It is often termed a test of 'executive functioning' and involves conceptual learning, planning, monitoring, working memory and flexibility of thought. Performance can be assessed in a number of ways but is usually measured by the number of correct categories sorted, perseverative errors and conceptual responses. The experimental paradigms of the laboratory-based studies were designed to investigate whether different remediation techniques could achieve change in the whole task or a component of a task.

Various reviewers have summarised the effects of studies of the WCST (e.g. Wykes, 2000; Kurtz et al., 2001; Wykes and van der Gaag, 2001). Figure 5.3 shows the effect sizes derived from a formal meta-analysis by Kurtz and colleagues (2001) for nine studies that contribute an effect size for sorting categories. Kurtz reports that the average effect size for categories is 1.08, for perseverative errors 0.93, and for conceptual learning 0.90. These effects are not modest. It was not possible for Kurtz and colleagues to identify possible contributors to successful remediation as the studies had much methodological heterogeneity, but it is clear that it is possible to improve neuropsychological test performance, at least on this task.

Three studies in particular highlight the issues in this area. The first is a novel study designed by Rossell and David (1997) which investigated whether a range of different types of intervention could increase performance on the WCST. Their comparison group was elderly (average age 76 years) who also had difficulty with the test but who were from the normal population. The main elements of training for successful performance in both groups were to increase planning, pacing and error detection. Verbalising the response did produce as in other studies (e.g. Stratta et al., 1994) improvements in responding, as did teaching categorisation by the use of scaffolded instruction (see below). However, only the normal control group were able to take advantage of one technique, increasing the verbal information contained in the task, and this was replicated in a further study by Young et al. (2002). This suggests that increasing verbal information may produce information overload in people with schizophrenia that may be detrimental to performance in the long term.

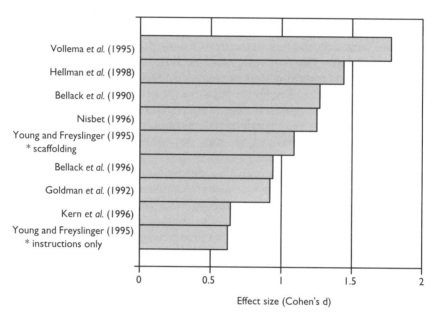

Figure 5.3 Effect of WCST on three aspects of the task (derived from Kurtz *et al.*, 2001)

The second study tried to improve performance using a technique that was first used to teach complex skills to children with a learning disability – errorless learning. Kern and colleagues (1996) compared two groups of trainees with schizophrenia. In one group the participants had two standard presentations of the task as well as modelling and feedback. The second group had no prior exposure to the task. The two groups then received training based on errorless learning principles, using 'self' and 'other' delivered cues. This facilitated the reduction of errors but did not abolish them. The group that had been exposed to the WCST training showed significant improvements in performance despite the large number of errors they had produced on previous opportunities. The number of categories achieved was an average of 4.6 compared to 3.2 before training and perseverative errors were halved. But perhaps the most interesting result was that there was durability of training over four weeks. These participants were less severely impaired than those in the Rossell and David study where their participants only achieved 1.4 categories before training and it has been suggested that level of initial performance can affect durability (Stratta *et al.*, 1997b).

Finally and more recently, in a pivotal study, Young *et al.* (2002) examined the usefulness of instruction as opposed to scaffolded instruction to improve performance on the WCST. In their study a comparison was drawn between three groups: two received the same level of instruction in two sessions (scaffolded or direct instruction) and a further control group were given opportunities to find another sorting rule but had no instruction. The scaffolded instruction group differed from the remaining direct instruction group by the instructions being presented in a collaborative manner, using open-ended questions, changing the tone of the instructions and giving the participants more choice. All groups improved the mean number of categories sorted. The scaffolded group increased from a mean of 0.6 categories to 2.9 categories at post-test, the instruction group from 0.6 to 1.6 categories and the control group from 0.6 to 2.1. Only the changes in the control and scaffolded groups were significant. The authors explain the improvement in the control group being due to the presence of a crucial factor – the element of discovery without the information overload probably present in the didactic instruction group. Self-esteem improved only in the scaffolded group, who also maintained positive affect during the study. But these changes were not directly linked either to the initial improvement or to the continuation of that improvement. However, it is highly likely that the improved self-confidence produced by the scaffolded techniques will encourage trainees to become engaged in other forms of training which will lead to further cognitive and social improvements. This study then highlights the efficacy of two main elements of training, collaborative discovery and the calibration of attentional demands.

After 15 years of research the rather pessimistic views of Goldberg and colleagues in 1987 on the possibility of remediating performance on the WCST have now been trounced. Some types of training seem to provide more learning than others but there is still room for further improvement (see Table 5.1). There is also some suggestion in the literature that providing monetary reinforcement may be detrimental to performance because it can divert attention away from conceptual issues towards some task irrelevant information. In a study by Vollema and colleagues monetary reward together with instruction may also be providing too much information which results in information overload and less efficient task performance (Vollema *et al.*, 1995).

Table 5.1 Types of successful training for the Wisconsin Card Sorting Task

Type of training	Successful reports
Calibration of attentional demand	Young et al. (2002)
Errorless learning	Kern et al. (1996)
Self-instruction (via verbalisation)	Rossell and David (1997) Stratta et al. (1994)
Scaffolded instruction	Young et al. (2002) Rossell and David (1997)
Element of discovery	Young et al. (2002)

Increases in the number of categories sorted can lead to performance within the normal range but this is generally dependent on how many categories the person could sort at baseline.

Positive results have been found for groups that vary in their clinical and demographic characteristics as well as in the same type of group in the original Goldberg *et al.* (1987) study. Stratta *et al.* (1997) and Wiedl (1999) suggest that there is still a group who are 'unremediable' and who show very low levels of categories sorted at the outset and who do not benefit from training. The study by Young and colleagues (2002) has now shown that this poor performance group, who are also usually more chronic and older, can benefit from training where this training is based on scaffolding. Although there have been few studies of sustained improvements following training, many recent studies have shown continued although sometimes reduced improvements over time, even up to one month following training.

Memory training

The description of memory problems in people with schizophrenia has often emerged from the results of studies specifically designed to remediate memory. They include the failure to use any strategy to aid recall such as rehearsal or elaborated encoding procedures. A first set of studies by Bauman (1971a, 1971b) set out to investigate whether an encoding strategy would be helpful. One group was provided with information on how to devise a strategy and the other group was given no specific instructions except to do their best. The result was no difference between the two groups in recall, which may lead us to assume that providing instruction on encoding strategies is not a useful exercise. However, further work by Bauman (1971b) and by Koh and colleagues (1976) led to more therapeutic optimism. What was missing from Bauman's first study was any indication that the encoding strategy provided (or rather merely hinted at) was actually used by the participants. Also, of course, participants with schizophrenia are variable and so some in the control group could also have used this same strategy without being instructed and therefore scuppered any chances of getting a between-group difference. Koh and colleagues (1973) tested elaborated encoding using a simple procedure that required patients to write down the degree of pleasantness of each of 50 words on a scale of 1 to 7. This enforced encoding produced increases in recall similar to those in both the psychiatric and normal control groups. Bauman (1971b) also provided a list of words which differed in their semantic grouping. When these groupings were made explicit in the list, by putting related words together, then people with schizophrenia were able to recall more words than a schizophrenia control group where the list was the same but not categorised. These list learning exercises were carried out under what is known as unintentional recall circumstances – the participants do not know that they are going to be asked to remember the lists. Under intentional recall conditions it would be expected that more elaborated encoding or mnemonic strategies might be utilised but in the majority of studies of people with schizophrenia few strategies are adopted spontaneously.

Practice can also increase recall. After ten weeks of practice on auditory verbal serial position memory tasks, two of eight participants with schizophrenia improved their average scores to above normal levels (Wexler *et al.*, 2000). In a similar computer-based study, Bell *et al.* (2003) used graded exposure to increase list lengths where moving from one list to another was based on achieving a performance threshold. There were significant improvements in working memory for those who were both severely and moderately impaired, with effect sizes at post-treatment and follow-up in the range 0.3 to 0.75. Half the schizophrenia group performed in the normal range following training and this was an increase over baseline performance for some of the group (Bell *et al.*, 2004). It is not clear how far the group of improvers were below the normal range so it is not possible to assess the rate of change. Clearly if all those who improved were only a few points below the normal levels then moving them up to a higher level might have been achieved without so much practice. These participants did also receive, in addition, large amounts of memory training on other computer-based tasks which may also have contributed to the increases. However, it is still an achievement to have improved memory performance with so little structured intervention on the task itself.

O'Carroll and colleagues (1999) tested errorless learning using a list learning exercise where in the effortful condition participants were asked to guess the ending for a pair of letters (e.g. the word begins with BR and the participants had to guess BRING). In the errorless condition, participants were presented with the same pair of letters but were told the actual word. In this study, individual memory performance was also accounted for in two schizophrenia groups, who were either in the normal range or showed memory impairment. These groups were compared to a group of people from the local community. Errorless learning was found to be successful even for the memory impaired group, whereas with errorful learning only the participants who were unimpaired or from the normal control group improved their scores. These results have provoked some controversy about why errorless learning should help people who have impaired explicit memory. One possibility is that the process of source monitoring is problematic (Vinogradov *et al.*, 1997) or it may be that residual explicit memory functioning may support this type of learning. This is a good example of how results of an intervention study provoke further hypotheses about memory deficits which would not have been obvious without an intervention.

A similar elaborated encoding procedure was adopted by Corrigan and colleagues (1995) in a study of the recall of social cues in a video. The participants were asked to produce the gist of the story, to put it in their own words, and were given a reminder of the instructional cue to repeat. At the end of the video presentation, the participants were asked to repeat aloud the story in the video and if they did not report all the key elements the trainer asked questions and provided key word lists of emotional descriptor words to elicit the information. The elaborated encoding together with a verbalisation procedure (repeating the information out aloud) increased the memory for social cues.

In summary, there appear to be a number of different training techniques that can aid memory (see Table 5.2). These overlap with training techniques for cognitive flexibility. Little work has been carried out on whether the elaborated encoding strategies are generalised to new memory tasks or even how stable this pattern of improved performance is at follow-up. Many of the training techniques are used together in a single study but it is not clear whether the sum of these strategies is more than the parts. Although practice can improve performance, there are many studies showing that performance is stable and poor over time despite practice.

Table 5.2 Types of successful training for memory tasks

Type of training	Successful reports
Elaborated and enforced encoding strategy	Koh et al. (1976) Corrigan et al. (1995)
Practice with increasing task difficulty	Wexler et al. (2000) Bell et al. (2004) Bell et al. (2003)
Errorless learning	O'Carroll et al. (1999)
Self-instruction	Corrigan et al. (1995)

Training attention

Until recently sustained attention has been the subject of few remediation studies despite its importance in everyday tasks. Many of the tasks in this area also involve some aspects of memory as well as attention. For instance, Wagner (1968) in a small study used contingent reinforcement and practice on an attention training task – a delayed matching to sample task (conventionally thought of as a working memory task). They compared the training group performance with a contact control and a treatment as usual group on a variety of tests after training. They showed improvements on four of the five outcome measures. This study suggests that some of the variance in poor performance must be due to inattention or distraction from the task. However, it is also possible that participants developed more elaborated coding on the delayed matching to sample training task that generalised to the outcome tasks.

Two studies by Benedict and colleagues showed improvements on tasks of attention using training programmes based on computer software. Benedict and Harris (1989) in a small study tested the effect of 25 training sessions versus an attention control and a further control group who received no training. Improvements in reaction time were noted only in the treatment group. Benedict *et al.* (1994) in a further study with 15 training sessions, used commercial software that had been designed for people with acquired brain injury. The software programmes provided extended practice on tasks that depended on high levels of sustained attention and showed little training effect. The authors concluded that there was little evidence from their study that practice on controlled cognitive processing can enhance performance on attention tasks. This is a similar result to the remediation effects in other areas of cognition – practice alone does not seem to offer a useful training tool.

In contrast to Benedict and colleagues, Kern *et al.* (1995) have shown more optimistic results. They investigated the possible remediation of difficulties on the Span of Apprehension Test. In this test the participant is required to identify target stimuli in arrays of varying sizes immediately after the array has been switched off. These tasks are dependent on early visual attention and the deficits found in groups of people with diagnoses of schizophrenia have been identified as a possible trait marker for the disorder; that is, a deficit that is not only stable over time but is by definition not modifiable. However, Kern and colleagues showed that there was an improvement in the Span of Apprehension when both monetary reinforcement and instructions were given together but not when these were given separately. The level of performance was similar in the effective training condition to that of normal control participants carrying out the same task. Effective training was also found in a study of computerised attention training using a software package called ORM which had been used with people with acquired brain injury (Medalia *et al.*, 1998).

For attention the results are more mixed than for other areas reviewed (see Table 5.3 for details). There are some indications of improvements but some pessimistic results and little evidence of a normalisation of behaviour on the tests. It has also been commented that there may be limits to training such that it may be possible to improve performance on the Span of Apprehension test only if the interval between the array presentation and the recall of the target is delayed. It is possible, however, to modify some seemingly uncontrolled responses such as an eye blink startle response by instructing the participants to attend or disattend to the alerting stimulus. But this instruction is only effective when the interval between the alerting stimulus and the puff of air is greater than 60msecs. (Filion *et al.*, 1998). It may be that attention to specific stimuli can be modified but only for very defined task characteristics and the important characteristic will depend on the severity of the difficulties. Research in this area is at such an early stage that these issues have yet been considered.

Table 5.3 Types of successful training for attention

Type of training	Successful reports
Self-instruction	Corrigan *et al.* (1995)
Salience cues	Corrigan *et al.* (1995)
Repeated practice in the context of other training strategies	Medalia *et al.* (1998) Corrigan *et al.* (1995)
Monetary reward plus instructions	Kern *et al.* (1995)

The results of laboratory analyses of change following treatment, usually compared to an untreated control, are on the whole favourable. A broad range of cognitive impairments have been targeted with a variety of techniques. There appears to be new therapeutic optimism that it is possible to improve the impairments with a variety of training techniques. It is not clear whether the same techniques will result in performance which is essentially normal (for instance, within one standard deviation of normal controls) as it is rare that such comparisons have been made. But in the few where they have, there have been increases in the number of people who would be considered cognitively normal. Others, however, although not making a direct comparison, have suggested that the majority of people still have substantial performance decrements after training compared to controls. The level of improvement may depend on a number of different task and participant characteristics.

Again individual cognitive skills that have been trained are not identified in the outcome measures. Rather it has been assumed that gross behaviours such as those encompassed by performance on a cognitive task, such as WCST or Span of Apprehension reflect 'executive function' or 'attention' or 'memory'. It is not clear whether the techniques adopted in these studies do target specific parts of a cognitive model but this could be tested in many of the studies by investigating the outcome measures in more detail. For instance, improvements in metacognitive processes might account for improvements across all tests and with all training techniques rather than training techniques being specific to a cognitive component or set of components.

Transferring skills from one task to another

The majority of laboratory studies have investigated the effect of training on a single test. However, there are a few studies, generally occurring more recently, which also test generalisation of test improvements to other tasks that may contain similar elements. Clearly it cannot just be assumed that improved performance in one task is due to more efficient processing strategies that can be generalised, or that conceptual learning has taken place in a way which can be used in other tasks. There is also a further difficult issue in testing generalisation, the underlying performance characteristics of the generalisation tasks, such as their difficulty and dependence on a specific cognitive processing strategy. For a fair test of generalisation these would need to be equated. So for instance it would be a surprise if learning on one task generalised to another task which shared only a passing resemblance to the trained task or that performance on a simple task would generalise to a much more complex task. However, if it is possible with such small amounts of training on simple neuropsychological tasks to achieve generalisation, then this would have implications for the design of more complex training procedures.

Bellack *et al.* (2001) investigated transfer of skills and showed that people trained on one task had improvements in a generalisation task that were greater than for a control group which received no training. The different characteristics of the tasks seem to account for the differential levels of generalisation, such that training on a more complex task, WCST, generalised more to the simpler Halstead Category sorting task than vice versa. The high levels of generalisation also seemed to depend on good baseline performance on delayed memory and on a short intellectual status test, which implies that it is not merely the training paradigm involved which may improve generalisation but also individual characteristics of the trainee. Young and colleagues (2002) also included a generalisation test as well as a test for the differential effects on other tasks that do not share similar characteristics to the trained WCST. They reported that only for the group that received scaffolded instructions were there significant gains in other tasks that had similar components. More participants in the scaffolded group also grasped the underlying abstract concept in one of the generalisation tasks which suggests that conceptual learning has occurred. There was, however, no generalisation to tasks such as the Trail Making Test and the Stroop where there were few common cognitive processing elements. The effects on generalisation were specific to the training and not to the non-specific effects of receiving training such as improvements in engagement or attention.

The characteristics of participants have rarely been investigated as a source of variance in remediation studies. These may have an effect on the success of a remediation strategy and on their ability to generalise to other tasks. Memory difficulties, as in the learning of other skills (e.g. social skills) have been highlighted as one such characteristic that seems to hinder generalisation. This might be considered as learning potential which was first introduced by Vygotsky (1962) as a useful concept in education. Learning potential refers to latent capacity rather than developed abilities (Grigorenko and Sternberg, 1998) and measures the extent to which someone is able to acquire new skills using dynamic assessment. Vygotsky was interested in whether there were children who would not learn from particular types of teaching. This is not the same as suggesting that there are some people who are unable to learn, as is sometimes implied (e.g. Wiedl, 1999), but rather that learning is affected by the specific cognitive skills and style of an individual. This concept might also be relevant to the generalisation of thinking skills to new tasks. Its usefulness probably depends on the analysis of change at an individual rather than group level. Other relevant participant characteristics such as cognitive style and thinking capacity are also likely to vary along more than one dimension.

Training issues in laboratory studies

Although the methods differ considerably there seem to be some specific training techniques that are associated with improvements, some that are associated with inconsistent improvements and some that are hardly ever associated with improvement. Wykes (2000) considered 18 studies, mostly using the WCST. Although more studies have now been added to the corpus of data, the categorisation of successful training programmes has not changed. Clearly several studies had overlapping training paradigms and therefore produced positive outcomes that on occasion could not be disentangled. Figure 5.4 shows the relationship between positive outcomes and a training component based on a simple count of positive studies compared to all studies that used such a component. This shows that neither paying people nor practice is potent method of change.

Practice

Practice can of course increase cognitive skill, however, the effect tends to be specific to a task. This was pointed out over a hundred years ago by Thorndike and Woodworth (1901) and was shown dramatically by a mnemonist

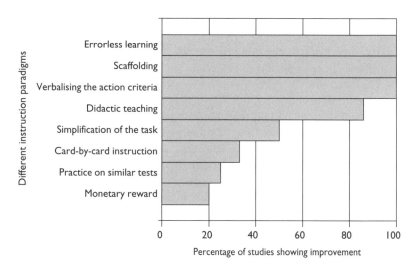

Figure 5.4 Success of instruction paradigms (from Wykes, 2000)

who by practice increased his digit span from 7 to 79 digits over several months. But even after all this practice he was only able to remember the same number of letters as ordinary mortals (Ericsson *et al.*, 1980). The task component to be increased through practice must then consist of something that is unlikely to change in the future.

Learning which occurs through practice is not well understood. One assumption is that it may increase the automation of cognition or behaviour. This means that the processes which are at first under conscious control can become automatic and this unconscious processing requires less cognitive effort. A real life example would be learning to drive a car. At first the movement of the gear stick, clutch and accelerator require much concentrated effort to time the sequence. With practice, subtasks become more efficient, require less cognitive effort and can become unconscious, as the individual becomes more of an expert. The effect is to leave more conscious processing available for other tasks such as remembering which way to go to the shops. Perhaps in Shallice's view (1988) the effect is to develop contention schedules appropriate for the task that then free the Supervisory Attentional System (SAS) for other processing requirements. For this automation process to work the cognitive processing strategies adopted must have the potential to be relatively efficient, or the processes that underlie performance must be relatively unimpaired. If neither of these are the case (and we certainly have doubts in the case of schizophrenia) then it is unlikely that practice could help task performance except in the simplest of tasks. In this case an initial assessment of the processing problem would have to show that even the component processing of the simple task was instantiated and unimpaired.

Alternatively practice could provide the time to develop more appropriate cognitive processing strategies that are more efficient for a particular task. For example, in a visual processing task, practice may allow an appropriate scanning system to be adopted. This must involve executive or metacognitive control. The spontaneous adoption of efficient strategies may be particularly hit or miss however. Not only are they dependent on individual characteristics, but also on chance variables occurring when completing the task from day to day. For example, we know that in general most people use a rehearsal strategy to improve verbal memory for lists and this strategy produces more words recalled at the beginning and end of a list. These are the well known primacy and recency effects. However, for individuals the presence of primacy and recency effects on the same task differs over time and for the same individual for different tasks carried out one after another (Della Sala and Logie, 1997). These individual differences show that there is variability of efficient strategy use in the general population. This variability is also likely to be present in the population of people with schizophrenia and it is not even clear that an appropriate strategy will ever be initiated. Furthermore difficulties in working memory may impair the ability to maintain a temporary schema and so even if initiated a strategy may be poorly implemented without specific external support.

Both explanations of the practice effect have been reported by remediation specialists to explain its adoption as a training method. They may account for the variability in findings within studies where only a minority of patients actually improves (Stratta *et al.*, 1994; Wexler *et al.*, 2000). Practice might, however, be useful when a strategy has been instantiated and may need more time to be practised to become more automatic. Automaticity here means not only the possibility of becoming an unconscious process but that the use of a strategy to solve the problem becomes normalised in a schema so that it is available for use in any similar tasks. This approach probably means that practice must follow explicit instruction since useful schemas for transfer are unlikely to develop without guidance. Even if contention schedules are built up by practice they may only be applied in the specific situation in which they were developed and still not be applied in new situations. In other words transfer of skills may not be helped by practice alone. In our opinion, practice alone is unlikely to provide people with schizophrenia and cognitive deficits with the opportunity to learn new and efficient strategies or to develop flexible responding, all of which are essential to solve problems in everyday life.

Positive and negative reinforcement

Positive reinforcement in terms of monetary reward was introduced as a method for improving motivation but money was also taken away contingent on wrong responses (negative reinforcement). The assumption is that motivation would increase engagement in the task and the initiation of efficient information processing strategies. In the case of the WCST it was thought that reward would help to sustain attention, particularly to parts of the task where the participant failed to take account of negative feedback. Negative reinforcement, loss of money, would reduce perseverative errors. However, just reducing one type of wrong response does not necessitate the production of the correct response and might just increase random responding. No conceptual learning would occur which is essential for completion of the task and which may support sustained improvement over time. One early detailed study of a comparison of reinforcement was carried out by Meichenbaum (1966). He allocated 64 people with a diagnosis of schizophrenia to four groups, with only one being provided with contingent positive reinforcement for responses on a test of abstraction. The remaining three groups received non-contingent positive or negative reinforcement or negative reinforcement of non-abstract responses. Only the group receiving contingent positive reinforcement increased the number of abstract responses on the trained task. They also increased performance on another test requiring abstract ability, the similarities subtest of the WAIS. Positive reinforcement alone may be relevant to cognitive rehabilitation but this may be limited to tasks where there are easily discernible elements and a complex response is not required.

There is another lesson to be learnt from this study – the place of negative reinforcement. The results show that there is no effect of contingent negative reinforcement. This may be because negative reinforcement has little information value when the majority of the responses are incorrect or it may be that behaviours leading to positive outcomes (in this case abstract interpretations) are not easy for the participant to identify when they are only denoted by an absence of reinforcement.

In a further similar study Meichenbaum (1969) showed that improvements in abstraction were greatest if there was contingent tangible reward rather than only social reinforcement. The tangible reward may be more discriminating for the participant, particularly for abstract tasks. The environment where Meichenbaum worked offered individuals little tangible reward so those offered in his study would have had high potency. But even so, it is still not clear that these high potency rewards could be helpful in the transfer of skills from one task to another.

Reward, although important, may also impair learning as it can direct attention to parts of the task that are not relevant for successful performance. For example, for the WCST alternating of types of response would reduce negative reinforcement and may produce some positive reinforcement, but would not produce the hoped for conceptual learning. This sort of extrinsic reinforcement has been shown in educational settings not to be helpful (Amabile et al., 1986). The process of cognitive rehabilitation should therefore be personally meaningful and as intrinsically rewarding as possible, particularly if the aim is to make the effects durable.

Errorless learning

Errorless learning is defined here as techniques that improve performance by ensuring a high degree of success during learning. It includes a number of different types of technique from backward chaining of responding, first used to teach people with learning disability to carry out complex tasks, to studies with people who have severely impaired memory. For amnesic patients the technique was first developed by Baddeley and Wilson (1994) to capitalise on intact implicit memory whilst reducing the impact of problematic explicit memory. People with schizophrenia have difficulties remembering which response was an error and which was correct. Errorless learning avoids this confusion by reducing the number of incorrect responses encoded in implicit memory which then do not have to be differentiated in explicit recall. This differs from practice as a training technique where it is merely fortuitous if people carry out a task with few errors.

The study by O'Carroll and colleagues suggests that for those people who have memory impairments, trying an effortful approach to learning which includes guessing the response is unlikely to be helpful when the possibilities for a response are numerous. This more effortful approach has been adopted in rehabilitation settings as it was believed that people with schizophrenia would be more engaged if they were given more choice. Clearly although engagement may be improved it is also likely that the individual characteristics of the participants will interact with this training paradigm to reduce benefits.

Self-monitoring

Self-monitoring by verbalising action criteria describes a process whereby the participant is required to repeat out loud the instructions to the task and their current response. This provides a number of different aids to the participant. First, it effectively provides spontaneously generated rehearsal for task instructions, something that may be forgotten otherwise, particularly by participants who are known to have poor memory. This is overt behaviour so it can be checked by the trainer for its veracity during the training period. Second, it provides support for control over behavioural disinhibition, where participants initiate responses that are not planned and produce initial errors. For some tasks these initial errors are difficult to recover from and the task may then require much more cognitive effort for correct completion. Finally, verbalisation is a method whereby self-monitoring can occur; i.e. where the action to be made can be compared with the action plan for the task, assuming that one has been made. These repeated cues, prompts and feedback on strategy use can take into account individual characteristics of the processing style as well as baseline performance characteristics to enable people at different levels of competence to improve performance. It should be noted that this is part of the method used in the original studies by Meichenbaum and Cameron (1973) to improve attention and behavioural style of severely disabled hospital patients with schizophrenia which are discussed in the next chapter.

Scaffolding

Scaffolding is a method of training described in the pedagogical literature to be the most successful, particularly at the early stages of learning in a child's life (Wood, 1998). Effortful processing is encouraged by increasing the complexity of a task to be just at the limit of competence. A degree of effort has to be made but a high degree of success is ensured and again errors are minimised. It describes the 'dynamic and bidirectional processes by which tutors fade support, titrate assistance and contingently shift guidance as they transfer task responsibility to the tutee' (Young et al., 2002). The term itself describes a general process, and not the specific types of support that are provided for task completion. In the classroom these will take into account the child's cognitive level and stage of cognitive development. For people with schizophrenia they will also take into account the strengths and weaknesses of the person's cognitive profile. A key ingredient to scaffolding is the transfer of task ownership from the tutor to the tutee and the absorption of performance responsibility. This collaborative style and the tutor's control of the attentional demands of the task distinguish it from didactic teaching.

Didactic teaching was often combined with other techniques such as monetary reward in laboratory studies of WCST improvement, and in some studies this produced a significant effect (e.g. Bellack *et al.*, 1990). However, on closer examination of the description of the instruction it is clear that although the instructions were didactic, they were provided in an interactive style which was dependent on the participant understanding that part of the task, and so was more like scaffolding. If the participant did not understand, then further correction and explanation was given. In other words the teaching was in response to training level.

Combined training elements

Combining training elements seems to produce greater improvements than single elements alone. For instance, Corrigan *et al.* (1995) combined vigilance and memory training. Participants were able to recall more social cues than those who received vigilance training alone even at follow-up. Similarly, reward and instructions can improve cognition because there is a focus on correct responding and away from incorrect responding, in addition to an explanation which may lead to conceptual learning.

Other training issues

Participant characteristics

Participant characteristics are likely to affect success. Some, like the original Goldberg study, involved chronic hospitalised patients whereas others included only outpatients, and we can only assume that there were symptomatic and general functioning differences between these groups. The samples also differed on their specific performance characteristics. For instance, even when similar training protocols were used the average number of card sorts differed in the WCST. The average number for Bellack *et al.* (1990) was about 1.5 whereas for Young and Freyslinger (1995) it was 0.43. It is therefore hardly surprising that there are some differences between studies purporting to measure similar training constructs. However, despite these differences there do seem to be some consistencies in the results although the individual differences in response to different methods of training have not yet been identified (Table 5.3).

Learning potential

Learning potential is the ability of a person to take advantage of the training programme offered. It has been suggested as one possible influence on the outcomes of CRT programmes (Green *et al.*, 2000). Both Stratta *et al.* (1997) and Wiedl (1999) present some data on people that they consider to have poor learning potential within their training paradigms. However, others have not found that dynamic measures of learning potential actually are predictive (Woonings *et al.*, 2003). In fact Woonings and colleagues suggest that the most predictive measures of outcome are the post-training levels of performance.

Generalisation

Generalisation or the transfer of skills has not been investigated in detail in this series of studies. The majority of the original studies tested and trained on the same tasks. Where new tests have been used, there are mixed results and these seem to be related to the training paradigm used. Some authors have concluded that practice mediated improvements may have a generalis-able effect in the absence of direct effects of training. For instance, Lopez-Luengo and Vazquez (2003) found that improvements were shown within attention training tasks and on executive functioning tasks that were not trained. However, there was no effect on tests of attention that were not trained. These authors conclude that practice can be a useful way to improve cognitive function. But we conclude that the mode of action is unclear and is more likely to be related to the non-specific effects of training than to practice per se. Bellack and colleagues (1996, 2001) too found little effect of practice on generalisation. But several studies have now reported generalisation based on scaffolded instruction.

What have laboratory studies told us about cognitive rehabilitation?

The general message is one of optimism. There are reports throughout this literature of people with diagnoses of schizophrenia and severe cognitive difficulties being able to improve their scores on standard tests with cognitive rehabilitation. Individual characteristics clearly interact with the type of training paradigm offered and this is essentially what Vygotsky, who defined learning potential, suggested. However, there is more optimism about learn-ing as more studies report improvements even in those whose performance falls into the severely disabled category. What we have to find is the right sort of training paradigm to fit the pattern of cognitive difficulties. However, the effects of training on specific component cognitive skills defined in Chapter 3 have not yet been tested. Furthermore, investigations of the response to training in relationship to the patterns of cognitive strengths and difficulties which will allow us to tailor our cognitive treatments have not been carried out.

These laboratory studies do not answer some of the more clinically driven questions which include whether the improvements noted on tests can be generalised to cognitive problems in everyday life. This not only includes general problem solving but whether participants in these studies notice that there have been marked improvements, for example, in their ability to concentrate on television programmes or to remember which medication to take. It is also clear that many tasks in everyday life require more than one cognitive process for their completion. The person has to attend to relevant stimulus attributes, disattend to attributes not relevant or redundant, sustain this attention throughout the task as well as use specific efficient information processing strategies. These generalisation issues tend to be considered in more clinically oriented studies which are reviewed in the next chapter.

Chapter 6

Changing cognition in clinical settings

Data from laboratory studies provide evidence of the improvement of scores on cognitive tests. There were a number of different training elements associated with this success. But these studies tended to concentrate on improvements in test scores in a single domain such as memory or attention or on a single test. Studies we describe in this chapter assess the learning of a variety of different tasks or component skills and incorporate tests of generalisation to other tasks not trained and to other general areas of functioning, such as symptoms. Again there were two main functions of these studies, to test cognitive training paradigms and to test models of the relationship between cognitive improvements and functioning outcomes. The key idea is not to show that it is possible to change performance on a single test, but to try to investigate whether the associations apparent between cognitive data and functioning outcomes continue after remediation; that when cognition is improved then functioning will improve. These studies are time intensive, if only because the effects on functioning are unlikely to appear just a few days after the training has been completed. Also, unlike the laboratory studies, they assume that cognition can be changed, rather than being designed to support a zeitgeist of stable and immutable cognitive deficits. Clinical investigations have run in parallel with little cross-connection, so that several training protocols now shown to have little effect on task performance were incorporated into these more general programmes.

The programmes all differ in the way in which they are implemented. The types are highlighted in Table 6.1. Different tools of training are shown as columns and almost every combination of characteristics can be found among the clinical programmes, making it difficult to interpret results as being attached to any specific set of characteristics. There is also a wide variety of target skills, as well as the methods of measuring improvement between programmes. This is in addition to differences in the actual experimental design of the studies themselves. Training incorporates elements of practice, strategy learning and new elements that were not explicitly tested in the laboratory studies. However, we will defy this heterogeneity and attempt to capture the roots of success for clinically oriented regimens.

Table 6.1 Variability in clinical cognitive remediation programmes

Setting	Information presentation	Therapist	Length	Incorporated with other rehabilitation
Individual	Social information	One-to-one	Single session	Not incorporated
Paired participants	Paper and pencil	Present	Between one and ten sessions	Part of comprehensive programme
Group	Computer	Absent	More than ten sessions	Other programmes run in parallel
More than one type	Video			
	At least two forms			

How successful are clinical programmes?

Idiosyncratic approaches

Single case study approach

Although much is to be learned from large group studies, individual cases often also provide some insight into the process as well as the outcome of a training paradigm. A single case was used in one of the earliest studies of cognitive rehabilitation, with a man diagnosed with schizophrenia who not only had low self-esteem but also experienced 'crazy thoughts'. In particular this person reported having difficulty in following conversations, with his thoughts wandering away from the topic and forgetting what was being discussed. As a consequence he appeared confused and disoriented, displayed a rigid posture and spoke strangely. Adams and colleagues (1981) devised a treatment plan aimed at improving the client's cognitive skills and to increase the quality and the quantity of his social interactions. The primary goal was to increase attention. The treatment package included the use of graded levels of attention to external stimuli, training in socially appropriate behaviour such as eye contact, and tasks to increase cognitive skills. A wide variety of tasks were used, including auditory, visual and conversation distraction tasks, which allowed some measurement of within-task improvement during the training. In addition, there were tasks to improve attention to appropriate internal stimuli and to disattend to 'crazy thoughts'. The distraction tasks increased in complexity throughout treatment. Improvements in skills were measured on non-trained tasks at one, three and six months following training. The client reported finding it easier to follow conversations and had increased his self-confidence. He also showed decreases in depression scores and no evidence of thought disturbance. By the end of the therapy the client had a part-time job. There have only been a few studies of individually tailored programmes to improve cognition following this report (e.g. Spaulding and Sullivan, 1992). The majority of subsequent studies have reported group data with protocol driven treatments.

Operant procedures for improving cognitive processing

A further idiosyncratic approach has been developed by Silverstein and colleagues (1999, 2001). Their approach is different from others in that they incorporate the shaping of attention skills within programmes designed to develop other skills. Shaping is the differential reinforcement of successive approximations of a behaviour. So rather than waiting for a complete behaviour to occur before offering reinforcement, reinforcement is provided for successive approximations or steps towards the final behaviour. Shaping can occur by reinforcing aspects of behaviour such as its duration, its form or its intensity. Early studies of unintegrated shaping procedures (e.g. Menditto *et al.*, 1991) showed that it is possible to improve attention to the point that the person can be enrolled in other skills programmes. Spaulding and colleagues (1986) showed that it was possible to increase cognitive skills in seven out of nine participants using shaping procedures so that they were then able to enter a more complex vocational rehabilitation programme. Silverstein *et al.* (2001) devised individual behavioural programmes for each participant by identifying the most problematic verbal and non-verbal behaviour through a functional assessment over a four-week baseline period. Then shaping procedures were carried out, with patients receiving tokens every 15 minutes if they exceeded their goals and the tokens were exchanged at the end of the session for money. The threshold for reinforcement was increased as the participants consistently attained their goals. The effects on their behaviour within the skills training demonstrated that most people in the programme showed skill improvements when shaping was employed.

These procedures have been employed specifically with patients who were the most disabled and who were unable to engage in many skills training packages. The addition of cognitive retraining using simple behavioural techniques allowed this group of patients to begin to engage more appropriately. There have however, only been a few published studies, each with a small number of participants. Some participants were not shown to gain, and it is not clear whether there are any predictors for this group of patients. Larger studies with control groups may enable us to identify which people of those with the most severe difficulties can gain specifically from this structured engagement approach. It is also not clear how long these gains are maintained following treatment.

The possibility of operant conditioning of behaviour was investigated in relatively large groups of participants by Meichenbaum (1966, 1969). He reported that when people with diagnoses of schizophrenia were trained on a cognitive measure (abstract proverb interpretation) with tangible reinforcement they not only improved their performance on the task but this generalised to another cognitive task (WAIS similarities subtest). In addition the amount of disordered or abnormal speech reduced when participants were provided with tangible and social reinforcement. Unusually this was tested a week later, which showed a durability of these effects.

Operant procedures do seem to have some benefit in improving both complex (abstract thinking) and more simple processes of sustained attention. Changing the environmental contingencies may therefore have a role to play in cognitive rehabilitation.

Self-instructional training

Meichenbaum and Cameron (1973) developed a training programme that, although based on operant conditioning, included concepts of developmental changes in cognition first proposed by Luria (1966). In their model it is assumed there is a loss of cognitive control of behaviour and that this control can be trained using a self-instructional training paradigm. Behaviours were first modelled by the therapist and then carried out by the participant under the trainer's control. This control was then passed on to the participant who spoke the instructions aloud. The self-instruction became covert with the participants being encouraged to repeat the instructions in their mind. Training was extensive and included learning to monitor their own behaviour and thinking, and responding appropriately to interpersonal cues. Not only was the extent of 'sick talk' reduced by 42 per cent but they also increased their levels of abstract thinking and recall of digits in a distraction condition. This method is perhaps the first to identify metacognitive activity as important in functional outcome and to show that training effects can have a widespread impact. In summary, these idiosyncratic approaches have been successful in improving performance on neuropsychological tests.

Nomothetic or prescriptive approaches

These approaches are based on therapies which have a set protocol and a manual for their implementation. There are few changes made to take into account individual characteristics even though the laboratory studies clearly identify this variation as important. The programmes are also often integrated into some overall rehabilitation programme for recovery.

Integrated psychological therapy (IPT; Brenner et al., 1994)

IPT is based on the premise that poor elementary cognitive processes feed forward to produce problems in more complex behaviours, such as social functioning. For example, poor attentional processing feeds into impairments of concept acquisition. These then feed into inadequate social skills which lead to impairments in the completion of complex tasks in social roles (Brenner *et al.*, 1994). It was one of the first clinical programmes to be well developed with manuals in both German and English. There are five sub-programmes each of which has both social and cognitive elements in differing amounts with more cognitive input at the earlier stages. The subprogrammes are: cognitive differentiation, social perception, verbal communication, social competence and interpersonal problem solving. The explicit cognitive sub-programme (cognitive differentiation) addresses a spectrum of cognitive abil-ities and includes aspects of attention (selective attention, shifting attention, sustained focused attention) and conceptualisation abilities (abstraction, concept formation, differentiation and recall). Activities are run in a group format where training is didactic. This method of training provides further social contact which may also boost social functioning.

Controlled studies of this approach have produced variable results but most do show improvements in cognitive functioning, although there is little support for the subsequent effects on social skills (Brenner *et al.*, 1994). In fact more recent evaluations have suggested that it is not possible to conclude that cognitive improvements are specific to the cognitive subprogramme rather than the remaining psycho-social subprogrammes (Hodel and Bren-ner, 1994). As cognitive rehabilitation continues in varying amounts through-out the training programme it is likely that it will improve following other subprogrammes. It is also clear from these data that cognitive improvements can be identified, but that these are not necessarily followed by changes in social functioning. However, these data do suggest that the original feed forward model may be too simple an explanation of the interrelationships between social and cognitive difficulties.

Many later studies investigated the effectiveness of the cognitive sub-programmes in the therapy. In a tightly controlled study, Spaulding and colleagues in Nebraska have addressed the problem of the specificity of cog-nitive subprogramme. They compared the cognitive subprogramme to a con-trol condition of groups providing supportive psychotherapy and both groups also received social skills training. The sessions took place either two or three times per week, lasted 45 to 60 minutes and were carried out over a 6-month period. There were several different domains of outcome measure-ment including cognitive assessments and functioning outcomes. Their results do suggest a specific effect of the cognitive subprogramme on improvements in social skills, although there are few unequivocal cognitive improvements (Spaulding *et al.*, 1998, 1999a, 1999b). They therefore investi-gated the effects of cognitive changes on outcomes as well as individual predictors of outcome. The main links appear to be between changes in 'top-down' modulation and social competence. In other words, the differen-tial change was in executive level processing rather than in attentional or pre-attentional processing. More recent analyses have suggested a direct effect of improvements in social competence with improvements on card sorting. Improvements in verbal memory were associated with improved psycho-social skill acquisition (Spaulding *et al.*, 1999b).

This study has also been used to test theories of the relationship of cognition to another outcome – paranoid symptoms. Social cognitive biases of misattribution were related to the level of paranoid symptoms but these biases were magnified by cognitive difficulties as measured by perseverative errors on the WCST. Following therapy both paranoid symptoms and cognitive difficulties had decreased but the social cognitive biases were still evident. This suggests that there is a stable relationship (although not yet a causal relationship) between measures of executive function and symptoms and that attempts to modify one might also have an effect on the other (Peer *et al.*, 2004).

Van der Gaag and colleagues (1992, 2002) also tested a programme derived from the work of Brenner and colleagues, but this programme had a stronger dependence on experimental research and on the deficits of people with schizophrenia, and provided individual training. His programme adapted IPT and used a number of specific training strategies, such as self-instruction previously found to be effective by Meichenbaum and Cameron (1973, see above), as well as some prosthetic training based on the work of Ekman and Friesen (1975). The cognitive training took place over 22 sessions, each lasting about 20 minutes and held twice a week. Perceptual abilities were trained first, followed by memory and then social cue perception. Homework was also assigned between sessions. They found improvements in the perception of emotion in faces, which was targeted in the training. There was some generalisation to executive functioning (Mazes, Word fluency and WAIS Picture Arrangement), but attention and memory functioning were unaffected.

In one of the recent tests of this cognitive subprogramme, Penades and colleagues (2003) compared two groups of 10 control patients and 27 people receiving the cognitive and social perception subprogrammes before and after the treatment envelope. The results suggest that cognition improved in the treatment group but not in the comparison group, although this was not specifically tested in a between-group analysis. In the treatment group 63 per cent of the participants did not show any impairment at post-test. There were also positive correlations between improvements in executive functioning and social behaviour scores with a correlation of 0.59 with interpersonal social behaviour. This suggests that changes in cognition were related to changes in social functioning. In another small study, Ueland and Rund (2004) showed that there were few changes between their treatment and control groups of adolescents, although the adolescents did show some improvements within the treatment group. However, both these studies were small and lacked the statistical power to detect anything other than large effect sizes.

The overall picture suggests that IPT improves cognitive functioning although the specific improvements differ between studies and depend on the level of experimental control. However, there are some replicated findings showing executive functioning can improve with this therapy although there are few methodologically rigorous tests. What has emerged recently is that cognitive functioning can improve even in control conditions. However, it seems that it is only the improvements that occur in the context of the programme that have implications for future social behaviour change.

Cognitive enhancement therapy

This therapy is an amalgamation of both group and partner working. It uses materials often adopted in brain injury training as well as a comprehensive approach to work therapy. The underlying model is neurodevelopmental, with the assumption that anomalies in development produce delays in social learning. Unlike most programmes which treat inpatients, this programme is aimed at higher functioning patients, i.e. 'stable outpatients'. The patterning of their specific problems is first assessed as either; (a) impoverished, (b) disorganised, or (c) rigid. For example, someone who is described as rigid would show relatively few hallucinations, but would persist with mild delusional thought. This group of participants is also characterised by having difficulties in developing alternative flexible responses to social problems, fixed and restricted cognitive schema and a reduced tolerance for ambiguity (Hogarty and Flesher, 1999a).

The goal of this therapy is to facilitate the attainment of social cognitive milestones by providing meaningful and self-directed experiences rather than responses based on role modelling in contrived situations. The programme therefore adopts a relatively unique approach of pairing participants so that they can help each other although there is a therapist present during sessions. In addition participants also attend groups where they present and discuss information on how they might solve individual social or work problems. The programme uses computerised training of memory and attention, based on software devised for the rehabilitation of people with traumatic head injuries (Bracy, 1995). The pairing is chosen so that the two people do not have the same sorts of difficulties. They collaborate on the software exercises, maintain records of performance and after three months enter larger groups of six to eight people who socialise and work together on the programmes. The group programme takes an additional six months and consists of exercises that focus on 'gistful' interpretations of information such as summing up an article in a newspaper to another person. The participant collaborator or the therapist will try to encourage the speaker to be as clear as possible in their communications. Non-participant members of the group remain silent during an exercise but they are expected to take notes and give feedback. Each of the group sessions for social cognition is concluded with 15 minutes of psychoeducation. The programme therefore offers cognitive training plus social contact during the paired computer training. Then there are also social support groups for practising higher level processes. The programme is therefore similar to IPT in that there is some integration of different rehabilitation targets.

Recently data on its effectiveness immediately following this long therapy (up to two years) has been published (Hogarty *et al.*, 2004). At the two-year assessment there were improvements in factor scores for processing speed and a general cognition score which included memory, flexibility, and language and manipulation skills. There were also effects on cognitive style which was defined in three categories (impoverished, disorganised and rigid). Although there were no changes in symptoms there were significant changes in observational measures of social cognition and social adjustment.

A similar cognitive programme has been adopted by Bell and colleagues (2001a) at Yale. However, although their programme uses both computerised cognitive practice as well as social groups these components run alongside each other. There is no pairing of individuals in the cognitive retraining sessions and no emphasis on the 'gistful' responses of individuals within the group. This cognitive rehabilitation is specifically part of a work rehabilitation programme. The cognitive training is carried out using computerised tests derived from Bracey (1995). These are presented in 45-minute sessions five times per week and the participants received a monetary incentive to attend. The attendance was on average 43 sessions, although some people received more than double this amount. An RCT of cognitive enhancement plus a work therapy programme compared to work therapy alone showed improvements in cognitive measures. These researchers measured not only the effects over a number of cognitive factors but also the number of people whose cognitive performance was within the normal range. Participants receiving the extra cognitive intervention showed larger effect size changes and the number of participants who showed normal performance following therapy changed from 45 per cent to 77 per cent, whereas it was relatively static in the control group. The effects of training were also durable six months after the end of therapy (Bell *et al.*, 2003) and were not affected by the severity of the initial difficulties. There is also now evidence that the training was relatively specific, in that there was no increase on an untrained reaction time task (Fiszdon *et al.*, 2004).

The evidence in the public arena suggests that this sort of integrated therapy provides positive benefits for cognition which are durable. The informal information from the two sets of researchers on their current projects is that these cognitive improvements have an impact on outcomes of work and social functioning. The mode of this improvement is not clear but it may be that to be effective cognitive rehabilitation programmes must be tied closely to other rehabilitation efforts in a comprehensive system. The effects of improved information processing can then be immediately implemented in training for other outcomes. It is also not clear if the 'gist' is the mode of action. Certainly what people are learning is metacognitive monitoring and control and this may be made more obvious when the participant takes an active part in the training of another person. Scaffolded instruction emphasises this as a powerful technique and a way of ensuring that the method of the instruction has been entirely understood.

Although Hogarty and Flesher (1999a) divide their participants into those with different cognitive styles, no data are currently available on whether these groups differ in their ability to benefit from therapy. Bell and colleagues, however, have shown that severity of disability is no bar to cognitive improvement in their programme. However, both programmes involve clinically stable outpatients who are performing at a relatively high level. As individual characteristics are likely to interact with the training programme, their isolation and test must be a key to resolving whether the most disabled can benefit from this type of programme which requires high levels of social participation from the outset.

Educational and remediation software programmes

Cognitive retraining following head injury advanced to use computerised retraining methods and these have been adopted in various forms by other CRT researchers (e.g. Bell *et al.*, 2001a). An alternative approach to this type of computer presentation is to use educational software that is easily available and was designed to be engaging. Both approaches have been reported to be efficacious and all seem to be engaging for people with schizophrenia. Although computer technology is being used here as the tool for cognitive rehabilitation, it is useful to review this form of rehabilitation separately as it does teach a variety of skills. It has not only tested within-training effects but also the transfer of trained skills to other tasks.

Both sets of programmes are based on models of practice and individuals progress through the various levels of the programme. There is no specific theoretical guidance on the presentation or inclusion of particular tasks. Rather they are chosen for their face validity, their appeal (in the case of educational software) and their comprehensiveness, in terms of the under-lying skills required. Specific programmes have been developed for attention (APT, Sohlberg and Mateer, 1987; ORM, Ben-Yishay *et al.*, 1987) and atten-tion, memory and conceptualisation (Captain's log; Sandford and Browne, 1988; Where in the USA is Carmen Sandiego? Broderbund software). One of the problems with computerised training is that although the programme might be specified, often individual tasks are chosen from the general corpus for each study. It is therefore not possible to compare efficacy even when the studies use the same general programme. Other studies use individual computerised tasks to 'pick and mix' the elements of training.

One of the first programmes developed for people with brain injuries was implemented by Burda and colleagues (1991). They randomly assigned participants to three half-hour sessions of computerised therapy, supervised by a computer technician, or to treatment as usual. They found significant improvements in memory and cognitive flexibility following training. This study also provided a novel approach to assessment – they included a self-report measure of cognitive difficulties which also showed fewer perceived cognitive problems following therapy in the treated group. Using similar procedures, Hermanutz and Gestrich (1991) randomised participants to computer training, training based on the IPT model which included social discussion on newspaper articles (see above), and a control group who received treatment as usual. There was evidence of improvement in cognition in both training groups compared to the control group but no difference between the two intervention groups. A similar result was obtained by Brown and colleagues (1993) in a comparison of two interventions, occupational therapy activities to improve cognition and an attention training computer programme. Several other studies with controls for non-specific effects of computer use have also found no improvements in attention (Medalia *et al.*, 1998). But there are reports of improvement (Benedict *et al.*, 1994) and the skills learnt using memory software did not generalise to tasks not trained. Field *et al.* (1997) in a comparison of specific tasks with a control group taking part in computer games showed no differential improvement and some improvements in the computer games group which were not shown in the experimental intervention group. Although Field and colleagues suggest that this is a negative finding, they did not have a control with no intervention. It is quite possible, as we will see below, for computer games to aid some cognitive functions.

Software designed for use within education has not only been tested for its efficacy but also provides the opportunity to control task level, and introduce complex problem-solving and concept formation tasks. The tasks have some ecological validity, although, of course, much of the presentation can be too child oriented. There have been few rigorous tests of this approach but Medalia and colleagues (2001, 2002) showed that problem-solving teaching in 'Where in the USA is Carmen Sandiego?' did improve cognitive skills. However, between-group differences were only apparent when problem solving was measured as a factor score on the Independent Living Scale (ILS; Loeb, 1996) but not when the Comprehension subtest of the WAISr was used. In comparison to other studies the outcome measures for this study are not those normally accepted, although the ILS, if reliable, is a more ecologically acceptable measure than some neuropsychological tests.

Further exploratory data analyses of the same Medalia data have investigated symptom changes using this computer software. Symptoms were measured on the PANSS and their relationship to the previously reported cognitive measures, Logical memory and the California Verbal Learning test were investigated (Bark *et al.*, 2003). Change scores showed that the group receiving problem-solving training improved significantly in their symptoms and these improvements were sustained 4 weeks after the end of the training. However, there were also no between-group differences on these measures. There were no basic correlations between changes in cognitive scores and change in symptom scores. Belluci, Glaberman and Haslam (2003) in a single blind RCT using Captains log software employed for 16 sessions over 8 weeks found that verbal memory and attention improved, as well as negative symptoms as measured by the SANS. Effect sizes were in the region of 0.3–0.4. In this study no attempt was made to tie together the cognitive changes and the symptom improvement so a model of related change was not tested. This group (and many others) also failed to consider the possibility of an interaction between treatment and improvements. An interaction has been observed by Spaulding and colleagues – cognitive changes were only effective if they were achieved through therapy.

Computerised training has shown mixed effects with some studies showing generalisation and durability but others showing no between group effects and no differential improvement compared to other types of cognitive skills therapy. The effects on functioning are again mixed with some positive results. The problem with the use of this therapy is that it is quite possible for the therapist to be involved and have high levels of contact, or for the participant only to interact with the computer. Higher levels of initial contact with a therapist may be responsible for cognitive improvement which enhances the learning of flexible strategies since the therapist can respond with sensitivity and flexibility to the strengths and difficulties of the participant. But little description is given in the current protocols to test this hypothesis. The assumption is that providing therapy via a computer is a high-tech way of providing cost-effective therapy. The only way it can be cost effective is if the amount of therapist contact is limited although the main protagonists of this approach do recommend the presence of a therapist (Revheim *et al.*, 2001).

Executive skills training

These interventions were developed specifically to practice executive functions such as planning and complex problem solving. These are skills known to be impaired in people with schizophrenia. The programmes described here therefore cover a wide variety of different cognitive processing components reflecting the multiple components of executive function.

Several programmes were developed with these targets. The first paper and pencil set of tasks is described by Olbrich and Mussgay (1990) who compared tasks of moderate complexity in which participants had to add or subtract numbers, find the common denominator for a set of words and link digits and symbols following set rules. The cognitive processes thought to be being practised were: mental arithmetic, reasoning and concept formation, as well as memory. The control condition focused on manual creativity such as painting. Participants carried out these tasks individually and the outcomes were measured on both simple and complex cognitive tests. The comparative results for the simple tasks were equivocal with both groups improving and these improvements were mirrored by improvements in clinical state. The more complex tasks produced clear results of more improvement in the cognitive training group. There were however, no effects on social behaviour, although it is not clear that the analyses would have been able to detect differential change given that everyone in the group was an inpatient and might be considered to improve during the short period of the trial (three weeks).

Following this, Brown *et al.* (1993) developed a set of activities from those used by occupational therapists which aimed to improve executive control of attention. These tasks were chosen according to a number of characteristics:

- type of task
- number and simplicity of task instructions
- time to complete
- problem-solving and decision-making requirements.

The final programme consisted of three 60-minute sessions each week for 12 weeks. The instructions for tasks were uniform and the order was from less to more complicated tasks. In this study the OT cognitive programme was the control condition with the experimental condition having computer training in attention in a single blind RCT. Both groups improved and although there were initial differences in favour of the computer training group, these disappeared when age (which differed between the groups) was covaried in the analyses. The structured programme of task-oriented activities did increase specific executive functioning through practice and possibly through guidance by the OT. However, these were not specifically measured. The improvements noted were on attention tasks but also on memory as measured by digit and visual span. In addition, there were improvements in efficiency, motivation and self-confidence. This was the first rigorous study of a more general individual cognitive rehabilitation programme and was unusual in providing process measures. Data on OT therapists' observations on implementing therapy indicated a number of different problems in implementing either intervention, including difficulty with maths, memory problems and auditory directions in the computer programme.

The first programme that was specifically designed to improve executive functioning was published by Delahunty and Morice (1993) – the Frontal/ Executive Program (FEP) – and consisted of a series of paper and pencil tasks that increased in complexity over time. There were three modules; cognitive flexibility, working memory and planning with 8, 16 and 20 sessions respectively. Each hour-long session contained different tasks, all of which had relevance to specific cognitive processing problems. The cognitive flexibility module included a range of tasks that required engagement, disengagement and re-engagement of various cognitive information sets. These relied upon oculomotor, perceptual, conceptual and fine motor flexibility skills. Working memory was targeted by a range of simultaneous set maintenance, set manipulation and delayed response tasks. Finally planning was aided by tasks involving set formation and manipulation, reasoning and strategy development.

The testing of the programme developed from three single case studies using the cognitive flexibility module (Delahunty and Morice, 1993). This showed normalised perseverative error scores on WCST even six months post-therapy. All three participants experienced improvements in social functioning following therapy, but some of these gains were lost at six-month follow-up. A study of the cognitive flexibility module in eight patients (Delahunty et al., 1993) also showed normalisation of perseverative error scores and improved planning ability. The first test of the whole programme was a randomised study of 22 patients who either received FEP or treatment as usual. One oddity of this study was that the treatment group experienced two pre-treatment assessments. Although this was ostensibly to assess practice effects, it was also likely to confound treatment with practice effects as participants in the treatment group received one more opportunity to practice the outcome measures. The scores in this study were analysed in two ways, by normalised performance and continuous measures and in both there were improvements in favour of the treatment group on the WCST, Prose Recall and Tower of London.

When the original manual was designed, it was assumed that the procedures would improve cognitive function through brain plasticity by practice at tasks involving sensory and motor areas as well as processes known to be limited by frontal/prefrontal neural systems. This sort of practice has certainly been shown to aid recovery in head injury and stroke (Cicerone et al., 2000). In the mid-1990s this programme seemed to our group to be a likely candidate not for practising neural systems but for developing strategic cognitive processing which fitted our cognitive approach. The programme was updated with this new emphasis in mind. Therapists guided participants on strategic processing. The participants gradually took responsibility for strategy use, ultimately carrying out strategic processing covertly. As the emphasis was on strategic processing, there were no right and wrong ways to complete a task, only a menu of possible strategies that could be used. The variety of different tasks using visual, verbal and motor information were now used to consolidate strategic processes and contributed to within session generalisation of strategic skills. The modules also changed slightly to include some new material and the working memory module was redefined as aiding memory; it includes working memory, short-term memory and long-term memory components and was shortened by four sessions. The final manual is a collaborative effort by the UK and Australian groups (Delahunty et al., 2002).

The first clinical results were on two case studies of severely ill patients who received the whole programme, and in addition to neuropsychological assessments they also had brain scans using SPECT imaging (Wykes, 1998). Both participants showed improvements across the cognitive outcome tests, but each showed a different pattern of behaviours to produce such improvements. The SPECT scans showed that changes in brain activation on a single task, word fluency, fitted both the behaviour within the activation task, as well as the profile of changes on the remaining independent cognitive tests. This was further support for the underpinning model of developing strategies rather than practise in neural circuits, as neural circuits showed different changes between the two individuals.

The first randomised control study followed, comparing people who received either the modified FEP, now known as cognitive remediation therapy (CRT) with a group who received intensive occupational therapy activities. This design allowed for the measurement of the effects of intensive therapist contact which may have a non-specific effect on cognitive outcomes. The OT activities were designed to be engaging but to have limited effects on cognitive components. This is because Brown *et al.* (1993) showed some improvements with a structured set of OT activities that were specifically designed to change attention. Therapy lasted for approximately 12 weeks with 40 sessions being provided. At post-treatment there were significant effects in memory, planning and cognitive flexibility with the majority of scores showing positive advantages for CRT (Wykes *et al.*, 1999). Figure 6.1 shows the effects of the treatment on flexibility and memory. These cognitive benefits changed little after six months post-therapy although the group effect

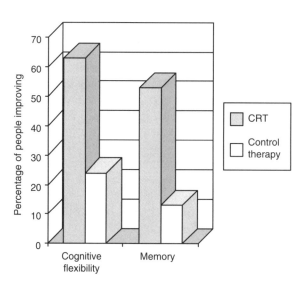

Figure 6.1 Percentage of people improving immediately following CRT (data from Wykes *et al.*, 2003)

was lost for cognitive flexibility not because of a reduction in the CRT group but rather that the control group caught up (Wykes *et al.*, 2003). There were no direct effects of therapy on symptoms or functioning, but there were improvements in social functioning in those people who had a clinically significant general improvement across tests of cognitive flexibility at post-treatment. This continued to follow-up. Self-esteem too improved following therapy but these effects disappeared at follow-up. This programme was not provided as part of a comprehensive rehabilitation programme and after its completion many participants returned to a daily activity schedule that often lacked the same level of positive reward. The changes in self-esteem are therefore fragile and may need to be specifically nurtured in future programmes. Further data from our group, as yet unpublished, from a larger RCT of 85 participants also shows clinical changes in cognitive outcomes with this therapy. These are greater in those aged under 40 but are not limited to those who have good pre-morbid IQ.

Several studies and reviews have suggested that memory is linked to functional outcomes (e.g. Green *et al.*, 2000) so this putative link was tested using data from this study. Reeder *et al.* (2004) defined the cognitive changes in terms of factor scores and showed that the memory factor was related to social functioning in cross-sectional analyses at baseline and post-treatment, replicating the results of others. However, although memory benefited from CRT these changes were not related to changes in functioning, rather change in another factor – called stimulus driven responding, predicted improvements in social functioning, but only when they occurred following CRT. In other words, as in the Spaulding study, spontaneous improvements in cognitive skill did not have the same force as those that occurred within the context of CRT. In our opinion this is because the therapy provides training that instantiates strategic processing that can be used in other spheres, i.e. it improved metacognitive skill. In terms of a model linking memory and functioning there are three possible interpretations of the Reeder *et al.* results. The first is that for social functioning to show improvements it must be related to larger changes in memory. Second, the model between functioning and memory was built on correlational relationships and these relationships gave the wrong impression of causality. Finally memory improvement could occur but with no transfer of skill to social contexts.

Further work on the theoretical underpinning of CRT was tested in a study using functional magnetic resonance imaging of participants before and after therapy using a working memory paradigm. The intervention group showed significant increases in activation in frontal areas compared to healthy and patient controls. The most significant results were found in the participants who had the most memory improvement observed in tests performed outside the scanner (Wykes *et al.*, 2002).

In summary, paper and pencil programmes for executive functioning have shown some increases in both cognition and social functioning. The cognitive improvements in this programme seem to be related to the increases in social functioning. The differences between the CRT programme and other cognitive training is that here there is an explicit recognition of the need for cognitive tasks to span a number of different cognitive processing domains. The use of strategic processing is explicitly built into this programme whereas others, particularly the computerised therapies, depend on chance learning of the most efficient approach.

Changing the environment

One group in Texas has approached the barriers produced by cognitive difficulties in a different way. Instead of changing the person's skills they have adjusted the environment so that cognitive demand is reduced (Velligan *et al.* 2000). In Velligan's therapy, Cognitive Adaptation Training (CAT), the individual is given a full psychometric assessment and then the environment is adjusted to fit with the specific problems that this throws up. The intervention involves visits by support staff who organise the environment, for example, by packing clothes into different containers for each day of the week and placing labels around the room as reminders of specific activities. These environmental interventions compensated for the memory, attention and planning problems experienced by the person. In a randomised control trial comparing a control condition, an experimental CAT intervention and a contact control group, positive outcomes were reported for the CAT group in terms of both symptoms and community functioning.

Improving cognition with medication

This chapter would not be complete without a discussion of the effects of neuroleptic medication on cognition. In Chapter 2 we discussed whether the effects of medication could be responsible for changes in cognition and in general concluded that treatment does not contribute to the onset of these difficulties. But recently there has been interest in whether treatments can improve cognition.

Treatment with typical antipsychotic medication

While it is clear that patients have benefited clinically from treatment with haloperidol and other typical medications, data on the cognitive effects have been sparse. Most studies suggest no effects. However, in a rigorous study Green *et al.* (2002) have shown that low dose haloperidol produced a beneficial effect of about 0.2 on cognition after two years of treatment.

Typical medications are associated with side effects, which even if subtle may change motor control and are therefore likely to reduce performance on some tests which have a large speed component. Keefe and Gold (2004) speculate that the lack of practice effects in people treated with typical medications is unusual and might be thought to be a cognitive cost of treatment. Given the large effect that medication has on symptoms it is surprising that there is little paucity of beneficial effects on cognition.

Treatment with atypical antipsychotic medication

Recently there has been a rapid increase in published studies investigating the potential beneficial effects of second generation atypical medications. To date three meta-analyses have tried to compensate for limitations in the design and analysis of the available studies (Keefe *et al.*, 1999; Harvey and Keefe, 2001; Woodward *et al.*, 2004). Woodward *et al.* (2004) report data from the largest cohort – 39 studies. Their analyses suggest that there are positive effects on attention, motor functions, executive functions, verbal fluency, working memory, verbal long-term memory and visual long-term memory even when the studies are more rigorous in their methodology. Different tests improved with different medications. Table 6.2 shows the most consistent changes over time for each medication where consistency is defined as changes established across two or more studies with no contradictory study.

Even with this relatively low level of proof, not all medications have effects on the same outcomes. In a rigorous double-blind study, the effects of olanzapine and risperidone were superior to both haloperidol and clozapine in terms of the percentage of people experiencing clinically significant gains (greater than 0.5 sd) on a global cognitive score (Bilder *et al.*, 2002). In this study the effects of clinical changes between different medications did not explain the cognitive change scores.

In summary, medication treatment may have modest effects on cognition,

Table 6.2 Consistent cognitive changes in different medications (adapted from Woodward *et al.*, 2004)

Cognitive function	Medication type			
	Clozapine	Risperidone	Olanzapine	Typical medication
Attention	Yes	——	Yes	——
Motor functions	Yes	——	Yes	——
Working memory	——	Yes	——	——
Visual memory	——	——	——	——
Verbal memory	——	——	——	——
Verbal fluency	Yes	——	Yes	——
Executive function	——	——	Yes	——

and specific types of medication may improve particular types of cognitive performance scores. The significance of this improvement is not yet known. These improvements have generally been measured over a relatively short period of time (about 14 weeks) with no control group so it is not clear whether these effects are the result of practice, but even if they are, it is clear they establish that people with schizophrenia are able to change their cognitive performance, thus suggesting more therapeutic optimism. However, what is salutary is that the changes in performance on the cognitive test scores, although of possible clinical importance, still leave the majority of patients with significant impairments.

Effects of putative cognitive enhancing agents

There have recently been a few reports of cognitive improvements with stimulant medications e.g. Barch and Carter (2005). Some of these produce a worsening of positive symptoms whilst having a beneficial effect on negative symptoms (e.g. amphetamine and methylphenidate). However, a new drug, Modafinil, has been shown to produce significant effects on attentional set shifting and cognition in a double-blind crossover study (Turner *et al.*, 2004). This new result may suggest novel approaches to enhancing cognition in people with schizophrenia.

The results from all the studies of psychological interventions were carried out on a variety of patients who received a variety of medications for their symptoms. Any improvements may have shown an interaction with type of medication but few studies investigated this. Wykes *et al.* (1999) showed an almost significant interaction with newer atypicals with the largest proportion being clozapine. Similarly Reeder *et al.* (2004) showed a significant interaction between type of medication and improvement, with greater improvement in those who received atypical neuroleptics. However, the most potent effect was for the cognitive intervention itself. These interactions clearly need further investigation if we are to have the most efficacious cognitive treatments.

Training components in clinical programmes

The majority of clinical programmes contain similar elements of training to those isolated in the laboratory tasks. The main difference from the laboratory tasks is in the content. The training tasks generally increase in complexity and difficulty, vary across different modalities and the types of cognitive skill required.

The main difference *between* clinical programmes is the role of the trainer. Some are there only to provide support and initial explanation, as in some computerised training. At the other end of the scale, the therapist takes an active part throughout the programme in supporting, instructing and reinforcing the participant or participants. Using the effect sizes produced in a meta-analysis by Krabbendam and Aleman (2003) we investigated the presence of a therapist comparing support and instruction versus low levels of involvement. Although the effect sizes were not significantly different between the two groups, the average effect size for cognitive changes was nearly twice as large when the therapist was an active participant (0.36 versus 0.69, t = 1.86, p = 0.125).

The presence of a therapist also covaries with the type of therapeutic procedures that were identified by Krabbendam and Aleman. Strategic procedures often, but not always, involved therapists and were associated with larger effect sizes (average 0.52) and although not significantly different from rehearsal learning (effect size 0.34) they point out that the average effect size for rehearsal learning spanned zero suggesting a less stable effect. It is not that the strategic procedures do not involve practice in any of the programmes, rather the efficient strategic processes are discussed and instantiated prior to practising the tasks.

Studies involving practice most often employ a few simple outcomes whereas the more intensive strategy-oriented approaches use varied outcomes across domains of functioning. This design difference is likely to affect meta-analytic reviews as simple outcomes are more likely to improve following treatment. In the meta-analysis by Twamley et al. (2003) the included programmes were described on two dimensions: whether a computer had been used and whether strategic instruction had been used. The authors do not provide the confidence interval for their effect sizes but in terms of negative studies there were more negative results in the computer assisted group. It also looks as though there is only a small effect size for computer-assisted studies and the lowest effect size was for the computer-assisted strategic training approach. They also report that for the three rigorously designed studies that used strategy training, there were positive outcomes in multiple domains including symptoms and functioning (Meichenbaum and Cameron, 1973; Spaulding, et al., 1999; Wykes et al., 1999).

Some studies also include explicit self-instructional training and these tend to be those emphasising strategic processing. Few include an explicit reference to self-monitoring apart from Wykes et al. (1999). It is not clear how much these two procedures are essential for improvements on the tasks but it seems likely that they would add to the value of reinforcement as well as increasing metacognitive skills and behavioural monitoring.

All programmes involve reinforcement of some form. The computer programmes explicitly reinforce correct behaviour and it is argued that working with a computer is a highly valued activity and so is intrinsically rewarding (Medalia et al., 1998). The role of the therapist in these programmes is one of encouragement and social reward and there is an emphasis on the intrinsic value of the programme. Some studies (e.g. Bell et al., 2001a) provided monetary reinforcement but only for attendance, not for performance on the tasks. On the other hand Wykes et al. (1999) in an intensive and lengthy programme did not pay for attendance, but the programme itself seemed to be intrinsically rewarding so that there were few drop-outs.

The issue of personal choice or style is not really attended to by many of these programmes which tend to be prescriptive. Within the strategic processing programmes there is room for the individual to select a specific method for solving the problem. In particular, this is emphasised by Wykes *et al.* (1999) and in some of the computer programmes. This may be pertinent to improvement, as the individual then owns the process and may be more likely to use it again. However, this has not been investigated explicitly and it is difficult to identify when this approach has been used. A within-programme investigation would be required to keep the sources of variation to a minimum.

The main factors to distinguish the programmes are not the specific methods of presentation but whether they use strategic or rehearsal types of learning. The other factors tend to fall into either of these categories. Strategic processing seems to produce the most increase in cognitive changes but it is not clear which training elements are effective for functioning changes.

Changes in functioning across CRT clinical programmes

Cognitive test improvement

There have been a number of reviews and meta-analyses of the outcomes of cognitive training programmes. Earlier reviews were based on narrow inclusion criteria and only a very small number of studies and were generally not well disposed towards the treatment (e.g. Hayes and McGrath, 2001; Suslow *et al.*, 2001; Pilling *et al.*, 2002b). But more studies became available in the late 1990s and early in the twenty-first century and meta-analytic methods applied to these suggest modest effect sizes overall on cognitive outcomes (Kurtz *et al.*, 2001; Krabbendam and Aleman, 2003; Twamley *et al.*, 2003). The average effect sizes are shown in Figure 6.2. These are based on different studies with different outcome measures. The Kurtz *et al.* (2001) figure is based on studies to improve the WCST many of which are laboratory type studies and those for the remaining two meta-analyses are dependent on slightly different inclusion criteria. The figures from Krabbendam and Aleman are based on analyses of 543 participants. They found homogeneity among the effect sizes so it must be concluded that we can improve cognition with these sorts of techniques.

Again the reviews amalgamate cognitive components so that cognitive outcomes are gross measures of a variety of functions. There is now a relatively large corpus of data on CRT outcomes and so this detailed analysis of cognitive outcome may soon be within our reach. But as well as improving cognition directly, we also set ourselves the target of trying to improve overall

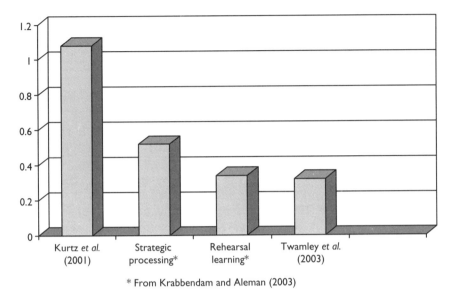

* From Krabbendam and Aleman (2003)

Figure 6.2 Average effect sizes for cognitive outcomes following CRT from meta-analyses

functioning and it is only these clinical studies that can give us some idea of whether that is possible.

Symptoms – positive, disorganised and negative

Symptoms have been shown to decrease following cognitive programmes. In the single case study of Adams *et al.* (1981) 'crazy thoughts', and depression as measured by the Beck Depression Inventory were reduced over a period of three months of treatment that was sustained at six-month follow-up. The disorganisation factor on the BPRS changed in Spaulding's study (Spaulding *et al.*, 1999a). Wykes *et al.* (1999) showed improvements in auditory hallucinations following therapy which were sustained at follow-up (Wykes *et al.* 2003). Negative symptoms have also decreased (Bellucci *et al.*, 2003; Bark *et al.*, 2003). The overall weighted effect size for symptom severity of the studies included in the Twamley meta-analysis is 0.26 suggesting modest effects.

Social functioning

Both Spaulding and Wykes showed improvements on social functioning following therapy, but in both these were not directly related to therapy but were associated with increases in cognition during therapy. Few studies have measured social functioning over a long enough period to detect subtle changes that may take some time to develop, for example, increases in friendships. Less than one-third of the studies reviewed by Twamley had included social functioning as an outcome measure but for these studies there was a significant mean weighted effect size of 0.51, suggesting again a modest effect.

Work functioning

Although there are currently two studies of work, few data are currently available on their outcomes. However Bell *et al.* (2004) have recently reported on 151 outpatients who were randomised to work therapy or cognitive enhancement plus work therapy. The work programme was effective in getting people into work and there were no group differences in whether individuals had a job. However, the people in the cognitive enhancement intervention group worked more hours and earned more money per week. In this study there was also a comparison between those who were in or not in treatment and normalised their performance on a digit span task. Those people whose performance normalised showed the best performance overall but only when normalisation was achieved through cognitive training. The effects were present at the end of therapy and were sustained six months after it ended. The cognitive intervention group increased the number of hours worked over the follow-up whereas the work therapy only group reduced their overall number of hours. So there does seem to be an effect of CRT on work.

Self-esteem

This is an area that has not been investigated in much detail in any study. Wykes *et al.* (1999, 2003) have shown improvements in self-esteem at the end of therapy that were specifically attributed to the cognitive remediation training rather than the non-specific effects of therapist contact. However, these improvements in self-esteem were not sustained at six-month follow-up. It seems hardly surprising, since CRT was not integrated into further rehabilitation programmes and therefore self-esteem changes would not have been further supported. These improvements may be sustained by developing maintenance CRT and by integrating cognitive training into other forms of rehabilitation.

Should we have independent or integrated rehabilitation?

Cognitive interventions have mainly been investigated independently of any other rehabilitation as the main aim was to identify the impact on cognition. However, it may be that there is now a need for more interventions such as those of Spaulding and Bell where the cognitive intervention is given immediately prior to or at the same time as other rehabilitation interventions. This would mean that any improvements in cognition can immediately be brought to bear on the rehabilitation programme, thus reinforcing the importance of the cognitive outcome and giving the person further experience of success in life outcomes that is meaningful. In this way the 'rate limiter' on rehabilitation outcome can be reduced. The measurement of subtle effects will be necessary in these sorts of designs as the most successful rehabilitation programmes will not have much room to show further improvement. It does seem clear to us that the poorest long-term functioning outcomes may result from stand-alone services. However, the relationship between cognitive improvements and functional changes is poorly understood. Until we have a specific model of how cognitive skills learnt in CRT are transferred to other activities, it will be difficult to delineate a set of cognitive targets and elements of training which will be successful in changing functioning.

Chapter 7

What is the effect of cognitive change?

We now know that CRT can have an impact on cognitive function and that functional improvements (in terms of symptoms, social and work functioning) follow cognitive change. Given these positive empirical results, it would be easy for rehabilitation specialists just to copy successful programmes. But the effect sizes are modest for both cognition and functional outcome and if we are to improve the effects, reduce variability between individuals and increase consistency across settings, we need to look for more sophisticated models. If we can discover how cognition has an impact on functioning, we may then be able to develop CRT to maximise functional improvement.

In the previous chapters, we have reviewed models underlying different CRT approaches to changing cognition. These have varied from strengthening neural pathways using practice (e.g. Delahunty and Morice, 1993; Bell *et al.*, 2004), improving cognitive control (Wykes *et al.*, 1999), to providing instruction associated with more mature thinking styles (e.g. Hogarty and Flesher, 1999a). The cognitive targets for individual therapies were mainly those processes that are deficient in schizophrenia (as many are), and the emphasis in training depended on the underlying model of cognitive dysfunction. So for those who adopted a neurodevelopmental model, CRT was intended to move people forward to later developmental stages of thinking. Those who adopted a more biological model assumed that practice would have an impact on neural structures that either compensated for the dysfunctional neural pathway through brain plasticity or rebooted neural pathways that were poorly regulated (Spaulding *et al.*, 1998). For those who considered that little change in fundamental processes could occur, environmental models were used to reduce the impact of cognitive difficulties.

Cognitive skills in each of these models have been assumed to be part of the pathway to functioning outcome and this has been explicitly tested in some of the intervention studies. But the improved outcomes we have seen following CRT may not only be associated with the specific attributes of the therapy but may also be affected by non-specific factors. So we need to consider the possible modes of action of different therapies on various outcomes. This process is important if we are to define the specific targets for intervention that may produce the most benefit.

Evidence for relationships between cognition and functioning was reviewed in Chapter 4. Here we will concentrate on relationships that are apparent following changes in cognition as these data illuminate causal relationships. Models of cognitive functioning have been described in biological or psychological terms and recently there has been some convergence between perspectives (e.g. Phillips and Silverstein, 2003). However, for the purposes of this book the model descriptions will remain at the psychological level.

The impact of cognitive change on symptoms

Is there a relationship between cognition and symptoms?

Models of the relationship between cognition and symptoms have emphasised executive functioning, especially in relation to positive symptoms. Frith (1992) suggests that defective self-monitoring leads to the misattribution of internally generated willed actions to external agents, resulting in delusions of alien control, certain auditory hallucinations and thought insertion. An inability to monitor the beliefs and intentions of others is said to lead to delusions of reference, paranoid delusions and third-person auditory hallucinations. Goldman-Rakic (1991) asserts more generally that an inability to keep appropriate internal representations (in the form of goals, instructions or concepts) 'in mind' is likely to lead to misinterpretation of causality and to an abnormal awareness of sensory experiences. Hemsley (1987) also implicates deficient self-regulatory mechanisms in the formation of positive symptoms, suggesting that hallucinations consist of intrusions into consciousness of redundant or irrelevant stimuli from long-term memory. Delusions are thought to result from attempts to account for the unstructured and ambiguous sensory input and memories, using a faulty reasoning style arising due to an abnormal experience of the covariation of events. All these theorists are suggesting that positive symptoms arise due to the abnormal self-regulation of sensory experiences and internal processing, and consequent erroneous conclusions about the perceptions of internal and external phenomena.

Related accounts have been given of disorganised symptoms. Working memory and context processing theorists suggest that thought disorder reflects the failure to keep prior speech and its context in mind, leading to a breakdown in the fluency of meaning within conversation (Goldman-Rakic, 1991; Cohen and Servan-Schreiber, 1992; Barch and Berenbaum, 1996). Frith (1992) also argues that problems in generating and regulating intentional actions lead to an inappropriate reliance on environmental stimuli to guide behaviour resulting in distractible, incoherent, disorganised or perseverative behaviour. Hemsley (1987, 2005) suggests that the overload of irrelevant information into consciousness leads to difficulties in organising thoughts and behaviour. Again, in each case self-regulation problems (in differing forms) lead to symptoms of disorganisation and incoherence.

Finally, negative symptoms are thought to result from the complete failure to regulate behaviour using internal processing. For Frith (1992), this takes the form of the failure to generate willed actions; for Hemsley (2005), the sufficient severity of the information overload of the cognitive system leads to a failure to carry out any goal-directed activities; and for working memory and context processing theorists, internal representations completely fail to lead to the generation of self-driven behaviour. These models consistently suggest that symptoms occur directly as a result of cognitive impairment. Therefore, if the relevant cognitive impairments can be reduced symptoms should diminish.

Is there evidence of a direct relationship with symptoms?

Cross-sectional studies of associations between symptoms and cognitive dysfunction in schizophrenia have produced mixed results. In particular, negative findings of an association between positive symptoms and cognitive deficits have frequently emerged (see Chapter 4). Whilst cross-sectional associations provide some support for psychological theories of a direct relationship between cognitive dysfunction and symptoms, to establish a causal relationship between the two, longitudinal studies investigating the impact of cognitive change on symptoms are needed. Some limited evidence for a longitudinal association between cognitive improvement and a reduction in symptoms comes from two studies of CRT. Evidence consistent with a direct relationship between cognition and symptoms was found by Wykes *et al.* (1999) and was replicated in a larger study by our group. In both studies improved cognitive flexibility led to a reduction in auditory hallucinations.

In a further analysis, Reeder *et al.* (2004) discovered that an increased tendency to rely on external or environmental (rather than internal) cues in selecting responses was associated with a reduction in symptom severity. However, this relationship was true only for those who received CRT and was not apparent at baseline. For the complete sample, poor verbal working memory was associated with high levels of negative symptoms and overall symptom severity prior to receiving therapy, but changes in verbal working memory were not associated with symptom changes. There are a number of important implications of these findings. First, the association between increased externally driven responding and reduced symptoms appears to be moderated by receiving CRT. We consider that the consistent use of cognitive strategies to improve accurate self-regulation and interpretation of experiences taught in CRT may produce more effect on symptoms than less structured cognitive changes which may occur within the course of the illness. The failure to find an association between improvement in verbal working memory and a reduction in symptoms, despite their initial association at baseline, also suggests that the relationship between verbal working memory and symptom severity is indirect. In other words a third or mediating factor may be important for this specific cognitive function to have an effect on outcome.

Factors likely to mediate between cognition and symptoms

Mediating factors are part of the vulnerability-stress model of schizophrenia described in Chapters 1 and 4. This model suggests that the response to stressors may mediate the relationship between cognitive function and symptoms (Zubin and Spring, 1977; Cromwell and Spaulding, 1978; Nuechterlein and Dawson, 1984). Cognitive deficits may act as vulnerability factors which may make the person more likely to relapse in the face of environmental stressors. Longitudinal data to support this proposition is reviewed in Chapter 4, but to date studies have not investigated the impact of cognitive improvement on vulnerability to relapse.

Hemsley (1987) postulates that avoidant coping may constitute this mediating factor. Negative symptoms such as poverty of speech, social withdrawal and retardation are thought to result from coping strategies employed to minimise the effects of the overwhelming and disordered cognitions. Therefore, cognitive improvement may not lead to reduced negative symptoms without a more active coping style.

A final putative mediating variable that has been investigated is an aspect of cognition: social cognition. Data from the Spaulding study were explored to investigate the relationship between social cognitive biases and paranoid symptoms following treatment (Peer et al., 2004). There was a correlation between social cognitive biases and paranoid symptoms that was amplified by the presence of executive functioning problems. After treatment, there were improvements in both cognition and symptoms but social cognitive biases remained static. Executive functioning problems continued to be robust predictors of outcome but social cognitive biases lost their predictive power. This suggests that the presence of social cognitive biases is important, but they only become potent predictors in the presence of other cognitive difficulties.

The impact of cognitive change on functioning outcome

Is there a direct effect of cognitive improvement on functioning?

The high degree of face validity for a relationship between cognition and social function in schizophrenia has led researchers to look for cross-sectional and longitudinal relationships between the two, assuming a direct link between them and generally failing to specify a theoretical model to account for the putative link.

Correlational studies have shown clear evidence of a link between cognition and functional outcome in terms of social and work functioning, rehabilitation potential, dependence on psychiatric services and cost. A number of pharmacological and psychological treatment studies have also attempted to identify a causal link by investigating the impact of specific cognitive changes on functional outcome.

The impact of cognitive change on functional outcome has been assessed in four studies of CRT. Two of these studies investigated the cognitive modules of Brenner's (Brenner *et al.*, 1994) Integrated Psychological Therapy (IPT) programme. In a recent small study (n = 27), Penades *et al.* (2003) showed that improved executive performance was significantly correlated with improvement in interpersonal social behaviour and life skills, and long-term verbal and visual memory improvements were associated with improvements in personal autonomy. In a larger randomised controlled trial (n = 94) comparing IPT with supportive therapy, Spaulding *et al.* (1999b) showed that for the whole sample, improved card sorting predicted improvements on the Assessment of Interpersonal Problem-Solving Skills. In addition, verbal long-term memory predicted improved social problem solving, but only for those who received CRT. In this latter case, the link between social function and cognition is indirect and CRT appears to act as a mediator between the two, suggesting that it is the means by which improvement occurs rather than improvement per se which is important in predicting changes in everyday living skills.

Our own group has carried out three randomised controlled trials investigating a CRT programme which targets executive functions and memory. Primary analyses of the first RCT, in which CRT was compared with a control psychological therapy, showed that improvements in cognitive flexibility and memory for the complete sample were predictive of a reduction in problems on the Social Behaviour Schedule (Wykes *et al.*, 1999). Subsequent analyses of data from the first and second RCTs were designed to investigate the role of factors which mediate the relationship between cognition and social functioning. Reeder *et al.* (2004) showed that while baseline verbal working memory predicted later social functioning, *change* in verbal working memory did not predict *change* in social functioning. Instead, an increased tendency to respond according to external feedback (rather than internal cues) was associated with a decrease in social problems, but only for the CRT group. Similarly, in the most recent and larger trial comparing CRT with treatment as usual, our group has shown that improved memory leads to improved social functioning only for those who received CRT. Consistent with evidence from Spaulding's study, these findings suggest that CRT may moderate the link between improvements in cognition and social functioning.

In a recent study by Bell *et al.* (2004), improvements in digit span (i.e. normalised performance) were predictive of the number of hours in paid work for the complete sample, suggesting a direct relationship. However, there was only a continuation of the improvements in work outcomes for those people with normalised working memory performance and who had received the cognitive intervention. This supports the moderating effect of treatment.

Evidence for an indirect relationship also comes from another area of treatment – medication studies where cognitive functioning has improved. For example, in a study of quetiapine compared to conventional neuroleptic medication, Velligan *et al.* (2003) showed that whilst there was significant differential executive and memory improvement for those who received quetiapine, there were no concomitant changes in everyday community functioning.

All these data support a direct link of cognitive change to improved outcome when, and only when, achieved as part of a cognitive intervention. Cognitive change by itself does not appear to be a sufficient condition for functional improvement. There appear to be no causal effects on outcome if improvements are achieved as part of:

- supportive therapy (Spaulding and colleagues)
- occupational therapy activities (Wykes and colleagues)
- work therapy (Bell and colleagues)
- medication (Velligan and colleagues)
- chance improvement in no treatment control conditions.

Are there factors that mediate between cognitive change and social or work functioning?

Social cognition has been suggested to be a mediating factor between cognitive function and social competence (Kee *et al.*, 1998). The only data on social cognition relate to paranoid symptoms (Peer *et al.*, 2004) where it acted in an interaction with cognition but was not a potent independent predictor.

Green *et al.* (2000) suggested that 'learning potential' might mediate the relationship between basic cognitive functions and outcome. In support of this mediating role Wiedl and Weinobst (1999) showed that non-learners tended to live in accommodation with higher levels of support and supervision. Non-learners also achieved a lower degree of success on a brief psychosocial rehabilitation programme. However, Woonings *et al.* (2003) in a more comprehensive study showed that learning, as assessed by measures of explicit and implicit learning and learning potential, was not associated with social functioning or rehabilitation outcome.

Other studies have implicated non-cognitive mediating factors. A reduction in active or problem-focused coping is associated with executive, memory and attentional impairments, which may result in greater functional impairments in stressful circumstances (Wilder-Willis *et al.*, 2002; Ventura *et al.*, 2003). This is consistent with a stress-vulnerability model of schizophrenia.

Fundamental cognitive change may also not be necessary for improved neuropsychological test performance because cognitive performance can be improved by providing monetary (Rosenbaum *et al.*, 1957; Kern *et al.*, 1995) or social reinforcement (Massel *et al.*, 1991; Silverstein *et al.*, 2001) for correct responding. This suggests that motivation may play a mediating role. Educationalists also emphasise that improved self-esteem or self-efficacy may lead to cognitive improvements.

Finally, Greenwood *et al.* (2003) showed that there were differential associations between executive functions and supermarket shopping ability, depending on symptoms. Participants were classified according to whether or not they were suffering from the psychomotor poverty syndrome and were assessed on measures of working memory, initiation or strategy use. Whilst verbal working memory specifically predicted functional accuracy and efficiency for the psychomotor poverty group, executive function was not associated with functional behaviour in the non-psychomotor poverty group. This finding of differential associations suggests that for the psychomotor poverty group only, a third factor mediated the relationship between verbal working memory and shopping skill.

The different ways in which cognition might have an impact on functioning and symptoms are illustrated in Figures 7.1, 7.2 and 7.3. In the first simple model, cognition has some direct effect on outcome, and therapy both directly improves cognition and moderates the link between cognition and outcome. Little evidence is available on the direct effects of cognition, irrespective of the presence of therapy. When cognitive changes take place randomly the effects of cognition on outcome tend to be negligible so in the model they are marked by a dotted line. However, there are data to support the notion of the moderating influence of therapy from a variety of different training methods, although most of these use a strategic instructional method.

The second model allows for a mediating variable such as coping or

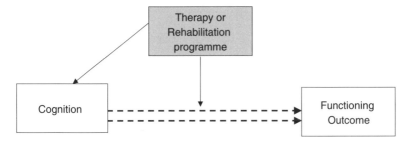

Figure 7.1 Model 1: Moderating role of therapy on functioning outcome

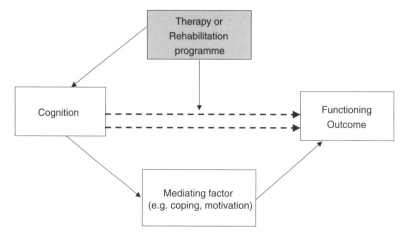

Figure 7.2 Model 2: Mediators and moderators of functioning outcome

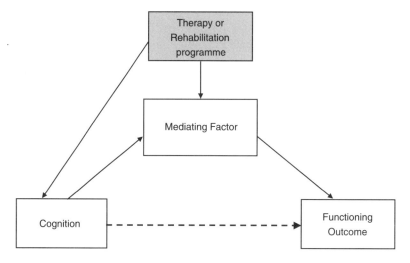

Figure 7.3 Model 3: Therapy moderates the cognition-outcome link via mediating factors

motivation to have an impact on outcome in addition to the direct and thera-peutic effects. There are some data to support the notion that mediating factors might be important but there are few actual tests. The ones that have been reported do not support the essential nature of the mediating factor (e.g. Woonings *et al.*, 2003; Peer *et al.*, 2004).

The third model suggests that therapy has an effect on the mediating factor as well as on cognition and this contributes to final outcome. In this model, therapy would have an effect of increasing motivation, self-esteem or metacognition and this may change outcome. Again there are few data; the Wykes study did improve self-esteem but this was not linked to the changes in cognitive function. However, it is common sense to assume that increased confidence may also have an impact on a person's work quality and the likelihood of them increasing their social contact. This is a particularly difficult model to test as the mediating factor contributes to cognitive change. It would therefore appear that cognitive change was the only predictive factor.

There are few data to test these models and none to differentiate them. It does seem to us that all the effects are plausible but some may only be subtle so the small samples currently available will never allow any separation. Evidence to date suggests that the links between cognition and functioning outcome depend on the presence of therapeutic change in cognition; it occurs as part of a cognitive intervention programme. These do seem to be significant which suggests that this should make cognitive change the main target for rehabilitation.

How does cognitive change have an impact on functional outcome?

Some models have been primarily descriptive in their specification of the links between cognitive and social functioning change (Brenner et al., 1992; Hodel and Brenner, 1994; McGurk and Mueser, 2004), whilst others (e.g. Spaulding et al., 2003) provide a more explanatory framework for the ways in which specific cognitive changes lead to changes in functional outcomes.

The reciprocal relationship model

Brenner suggests that two interacting vicious cycles can explain the disruptive effect of cognitive deficits on functional outcome (Brenner et al., 1992; Hodel and Brenner, 1994). The first of these cycles consists of a reciprocal relationship between impairments in basic cognitive functions, such as attention and early perception, and high order integrative processes, such as executive function and memory retrieval. This results in attentional and encoding deficits having a detrimental impact on retrieval and executive functioning and these processes in turn skew attention and encoding (see Figure 7.4). This downwards spiral of cognitive functioning eventually results in impaired perception and social functioning. The second cycle shows that cognitive deficits resulting from the first vicious cycle, lead to poor interpersonal coping and a consequent increased exposure or susceptibility to stressors. The resulting high levels of arousal lead to a deterioration in cognitive capacity and heightened cognitive impairment. This may produce not only functional impairment, but also the onset of psychotic symptoms. The interaction of the two cycles leads to a gradual deterioration and a maintenance of dysfunction in the absence of environmental changes.

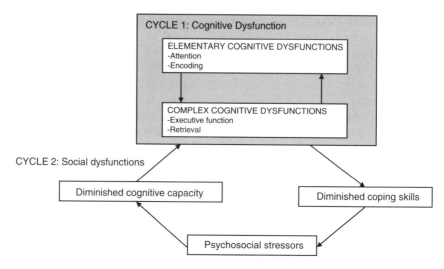

Figure 7.4 Brenner's model of vicious cycles

Support for this model comes from a study by Penades *et al.* (2003) who showed that change in basic cognitive functions (encoding and attention) was linked to change in more complex cognitive functions (memory retrieval and executive functions), and that changes in both types of cognitive function (encoding and executive function) were associated with changes in functional outcome (personal autonomy and general functioning).

A hierarchical cascade model

McGurk and Mueser (2004) propose a model specifically to account for the impact of cognitive dysfunction and symptoms on work outcome in supported employment. Like Brenner, they postulate a hierarchical structure of cognitive processing, ranging from basic functions such as perception and attention to more complex processes such as executive function (see Figure 7.5). It is assumed that deficits in the basic cognitive functions interfere with complex processes of learning and memory and that these in turn interfere with executive functions, assumed to be yet more complex. Impairment in lower level functions is not a sufficient condition for impairment further up the hierarchy, but it creates a risk factor for impaired complex cognitive processing. Since cascading impairments lead up the hierarchy, it may be easier to improve vocational functioning problems (e.g. using supported employment services) resulting from basic cognitive impairments than those resulting from more complex cognitive processing deficits. For example, practising tasks so that they become overlearnt and eventually automatic may help to compensate for impaired psychomotor speed so that it no longer has an

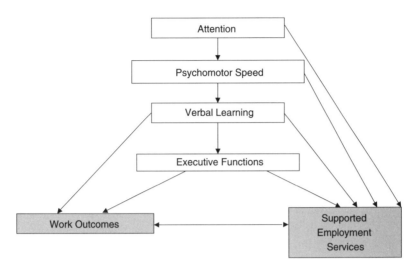

Figure 7.5 McGurk and Mueser's model of cognition, symptoms and work in supported employment

impact on performance at work. This is supported by findings that psychomotor speed is generally associated with work outcome (Bellack *et al.*, 1999; Gold *et al.*, 1999), but not in populations of people in supported employment services (McGurk *et al.*, 2003).

According to this model, improvements in attention and psychomotor speed will result in a reduction in the need for supported employment services and an improvement in other more complex cognitive processes should lead to improved employment outcomes. Furthermore, work outcome may be improved by further compensating for the effects of impaired executive or memory functioning on work, using either self-management strategies or by manipulating the environment. Recent data from Bell and colleagues (2004) show that improvements in one complex process, working memory, through cognitive enhancement therapy result in a trend towards less dependence on supported employment. This is only indirect support for the McGurk and Mueser model as a better work outcome only follows the combination of supported employment and higher order cognitive change. The argument has to be made that the improvements allowed participants to make better use of the support offered.

Both Brenner's and McGurk and Mueser's model describe links between specific types of cognitive function and functional outcome but they suggest the need for different levels of direct intervention. McGurk and Mueser would support a focus on executive difficulties as other therapies may not be able to compensate for these problems. But Brenner would suggest that interventions for basic information processing as well as executive functioning would lead to beneficial effects. They also suggest the way in which both direct and indirect relationships between specific cognitive functions and functional outcome are formed. However, these models are primarily descriptive and provide little explanation as to how cognitive change may influence social or work functioning.

Cognitive microskilling

A more comprehensive explanatory model is proposed by Spaulding (2003). He postulates a central cognitive mechanism for the appropriate selection and implementation of specific cognitive operations, or 'microskills', in response to environmental demands. More complex or molecular skills are composed of different combinations of microskills. Behaviours and their associated microskills are differentially selected depending on their 'activation thresholds' which are determined by a combination of the environmental demand for those behaviours (i.e. the frequency with which they have been recently used) and the rate at which they are positively reinforced (e.g. by social approval). Therefore, microskills which are frequently used and reinforced have a low activation threshold and are consequently activated more quickly. Cognitive information is said to be organised within memory hierarchically according to these activation thresholds. For microskills such as those used in social interactions, which are used on a routine basis (e.g. visual scanning of the features of a person's facial expression, interpretation of the person's emotional state, selective attention to a single person within a distracting environment), the continuous high demand results in ongoing ready access to them.

It is proposed that during an acute episode, the cognitive mechanism for the selection and implementation of cognitive operations fails, resulting in disorganisation of the hierarchy of activation thresholds. Therefore, access to the highly rehearsed microskills required for routine social functioning is reduced. On resolution of the psychotic episode, reorganisation of the microskills does not occur spontaneously but relies upon an interaction with the environment, with response hierarchies of activation thresholds being re-established according to environmental demand and reinforcement. It is argued that institutional environments with low demands and little reinforcement, characteristic of the living environments of many people with chronic mental health problems, lead to poor response reorganisation. Conversely, through increasing demand and reinforcement, rehabilitation may lead to improved reorganisation of activation thresholds of routine microskills. Specific cognitive rehabilitation, or CRT, gives additional benefit from focusing more specifically and intensively on the activation of microskills relevant to particular tasks. This implies that cognitive improvement should result both from CRT and from other rehabilitation programmes not specifically designed to improve cognition. This is supported from findings that control therapy groups in randomised controlled trials of CRT show signifi-cant but limited cognitive improvement (Spaulding *et al.*, 1999b; Wykes *et al.*, 1999, 2003; Bell *et al.*, 2004). However, these cognitive improvements do not impact on functional outcome.

The ability to select and implement microskills itself relies upon a wide and complex range of microskills and this repertoire falls within the domain of executive functioning. Executive microskills are considered to be of funda-mental importance since other microskills cannot function without them. Similarly, the allocation of cognitive resources to support appropriate responding is of crucial importance and this is reflected in short-term mem-ory performance. Like Brenner's model, Spaulding suggests that the acquisi-tion or recovery of complex skills does not proceed in a linear sequence, but depends upon interactive cycles of improvement, with improved executive skills leading to improved performance skills and vice versa. This model suggests that an intervention to enhance cognitive recovery should have a number of specific targets:

1   The environment should be tailored so that:

- there are frequent opportunities and support for appropriate behaviour or microskills
- appropriate or effective responding is highly reinforced
- the relationships between specific behaviours and their antecedents and consequences are predictable and consistent.

2   Cognitive microskills relevant for effective social functioning should be specifically practised.
3   The ability to identify situations and task demands which require specific microskills, and to allocate the necessary resources, should be specifically rehearsed using self-instructional training to direct attention and to encourage self-monitoring and problem solving.

It is assumed that whilst recovery of executive function and memory mediate recovery of everyday and social functioning, their recovery is not a necessary condition for improved social functioning, and more complex executive func-tions may only emerge following the recovery of more basic performance skills. This suggests that executive function and memory should not be exclusive targets for intervention, and that rehabilitation should target other lower level microskills.

How does cognitive change occur?

These models have a number of implications for the mechanisms of change, which may help to inform CRT programmes. Spaulding *et al.* (1998) have proposed that cognitive change may occur via three hypothetical mechanisms: (a) prosthetic mechanisms, by which new skills compensate for persisting deficits; (b) remediational mechanisms, by which impaired processes undergo actual repair; (c) reorganisational mechanisms by which environmental conditions enhance the functional reorganisation of processes disrupted by acute psychosis.

Both Brenner and McGurk and Mueser's models suggest that cognitive functions can improve directly or through the improvement of related cognitive functions. Whilst the latter may imply some compensation, they both assume that cognitive functions can undergo fundamental improvement, suggesting remediational or reorganisational mechanisms, although neither distinguish between the two. McGurk and Mueser also suggest that some compensatory skills, in the form of improved self-management, may also facilitate a reduction in the negative impact of existing cognitive functions.

All three models emphasise the interactive nature of cognitive functions and this has been well established empirically. The distinction between learning new compensatory cognitive skills and changing existing cognitive processing is therefore difficult to draw. For example, learning improved self-management techniques will inevitably lead to improved executive function. In fact, this is presumably a tautologous statement, since self-management falls within the domain of executive functioning. Furthermore, improved self-management is likely to result in improved attention and learning for example. Therefore, the emergence of any new cognitive skill is likely to lead to the improvement of a range of other aspects of cognitive processing.

Counter to this suggestion, in explanation of their findings of improved performance on the Span of Apprehension, Spaulding *et al.* (1998) suggested a prosthetic model of change in which a deficit in early visual information processing is considered to be compensated for, remaining fundamentally unchanged. Improved task performance is hypothesised to reflect an improved 'top-down' modulation of pre-attentional processes, or the ability to evaluate the processing requirements of the task and to allocate relevant processing capacities in response, rather than an improvement in the fundamental rate or quality of early visual information processing itself. This is an example of a prosthetic mechanism of cognitive change, with self-monitoring and attentional control capacities compensating for deficits in early visual information processing.

Spaulding and colleagues (1998, 2003) argue that prosthetic and reorganisational mechanisms could operate according to familiar models of learning, conditioning and cognitive development. However, the prospect of finding a remediational model for the normalisation of stable cognitive deficits is poor, due to a conventional understanding of the biology of the brain that suggests that congenital or acquired structural abnormalities cannot be repaired. More recent data following traumatic brain injury now attests to the malleability of brain functioning. Spaulding's (2003) model of response hierarchies suggests that cognitive improvement occurs due to reorganisational mechanisms.

Evidence for the mechanisms of cognitive change is hard to find. Most data on these changes are correlational. For instance, brain scanning has offered us a window into the brain so that we could investigate whether there are changes in the way the brain functions that correlate with cognitive change. If different brain areas were activated then we might reasonably suggest that the changes were not brought about by remediational mechanisms. There have been some neuroimaging studies of people undergoing cognitive interventions and following the receipt of a new medication. For example, Wykes *et al.* (2003) investigated brain activation during a working memory task before and after CRT. Normal performance on the working memory task was associated with frontal lobe activation, which gradually decreased over time as the participants became more skilled at the task. Participants with schizophrenia at first showed significantly less frontal lobe activation but increased over time in comparison to a control group who received only occupational therapy activities. These findings seem to suggest either that impaired cognitive processing undergoes repair (a remediational mechanisms model), or that CRT increases the efficiency of cognitive function (perhaps through the influence of a third factor) which is essentially unimpaired (a reorganisational model).

In a SPECT study, Penades *et al.* (2002) showed consistent results of increased prefrontal blood flow during the Tower of London task relative to a control task in eight people with schizophrenia, after receiving the cognitive differentiation and social perception components from the Integrated Psychological Therapy programme. This was consistent with earlier findings from a preliminary pilot by the same group with two patients with chronic schizophrenia, one of whom showed increased prefrontal blood flow during the same executive task (Penades *et al.*, 2000). Wexler *et al.* (2000) also showed that patients who demonstrated performance gains after receiving ten weeks of verbal memory training also showed increased activation in the left inferior frontal cortex during a verbal memory task in an fMRI study. All of these studies are consistent. The same brain regions associated with normal performance increase their activation following CRT.

Evidence for a mechanism in the form of a change or exaggeration of an existing behavioural style comes from two case studies of schizophrenia patients who received CRT (Wykes, 1998). She showed that following CRT one person increased his verbal output without close monitoring, but also increased his errors. The other participant decreased his output but monitored it more closely, and so decreased the errors. These different styles both produced increased overall scores but in completely different ways. The changes in brain activation shown (using SPECT scans) reflected these strategies and were different for both participants. The results from other neuropsychological tests carried out outside the scanner and everyday behaviour also reflected this same behavioural style. Most studies still report the results of CRT as group data and have failed to consider these individual characteristics, which may shed much needed light on the process of cognitive change. These findings suggest that we might be changing thinking dispositions rather than the actual capacities of the processes themselves and these changes in strategic thinking might be different between individuals.

The bottom line

There are direct and indirect links between cognition and both symptoms and functional outcome. However, the nature and mechanisms of these links are poorly specified and understood, and theories of the relationships between cognition and outcome currently have little empirical support or limited explanatory power.

The theories of the relationship between cognitive change and its impact describe just that – the relationships between one function and another. They tell us what will change and even point to possible targets such as executive functions. But the key question for CRT is not what to change but *how* to change it. Spaulding's model is the most helpful in suggesting some underlying mechanisms and does give us some clues for developing a therapy protocol. Since most functioning change has occurred when cognition has changed during CRT, an understanding of the mechanisms involved in this process should be developed to lead to more effective therapy.

Part III

The process of therapy

Chapter 8

A theoretical model for cognitive remediation therapy

Improvements in cognitive functioning are valued by people with schizophrenia. However, throughout this book we have emphasised that CRT should also facilitate the transfer of improved cognitive skills to other areas of behaviour and there is evidence that it does for those receiving therapy. This suggests some therapeutic optimism and hints that particular attributes of therapy specifically aid transfer from the cognitive to the functioning domain, since cognitive improvements brought about by non-specific effects (such as non-cognitive treatments or natural recovery) are not as helpful in facilitating functioning change. But these specific attributes have not yet been identified.

A number of models have linked the cognitive and functional domains but these are mostly descriptive, specifying the types of links that exist but not how these links are formed. Therefore, although they offer possible targets for intervention, they do not inform the development of the mechanisms of intervention. Furthermore, although there are empirical data to support the models, these data are mostly correlations and few studies have aimed to test causal links.

To our knowledge only one model suggests *how* interventions should proceed and this is being developed by Spaulding (2003). This model emphasises the importance of 'exercising' or practising 'microskills', which leads to lower thresholds for their activation and the consequent increased likelihood of their selection and implementation. In addition, the selection and implementation of specific 'performance microskills' is said to be governed by higher level 'executive microskills' which themselves are said to benefit from practice and consequently reduced activation thresholds.

Like Spaulding, we think that practice and reinforcement are important in facilitating learning, and that executive functions are important targets in teaching self-regulatory skills. But our model differs in emphasising the primary importance of teaching skills to improve self-regulation of *thinking* or *metacognition*. Participants then learn to transfer existing cognitive knowledge and skills to new situations. In this model the teaching style encourages active, reflective processing in addition to practice. The mechanisms of change specified by the two models overlap yet differ in their priorities and consequent proposed methods of intervention. It seems to us that Spaulding favours practice (with some instruction on reflective processing), whilst we will argue strongly in favour of explicit teaching of reflective processing (with some subsequent practice of these functions).

In this chapter we will outline our own model of the interrelationship between cognition and functioning, emphasising the mechanisms by which specific cognitive changes will have an impact on functional outcome. This allows us not only to propose a content for the therapy (i.e. the cognitive targets) but also the process of therapy. Whilst we have drawn upon empirical data in developing our model, at present, evidence in favour of differing methods of cognitive change comes from studies which vary in their participant samples, outcome measures and analyses of change. The model therefore offers a set of hypotheses about cognitive change which may be tested in future research.

How cognition influences everyday actions

If we are to improve everyday functions by changing cognitive functioning, we must first explain how cognition affects actions. We propose that different sorts of actions are influenced by cognition in different ways. First, we distinguish between automatic and controlled routes to action. These routes are analogous to those specified by the Contention Scheduling System and the Supervisory Attentional System respectively in Shallice and Burgess's (1990) model of information processing and to the automatic and willed routes to action proposed by Frith (1987).

The automatic route

The automatic route occurs when single or multiple actions are triggered by the environment and which consequently can proceed automatically without internal control. We will refer to multiple actions that form a string of behaviours which are overlearnt and run according to a fixed automatic routine as 'behavioural routines'. The automatic route is shown in Figure 8.1.

Figure 8.1 Automatic actions

The controlled route

The controlled route occurs when actions are triggered by internal goals and intentions, which then drive the selection and regulation of these actions. We differentiate between two types of controlled actions. The first type relies *only* upon a goal being formed and an intention to carry out actions to achieve that goal. These actions do not require the actor to select from a range of possible actions, because having an intention to reach his or her goal is presumed to trigger an associated cognitive schema which specifies, in full, the set of actions or behavioural routines which is required to achieve the goal.

Cognitive schemas are described in Chapter 2 as generic knowledge structures or templates that are stored within long-term memory and are the means by which mental representations are organised. They prime certain actions and set up a context for their use. This first subset of controlled actions relies on highly specified schemas which prime a complete set of actions so that additional internal selection of actions according to current goals is not required. Therefore, they proceed in the same manner each time they are carried out and do not depend on specific circumstances. Controlled processes such as executive functioning or explicit memory retrieval may be required to implement the set of actions in full, but the selection of actions and their temporal sequence is specified by the cognitive schema. For example, if I am watching TV and a film starts showing, I may have the intention to watch the film. In this case, my understanding of what is required to watch the film (i.e. my filmwatching schema) is such that I do not need to reflect upon what to do in order to watch the film, I can just watch it. My ability to watch the film then may depend upon controlled processes (e.g. executive control) to direct my attention towards the screen in a sustained fashion, but use of these processes is directly entailed by my continued intention to watch the film and the subsequent activation of my film-watching schema. Executive control may also be required to start and stop specific controlled actions or behavioural routines (e.g. lift the kettle once boiled and pour the water into the mug), but again the decisions to make these changes are specified by the activated cognitive schema rather than by an internal reflective process. The controlled route for this subset of routine actions is shown in Figure 8.2.

A second subset of controlled actions does not follow directly when an intention to act is made. These rely upon the ability of the actor to select actions appropriately from a range of options (which may be specified in part by an existing schema). The actions required for film watching given in the example above may shift to fall within this second subset of controlled actions if I reflect upon my actions and decide to change or improve the routine (e.g. I get up and close the door to shut out extraneous noise that is distracting). Alternatively the action may be more novel (e.g. if I intend to make a meal, I need to decide what kind of meal I would like to make, look in

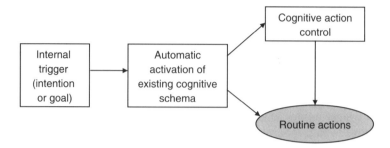

Figure 8.2 Routine controlled actions

a recipe book, consider what ingredients are available and so on). Thus, I must reflect upon my intention, my goals, my past experience and the way in which these interact with the current circumstances in order to select a certain set of appropriate actions which will allow me to achieve my goal. This ability to reflect upon and regulate one's own thinking is referred to as *meta-cognition*. This type of controlled action is shown in Figure 8.3.

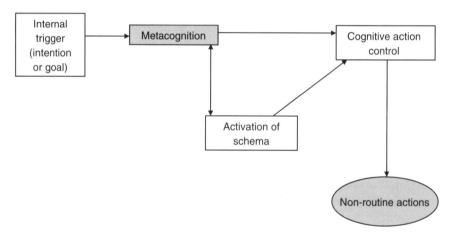

Figure 8.3 Non-routine controlled actions

Two types of action

We propose that for tasks that rely upon actions which occur via both the automatic and first of the controlled routes, improved performance will necessarily result from the increased efficiency and/or capacity of the associated cognitive processes: there is a direct relationship between the two. For example, in the first case of film watching, if my sustained attention improves, then my film watching will also improve. We label this category of actions for which there is a direct relationship with cognitive function as *routine actions*.

For actions that occur via the second of the controlled routes, improved cognitive processing will not necessarily lead to improved behaviour, since the use of particular cognitive processes is not specified in full by the cognitive schema associated with the intention to carry out this behaviour. Behaviour may only benefit from improved cognitive processing if the person decides to use these processes to carry out the task. For example, improved planning ability may only impact a particular task if the person decides to actually generate and use a plan, and this decision will be depend upon the person's metacognitive skills. Therefore, for these actions, rather than change behaviour only by improving specific cognitive processes (e.g. planning ability), we should also aim to improve the ability to reflect upon and use the relevant and most effective existing knowledge and skills, for example, to help the person to decide to use a plan. We term this category of actions *non-routine actions*.

Fundamental to carrying out non-routine actions is the ability of the person to use existing knowledge, experience, motivations and skills in new contexts. This is known as *transfer* (De Corte, 2003). Effective transfer depends crucially upon the person's metacognitive abilities, the cognitive resources upon which the person can draw in planning, implementing and monitoring his or her actions, as well as both internal (e.g. motivation) and external (e.g. the nature of the task) non-cognitive factors. This model for the differing relationships between cognition and action (or functioning outcome) is shown in Figure 8.4

Impact of improved cognition and metacognition on symptoms

We have based our model on the relationships between cognition and everyday behaviours. However, improved cognition may also impact symptoms.

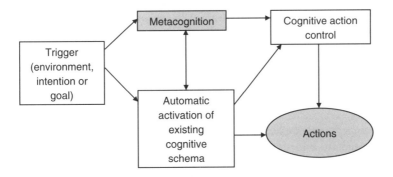

Figure 8.4 A model for routes to action

Positive symptoms

Positive symptoms have been attributed to deficits in self-monitoring, monitoring the intentions of others and metarepresentation (Frith, 1992), reasoning biases (Garety and Hemsley, 1994), and difficulties in inhibiting intrusive material from long-term memory (Hemsley, 1987). The processes by which these deficits may result in the symptoms of schizophrenia are discussed in Chapter 5. They may all be attributable to deficits in the functioning of the central executive, and particularly metacognitive processes, suggesting that improved executive functioning (particularly improved metacognition) may result in a reduction in positive symptoms. In support of this, are findings that cognitive behaviour therapy (CBT) can lead to fewer positive symptoms. CBT aims to reduce positive symptoms by encouraging reflection on thinking processes and the reappraisal of faulty attributions by reality testing and cognitive challenging. These processes all rely on metacognitive processing of affectively laden material. CRT serves a similar purpose in a non-affect-related domain and aims to improve generic metacognitive skills. Wykes *et al.* (1999), Bark *et al.* (2003), and Peer *et al.* (2004) all show improvements in positive symptoms that might be explained by metacognitive regulation (i.e. flexibility of thought).

Disorganised symptoms

Disorganised symptoms have been attributed to difficulties in self-regulation and self-monitoring (Hemsley, 1987; Frith, 1992). These are explicitly targeted and the organisation of cognitive function and behaviour is a consistent goal of CRT. Therefore, cognitive improvements following CRT may directly result in a reduction in disorganised symptoms.

Negative symptoms

Negative symptoms have been attributed to difficulties in generating internally cued actions and intentions (Frith, 1992) and to coping with information overload by avoidance (Hemsley, 1987). Via improved metacognitive regulation, CRT aims to improve self-regulation of behaviour which may lead both to increased or better regulated self-driven behaviour and to more adaptive coping with overwhelming cognitive material.

Insight

There is considerable evidence to suggest that poor insight is associated with executive deficits and generalised cognitive impairment in schizophrenia. Therefore, if cognitive function improves, we may expect insight to improve. Support for this possibility comes from the likelihood that good insight relies upon the self-appraisal of behaviour, interactions with others, and internal experiences. This entails the use of metacognitive skills. Therefore, CRT may lead to improved insight due to an emphasis on improving metacognitive processing.

The distinction between cognition and metacognition

Whilst cognition has a direct impact on both routine and non-routine actions, an additional necessary and sufficient condition for the implementation of non-routine actions is the use of metacognition. 'Metacognition' refers to 'thinking about thinking' (Flavell, 1979) or to cognitive processes which relate not to immediate perceptions of the external world but to internal mental representations of reality. Flavell *et al.* (2002) highlight the distinction between the 'static' component of metacognition (metacognitive knowledge) and its 'dynamic' component (metacognitive experience or regulation). Meta-cognitive knowledge is knowledge about cognitive processes which can be used to make cognitive function more efficient. Metacognitive experience or regulation refers to the monitoring and regulation of one's own thinking processes (Kluwe, 1982). We will refer to it as *metacognitive processing.*

Whilst metacognition forms part of general cognition, for the rest of this chapter, in describing our model, we will use the term 'cognition' in a specific, narrow sense, to describe only that cognition which cannot be labelled 'meta-cognitive'. In other words, we will use 'cognition' to refer only to processes which relate to primary mental representations of the world. We will also distinguish between knowledge and cognitive processing within the general domain of 'cognition'.

Similar thinking processes may be described as metacognitive or non-metacognitive according to their object: metacognition relates specifically to secondary representations; non-metacognitive cognitive processing relates to primary representations of the external world. Monitoring is a metacognitive strategy when it refers to self-monitoring of one's thinking processes, for example, noticing when one has made a mistake, but it is a cognitive strategy when it refers to monitoring external reality, for example, noticing typographical errors.

Cognitive and metacognitive processes can also be distinguished according to the types of functions they involve. Cognitive processing can involve any type of cognitive function (e.g. attention, memory, executive functioning) whose object is a primary representation. Metacognitive processing, by its nature since it involves processing only using secondary representations of reality, can refer only to executive functioning, and specifically those processes which are used to regulate thinking. Executive processes which regulate behaviour and all other lower order cognitive functions form part of cognitive processing.

Evidence for a distinction between executive processing and metacognition come from recent studies by Koren (personal communication) which suggest that performance of participants on the WCST was not highly correlated with their performance on a test measuring their metacognitive abilities to monitor and evaluate their own performance. Therefore, some people may be able to monitor their actions but not their cognitive processing and may thus be able to succeed on tasks without explicit awareness of the processes involved in achieving their success.

Improving routine actions

We have argued that routine actions can be directly improved by improving cognition. We propose that there are a number of ways in which this may occur:

1   Increasing the number of behavioural routines or cognitive schemas which guide action.
2   Improving the quality of the behavioural routines or cognitive schemas which are stored:

  • by improving encoding so that the memory is more robust and less susceptible to interference, etc.
  • by elaborating the routine or schema so that it is more complex
  • by improving retrieval processes, so that useful behaviours or schemas are readily retrieved where appropriate.

3   Improving the ability to create and realise intentions which may trigger routine controlled actions.
4   Increasing cognitive processing capacity or efficiency so that cognitive processes which form part of a behavioural routine or which are triggered by the activation of a cognitive schema are more effective. For example, an improved ability to sustain attention for long periods of time would result in more effective film watching. Or for someone who has a schema which includes mental rehearsal when trying to remember telephone numbers, their telephone number memory may improve if sustained attention (which may facilitate effective mental rehearsal) improves.

The last two of these possibilities provide broad goals which may affect not only routine actions but also non-routine actions. The ability to create and realise intentions is required for non-routine actions since these are also triggered by internal cues and seem likely to require metacognitive processes. Cognitive processing provides the resources upon which a person can draw when reflecting upon and carrying out a non-routine task. However, increasing the number or quality of behavioural routines or cognitive schemas (i.e.

the first two possible ways to improve cognitive function to have an impact on routine actions) so that a complete set of actions is specified to carry out associated tasks will lead us to teach every skill individually, in all their possible iterations across tasks. This is not only extremely difficult given the constraints of time and complexity (as well as tedious for both the learner and teacher) but would restrict people to carrying out only well-known actions in familiar situations. It would not affect the ability of the person to respond flexibly to new tasks or behaviours.

An alternative to teaching individual behavioural routines and cognitive schemas which may expand or firm up the existing repertoire of routine actions, may be to teach: (a) new behavioural routines and cognitive schemas which may be easily transferable to a wide range of circumstances, and which are not bound by particular circumstances; (b) transfer skills to ensure that new or existing routines or schemas are effectively utilised in novel situations, or routine actions are adapted (shifting them to become non-routine actions) to make use of improved skills. We therefore have four revised goals that are important for improving both routine and non-routine actions:

- to improve the ability to create and realise intentions
- to increase the efficiency and capacity of cognitive processing
- to teach transferable behavioural routines and cognitive schemas
- to improve transfer skills.

These are all crucially associated with transfer.

Improving non-routine actions

The primary goals for improving non-routine actions now overlap with the goals for improving routine actions: we want to: (a) increase the efficiency and capacity of cognitive processing; (b) improve transfer skills. The first of these has been the target of many CRT programmes, although the specific component processes taught and the tests for showing improvement have never been well specified. Cognitive skills transfer has never been an explicit target and in the following sections of the chapter we will explore transfer in more detail and discuss how improving transfer may help us to reach our goal of improving routine and non-routine actions.

Transfer

Transfer is not a new phenomenon. Thorndike and Woodworth described it in 1901 and there are references within Gestalt psychology in the 1940s (Katona, 1940; Wertheimer, 1945). But we will rely on a contemporary definition: 'the broad, productive, and supported use of acquired knowledge, skills, and motivations in new contexts and learning tasks' (De Corte, 2003).

Transfer is conceptualised as: (a) near transfer or the 'low road', in which the transfer situation is closely related to the original learning situation; (b) far transfer or the 'high road', in which the transfer situation is discrepant from the original learning situation. Near transfer can be achieved when tasks and behaviours are well learnt through extensive and varied practice, and there is a high level of similarity between the learning situation and where these skills need to be implemented. This form of transfer is analogous to the use of existing cognitive skills and knowledge in highly specified routine controlled actions. Far transfer, however, involves the effortful and deliberate abstraction of principles which can be used to guide task behaviour in novel and complex situations. Therefore, metacognitive processes are of fundamental importance. Far transfer is required for non-routine actions.

Most CRT studies have concentrated on the near or low road to transfer, by teaching specific cognitive skills for cognitive tasks which are similar to the neuropsychological tests on which the participants are assessed. Meta-analyses of randomised control trials of cognitive training suggest that near transfer (from one cognitive task to another similar one) has been accomplished (Krabbendam and Aleman, 2003).

There is also some evidence of cross-domain or far transfer although few studies to date attempt such outcome measurement (Twamley et al., 2003). Studies which have targeted far transfer, have either unknowingly specifically targeted metacognitive skills, or assessed the impact of CRT on non-cognitive tests of everyday life skills. For instance, in the trials by Medalia and colleagues it was the problem-solving therapy (which necessarily involves metacognitive processing) that affected levels of symptoms (Bark et al., 2003). Wykes et al. (1999, 2003) also included a specific problem-solving and planning focus to the therapy with an emphasis on metacognitive regulation. This therapy had a positive effect on both social functioning and cognition.

Improvements in non-cognitive domains following CRT also seem to be specific to programmes which address metacognitive skills. CRT programmes which have targeted sustained attention or memory have shown little transfer of improvements to tasks or domains different to those used in the training situation (e.g. Medalia et al., 2000a; Benedict et al., 1994; Stratta et al., 1997). We suggest that it is only by expanding the focus of therapy to take into account the prerequisites of far transfer that it will be possible for CRT to maximise its effects on quality of life.

The efficiency with which transfer takes place (or even if it takes place at all) depends on a number of interacting factors. These fall into two main categories: internal factors or personal resources, including cognitive and metacognitive processing, knowledge, and motivation; and external factors, including the nature of the task, the context in which relevant skills and knowledge useful for the task were learnt, and the current environment (the context of the task and relevant support from other people).

Effects of personal resources on transfer

Cognitive processing

The capacity and efficiency of cognitive processing skills will determine how well various elements of a task can be carried out. They form the cognitive resources which can be transferred from one situation to another. For example, someone entering a new shop and deciding how to go about buying the items on their shopping list may be able to decide that they need a plan (i.e. use appropriate metacognitive skills), but may be easily distractible (i.e. have cognitive processing impairments) and so quickly lose sight of their plan. Thus, in this case, it is their cognitive processing rather than metacognitive skills which may hinder their progress.

Knowledge

Here we refer to knowledge which is not metacognitive in nature, and like cognitive processing, existing knowledge provides the resources which can be transferred from one situation to another. Within the literature, two types of knowledge have been identified as particularly important for transfer.

1 *Generic schematic knowledge.* In order for transfer to occur, schemas must be identified within long-term memory for problems which require similar solutions to those of the current task (Cooper and Sweller, 1987). The broader the schemas, the greater the likelihood that the person will notice connections between familiar and novel situations and that transfer will occur. Transfer therefore depends upon the quality and breadth of the person's generic schematic knowledge base.

2 *Task-specific knowledge.* Well-developed and expansive domain-specific knowledge tends to be more principled in form than knowledge which is patchy or limited (Gelman and Greeno, 1989). This allows the person to make connections between existing knowledge and the current situation on the basis of a deeper, more abstract understanding of the task than may be afforded by a superficial understanding of specific task-related concrete or surface elements.

High levels of domain-specific knowledge can also be used to compensate for lack of interest or motivation as well as poor general strategic skill. Alexander and Murphy (1998) showed in a cluster analysis of student outcomes that those who had a strong domain-specific knowledge base could use it to compensate to achieve reasonable outcomes even if they were not motivated to learn. This suggests that people with schizophrenia might, if given high levels of domain-specific knowledge, be able to overcome strategic or motivational problems. Domain-specific cognitive schemas may be particularly important in specifying necessary actions to a high degree. There is now emerging evidence that 'shopping knowledge' is predictive of performance on a grocery shopping skills test, even when there are gross cognitive impairments (Rempfer *et al.*, personal communication).

Transfer-relevant knowledge is likely to be limited in people with schizophrenia for a number of reasons:

1 Impairments in encoding and retrieval in explicit memory result in a reduction in stored knowledge of any form.
2 The experiences of people with schizophrenia have frequently been limited often from a very early age. There is now increasing evidence to suggest that educational and social difficulties are apparent in very young children before the onset of symptoms of schizophrenia or a prodrome (Cannon *et al.*, 2002). Education is frequently disrupted for people with schizophrenia, there is a significantly lower chance of being in employment (Cook and Razzano, 2000), social networks are reduced (Bengtsson-Tops and Hansson, 2001), and people frequently spend considerable periods in hospital or in supported accommodation. Therefore, the breadth and depth of experiences have frequently been significantly limited, reducing further opportunities to gain general and domain-specific knowledge.
3 There is significant evidence to suggest that people with schizophrenia not only have difficulties in organising and categorising information, but there are abnormalities in their semantic associative networks. In combination, these factors are likely to result in schemas which are poorly organised and lacking in coherent internal structure.

Metacognitive processing

This allows the person to reflect upon and regulate their own thinking or cognitive processing which is important in generating and realising intentions, goal setting, generating and implementing strategies, problem solving and sequencing, self-monitoring of thinking, and evaluating plans and strategies.

Metacognitive processing is equivalent to executive control of thinking processes and there is substantial evidence (reviewed in earlier chapters) that this is significantly impaired in the schizophrenia population. In fact, Frith (1979) argues that metarepresentation or the ability to represent (or think about) internal representations of reality is the core deficit in schizophrenia (see Chapter 3 for a more detailed explanation). Metarepresentation is a constituent part of metacognition.

Metacognitive knowledge

We argued earlier that metacognitive knowledge provides the person with information about how to improve the efficiency of task performance. It relates to three domains: (a) strategy variables, which include knowledge about cognitive strategies (to make progress towards goals) or metacognitive strategies (to monitor and evaluate progress) as well as how to ensure the most effective use of these strategies; (b) task variables, which include knowledge of the nature of the task and the demands it will place upon the person; (c) person variables, which include knowledge about how people in general learn and process information, as well as knowledge of one's own knowledge, cognitive strengths and limitations, motivation, affective states, cognitive style or characteristics as learners and how these factors may impact task performance. In this final respect, it includes an aspect of self-appraisal which contributes to a person's sense of self-efficacy (Paris and Winograd, 1990).

Metacognitive knowledge is likely to be reduced for similar reasons as for the reduction of knowledge in general (outlined above), for example, due to impairments in explicit memory (affecting encoding, storage and retrieval) and in metacognitive skills (affecting the self-reflection required in the acquisition of metacognitive knowledge).

Motivation

Motivation to complete the task in hand, and particularly interest in that task or the extent to which it is personally meaningful, is a primary ingredient in predicting transfer of information from one domain to another. Alexander and Murphy (1999) showed that the most highly achieving students were those who were oriented towards learning, despite having an initial poor knowledge base. Therefore, high levels of motivation seem to compensate for deficiencies in domain knowledge. Motivation may affect how likely someone is: (a) to engage in any particular activity; (b) to devote sufficient effort to the task and the problem solving which may be required to achieve the task; (c) to persevere with the task in the face of adversity. Motivation is likely to be significantly reduced in people with schizophrenia for all areas of functioning for a variety of reasons:

1 *Past experience.* Schizophrenia is frequently associated with low levels of attainment in education and employment, limited social networks and serious disability. Therefore, past experience leads many people to predict failure and to have a reduced sense of self-efficacy.
2 *Self-esteem.* There is significant evidence to suggest that people with schizophrenia suffer from pervasive low self-esteem (Bradshaw and Brekke, 1999). This can lead to negatively biased appraisals of

self-efficacy and a tendency to avoid taking up opportunities which are perceived to be likely to lead to failure.

3 *Depression and anxiety.* Depression is common in schizophrenia (Koreen *et al.*, 1993) and is associated with loss of interest, pleasure, motivation and energy. Co-morbid anxiety is also extremely common and associated with high levels of avoidance (Wetherell *et al.*, 2003).

4 *Negative symptoms.* These include apathy and avolition which are specifically related to motivation.

5 *Positive symptoms.* Delusional thinking may lead to unrealistic goals, which may also be inconsistent with those which are valued when the person is well. Furthermore, they are frequently distressing and disruptive and can lead to a loss of motivation.

6 *Opportunity.* People with schizophrenia frequently lead lives which are limited by disability. These factors are all likely to reduce the opportunities for independent living, developing new interests and striving for lifelong goals.

7 *Future and goal-directed thinking.* Impaired metacognitive regulation and explicit memory are likely to lead to a reduction in the generation and implementation of long-term goals and plans, from which much motivation is derived.

Personal resources are therefore challenging for transfer in the field of schizophrenia but we do not need to be too pessimistic as it is clear that we already have some evidence that these things can be improved. Meta-analyses of randomised control trials of cognitive training suggest that improvements in cognitive processing (as well as metacognitive processing, in the form of problem solving, for example) are possible (Krabbendam and Aleman, 2003). We also know that people with schizophrenia are therefore able to learn, suggesting that knowledge may be increased, and studies have shown that motivation can be increased in people with schizophrenia. These factors therefore all seem to be reasonable targets for CRT if we are to improve transfer.

Improving transfer

To have a positive impact on transfer, we need to account not only for internal factors which affect transfer, but also external factors. These include the nature of the task, the context in which relevant skills and knowledge useful for the task were learnt, and the current environment.

The task

For transfer to occur, the participant must notice conceptual similarities between the current task and tasks or schemas held in long-term memory which provide clues to the ways in which the new task may be approached. This process of comparison with past experience will be facilitated if: (a) the current task *contains familiar constituent parts*, since this will help trigger memories of previously solved problems; (b) the current task *falls within a well-developed domain of knowledge*, since this sort of knowledge is known to be well organised and principled in form, which encourages deeper level, more abstract processing.

The learning context

The following aspects of the learning context have an impact on transfer.

Similarity between the learning context and the current context

Traditionally, the transfer of information from one domain to another has been considered to involve the direct application of acquired elements from one situation to another. Many have argued that transfer therefore depends on the degree to which tasks share identical elements and that knowledge and skills are very strongly embedded in and tied to the context in which they were acquired (Thorndike and Woodworth, 1901; Singely and Anderson, 1989; Anderson *et al.*, 2004). Whilst it is now generally acknowledged that people can use problem solving to increase the likelihood of the transfer of skills to new domains (Mayer and Wittrock, 1996), it is well established that transfer of information is more likely to occur the more similar are the learning and transfer tasks.

In support of this is much evidence to suggest that skill acquisition frequently fails to generalise to tasks which differ from those in which the skills were learnt. Examples of this are apparent within the schizophrenia literature. Medalia *et al.* (2000b) showed that whilst people with schizophrenia demonstrated improvements on a memory remediation task, they did not make greater gains than a control group on measures of immediate paragraph recall or list learning.

Training methods used

Training methods should explicitly promote the development of the personal resources needed for successful transfer. Thus, for example, participants may be encouraged to articulate their cognitive and motivational processes during learning and problem solving to promote metacognitive processing and knowledge. The development of broad generic schemas may be facilitated by the use of multimedia learning environments and helping people to connect verbal explanations to visual representations (Mayer, 1999).

The environment

The environment may contribute to transfer in a number of ways.

Current environment

This may include the extent to which the current environment is conducive to the implementation of effective metacognitive and cognitive processes. For example, since people with schizophrenia frequently suffer from attention and working memory impairments, keeping disturbances and extraneous noise to a minimum is likely to reduce distractibility and the amount of irrelevant information which gains automatic access to working memory.

Support from other people and other sources of information

Bransford and Schwartz (1999) emphasise the extent to which people live in resource-rich environments. The ability to make use of existing skills and knowledge is enhanced by judicious help and support from other people and from other sources of information within the environment such as recipes or maps. This relies not only on the availability of potential supports and their usefulness, but also the extent to which the actor is able to seek, request, accept and make use of appropriate support. Factors relating to both the task and the environment therefore emphasise two main points at which transfer is affected by external factors:

- the context and nature of the current task
- the context and nature of the learning environment.

Whilst CRT therapists may be able to advise about the tasks and types of environments which might facilitate transfer for people with schizophrenia and teach them to recognise and shape aspects of their environment to increase the likelihood of transfer, the point at which CRT can have most impact is at the learning stage. There are a number of implications for enhancing the learning stage that can be drawn from these findings.

1 Ensure participants are trained using *tasks which are personally meaningful* (i.e. they are relevant to their goals) and hold some broad similarities with those used in everyday life. (Note that we would not advocate teaching identical tasks since the aim is not to teach a series of new routine actions but the ability to *transfer* skills to non-routine actions.)
2 *Capitalise on well-developed domains of knowledge* in teaching new skills (e.g. develop strategies which draw upon existing knowledge bases).
3 Teach participants *to seek and make use of appropriate help and support* from within the environment.

The goals and processes of CRT

We have emphasised the importance of transfer and have used the concept in the development of our final model of the relationship between cognition and functioning. We discussed above how a number of non-cognitive factors in addition to metacognition are important in facilitating transfer and so have also been included in the model. This more comprehensive model is shown in Figure 8.5.

Our findings have also suggested that if we are to improve functioning in people with schizophrenia we need to improve transfer by the following means:

1   Providing a learning environment which promotes transfer.
2   Improving the personal resources of CRT participants upon which transfer depends, including:

    • cognitive processing
    • knowledge
    • metacognitive processing
    • metacognitive knowledge
    • motivation.

3   Encouraging participants to seek and use environmental help and support.

This needs to occur within an environment that accounts not only for the difficulties associated with schizophrenia, but which continuously promotes

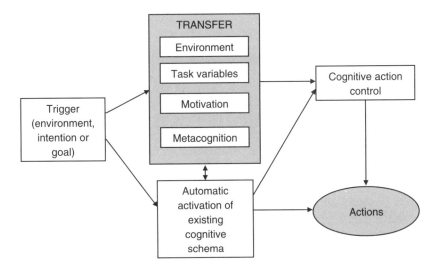

Figure 8.5 A model for cognitive remediation therapy

the use and development of these personal resources and which uses tasks which are personally meaningful (i.e. goal related) and relevant to everyday life. Each of the different personal resources which act as targets for CRT will benefit from different elements of a learning environment. We will discuss these in turn in the following sections.

Targeting cognitive processing

Whilst CRT may need to aim to improve a wide range of cognitive functions if we are to impact a broad range of everyday functions, we suggest that the primary and consistent focus of attempts to increase cognitive processing capacity and efficiency should be executive functioning, although the practice of non-executive cognitive processing skills is inevitable. We propose that executive functions are generally the only cognitive functions which are directly amenable to conscious control and deliberate change. Examples from each of the other cognitive processing systems (long-term memory, working memory and the brief sensory store) may help to elucidate this point.

If we try to improve explicit long-term memory we can target encoding, storage or retrieval. Encoding can be improved by increasing the depth of processing of the to-be-remembered material or by spending longer undertaking superficial encoding. In both cases, this relies on executive functions: either to organise, categorise and structure the information more fully, or to direct attentional resources towards the information and initiate rehearsal of that information. Alternatively, retrieval may be improved by making search strategies within memory more systematic. Again, this relies on executive functions. Once a memory is encoded, we may not consciously influence that memory again by cognitive means, except to improve encoding, until the memory is retrieved. We may be able to facilitate the storage of the memory, for example, by ensuring we get enough sleep, but we cannot actively control the memory, except by using executive functions. Similarly, suppose we try to improve working memory. We could attempt to improve the encoding of the memory, by directing attention in a more focused way towards the to-be-remembered material, or we could maintain the memory more effectively by rehearsing the information. In each case, these facilitatory processes rely on executive functions. Finally, suppose we try to improve early visual processing such that brief iconic memories are stored in a stronger form. Presumably the way to do this is to direct sufficient attention towards the stimulus to ensure sufficient and accurate encoding – again, a function of the central executive. Therefore, whilst we may practise the use of certain non-executive functions, we suggest that we cannot consciously attempt to change any of these functions directly. To change the operation of these functions, we must target executive functioning.

This suggestion is consistent with ideas promoted by Baron (1985, 2000) who postulates two main components to thinking – cognitive capacities and

thinking dispositions. Cognitive capacities he defines as 'ability parameters
. . . which affect success at tasks and which cannot be improved by instructions' (Baron, 1985: 14). These include perceptual speed, working memory
capacity and response inhibition. In contrast, thinking dispositions are those
factors that 'affect success in psychological tasks and that *are* subject to
control by instruction' (Baron, 1985: 15, italics in the original). These last
parameters affect the amount of time someone will spend on a task, their
willingness to switch perspectives (i.e. be cognitively flexible) and the dis-
position to weigh evidence. Baron's division of cognitive processes into cognitive capacities and thinking dispositions is similar to (although not identical
with) our division into non-executive and executive processes. In each case,
the former are hypothesised to be amenable to change only via practice,
whilst the latter may be changeable following instruction and active control.

Evidence to support adopting primarily executive targets comes from the
CRT literature which suggests that training in strategy use (i.e. executive functioning) may be more effective in promoting cognitive improvements than
practice alone (Krabbendam and Aleman, 2003). There is also considerable
evidence in the educational transfer literature to suggest that strategy use (an
aspect of executive functioning) aids transfer and metacognitive processing
(Sawyer *et al.*, 1992; Nietfeld and Schraw, 2002; Fuchs *et al.*, 2003a).

We suggest that specific executive functions which can promote improved
functioning in impaired cognitive processes should be identified and targeted.
These should then be promoted using the broad principles of transfer and
metacognitive self-regulation, discussed in greater detail below.

Targeting knowledge

Whilst enhancing domain-specific knowledge is likely to enhance performance in associated areas of everyday living, we suggest that the aim of CRT
should be to promote transfer abilities across a very wide range of domains
so that participants are able to flexibly and effectively approach any new task
with which they are faced. Therefore, we advocate that CRT should teach
people to develop broad-based, conceptual problem-solving schemas, which
can be used as templates for undertaking a wide range of tasks.

Evidence for the success of developing broad-based schemas in promoting
transfer can be found within the literature. For instance, Fuchs *et al.* (2003b)
investigated different approaches to teaching mathematics, all of which
included teaching the rules for solving different types of problem and how to
group problems (i.e. creating a problem schema). The schemas in the first
condition were expected to be narrow, as all the problems of a particular type
were described in the same way, with only the content and the quantities
differing. In the other conditions they expected broader schemas to be
developed because they explicitly changed superficial features of the problem
categories without affecting the rules by which the problem would be solved.

Students in the conditions designed to promote the development of broad schemas showed better far transfer than the students in either the narrow schema condition or a control condition (teaching as usual). There was no difference between students in the narrow schema condition and the control group. This suggests both that the development of broad schemas is important for flexible responding and that they cannot be achieved through the provision of the same task information; i.e. tasks must vary in their superficial content.

Others have shown that transfer is enhanced through the use of learning with multimedia learning environments (Mayer, 1999), helping people to connect verbal explanations to visual representations (Mayer, 1999), multiple learning contexts (Stark *et al.*, 1999), the use of diagrams (Cuevas *et al.*, 2002) and training variability (Shute and Gawlick, 1995). In each case, encoding across a range of modalities encourages the abstraction of deep structure rather than superficial features, leading to the development of broad schemas.

Targeting metacognition

Good metacognitive processing allows someone to suppress an initial response, deliberately reflect upon and examine the task in hand and generate alternative solutions and strategies for completing the task by considering ways in which the novel task shares connections with familiar tasks. This process facilitates transfer and relies upon the participant's ability to:

- understand and use rules for problem solving
- identify categories for sorting problems that require similar solutions
- recognise that novel problems are similar to previously solved problems.

A number of ways of teaching these processes have been developed and tested.

Teaching by instruction

In the study by Fuchs *et al.* (2003b) described earlier, which investigated teaching problem solving in mathematics, students who were taught by developing broad schemas were also divided into conditions which differed in whether or not they were explicitly instructed about the concept of transfer to increase the use of metacognitive processes. In particular they were taught that in the face of novel problems they should search for connections to previous problems. Metacognition should be improved by both learning about abstraction and by triggering awareness of connections between familiar and novel problems.

On immediate transfer tasks the students were better when they had a combined treatment of explicit full instruction on the concept of transfer plus the promotion of broader schemas. This comparison produced an effect size of 1.45 over simpler solution methods. For far transfer, the effect of transfer teaching in comparison to a control group (who only received teaching as usual) was 1.16. This study, the culmination of a series of studies by various authors in educational psychology, shows that instruction improves far transfer. This mirrors the results found in studies of people with schizophrenia where cognitive change is observed, but this has no effect on far transfer (e.g. in some medication studies), when no instruction has been given (e.g. non-specific effects in control conditions) or when programmes have concentrated on learning only by practice rather than instruction (Krabbendam and Aleman, 2003).

In the same study Fuchs *et al.* (2003b) investigated the effect of students' prior abilities, which is relevant for the design of any intervention programme for people with schizophrenia. They found that for those with high levels of disability, the rate of non-responding to the intervention was highest when the rules of the problems had not been explicitly and thoroughly taught. The lowest rate of non-responding was when broad schemas were promoted together with metacognitive training. CRT approaches in the recent past which did not emphasise broad cognitive schemas and which often lacked explicit instruction would not have been helpful, particularly for those with the most disability. This may explain some of the variation in the results of CRT. For instance, for those with better cognitive abilities, CRT could have a large effect on near transfer but for those with poorer ability prior to the training then fewer effects on near transfer and little effect on far transfer would be expected. These were the results from the study by Stratta *et al.* (1997b). The lack of evidence of large or stable effects over time following CRT is therefore understandable given the preponderance of people with poorer cognitive function in the population of patients.

Teaching analogical reasoning

One of the ways of improving the identification of problem rules – the first step to transfer – is to use reasoning by analogy. It is possible to extract the rules of one type of task by using instructional techniques for individual task problems. In cognitive enhancement this technique is perhaps the most clearly described as getting the 'gist' of a problem (Hogarty and Flesher, 1999a). Extracting the gist depends on the extent to which the person has task-specific knowledge, with high levels tending to be more abstract in form, allowing the person to make connections between existing knowledge and the current situation on the basis of a deeper understanding of the task than may be afforded by concrete or surface elements (Gelman and Greeno, 1989). Hogarty and Flesher (1999a) suggest that extracting the gist occurs through the identification of the principles underlying one task. However, we have seen that transfer relies upon the use of multiple exemplars and the creation of broad schemas, so this may not be the most persuasive technique.

One alternative is drawn from management training where a new technique of *analogical encoding* has been identified. This might be particularly helpful for cognitive interventions for people with schizophrenia because it can be used even before the underlying structure of a problem has been well understood and encoded. In the past, analogical reasoning has been carried out with reference to the knowledge that the learner already possesses. The instructor encourages the learner to make comparisons of old knowledge with the new target situation (this is similar to the descriptions by Hogarty and Flesher, 1999a). But its applicability is limited to those situations where the learner has an adequate knowledge base. The technique adopted by Gentner *et al.* (2003) uses comparison of two examples before either one is clearly understood. Analogical encoding is not used to transfer knowledge per se but to highlight and clarify the new concept. It promotes attention to commonalities including common principles or schemas and reduces the effects of surface properties which are known to be highly accessible to people with schizophrenia (see the results of latent inhibition studies in Chapter 2). Genter and colleagues (2003) found that comparison was a more effective strategy than the abstraction of principles from single cases. The group IPT manual of Brenner *et al.* (1994) highlights that this sort of comparison is sometimes used in their procedure. Again this might account for the variability in the data from IPT if these techniques are sometimes used to good effect but at other times are not emphasised.

Teaching regulation and control of strategy use

A crucial element of problem solving is the controlled generation and implementation of strategies. This occurs as part of a conscious metacognitive evaluation of task needs (Garner, 1990) and not as part of an automatic response set to tasks in a very familiar domain. There is considerable evidence to suggest that teaching controlled strategy-use aids transfer (Graham and Harris, 1989; Sawyer *et al.*, 1992; Rojas-Drummond *et al.*, 2001; Fuchs *et al.*, 2003a).

Teaching self-regulation through articulation

Meichenbaum and Cameron (1973) used verbalisation of task instructions, cues, prompts and responses for self-guidance. This was first modelled by the therapist. Next, the participant spoke the instructions out loud, then whispered them and finally repeated them covertly. They found improvement on a variety of cognitive and symptom measures which remained at follow-up.

An alternative way in which we may be able to encourage participants to regulate behaviour in an articulated way is by changing the training situation so that the trainee takes on the role of the trainer. By requiring the trainee to give the task instructions and to evaluate performance, the role of metacognitive regulation is again highlighted. The CRT model described by Wykes *et al.* (1999) contains these elements and some manuals allude to the use of the trainee/trainer role reversal (Revheim *et al.*, 2001) but this is not systematic.

Improving motivation

Numerous authors have highlighted the importance of a sense of purpose in the information to be learnt and in situations in which knowledge and skills can and should be transferred (Campione *et al.*, 1995; Holyoak and Thagard, 1997). To this end, participants should be engaged in goal-related activities which depend upon effective problem solving, and the knowledge and skills acquired should be seen as a means to accomplish further goals, rather than for their own sake. Therefore, goal setting is also important, providing personal meaningfulness to the training and motivating someone to continue effortfully to engage in treatment (Cervone, 1993).

A sense of self-efficacy is also important in sustaining motivation (Schunk, 1986, 1996; Zimmerman, 1995) and so participants should have frequent experiences of success which are positively reinforced. Finally, metacognitive self-regulation of the participant's own motivation and the factors which may influence it should be consistently encouraged.

Creating a learning environment to promote transfer

A powerful learning environment in CRT programmes for people with schizophrenia should provide the following elements.

1   Support the development of *broad schemas*, particularly those which support problem solving, by the use of learning in *multiple modalities* and with *multiple exemplars* which highlight aspects of deep rather than superficial structure of problems.
2   Support *constructive, reflective learning* and encourage participants to *articulate and regulate their cognitive and motivational processes* during learning and problem solving, to promote the use of metacognitive processing and knowledge.
3   Use *explicit instruction* to teach the principles of metacognition, transfer and ways in which deep structure can be extracted.
4   Teach *analogical reasoning skills*, or the ability to recognise similarity between tasks (particularly in terms of deep structure), and to apply familiar solutions to new problems.
5   Encourage the *regulation and use of a broad range of strategies*.
6   Provide and encourage the use of *sociocultural and material supports for*

learning and problem solving (e.g. interaction and collaboration, written information).

7　Use *personally meaningful problems* which have similarities with tasks encountered in activities of daily living.

8　Establish personally meaningful goals for therapy and then provide positive reinforcement and experiences of success to increase motivation.

Moving from models to therapy

Our model of the relationship between cognition and functioning outcome, and the means by which cognition can be effectively changed to enhance everyday functioning emphasises the importance of controlled processing, particularly executive function and metacognition, and the transfer of cognitive skills from one domain to another. We advocate direct instruction of these reflective skills, and in this way our model differs from others (such as Spaulding's recent model) which advocate more 'bottom-up' approaches to modifying cognition. We suggest that practice alone is insufficient to generate meaningful cognitive changes and that we should focus on the use of instruction to promote strategy use rather than increased speed of processing.

Others have attempted to intervene at different points and have provided support for low level cognitive processes, such as attention (in the case of McGurk and Mueser) or for higher level thinking, such as decision making (in the case of Velligan's Cognitive Adaptation Training). Our model suggests a more hopeful outcome and aims to give participants the skills to be able to respond flexibly to new environments and demands according to their own choices and decisions.

Chapter 9

The content and process of therapy

According to our model of cognitive change and the relationship between cognition and functional outcome, the primary goals of CRT should be:

- to increase the capacity and efficiency of cognitive functions
- to teach broad, transferable cognitive schemas to guide action
- to improve metacognition
- to increase motivation.

CRT should be carried out in an environment that promotes transfer, and participants should be encouraged to use environmental help and support.

Our own programme of CRT aims to achieve these goals using theoretically driven and empirically sound principles and training techniques. We adopt a multifaceted approach and a variety of cognitive and non-cognitive factors are taken into consideration. We propose that it should be based upon: (a) a model of healthy cognitive processing and a clear understanding of the cognitive strengths and difficulties associated with schizophrenia (outlined in Chapters 2 and 3); (b) a model of the relationship between cognitive function and everyday behaviour (outlined in Chapter 8); (c) theoretically and empirically driven methods of improving cognitive function (outlined in this chapter); (d) an understanding of the impact of additional environmental, personal and interpersonal factors on cognitive and functional change.

We are clear not only about the particular training approach that should be adopted for CRT, but also about what should not happen. There is clear evidence from studies in the field of education that barriers to the transfer of skills can be established through the instructional method adopted. For instance, time must be allocated to exploring 'knowledge and strategies both richly and deeply' (Durkin, 1978) and that merely 'mentioning' is not the same as teaching. This is from a paper that is more than 20 years old, but nearly 100 years ago Dewey (1910) described some schooling as covering the ground rather than nurturing the mind. 'Mentioning' may also deter domain specific learning by highlighting less central concepts. Given the propensity of people with schizophrenia to give equal weight to many different features of a task, it is highly likely that this would be a deterrent to adequate learning.

It has also been shown that presenting a cognitive strategy as if it were a precise series of steps to be executed in a ritualistically practised manner so that it becomes automatic may strengthen some skills but be 'fatal to reflective power' (Dewey, 1910: 51). Our theoretical model relies on the engagement of metacognitive processes in order for far transfer to be achieved. So for strategy instruction to contribute to transfer, the learner must: (a) be shown the value of effortful processing; (b) be encouraged to modify and personalise the general heuristic; (c) be provided with opportunities and incentives for such activity (Alexander and Murphy, 1999).

Finally, whilst the development of behavioural routines may increase someone's repertoire of skills, a focus on specific task-related routines will not facilitate transfer, and a huge number of routines suited to every occasion will need to be taught individually. Instead, the creation of generic schemas, which can provide the principles for the solution of broadly similar problems facilitates transfer and flexible responding (Cooper and Sweller, 1987).

So, in summary, we advocate instruction, not mentioning; the flexible use of a range of strategies and not adherence to specific strategies in a rigid manner; and the development of broad, generic schemas, and not behavioural routines which are not easily transferable between situations.

The environment

CRT begins within a structured therapeutic environment, separate from activities of daily living. This may seem counter to the principles of transfer which suggest that the likelihood of transfer is increased with a close match between the learning environment and the tasks in hand, but its use in the initial stages of therapy has a clear rationale. Furthermore, whilst the setting is not one in which activities of daily living take place, the use of ecologically valid, task-relevant and personally meaningful materials and exercises is advocated.

Our rationale has three points. First, CRT is intrinsically relatively non-emotive as it aims to target cognitive function rather than beliefs or affective states. However, a neutral and structured therapeutic environment allows the emotional valence of therapy to be kept low, to minimise distress and to reduce the cognitive load. It aims to pair the therapy with few situations in which the participant may have experienced past failure, to facilitate engagement and to limit associations with existing inefficient cognitive habits. It may be couched in terms of individual educational coaching, which may be socially normative and associated with little stigma.

In addition, CRT aims to provide the participant with a comprehensive cognitive structure to reduce stimulus overload and facilitate efficient cognitive processing. The responsibility for providing this structure at first lies with the therapist, but is gradually surrendered to the participant as his or her skills improve.

Finally, our goal is to teach people to adapt flexibly and efficiently to novel situations. Therefore, we suggest that skills should not be taught in a way which is context bound but allows for the development of a new style of thinking which is brought to bear on all aspects of the participant's life.

The therapeutic relationship

The process of CRT begins on a one-to-one basis with the participant and a therapist. There are two reasons for this. First, it provides the opportunity to establish a good therapeutic relationship. People with schizophrenia may have had difficult past experiences of treatment and relationships, and sustaining relationships may be onerous due to social cognitive impairments, co-morbid mood disorders and low self-esteem. A one-to-one relationship can reduce social demand, instil a sense of being valued and provide a forum for the therapist to offer positive feedback about healthy cognitive behaviour (thus promoting self-esteem), help correct negatively biased self-appraisals and increase motivation. There is significant evidence in support of the therapeutic relationship in promoting change within the general psychological therapy literature (e.g. Bentall *et al.*, 2003).

Second, one-to-one therapy allows the therapist continuously to assess and formulate the participant's strengths and limitations, to tailor the treatment on the basis of the formulation, and to carefully monitor and guide the participant's thinking and behaviour. These processes are crucial for successful CRT and will be described in more detail below.

The therapeutic relationship in CRT follows similar principles to those in other cognitive-behavioural therapies. A collaborative working alliance is fundamental. The therapist aims to give unconditional positive regard for the patient, to reinforce desirable behaviour and to offer empathy for the participant's difficulties. He or she should be non-judgemental in approach to the participant's strengths and difficulties and open-minded in encouraging strategies which are personally meaningful or useful for the participant, even if the therapist considers them to be unorthodox or second rate. A balance should be struck between ensuring strategies which are effective and valid, and encouraging the participant to find his or her own solution to problems.

The therapeutic relationship may differ from that within traditional CBT in some ways. The therapist may be relatively directive at first to provide high levels of structure to support cognitive functioning, although the direction is non-dogmatic and sensitive to the participant's responses. He or she should be given frequent choices, the therapy should be tailored to the participant's own goals, and the therapist should avoid a confrontational stance. The participant's own words should be used to discuss problems, and the participant's own expertise in his or her difficulties and finding ways to cope with them should be acknowledged and respected. The therapist may frequently act with little verbal explanation to minimise cognitive demands, particularly for participants whose verbal or working memory skills are impaired.

Engagement

Whilst some participants may have specifically requested to work on cognitive problems, it is sometimes the case that referrals for CRT (and other) services are made at the instigation of professionals rather than service users. Therefore, the first task of engagement is to explain the aims of CRT and to offer a clear rationale for treatment. Some but not all patients are well aware of cognitive problems they experience in everyday life and find them distressing. An open discussion regarding common cognitive problems associated with schizophrenia, other mental health or physical problems, as well as normal ageing, can help to elucidate problems, to normalise cognitive difficulties and to provide the therapist with an opportunity to respond sensitively and empathically to the participant's difficulties. This whole process can help to build rapport and to begin to educate the participant in the role of cognitive function in everyday living skills.

Engagement is often aided by the assessment procedure and a sensitive discussion of the results can help to provide external validation for the person's own experiences (see Chapter 10). This should not be used to explain the participant's range of 'deficits' but to discuss cognitive strengths and difficulties, particularly highlighting the ways in which the participant copes with cognitive problems and is able to find ways to compensate for them. This not only helps to ensure the experience is a positive one, but also provides essential information for the therapist about the participant's natural coping strategies which can be used in therapy. Information about current or past interests, hobbies or employment can be particularly helpful.

The way in which CRT is presented may differ depending on the experiences and beliefs of the participant. For some, explaining it as an educational treatment where thinking skills and knowledge are taught and practised is non-stigmatising and relevant to goals, such as going to college or into employment. Others, particularly those whose past educational experience may not have been positive, may respond better to an explanation relating to everyday activities and how the participant may increase his or her competence or enjoyment of these activities if, for example, memory or concentration were better. Many participants respond to the idea that CRT is like a 'mental gym' and that for thinking skills to remain 'in trim' regular mental exercise is important.

Goal setting

Setting goals will form one of the first parts of the engagement process for some, whilst for others (especially those referred on the recommendation of mental health professionals), the participant may not identify specific goals initially but only as his or her engagement and understanding of the role of CRT increase. For those who have specific goals at the outset, this may help to inform the assessment process, since a clear understanding of what is needed to achieve the goals and the participant's strengths and difficulties in relation to these goals is important.

Participants' goals may relate directly to cognitive functions (e.g. to improve concentration) or to non-cognitive activities which may at present be hindered by cognitive difficulties (e.g. to improve concentration sufficiently to be able to watch a complete film). Many people are motivated by going back to work or college. Goals should be concrete, specific, measurable and realistic. They should be subject to revision throughout the treatment in response to changing insight and motivation. The presence of negative symptoms or chronic low self-esteem may make the development of realistic goals particularly difficult for some. In these cases the therapist may need to adopt a motivational interview approach (Miller and Rollnick, 2002), in which the benefits and disadvantages of making changes are discussed, the participant's ambivalence to change is acknowledged and the routes by which they may achieve long-term goals are explored. For others, the therapist may need to be proactive in suggesting a range of possible goals from which the participant can then choose.

Clear goals not only provide a rationale and framework for therapy, but also ensure the participant is motivated to engage with the therapeutic process, is interested in the focus of therapy and can appreciate the rationale for therapeutic tasks.

Continuing engagement throughout treatments

The engagement process continues throughout the course of therapy and it is important to ensure that the treatment remains a positive and rewarding experience. Intrinsic to CRT is the consistent constructive feedback to the participant regarding their performance. It is pitched at a very basic level so that even the most impaired participants find it manageable, although therapists can make sessions more challenging for more able participants. These factors help to keep participants engaged. In addition, the therapist can aim to do the following:

1 Use appropriate positive reinforcement, particularly pointing out improved performance.
2 Tailor sessions to an appropriate length, depending on mood, mental

state, level of fatigue, etc., and include a variety of tasks which make varying demands in terms of the types of skills required and the level of complexity.

3   Give breaks within or even between sessions. Many participants need a substantial break (e.g. a week) mid-way in treatment. In this case, its purpose and usefulness should be explicitly discussed with the participant and flagged up as a coping strategy which may be useful in other circumstances.

4   Respond carefully to the sensitivities of the participant. For example, therapists frequently need to adjust the extent to which they are directive in sessions, as many people may feel criticised or undermined by instructions about how to undertake tasks.

5   Continually explain, draw attention to and reinforce the rationale for therapy and the relationship between cognitive skills and tasks and everyday living skills (particularly those relating to the participant's goals).

Assessment and formulation

Intervention begins with a detailed assessment and formulation in which the specific cognitive strengths and difficulties of the participant (particularly those which are required to achieve his or her goals for therapy) are identified. This process is described in detail in Chapter 10. Each formulation is highly individualised and identifies specific cognitive deficits (rather than generic difficulties, such as 'executive impairment'). The formulation is guided by the simple framework of cognitive processing outlined in Chapters 2 and 3. Hypothesis testing should be used to elucidate the specific deficits which may account for anomalies in cognitive function (described in more detail in Chapter 10). This is then used to select domains for intervention and to guide the development of coping strategies.

The learning environment

In the previous chapter we identified a number of principles to promote a powerful learning environment, which are also well established in the literature (De Corte, 2003):

1   Learning should be constructive and reflective rather than passive, although it should be clearly guided by the therapist.

2   Explicit instruction should be used to teach the principles of metacognition, transfer and ways in which deep structure can be extracted.

3   Participants should be taught to recognise similarity between tasks (particularly in terms of deep structure) using analogical encoding, and to apply familiar solutions to new problems.

4 Multiple modalities and multiple exemplars which highlight aspects of the deep structure of problems should be used to support the development of broad schemas.
5 The regulation and use of a broad range of strategies should be encouraged.
6 Sociocultural and material supports for learning, such as interaction and collaboration with other people, or the use of informational tools (e.g. maps, recipes, books, etc.) should be supported.
7 Personally meaningful goals for therapy should be agreed upon and positive reinforcement and experiences of success should be provided to increase motivation.
8 Cognitive and motivational self-regulation should be enhanced to promote metacognitive processing and knowledge, and external regulation of learning gradually withdrawn as the student begins to master his or her own learning and transfer.

To achieve the final aim, the process of therapy is continuously driven by an interactive, collaborative and supportive 'scaffolding' approach to teaching. 'Scaffolding' is a metaphor for the way in which the educator provides the necessary supports for the learner to complete a task at the limits of his or her competency, just as builders may provide scaffolding to support a building (Wood et al., 1976). The supports are removed as the learner's skills increase and the responsibility for completion of tasks is gradually transferred to the learner. Tasks are approached from a shared collaborative perspective, although the level of responsibility for the task is uneven, with the learner's position shifting from being dependent on guidance to being the leader. Through this process the learner gains new skills, in addition to independence, and learns to construct ways in which solutions to tasks can be achieved. The concept of scaffolding is closely related to Vygotsky's notion of the zone of proximal development (Vygotsky, 1962) which refers to the distance between what a child is able to do with help and what he or she can do independently. The child learns through communication and social interaction with the adult and gradually develops the ability to carry out tasks without help.

Scaffolding takes place both at the macro and the micro level. At the macro level, the whole of the therapeutic process is scaffolded so that the high levels of structure are provided at the start of therapy and gradually faded out as the participant becomes increasingly competent. At the micro level, performance on individual tasks is scaffolded.

Scaffolding at the macro level

For ease of explanation, we will explain the process of scaffolding at the macro level according to a series of stages within therapy. However, in reality these stages are not distinct, and follow a cascading course, with a great deal of overlap. Different stages frequently run concurrently and some stages continue throughout therapy. The emergence of each step follows gradually and organically from the previous step according to the participant's progress.

Initially, CRT takes place within a quiet undisturbed environment and the information used is designed and presented in a highly structured format which is constantly regulated by the therapist. The participant gradually learns to structure and regulate his or her own cognitive environment, and as he or she does so, the responsibility for the learning process is increasingly handed over to the participant and the task material becomes increasingly complex.

The first stage in therapy is that of *engagement* in the process of therapy, although throughout, the therapist aims to keep the participant engaged, encouraging and helping them to generate, monitor and revise their goals, as metacognitive knowledge (understanding their own cognitive strengths and difficulties and the relationship between cognition and functional outcome) and motivation increase.

The next phase of therapy begins with the presentation of CRT tasks. The core feature of this phase is that for each task, the *therapist provides structure and regulates performance*, sufficient to compensate for the participant's cognitive impairments, and to ensure a consistently high degree of success in task performance. At first during this phase, the therapist keeps verbal instruction and description to a minimum and teaches tasks primarily using demonstration and behavioural shaping. The participant's errors are rarely corrected and teaching relies mainly on behavioural reinforcement, errorless learning and scaffolding methods which target implicit rather than explicit memory processes.

As the therapy progresses, the therapist embarks on the third phase. Now, whilst a high level of structure and behaviour regulation continues to be provided, the therapist also begins to *teach and reinforce the use of cognitive strategies and metacognitive knowledge*, so that (regulated by the therapist) the participant can begin to provide some of the structure to tasks and compensate for their own deficits.

The teaching of cognitive strategies occurs in a number of steps. First, the strategies are presented as intrinsic to the task, carried out *overtly by the therapist*. For example, to regulate attentional processes, the therapist may point out each item in turn in a line of items (e.g. numbers) to be scanned, thus directing the attention of the participant in a systematic way. Second, the therapist gradually relinquishes responsibility for the use of the strategy and it is carried out *overtly by the participant* (e.g. the participant points to each item as it is scanned). Third (although some participants may never achieve this stage for all tasks), the responsibility for the use of the strategy is completely relinquished by the therapist and the strategy is carried out *covertly by the participant* (i.e. the pointing out of each item to be scanned happens internally, so the participant learns to regulate his attention using internal, rather than external control processes). One of the aims of this phase is for the participant and therapist to identify a small set of core strategies (e.g. four or five) which the participant finds particularly useful and meaningful, and which fully support his or her cognitive functions, particularly those which are impaired.

The fourth phase of the therapy occurs when the *participant provides structure and regulates performance* sufficiently to support cognitive function and to achieve a high degree of success on CRT tasks. Thus, it is the participant's responsibility not only to carry out a particular strategy, but also to initiate the decision to use a strategy, to generate a range of possible strategies, to choose an appropriate strategy and to monitor and potentially modify its use. In other words, the participant is now responsible for the use of metacognitive skills and metacognitive knowledge in transferring existing skills and knowledge from one domain to another.

The final stage of therapy consists of the *incorporation of the new metacognitive and cognitive skills into environments in which activities of daily living take place*. Therapists may enrol the support of other members of the multidisciplinary team who reinforce learning, and the participant continues to take an increasing role in regulating and organising his or her own behaviour and environment, incorporating the use of social and other support. The scaffolding process at this macro level is shown in Table 9.1.

Scaffolding at the micro level

Performance on specific tasks should also be scaffolded. This can be facilitated using a number of related teaching techniques:

- errorless learning
- modelling and shaping
- operant conditioning
- explicit instruction
- Socratic questioning
- multimodality practice.

Errorless learning

Errorless learning relies on the consistent presentation and use of correct material to ensure the implicit encoding of accurate information. This avoids the confusion exhibited by people with schizophrenia between correct and erroneous material in explicit memory.

The first stage of errorless learning is the breaking down of a task into its constituent components. Training then begins with the simplest components and very gradually includes additional components and the task demands

Table 9.1 The macro-level scaffolding process

Stage	Therapeutic process
Engagement	• Provide rationale • Discuss subjective cognitive problems • Feedback results of cognitive assessment • Describe CRT • Set goals • Use positive reinforcement to make it a rewarding experience • Tailor sessions • Respond to sensitivities • Develop a good therapeutic relationship
Therapist gives structure	• Fully compensate for cognitive impairments • Minimise verbal instruction • Demonstrate tasks • Use shaping and positive reinforcement • Use errorless learning • Use scaffolding • Target implicit not explicit memory • Rarely correct errors
Teaching strategies	• Therapist continues to provide structure, but participant takes on some responsibility • Teach strategies stage-wise: (a) presented as intrinsic to task; (b) carried out overtly by therapist; (c) carried out overtly by participant; (d) carried out covertly by participant • Identify set of core strategies
Participant gives structure	• Participant initiates and implements strategies • Participant controls use of metacognitive knowledge and skills
Generalisation	• Other staff reinforce cognitive skills in other areas • Participant organises own behaviour and environment • Participant uses social support

become more complex. Each component is overlearned before moving on, through repetitive and successful practice which is frequently positively reinforced. Thus, trial and error learning is completely eliminated and the participant is assured a high degree of success. A number of techniques can be used to facilitate errorless learning:

1 Simplify tasks to a level within the participant's capabilities.
2 Use directive questioning, prompting and cues to ensure the participant reaches a correct or appropriate response immediately, rather than encouraging erroneous reasoning, trial-and-error learning or guessing.

3 Ensure the participant sets off with the task at a manageable speed.
4 Ensure the participant is using sufficient cognitive strategies to compensate for impairments.
5 Reduce the amount of information the participant is to be faced with or shorten the task.
6 Provide adequate breaks to ensure the participant's concentration is not overtaxed.
7 Provide help as soon as the participant begins to struggle with a task – do not leave him or her to flounder.

Modelling and shaping

These are behavioural learning techniques whereby the teacher models desirable behaviour, gradually introducing the next stage in a process, so learning is stepwise and consistently accurate.

Operant conditioning

Accurate or efficient processing is consistently rewarded by social reinforcement and inaccurate or inefficient processing is ignored.

Explicit instruction

This is carried out in a non-dogmatic and sensitive way, incorporating input from the learner. This includes instruction of the key strategic thinking processes.

Socratic questioning

This technique is drawn from traditional CBT and consists of posing open-ended questions to draw information from the participant. Questions are framed to guide the learner to push forward the boundaries of his or her competence. This is particularly important for building metacognitive skill and broad cognitive schemas and comes later in therapy.

Multimodality practice

All strategies are subject to massed practice within a wide range of tasks, formats and modalities. Multimodal encoding facilitates the development of broad cognitive schemas (Cuevas *et al.*, 2002). The process of scaffolding at the micro level is summarised in Table 9.2.

Table 9.2 Scaffolding at the micro level

Training approach	Techniques
Errorless learning	• Simplify task • Be directive • Use manageable speed • Ensure use sufficient strategies • Provide adequate breaks • Provide help
Modelling	• Model behaviour • Use step-wise learning • Reinforce appropriate behaviour
Operant conditioning	• Provide social reinforcement for appropriate behaviour • Ignore inappropriate responses
Explicit instruction	• Be sensitive and non-dogmatic • Use input from the learner • Teach strategic processing
Socratic questioning	• Pose open-ended questions • Frame questions to guide learner
Multimodality practice	• Use a range of tasks, formats and modalities

Targeting specific cognitive functions

The sections above describe general techniques which are used to improve cognitive functioning and motivation throughout the therapy. In the following sections, we will describe ways in which the specific targets of CRT are approached. These targets are to:

• teach broad, generic, transferable cognitive schemas
• increase cognitive capacity and efficiency
• improve metacognition
• increase motivation.

The selection of specific targets for improvement (e.g. specific cognitive functions) relies entirely on the formulation which should be used as a constant reference to guide the process and content of therapy. These target processes will then be improved by increasing executive control of them. Strengths should be capitalised upon and used in the formation of strategies and coping, and difficulties which are relevant to the participant's goals form the targets for intervention. In Chapter 10, we describe ways in which the participant's difficulties are subject to continuous investigation, through observation and hypothesis testing, and through comparison with a model of healthy cognitive functioning.

In the sections below, we outline methods by which cognitive functions and motivation may be targeted. But other non-cognitive factors which influence performance should also be addressed. These might include low mood, medication side effects, unhelpful behavioural coping strategies (e.g. avoidance) and should be tackled using the normal clinical armamentarium which the therapist and clinical team has at their disposal.

Building generic cognitive schemas

The development of generic and broad schemas which are of most benefit to guide irregular actions relies upon the abstraction of principles and structure from any given situation. A number of techniques can be used to encourage people to rely on abstract rather than superficial similarities between situations:

- use diagrams
- use multimodal presentations
- use multimedia
- help the person to connect verbal explanations to visual representations
- use multiple learning contexts
- use analogical encoding.

Increasing cognitive capacity and efficiency

In Chapter 8 we suggested that executive functions may be the only cognitive functions which are directly amenable to conscious control and deliberate change. Other lower level cognitive functions are likely only to improve with practice. Therefore, the emphasis in our CRT programme is the improvement of executive functions.

Executive function is taught using the broad range of teaching techniques outlined above. The selection of appropriate executive functions is guided by the types of impairments in component cognitive processes they need to support. CRT allows the development and teaching of a broad range of cognitive strategies by which the participant can compensate for lower level deficits and regulate his or her own behaviour. The specific strategies which are adopted will depend upon:

- the cognitive strengths of the participants, with strategies relying on natural abilities and interests more likely to succeed and be utilised
- the cognitive deficits of the participant, with appropriate strategies generated to compensate for relevant deficits
- the cognitive behavioural style of the participant, so that strategies are either compatible with the style (e.g. use visual techniques for visualisers) or compensate for unhelpful styles (e.g. provide structure for people who

have a disorganised style of responding, or encourage attention to the gestalt for those who tend to focus only on details).

The strategies should be effective and personally relevant. To achieve these ends, the therapist and participant must work together in a highly collaborative manner and be creative in devising highly individualised, pragmatic and simple strategies. This may lead to strategies that are idiosyncratic or unusual, but which hold considerable personal meaning for the participant. Strategies that are too complex, impractical or are inconsistent with the participant's cognitive style, model of the world and understanding of his or own cognitive strengths and difficulties are unlikely to be effective or used consistently enough to be helpful. In many cases, strategy learning at first takes place in a number of steps:

- demonstrated by the therapist
- copied by the participant (with help and prompting from the therapist if necessary)
- used overtly by the participant following reminders from the therapist.

The ultimate goal is for strategies to be internalised by the participant and to be used spontaneously to regulate behaviour. As the participant becomes more familiar with strategy use and understanding of their cognitive strengths and difficulties increases, the development of strategies can become more collaborative and strategies may become more idiosyncratic. Common strategies include the following:

1 *Verbalisation:* of task instructions cues, prompts and strategies relating to the task in hand. Verbalised prompts are often used very repetitively (and so are continuously refreshed within the phonological loop) and may at first be carried out in conjunction with the therapist, with the participant becoming increasingly independent in providing him or herself with verbal cues. This is akin to Meichenbaum and Cameron's (1973) self-instructional training.

2 *Rehearsal:* related to the concept of verbalisation is the rehearsal of the target information.

3 *Use of imagery:* a non-verbal equivalent to rehearsal, maybe to maintain a visual image in mind of the target item. The creation of images may also be helpful in verbal comprehension or planning.

4 *Information reduction:* stimulus overload is well known to impair performance in people with schizophrenia (Nuechterlein and Dawson, 1984). Information reduction may entail the physical limiting of the amount of information to be perceived or reducing the demands of the task.

5 *Breaking the task into smaller steps:* tasks are broken down according to component parts, so that the participant only partially completes the task, or completes the task a step at a time.

6 *Chunking:* within the context of memory tasks, information reduction may entail that the information to be remembered is divided into manageable chunks to facilitate encoding.

7 *Simplifying the task:* tasks instructions or expectations can be simplified to a level appropriate for the participant. Tasks can also be simplified by making them shorter, breaking them into steps, including verbal or written prompts, and encouraging strategy use.

8 *Providing verbal or visual prompts:* these can be used to keep track of task instructions, to monitor timings or sequences within tasks, to remember information, to aid prospective memory.

9 *Categorisation:* categorising to-be-remembered information can facilitate memory.

10 *Organisation:* this can make information more manageable and aids memory. It may include strategies such as ordering information, restructuring the task, and so on. This may also include identifying patterns within information or imposing structure within information, or linking new material to existing knowledge.

Whilst some of these strategies appear to target certain cognitive processes, their use may be versatile. For example, although rehearsal may most obviously be a means of refreshing information in the phonological loop, thus providing a strategy for short-term memory, it may also be used as a self-instructional tool to direct attention. This is not an exhaustive list of strategies, and the therapist should be creative in identifying techniques that may be useful for different participants.

Improving metacognition

The therapist must explicitly teach the participant both metacognitive regulation and metacognitive knowledge. If generalisation is to be achieved, the participant must learn to put what they have learnt into some kind of mental representation such as language or diagrams (i.e. a generic schema) (Biemiller and Meichenbaum, 1998). The constant reflection upon current and past experience, comparison between learning situations to abstract the deep structure of problems and reasoning by analogy are modelled, explicitly taught and reinforced when implemented spontaneously.

Teaching metacognitive skills

A number of skills are explicitly taught to facilitate metacognitive regulation:

1 *Problem solving and strategy use:* this includes a number of steps:

   • the task is analysed and a shared understanding of the problem established

- a range of possible strategies or solutions are generated via brainstorming; each solution is evaluated and the most appropriate and effective solution is selected
- the strategy or solution is implemented
- the strategy or solution is monitored and evaluated
- it is modified or adapted if necessary, or an alternative strategy or solution is selected.
  Problem solving or strategy-use schemas incorporating these steps should ideally be developed.

2 *Materialisation:* this refers to the use of physical prompts or aids (such as diagrams, pictures, notes, lists, etc.) to guide behaviour.
3 *Verbal self-instruction.*
4 *Generalisation to non-routine behaviours:* encouraged by reflection on the way that strategic thinking can be implemented in everyday life situations. This again enables further practice of metacognitive skills.

Teaching metacognitive knowledge

Relevant metacognitive knowledge includes an understanding of the participant's own: (a) cognitive strengths and difficulties and ways in which to compensate for deficits and make use of existing strengths; (b) cognitive behavioural style, and the strengths and pitfalls associated with this response style; (c) motivational (e.g. mood) and other factors (e.g. drug or alcohol use, symptoms) which may affect his or her performance. In addition, metacognitive knowledge should include knowledge about the general demands of tasks and the role of cognitive and non-cognitive factors in influencing performance.

The teaching of metacognitive knowledge involves explicit instruction by the therapist in relation to specific tasks and the participant's skills. Participants are repeatedly asked to reflect on their own performance and on the task. The therapist begins by modelling the use of metacognitive knowledge to inform strategy use, and the participant is gradually required to take responsibility for using this knowledge to regulate his or her performance. Metacognitive knowledge is also taught through the continued use and collaborative revision of the shared formulation and education about cognition and factors influencing cognitive performance. CRT aims to achieve a number of specific aims with respect to the improvement of metacognition by the end of the initial individual phase of therapy:

1 For the participant to generate a repertoire of idiosyncratic, personally meaningful strategies that capitalise on their cognitive and behavioural strengths and compensate effectively for their cognitive difficulties. They should have a high degree of face validity for the participant and be

used flexibly to facilitate a wide range of cognitive and behavioural activities.

2 For the participant to monitor and regulate his or her own behaviour using self-talk.

3 For the participant to develop a limited understanding of their own cognitive strengths and difficulties and to use this to guide behaviour.

4 For the participant to understand a small set of principles governing cognitive function in general, for example, that encoding is facilitated by semantically organising the to-be-remembered material.

These aims are limited and specific, but the extent of the complexity of metacognitive thinking and knowledge which is encouraged depends on the relative cognitive abilities of each person.

Increasing motivation

We propose that a number of factors intrinsic to our CRT programme will have a positive impact on motivation, such as the development of a collaborative therapeutic relationship, the engagement process and use of personal goals to guide therapy. In addition, many of the teaching techniques, such as scaffolding, errorless learning and operant conditioning, automatically entail experiences of success and reward. Whilst not explicit in some of the other techniques, the therapist consistently attempts to make learning a positive, rewarding and meaningful experience for the learner. This is advantageous in promoting self-esteem, a more positive sense of self-efficacy and motivation. The ways in which the various cognitive and motivational elements important for transfer are taught, are summarised in Table 9.3.

The tasks of CRT

Whilst in the final stage of CRT we advocate using activities of everyday living to practise new cognitive and metacognitive skills, specific CRT tasks are required in the earlier stages of therapy. We recommend that these tasks should be relevant to everyday living skills and as far as possible personally meaningful for the participant. Tasks generally should comprise pencil and paper problem-solving exercises which are pitched at a basic level to make them manageable for those with high levels of cognitive impairment. It should also be possible to tailor tasks, and they should vary in difficulty, to ensure the participant is neither overwhelmed by continued high demands, nor bored. These tasks may also be presented on a computer, but the therapist (rather than the computer) should, at least at first, continue to take responsibility for:

Table 9.3 Targeting factors contributing to transfer

Target function	Techniques
Building broad cognitive schemas	• Use diagrams • Use multimodal presentations • Use multimedia • Help the person to connect verbal explanations to visual representations • Use multiple learning contexts • Use analogical encoding
Increasing cognitive capacity and efficiency (i.e. executive functions)	Develop strategies based on: • strengths • deficits • cognitive style Strategies should be: • personally relevant • pragmatic • simple • individualised Possible strategies: • verbalisation • rehearsal • imagery • information reduction • breaking into small steps • chunking • simplifying • visual/verbal prompts • categorisation • organisation
Teaching metacognitive skills	Develop metacognitive skills: • problem solving • strategy use • materialisation • verbal self-instruction • reflection
Teaching metacognitive knowledge	Teach understanding and knowledge of: • personal strengths and difficulties • compensation techniques • ways to use strengths • personal cognitive behavioural style • personal motivational factors • task demands • influence of non-cognitive factors
Increasing motivation	• develop a collaborative therapeutic relationship • use personal goals • use successful and rewarding teaching techniques

- individually tailoring the structure and progress of the therapy
- closely monitoring the strategic processes and performance of the participant
- encouraging the participant to reflect upon his or her own performance and strategic processing and to generate strategies to complete tasks more effectively.

These processes cannot be effectively carried out by a computer since it is unable to monitor a wide range of the participant's behaviours (e.g. eye movements, self-monitoring, decision processes, and so on) and it cannot be sufficiently flexible to guide behaviour, strategy generation and thinking according to the participant's strengths and difficulties in both cognitive and non-cognitive domains. For instance, unless the software is particularly sophisticated, it will not be possible for a computer to positively reward a person who has only partly completed a task; nor will it be possible to simplify the tasks or choose strategies to solve the problem. Computer programmes for cognitive rehabilitation have been designed so that the user 'discovers' the rule for the problem. We maintain that this general discovery method is inefficient in schizophrenia and will not develop the metacognitive abilities that we have emphasised. However, the material for tasks may be presented in an interesting and engaging format using computers and in a modality which is socially valued and normative.

As therapy progresses and the participant becomes increasingly skilled, tasks should become gradually more complex. Whilst tasks should be varied and progressively complex, they should also frequently be repetitive. This allows learning to be directed towards cognitive strategies rather than towards grasping numerous new task instructions. It also gives participants the opportunity to observe their own improved performance over time and to experiment with and observe the results of using different strategies for similar tasks. Tasks should involve a wide range of cognitive skills in verbal, non-verbal and social domains, which are varied to maintain interest, and should be as diverse as possible in their design, modality and content. The use of multiple exemplars, multimedia and variability in tasks can promote transfer of skills (Gick and Hollyoak, 1983; Mayer, 1999). These tasks should then be used to practise cognitive strategies to the extent that they become overlearnt.

For instance, 'Comprehension' is a task from the CRT programme designed by Delahunty *et al.* (2002). This presents participants with increasingly complex passages of information which are presented orally or in a written format, and asks them to learn the gist of each passage and to answer a series of questions about its content. At first, the verbal material consists of only a couple of sentences, but competent participants may be given a section from a newspaper to read. Participants are taught a variety of strategies (consistent with their own cognitive strengths and difficulties) to improve attention, memory and comprehension of the passage, such as rehearsal, breaking the passage into small sections (chunking), visualisation, creating visual prompts, and so on. They may also be taught basic language rules, for example, about how to identify the subject of the sentence, and to monitor their own level of understanding and recall. This requires teaching metacognitive processing skills as well as metacognitive knowledge relating both to the participant's own verbal and memory skills and the ways in which these can be supported, and to the nature of written material and ways in which information can be extracted from it and remembered. The various elements to this task and its training are summarised in Figure 9.1.

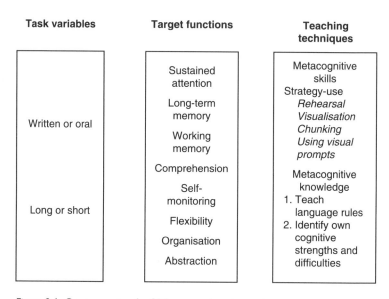

Figure 9.1 Components of a CRT comprehension task

Frequency and length of CRT sessions

Since CRT aims to create new schemas that can be used in a variety of contexts, it is recommended that CRT sessions during the one-to-one classroom phase be conducted on a frequent basis. Whilst there is no research evidence relating to this point, our own experience suggests that whilst most participants do not manage to attend on more than four days per week, those who attend for less than three days per week gain significantly less benefit from CRT. With extended gaps between sessions, participants forget what they did last session, which not only hinders the learning process, but also leads to a loss of motivation as improvements are not maintained. With respect to the length of sessions, this must be guided to a large extent by the attentional capacity and motivation of the participant (which can vary on a day-to-day basis), as well as available resources. However, in our experience after one or two weeks of CRT in which the attention span is gradually shaped up, most participants are able to attend for an hour on most days.

CRT programmes in the literature have varied in length from less than an hour to several months. The optimal length of treatment will obviously depend in a large part on the goals of therapy. In our view, in order to create lasting changes which are likely to impact everyday living skills in a clinically significant way, this initial learning phase in CRT needs to be delivered on an intensive basis for several months.

Generalising CRT skills

When the initial one-to-one training phase has been delivered, CRT begins to be implemented within an everyday setting. This may be a good point at which to involve other mental health professionals within a multidisciplinary team who can be taught about: (a) the participant's cognitive and motivational strengths and difficulties; (b) the participant's individualised set of strategies identified within the classroom training; (c) the ways in which these strategies can be used and reinforced in a variety of rehabilitation and everyday living settings. Ideally, a CRT milieu would provide consistent support for the use of metacognitive skills and knowledge to help transfer existing knowledge and skills to new situations, but the less intensive involvement of a multidisciplinary team can facilitate the use of CRT principles in a wide range of domains and modalities which is likely to lead to significantly better learning and transfer (Mayer, 1999).

In addition to this general reinforcement of CRT principles, at this stage, the participant may need continued dedicated CRT sessions which seek to teach the participant to use his or her new skills and knowledge in a variety of everyday settings. Whilst individual work may continue to be optimal, since an individualised set of strategies should by now have been developed, group work may also be possible.

This phase should be highly goal oriented and metacognitive strategy use should be taught and repeatedly reinforced in everyday living settings. The change in environment may lead to considerable deskilling for the participant. Therefore, the earlier stages of therapy may need to be repeated in a variety of new contexts. At this stage it may be appropriate to modify or increase the strategies available to the participant. For example, the strategy of asking for help and support from others can be highly adaptive in an everyday living setting.

Ideally, the principles of CRT will continue to be used in all rehabilitation programmes and to be reinforced by staff involved in the participant's care, but where this is not possible specific booster sessions to maintain the use of metacognitive strategies are likely to be vital to ensure their use becomes habitual. CRT should perhaps be seen as a learning process which takes place throughout life, as for all of us, we continue to learn and develop new skills.

Ending CRT

The ending of any one-to-one therapy can be prepared for in a number of ways. These are not specific to CRT:

1 How long the therapy will last is explained at the beginning of therapy.
2 Frequent reminders should be given about how many sessions are remaining. It may be useful to mark off the sessions on a calendar.
3 Participants' feelings about ending therapy (such as disappointment, sadness, or a sense of loss or rejection) should be explicitly acknowledged, normalised and addressed.
4 If the generalisation aspect of CRT is to be continued by other professionals, the one-to-one therapist may offer a series of gradually less frequent follow-up sessions.

Therapist characteristics and supervision

Whilst there may be no set CRT tasks (although various groups have developed CRT manuals), the therapist must have a good (if relatively simple) understanding of:

- cognitive deficits associated with schizophrenia
- theoretical models of cognitive systems (e.g. working memory, attention, executive function) which are impaired in people with schizophrenia
- a model of the relationship between cognition and everyday functioning schizophrenia.

Furthermore, the therapist should be able to use these models to guide his or her CRT. CRT should never be reduced to the practice of a range of cognitive tasks to improve accuracy.

Ideally, CRT therapists should receive regular supervision from a clinician who has a good understanding of cognitive function in schizophrenia and the principles of CRT and cognitive assessment. Some of the issues that may be useful to cover in supervision include the following:

1 The continued assessment and formulation of cognitive strengths and difficulties. After the initial assessment, this may particularly focus upon:

- identifying problem areas of performance
- generating hypotheses concerning the underlying cognitive deficits
- testing and revising the hypotheses.

2 Tailoring tasks and sessions to suit the level of the individual participant.
3 Overcoming or compensating for particular difficulties for the participant.
4 Administering tasks smoothly and effectively.

5 Engagement issues.
6 The therapeutic relationship (e.g. boundaries issues; ruptures in the relationship, ending therapy).

Why choose our CRT programme?

In developing our programme we have drawn upon the evidence relating not only to schizophrenia and changing cognitive function, but also to that of the general psychological therapy literature. It is unique in specifying the relevance of functional outcome and building on a model of the relationship between cognition and everyday behaviour.

The CRT described here is goal oriented. This means it differs from other programmes that only target cognition. The outcome of our therapy includes improvements in overall cognitive performance, but these are expected to affect functional change and are generally the primary goals.

We emphasise improving effective metacognition and the formation of generic broad schemas rather than accurate performance, so we do not expect participants to achieve particular levels of performance before moving on to other cognitive tasks. This also makes CRT different from many programmes where accurate performance determines the rate of progress. This is particularly true in current computerised therapy programmes. In addition, our individualised programme can take into account cognitive behavioural style which is also likely to enable transfer to real-life tasks since this is a natural way of responding. The inclusion of material on social cognition within the programme will also transfer to real-life tasks by building broad schemas within the social domain.

Chapter 10

Assessment and formulation

Assessment and formulation are fundamental ingredients in carrying out any psychological therapy. Whilst CRT researchers have used a broadly similar assessment process, mainly covering cognitive function, social or other functional outcome and symptoms, the formulation process has been neglected. A detailed, individualised and theoretically driven formulation is vital if we are to deliver sophisticated, individually tailored and theoretically sound treatment which will be effective in improving both cognition and functional outcome.

The content of the assessment should also vary according to the therapeutic context, the characteristics and goals of the participant, the resources available and the demands of the service setting.

In this section on practical considerations for carrying out CRT, we discuss: (a) the rationale and uses of assessment in CRT; (b) important scientific, clinical and pragmatic considerations to be taken into account when compiling an assessment battery; (c) the core and discretionary content of a CRT assessment, with reference to our model of cognitive and functional change outlined in Chapter 8; (d) the way in which the results of the assessment can be used to create a detailed and informative formulation to guide therapy.

The rationale for assessment in CRT

The reasons for assessment are multifaceted and can depend upon the context of the therapy, but in CRT the main ones are:

- assessing the person's suitability for CRT
- formulation
- engagement
- monitoring and evaluating change.

The rationale will drive the selection of appropriate assessments.

Assessing suitability for CRT

Whilst it may be possible to improve cognitive function even in those whose cognitive function is relatively intact, CRT has been designed and evaluated for people whose cognitive function is impaired or markedly inefficient. It is most applicable for those whose cognitive deficits have a detrimental impact on their everyday functioning or their ability to make use of rehabilitation or treatment programmes. Therefore, the first goal of assessment is to establish whether cognitive impairment plays a role in the person's real-world difficulties.

At the other end of the spectrum, a lower limit of cognitive function below which CRT does not appear to be beneficial has not been established to date. In fact, there is evidence from a number of studies (e.g. Bell *et al.*, 2001a; Reeder *et al.*, 2004) which suggests that even those with very severe cognitive impairments can make improvements. Despite this, studies of the efficacy or effectiveness of CRT have presumably not included those people for whom cognitive function is so limited that they are unable to complete the assessment process. There are currently a number of indications which need consideration before embarking on standard CRT:

1   *Acquired brain injury.* It is well established that people with schizophrenia may suffer from brain abnormalities, but CRT trials to date have generally excluded people with acquired brain injuries, not attributable to the schizophrenic disease process. There is a large literature regarding cognitive rehabilitation for people with acquired brain injury, and the models and techniques for such treatment differ from those for people with schizophrenia. Therefore, standard CRT is unlikely to be applicable to people with acquired brain injuries in addition to schizophrenia.

2   *Significant substance abuse.* Substance abuse is common in people with schizophrenia, but CRT is not appropriate for people with a diagnosable problem of drug or alcohol abuse. Substance abuse may result in additional brain damage, but most importantly, the detrimental short-term impact of substance use on cognitive function (for example, attention or memory) and motivation is likely to significantly limit the benefit of CRT. Therefore, it is recommended that any substance abuse problem is tackled before beginning any cognitive remediation programme.

3   *Florid psychotic symptoms.* Cognitive function frequently worsens during a psychotic episode and people are often distracted by internal phenomena such as auditory hallucinations. The presence of even high levels of current psychotic phenomena does not appear to preclude someone from benefiting from CRT and for some people CRT can lead to a reduction in positive symptoms (Wykes *et al.*, 1999). However, people who are

currently floridly psychotic or continuously distracted or highly distressed by psychotic phenomena are unlikely to respond well to the additional stimulation of CRT.

4   *Lack of motivation.* The assessment of motivation and insight into cognitive difficulties may be important to establish the level of potential engagement in therapy. Whilst engaging the client forms part of the therapeutic process and engagement may increase as therapy progresses, very poor motivation to change or a complete lack of understanding and acceptance of the presence of cognitive difficulties is likely to limit the extent to which the participant can be meaningfully engaged. Our current clinical evidence suggests that few people cannot be initially engaged in treatment (see case studies, Chapter 11), although the process of therapy may need adaptation.

Formulation

The aims of CRT are threefold:

- to improve cognitive processing skills
- to improve metacognitive abilities to facilitate transfer of cognitive processing skills and knowledge to novel or non-routine activities of daily living
- to improve motivation to change, by improving self-esteem and self-efficacy and by clarifying the rationale for making cognitive changes to achieve personally valued goals.

These aims rely on a detailed individual formulation of the cognitive strengths and difficulties to enable the therapy: (a) to directly target cognitive difficulties; (b) to develop metacognitive and cognitive skills in domains of cognitive strength; (c) to provide the participant with an accurate understanding of his or her own cognitive strengths and difficulties which can be used to guide behaviour and responses to new tasks; (d) to reinforce areas of cognitive strength to improve self-esteem and self-efficacy.

Engagement

A skilful assessment can provide an opportunity for the assessor to engage the participant in the therapeutic process, exploring and feeding back the participant's cognitive strengths and difficulties and their perception of and insight into their difficulties, as well as educating them about the role of cognition and the ways in which impairments can contribute to everyday difficulties. People with schizophrenia are often painfully aware of their cognitive difficulties, and a frank and empathic discussion about these can help to normalise someone's difficulties and to provide an opportunity to acknowledge difficulties which are relatively common and not associated with high levels of stigma.

Many people can find some neuropsychological assessments enjoyable and this can provide the opportunity for the assessor and participant to begin to develop a healthy rapport. It may be helpful to frame the assessments as brainteasers or puzzles to identify strengths and difficulties in thinking skills rather than 'tests'.

In the final stages of the assessment process, the assessor presents the findings of the assessment in a sensitive and non-confrontational manner, highlighting strengths and framing difficulties so that they are seen as neither catastrophic nor stigmatising for the participant. The assessor then begins to formulate the strengths and difficulties with the participant in a collaborative and empathic way, providing a clear rationale for the following course of therapy and identifying and shaping personal goals.

Monitoring and evaluating change

An initial assessment is vital if therapeutic progress is to be monitored. The monitoring and evaluation of change may be carried out for a variety of reasons, which may have an impact on the type of assessment conducted. To date, CRT programmes have frequently been monitored for research purposes. This may be within a formal research context, for example, a randomised controlled trial, or as part of a clinical audit or research programme designed to support the development of clinical services. Given the current equivocal evidence for the efficacy and effectiveness of types of CRT, formal evidence of therapeutic change may be required by service managers to encourage investment in new clinical services.

The monitoring and evaluation of change for clinical purposes is in keeping with the scientist-practitioner model adopted by many mental health professions. It enables the clinician: (a) to modify the therapy or practice during treatment according to progress already made or persisting areas of need; (b) continuously to appraise and update the formulation which guides the therapy; (c) to assess whether the participant's goals have been achieved and to plan for future services or treatment on the basis of remaining areas of need; (d) to provide accurate feedback to the participant regarding therapeutic change, as well as strengths and difficulties.

A summary of the rationale is shown in Table 10.1. If CRT is to be useful in services, the purpose of the assessment should be considered in some detail when selecting appropriate measures. This process may change as we come to know more about the characteristics which make someone suitable for CRT as research studies report their findings.

Table 10.1 Rationale for assessment

Suitability for CRT	Formulation	Engagement	Monitoring and evaluating change
Brain injury?	Cognitive processing skills	Exploring cognitive strengths and difficulties	Evaluating efficacy in evidence-based approaches to treatment
Substance misuse?	Metacognitive abilities	Investigating insight into difficulties	Modifying therapy during treatment
Symptoms?	Motivation to change	Education–cognition can contribute to everyday difficulties	Appraise and update the formulation
Motivation	Personally valued goals		Assess whether goals achieved
			Feedback to the participant

Compiling an assessment package

Broadly, an assessment for CRT will be guided by the model of the relationship between cognition and functional outcome (see Chapter 8). The extent to which factors such as motivation that contribute to or influence cognitive processing, functional outcome or the transfer of skill, are assessed will vary widely and will depend on: (a) the purpose of the assessment and the goals of the therapy; (b) the resources available; (c) the characteristics of the participant. There is no ideal assessment battery and these three factors will result in a highly individualised assessment process which takes into account a combination of pragmatic, scientific and clinical considerations. Whilst standardised tests should form the mainstay of the assessment, non-standardised assessments (which utilise clinical judgement) may also be used and will target a range of cognitive and non-cognitive domains. Comparison with normative samples should be made to establish the relative level of functioning and the assessment should be consistent with the goals of the therapy.

Purpose of the assessment and the goals of therapy

In general, *for research purposes*, it is important to include highly standardised and well-established assessments which are frequently cited in the literature, to ensure findings are reliable and valid, to allow for comparability with other findings and to make them easily interpretable by the reader. However, the construct validity of many such tests (e.g. the Wisconsin Card Sorting Test) is often conceptually unclear and thus may be of limited use clinically and for understanding some of the underlying mechanisms of change. Thus, whilst it may be necessary at present to include some traditional, less transparent assessments, the use of novel or little known tests which are more specific in their target functions should be encouraged.

The monitoring and evaluation of change *for clinical purposes* potentially has a wider scope as it is not necessarily intended for a wider audience. It may still be advisable to include standardised and well-established tests to ensure the measures are sound and objective, in addition to more idiosyncratic measures or the clinician's judgement.

The purpose of the research or clinical assessment will then guide the inclusion of particular tests. In the case of research, the particular hypotheses to be addressed should be the primary influence in selecting measures, whilst for clinical purposes, the assessment may account for the participant's and clinician's goals for change. A minimum requirement should be the collation of sufficient data for the therapist to generate a formulation of the strengths and difficulties to be addressed to guide therapy.

Resources available

Relevant resources required for assessment include time, personnel (particularly their area of expertise), equipment and materials, and space. The assessment should be consistent with the model and purpose of therapy, but beyond this should be tailored to accommodate and make full use of the resources available. For example, social functioning may be equally well assessed by psychologists, nurses, occupational therapists, or social workers, who may each use a slightly different model or means of assessment. The use of a multidisciplinary approach may not only provide an effective means of using available resources but can also give a rich source of data from multiple perspectives. It also has the advantage of facilitating communication between professionals and the development of a consistent multidisciplinary approach to patient care.

Characteristics of the participant

The following personal characteristics should be taken into account in selecting tests for inclusion in an assessment battery:

1 *Attention span*, which may limit the use of particular lengthy tests, or the length of time which can be spent on assessments on any single occasion.
2 *Cognitive strengths and difficulties*, which may result in *floor or ceiling effects*, or preclude the use of tests with more complex task instructions.
3 *Literacy, numeracy or colour blindness.*
4 *Ethnicity*, which may result in differences in culturally specific knowledge.
5 *Language*, since many verbal tasks are required to be carried out in the first language.

6 *Responsiveness to feedback*, which may preclude tests in which poor performance is clearly aversive for more sensitive participants.
7 *Current psychotic symptoms*, which may lead to (a) distractibility, (b) distress, or (c) idiosyncratic or distressing interpretations of the test or tester.
8 *Mood*, particularly depression, anxiety or mania, which can lead to additional transient cognitive deficits.
9 *Disorganised symptoms*, particularly thought disorder, which may hinder the ability to maintain focus and communicate.
10 *Motivation* to undertake the tasks.

In addition, participants who are currently within a clear psychotic episode are likely to demonstrate additional transient cognitive impairments which are not stable characteristics of the disorder. Therefore, whilst the presence of some psychotic symptoms does not preclude carrying out a cognitive assessment, frank psychosis makes assessment inadvisable.

The cognitive strengths and difficulties of a participant will also influence the choice of cognitive domains which may be subject to more or less rigorous investigation. For example, on discovering that a person has executive impairments, the clinician may decide to explore this area in more depth, attempting to operationalise the specific executive impairments. However, for someone who scores within the normal range on a global test of long-term memory, a more detailed examination of memory function may be forgone.

Formal assessments

In selecting formal or standardised assessments, a number of test characteristics should be taken into account:

1 *Reliability*: this refers to the repeatability or consistency of measurement. A variety of forms of reliability exist, but of particular importance in this context are inter-rater reliability (the consistency of results between assessors) and test-retest reliability (the consistency of results between repeated test administrations). Cognitive tests are frequently subject to problems in repeatability as the participant brings previous learning on the same test to subsequent trials. The use of parallel forms can avoid this problem. Data relating to the reliability of a particular test is frequently presented in the user's manual.
2 *Validity*: this refers to the extent to which the measurement is an accurate reflection of the construct being measured. Reliability is a necessary but not sufficient condition for validity. Again, there are a variety of types of validity, but particularly important is construct validity, or the extent to which the measurement accurately reflects a particular construct or cognitive process. High construct validity is required for an accurate

assessment of a particular construct and data relating to this is frequently reported in the user's manual.

3 *Ecological validity*: this is related to the more formal concept of 'external validity' and refers to the extent to which findings can be generalised to the 'real world'. In establishing a controlled test environment which is relatively impervious to contaminating factors, cognitive tests frequently suffer from being far removed from activities of daily living.

4 *Sensitivity to change*: tests should be sufficiently sensitive to levels of performance to be able to detect clinically relevant changes. Whilst offering a useful characterisation of the level of performance relative to standardisation samples, some tests are too global to identify specific changes which are important in predicting concomitant changes. For example, some tests have very narrow limits to their measurement, e.g. a range of 1 to 3. Subtle changes are therefore unlikely to be identified. Alternatively, assessors should be aware of over-interpreting relatively insignificant changes which are numerically large. The standard error of a test provides a measure of the extent to which fluctuations in performance can be accounted for by measurement error as opposed to actual change.

5 *Availability of normative comparison data*: to assess the relative level of performance, comparisons with standardised samples are required. Performance that falls more than two standard deviations below the normative mean is generally considered impaired. Since performance on cognitive tasks is frequently dependent on age, gender, level of education or pre-morbid or current IQ, norms which take into account these characteristics are often available. These are important in ruling out the possibility that apparent impairments are due to real deficits rather than to contaminating factors (e.g. poor education).

6 *Acceptability*: this may depend to some extent on the motivations and sensitivities of the participant. For example, many people with schizophrenia find completing the Wisconsin Card Sorting Test aversive, due to repeated feedback from the tester that their performance is wrong.

7 *Ease of administration and interpretation*: accurate administration, scoring and interpretation are vital to gain a meaningful and precise estimate of a person's performance. Some tests are notoriously difficult in this respect and should be avoided unless the tester is sure of his or her competence and understanding.

In relation to this final point, the qualifications, training and supervision of the assessor should be taken into account to ensure accurate administration, scoring and interpretation of formalised assessments. With respect to cognitive tests, these frequently specify that they should be undertaken by specially trained professionals, such as clinical psychologists. Whilst such strict criteria are not frequently necessary, adequate training and supervision of assessors are essential. Similarly, the assessment of symptoms or social functioning often requires considerable clinical skills of the assessor and a lack of relevant experience may lead to inaccurate and potentially damaging results. The importance of accurate, thoughtful and careful assessment cannot be underestimated, particularly given the tendency for test results to repeatedly appear in case notes and to have far-reaching consequences in terms of service planning.

The assessment process

In our model we have made it clear that a number of key areas need to be assessed to develop treatment protocols. These include cognitive processing, functional outcomes and, most importantly, transfer of cognitive skills across different domains and tasks.

Assessing cognitive processing

A brief assessment should be made of all the main cognitive systems:

- brief sensory store
- working memory slave systems
- episodic buffer
- long-term memory
- central executive.

In addition, an assessment of the person's current and pre-morbid intellectual functioning should be made to establish relative strengths and difficulties and to identify the level of likely decline. In combination with information about the person's educational and occupational history, this may identify areas of existing strength which may be currently underutilised. Domains of current interest or leisure activity may also help to identify islands of ability or cognitive strength.

Whilst it is important to have an understanding of both strengths and difficulties, a more thorough understanding of difficulties is required, since these are likely to impede progress, and therapy will explore ways to improve or compensate for them. Thus, for each cognitive domain, an initial global assessment of the level of function can be made, and only for those domains in which impairment is identified should a more in-depth assessment of the component processes be conducted. For all domains, an assessment of both verbal and non-verbal domains is helpful. A clear understanding of executive processes, including attentional control (e.g. sustained attention, distractibility) is particularly important since these form the main targets for intervention. Assessments of various aspects of social cognition hypothesised to have an impact on functional outcome for that participant may also be included.

An alternative means of assessment to the traditional neuropsychological model is through the observation of the participant's performance on specific cognitive or functional tasks, which can take place before and particularly during the CRT programme. Such observation forms part of the ongoing process of assessment and formulation and is particularly useful for identifying specific component cognitive processes which may be impaired or particularly strong. Observation may primarily be made by the therapist as part of the therapeutic process, but also by the participants themselves and other informants. An informal discussion of the participant's own experience of their cognitive difficulties can also be a good means of engaging the person in therapy.

Common themes in the information from the participant and other informants can be extracted and used to identify: (a) cognitive processes which appear to be most influential in resulting functional problems; (b) current cognitive or behavioural coping strategies. These strategies are important since they are likely to be longstanding, rely on the natural capabilities and cognitive style of the participant and to have been consistently reinforced by the environment.

The therapist's observations should be used as part of a process of identifying and testing hypotheses regarding the specific impairments a participant shows. This process is summarised in Table 10.2. The observations of informants or the participant outside the session can be used as corroborating evidence.

First, a cognitive task on which the participant has difficulties is identified. The nature of the difficulties is precisely specified and the therapist generates hypotheses about underlying cognitive deficits. For example, problems in repeating a single auditorily presented sentence may be hypothesised to result from: (a) distractibility, leading to the encoding of inaccurate or weak memory traces, or to inefficient retrieval; (b) comprehension deficits; (c) lack of rehearsal or maintenance so that the memory trace suffered significant decay; or (d) poor retrieval strategies, so the participant is unable to recall the

Table 10.2 Observational process to identify impairments in component cognitive processes

Stage 1	Identify problem
Stage 2	Specify precise nature of problem
Stage 3	Generate hypotheses about underlying cognitive impairment
Stage 4	Test hypotheses using the following evidence from: • self-report of patient • performance on other tasks • functional analysis of the problem behaviour

memory. The therapist attempts to distinguish between these hypotheses using a number of strategies:

1   Ask the participant about his or her experience of doing the task. This evidence should be treated with caution since introspection is unreliable, but participants are often able to give clues as to what they find difficult (e.g. 'I am easily put off by noises outside', or 'I didn't completely understand what you said').
2   Compare performance across tasks to identify similarities and differences which may hold some explanatory power. For example, if the participant has comprehension difficulties in a range of other circumstances (e.g. reading a magazine, understanding instructions), this might suggest that comprehension difficulties are likely to contribute in these circumstances too.
3   Carry out a systematic functional analysis of the problem, by helping the participant to compensate for each hypothesised deficit in turn, and identifying the process, which when compensated leads to improved performance. For the example given above, the following measures may be taken to compensate for each of the hypothesised deficits:

   •   *distractibility* – remove all sources of possible distraction, ensure the person is not experiencing distracting internal events (e.g. auditory hallucinations) and that the sentence is read out clearly and accurately
   •   *comprehension* – use a sentence which the participant has easily understood in other circumstances
   •   *lack of rehearsal or maintenance* – explicitly prompt the participant to devise an appropriate maintenance strategy (e.g. rehearsal, creating a visual image to which the participant continues to attend throughout the delay), check the participant has used the strategy
   •   *poor retrieval strategies* – provide a prompt in the form of the first word of the sentence or a visual clue.

A final note: deficits may not be unique and a combination of problems may account for poor performance. This will need careful and repeated hypothesis testing which should be continuously subject to reassessment and revision.

Assessing functional outcome

The domains of outcome to be assessed will depend on the purpose of the therapy and the monitoring process, as well as the participant's goals. Outcome domains typically include social functioning and activities of daily living, with respect to both level and frequency of activity; symptoms, including positive, negative and disorganised symptoms, as well as co-morbid affective symptoms; self-esteem; insight into symptoms or cognitive difficulties.

Assessments can rely on self-report or the observations of others (usually a care provider who knows the person well) and may take a number of forms:

*   questionnaires
*   interviews with the participant or an informant (structured, semi-structured or open)
*   standardised assessments where the behaviour of the person is observed under controlled and formal circumstances (e.g. the Assessment of Interpersonal Problems-Solving)
*   observation of behaviour in naturalistic settings.

Assessing transfer

We have argued that one of the goals of CRT is to encourage transfer. Transfer may be defined as the 'broad, productive, and supported use of acquired knowledge, skills and motivations in new contexts and learning tasks' (De Corte, 2003). A number of researchers have argued that learning transfer takes place in a resource-rich context and the success of transfer depends partly upon the participant's ability to make good use of these resources (Bransford and Schwartz, 1999). Hatano and Greeno (1999) have also emphasised that the use of existing knowledge and skills takes place in contexts in which the actor has access to support in the form of other people, prompts, written information and so on. Successful transfer therefore relies on the ability to use these sociocultural supports to maximise performance, rather than the ability to independently carry out actions in an isolated context. Therefore, whilst it may be argued that performance on any new task may indicate the ability to use acquired skills and knowledge in a new situation, this may actually be an artificial test of transfer since often it does not allow the participant to make use of everyday sociocultural supports. A more realistic assessment of transfer may come from more ecologically valid tests which take place in everyday supported contexts.

A good example of such a test is the Grocery Shopping Skills Test (Hamera and Brown, 2000) which assesses the ability to buy a list of specific grocery items in a supermarket using any available resources. It is considered to be a test of executive function, but in which executive skills are assessed in a real-world context.

Assessing factors which contribute to cognitive transfer

The model of the relationship between cognition and functional outcome, set out in Chapter 8, suggested that a number of factors contribute to the likelihood that existing cognitive skills and knowledge will be transferred to a new domain or novel task: cognitive processing, metacognition and motivation of the participant, as well as the environment and nature of the tasks involved. The assessment of these factors may help not only to identify areas of existing strength or difficulty but also to monitor the process of change which may allow hypotheses regarding the mechanisms by which potential changes may occur to be tested. The factors which facilitate transfer may also overlap with elements of functional outcome (e.g. symptoms, insight). An assessment of cognitive function should always form a fundamental part of an assessment, but optional additional measures may be included to assess:

- metacognition, including meta-knowledge of cognitive strengths and difficulties (i.e. insight relating to cognitive function)
- self-esteem
- self-efficacy
- depressive symptoms
- anxiety symptoms
- engagement with treatment
- therapeutic alliance
- support within the environment.

The assessment of metacognition in schizophrenia is in its very early stages within the schizophrenia literature. There are specific theory of mind (ToM) tests that can assess whether a person has an understanding of another person's point of view or belief which to some extent also measure metacognition. There are also neuropsychological tests that purport to measure metacognitive knowledge and metacognitive regulation that can be built on Koriat and Goldsmith's (1996) two-stage process (e.g. Koren *et al.*, 2004). These tests first investigate what the person knows about their performance and then whether they use this knowledge to change their behaviour. But these tests are in their infancy. We have no information on their reliability or validity. Metacognition can, however, be assessed informally throughout the process of therapy by questioning the trainee on what is currently guiding their behaviour.

So far in CRT studies metacognition has been assessed as the ability to use the skills taught in therapy to new tasks which are usually assessed in an independent context. This can be assessed before the beginning of therapy as well as during and following therapy. Transfer is indicated by the use of skills across tasks requiring the same sorts of cognitive skill. Here it is the variability of responding during tests that will provide information on what is transferred and whether transfer is erratic or non-existent. For instance, it may be that on some tests of memory the person does rehearse, encode more deeply and retrieve appropriately whereas on other tests within the same cognitive domain this does not occur. Knowledge of the necessary strategies for skill improvements in other contexts is important to note as this means that the participant needs not to be taught *how* to use them, only *when* they should be used.

The ability of the participant to transfer existing cognitive skills to new tasks can also be assessed directly. This can occur informally through the observation of the use of self-regulatory strategies or using cognitive or functional tests in which process factors are monitored. For example, following therapy which teaches flexible strategy use, transfer of this new skill can be assessed using the Hayling Sentence Completion Test. In the first part of this task, the participant is asked to complete 15 sentences as quickly as possible with a word that makes sense (e.g. 'He posted the letter without a . . . .'; 'stamp'). The second part requires the participant to inhibit the strongly primed missing word and to complete a second set of sentences with a word that doesn't make sense in the context (e.g. 'The captain wanted to stay with the sinking. . . .'; 'banana'). Responses are rated as to whether a strategy was used in their generation.

Assessing cognitive behavioural style

People vary not only according to individual strengths and weaknesses in specific cognitive processes but also according to the habitual style in which they cognitively process information (Robertson, 1985). This is frequently referred to as a person's 'cognitive (or learning) style' (Allport, 1937). A cognitive style is thought to be a relatively stable personality characteristic (Riding et al., 1993) which corresponds to dichotomous dimensions. A number of dimensions have been proposed, although there is no generally agreed or well-established set of cognitive styles (Messick, 1976). Field independence versus field dependence is probably the most well known (Witkin, 1961). This refers to a tendency to approach the environment in an analytical, as opposed to global, fashion. Other well-known styles include levelling versus sharpening, which refers to the extent to which people recall distinct memories rather than merging similar events in memory (Holzman and Gardner, 1960), impulsivity versus reflectivity (Kagan, 1965), visualising versus verbalising (Riding and Buckle, 1990) and left hemisphere versus right hemisphere, which refers to analytic versus visual cognitive processing (Sonnier, 1991).

Closely related to the concept of cognitive style is that of 'learning style' which refers specifically to characteristic modes of learning. Kolb (1984) proposed that there are four types of learners – divergers, assimilators, convergers, and accommodators – who vary in the extent to which they rely primarily on concrete experiences, reflective observation, abstract conceptualisation, or active experimentation in order to learn. Others have suggested that three learning styles relate to sensory preference and that people learn primarily according to visual, auditory or kinesthetic senses (Dunn and Dunn, 1979).

It may be argued that schizophrenia is associated with particular cognitive styles. For example, people with schizophrenia frequently identify constituent parts rather than the gestalt and can be easily distracted by detail. This may correspond to falling toward the analytic pole of the holistic-analytic dimension (Riding and Cheema, 1991). People who tend towards the holistic pole tend to view situations as a whole, while those who tend towards the analytic end of the dimension tend to view the whole as a collection of parts and focus on just a few aspects at once.

There is also likely to be considerable inter-individual variation in cognitive styles within schizophrenia samples, although there is little research in this area. Whilst the impact of cognitive styles in CRT may make an interesting and useful avenue for future research, we propose that at present formalised assessment of an individual's cognitive styles may be unnecessary for the purposes of CRT, but that it is useful to observe and informally assess the general cognitive and behavioural style by which each person undertakes a task. This 'cognitive behavioural style' should be used to formulate the patient's strengths and difficulties to inform a CRT programme and may encompass:

- cognitive or learning styles
- common behavioural manifestations of symptoms (e.g. disorganised behaviour or poverty of action)
- common behavioural manifestations of cognitive deficits (e.g. slow response initiation resulting in an overall slow response style)
- habitual coping responses (e.g. avoidance of material which is poorly understood)
- other habitual cognitive or behavioural responses (e.g. constant self-monitoring).

For example, one patient may generally approach tasks in a chaotic and impulsive manner and tend to rush his or her responses with little reflection and monitoring. Another person may show consistent difficulty in initiating responses and act in a slow but considered manner.

The two cases discussed previously and reported by Wykes (1998) showed distinct responses to CRT. One person increased his already high verbal output without close monitoring, which led to even higher output but with a high proportion of errors. The other was initially slow and over time decreased his output but monitored it more closely and so decreased the errors. These changes suggest that in each case, performance changes may reflect an exaggeration in existing cognitive behavioural styles. Inclusion of information regarding cognitive behavioural styles in the CRT formulation may be useful in the following ways:

1 To adapt the teaching style to match the cognitive or learning style (e.g. use visual prompts, instructions and strategies and imagery for participants who are 'visualisers' rather than 'verbalisers').
2 To teach and develop strategies to compensate for ways in which the cognitive behavioural style hinders cognitive processing (e.g. develop rules to create structure to tasks for participants who work in a chaotic and disorganised manner).

3   To teach and develop strategies which are consistent with existing cognitive behavioural styles and capitalise on strengths (e.g. develop detailed step-by-step instructions, rather than providing more general prompts, for people who respond better to detail rather than the global picture.

4   To inform metacognitive knowledge about the participant's cognitive strengths and difficulties.

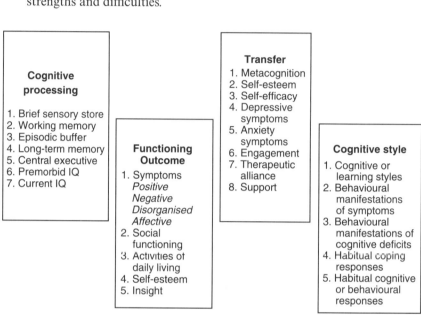

Figure 10.1 Assessment domains

Figure 10.1 shows the range of functions which could be included in the assessment process.

Formulation

The formulation is a systematic and coherent integration and interpretation of the findings of a detailed cognitive assessment and should take into account the problems identified by the participant and clinicians and the participant's goals for therapy. It should be based on the model of cognitive processing outlined in Chapter 2 and should be simple and clear enough to guide all aspects of therapy, whilst containing sufficient detail to facilitate an accurate understanding of the strengths and weaknesses of the participant. This formulation can be shared collaboratively with the patient and with the professionals involved in the person's care to inform other aspects of treatment or routine care. The therapist should also be guided by the model of the relationship between cognitive function and functional outcome (described in

Chapter 8), and broadly formulate the ways in which cognitive strengths and weaknesses as well as non-cognitive factors contribute to problems in functional outcome.

The information to be included in the formulation and a means of presenting this is shown in the formulation plan in Table 10.3. In addition to information regarding pre-morbid and current intellectual functioning, age and education level, information on previous and current employment and interests can provide useful clues regarding possible cognitive strengths and ways in which to motivate the participant. Each set of factors contributing to the formulation should then be conceptualised in terms of strengths and weaknesses, with the most marked of each particularly highlighted. This allows for areas of difficulty to be targeted in treatment, using areas of strength to support and compensate for difficulties. Areas of functioning should include:

- cognitive processing, which is assessed using neuropsychological and cognitive tests and informal observation and hypothesis testing
- cognitive behavioural style, assessed informally through observation
- non-cognitive factors influencing performance (specified in the model of cognitive change outlined in Chapter 8), including, for example, motivation, mood, self-esteem, symptoms, insight and future and goal-directed thinking
- coping and strategies that compensate for cognitive deficits, which might include behavioural strategies such as avoidance of difficult cognitive tasks, or specific cognitive strategies, such as rehearsal to improve memory.

The formulation should conclude with a problem list, which may contain both cognitive and functional problems. In the case of functional problems, the hypothesised influence of cognitive deficits should be clearly identified. The goals for the therapy should then be generated from the problem list in collaboration with the patient, but also with other clinicians.

The formulation should be constantly updated and revised throughout the assessment and therapeutic process in collaboration with the participant. Not only should it inform treatment, but it can also be used to record new and developing strengths to monitor progress and to serve as a reminder of techniques learnt, and to improve the participant's metacognitive self-knowledge.

Table 10.3 Formulation plan

CRT FORMULATION	
Name	Age (in years and months)

Premorbid abilities

Education

Current and previous employment

Current and previous interests

Cognitive function
Current estimated full-scale IQ
Current estimated verbal IQ
Current estimated performance IQ

Difficulties	Strengths
1.	1.
2.	2.
3.	3.

Cognitive behavioural style

Difficulties	Strengths
1.	1.
2.	2.
3.	3.

Non-cognitive factors

Difficulties	Strengths
1.	1.
2.	2.
3.	3.

Coping and use of compensatory strategies

Problem coping and strategies	Effective coping and strategies
1.	1.
2.	2.
3.	3.

Problems	*Goals*
1.	1.
2.	2.
3.	3.

Chapter 11

CRT in action

Case studies

In this chapter we will try to illustrate the process of CRT using case studies derived from our own clinical work. We also highlight some of the difficulties often found in therapy and the clinical solutions we have found to these difficulties over the last ten years.

In our CRT programme, each person completes a general set of assessments and then we pick up on issues that have been highlighted by this process, or by the participant and other professionals. The general principles of the assessment are given in some detail in Chapter 10, so here we will only comment on tests we have found useful. It is important to assess the cognitive difficulties and general cognitive behavioural style as well as non-cognitive factors that might influence transfer. We need to bear in mind the overall aims of the assessment:

- to engage the participant
- to produce a set of agreed difficulties
- to produce a set of goals that can be a focus for treatment
- to provide enough information to define the process of therapy.

At the end of this process we need to have a formulation of the relationships between the cognitive difficulties and the functional problems experienced by our clients, in order to inform therapy and, where possible, to share with the client.

While we would advocate doing as full an assessment as possible, in practice we have found that assessment of pre-morbid and current IQ, long-term and working memory, a range of executive functions and some attention tasks are sufficient to create the initial formulation which can be elaborated by clinical observations. The case studies described below illustrate particular issues that arise in therapy or assessment. They represent cases but are not specific cases in our practice.

Case Study 1: Donald

Background information

Donald was a 36-year-old Caucasian man, born in England, who had been diagnosed as suffering from schizophrenia at the age of 23. He was an only child. He left home for a brief period at the age of 18 when he went to college to study technical drawing. A year later, he experienced a psychotic breakdown and eventually gave up his college course. He moved back to live with his parents and was still living at home with his elderly and frail mother (his father had died three years previously) when he was referred for CRT. Donald's father had been a draughtsman and his mother a housewife during her married life, and prior to that she had been a nursery assistant. Donald was employed briefly in an office after recovering from his psychotic breakdown, but he struggled to attend daily and gave up the job after only four months. He has not been employed since.

Donald attended a day hospital four days a week. He was referred for CRT by his key worker, who felt that Donald's poor concentration and chaotic style prevented him benefiting from both the rehabilitation and recreational programmes offered by the centre.

Donald presented as a friendly, cheerful man who appeared to be frequently preoccupied with internal experiences. Apparently in response to these experiences, he often spoke or laughed quietly to himself, but this also appeared to be as though he was articulating his thoughts out loud. His speech was generally thought disordered, pressured and repetitive and it was often difficult to understand what he was saying. He was physically active, and frequently appeared restless. He rarely persisted at any one task for more than a few minutes, although his attention could be successfully redirected with some prompting.

Donald was a popular man who had a number of friends at the day hospital, although these relationships appeared to be relatively superficial. He was socially outgoing although his conversation was extremely limited due to his distractibility, and on some days Donald appeared to be particularly preoccupied and was irritable with others. At these times, he tended to isolate himself and could rarely be engaged in activities at the hospital. Donald had had five psychiatric admissions since his first contact with psychiatric services and was currently prescribed clozapine. His last psychotic episode was over a year ago.

Assessment

His initial assessment on the Wechsler Adult Intelligence Scale, version III UK version (WAIS-III-UK), and Wechsler Test of Adult Reading (WTAR) showed that there had been a decline in functioning. His performance skills were better than his verbal skills but he was generally chaotic when carrying out these tests. His performance on executive functioning tests confirmed that this was a specific problem. He was assessed on the Hayling and Brixton tests which showed that his self-monitoring was particularly poor and planning was consistently impaired on subtests within the Behavioural Assessment of the Dysexecutive Syndrome (BADS). He was poor on the AX version of the CPT. On tests of long-term memory (Doors and People Test) and working memory (Letter Number Span) his performance was in line with his current IQ, although his visual long-term memory was better than predicted.

Information on non-cognitive and other functional problems or factors which may influence performance was drawn from discussions with other professionals involved with his care, his mother and Donald himself as well as from case notes. The main non-cognitive factor that emerged from this part of the assessment was his occasional irritability and withdrawal, which seemed to be associated with low mood. His score on the BDI was within the normal range.

Formulation

Donald is a 36-year-old man who has been involved with the psychiatric services for 13 years. He has been dependent on his parents all his life and this is becoming more of a problem as his mother becomes increasingly frail. He still seems to experience some anomalous sensory experiences but the main aspect of his presentation is his high degree of disorganisation and impulsivity which is reflected in his consistently poor executive functioning with clear difficulties in response inhibition, self-monitoring, planning and sustained attention. His coping style is enthusiastic and persistent at best but can veer into impulsivity and perseveration. Similarly his willingness to ask for help can sometimes mean that he is not able to complete even manageable tasks independently as he constantly asks for reassurance. This seems to have been reinforced by his parents (now his mother). He also appears to use self-talk to carry out tasks but in everyday functioning this is sometimes too loud and appears to staff also to be related to anomalous experiences. So although he has some coping responses they are not always well regulated and can therefore be a strength or a weakness.

His memory seems relatively unimpaired compared to his other difficulties and he has particular strengths in visuo-spatial processing and memory as well as attention to detail. He is not particularly slowed in his responses.

Donald is motivated but this is sometimes affected by low mood and associated irritability. He manages these mood states by withdrawal. His problems which were primarily identified by his key worker included not being able to take part in groups due to high levels of distractibility and impulsivity, which tended to produce disruption in group activities. Donald was aware of many of these difficulties. He also had problems completing

Table 11.1 Donald's formulation

CRT formulation

Name Donald

Age (in years and months)
36 years 5 months

Pre-morbid abilities
WTAR standardised score 105

Education
School attendance good until 18 years. Few post-16 qualifications and few post-16 retakes at 18. Vocational course in technical drawing at college – not completed

Current and previous employment   Brief office job

Current and previous interests   Technical drawing, airplanes

Cognitive function
Current estimated full-scale IQ   85
Current estimated verbal IQ   75
Current estimated performance IQ   95

Difficulties	*Strengths*
1. Planning	1. Long-term memory
2. Response inhibition	2. Speed of response
3. Self-monitoring	3. Visuo-spatial processing
4. Sustained attention	

Cognitive behavioural style

Difficulties	Strengths
1. Disorganised	1. Visually able
2. Impulsive	2. Attention to detail
3. Distractible	3. Memory

Non-cognitive factors

Difficulties	Strengths
1. Occasional irritability	1. Friendliness
2. Incoherent speech	2. Happy to join in
3. Disinhibition	3. Motivated

Coping and use of compensatory strategies

Problem behavioural coping	Effective coping and strategies
1. Failing to reflect (impulsive)	1. Self-talk
2. Sometimes overly persistent	2. Asks for help
3. Constantly asking for reassurance	3. Persistent

Problems	Goals
1. Not able to take part in groups	1. Take part in three groups per week
2. Can't finish everyday tasks	2. Can finish cleaning room
3. Can't work independently	3. Can shop and cook meal for himself

everyday tasks independently due to his disorganisation, lack of planning, perseveration and tendency to ask for a lot of help.

Donald's goals included taking part in groups as well as some daily activities in his home to help his mother. To make these measurable and concrete we agreed on cleaning his room and shopping and cooking two meals per week. A summary of the formulation is given in Table 11.1.

Treatment plan

The goals of therapy were to decrease Donald's disorganisation, impulsivity and distractibility. This was achieved by targeting metacognitive skills associated with plan generation and self-monitoring. The necessary executive skills included focusing attention on the key elements of the task. These were aided by his current coping strategies of self-talk and his cognitive and behavioural strengths. Coping based on his visual skills was helpful as well as his attention to detail. Both metacognitive knowledge and metacognitive regulation were taught, as they affect independence in tasks. Metacognitive knowledge was encouraged by focusing on his self-efficacy and by discussing his tendency to rely on others, even when he was able to carry out the task. The amount of the task he carried out before asking for help was gradually increased. Then he was taught to evaluate his capabilities to complete the task and finally to check his own performance.

In the second phase of therapy, which moved into the functional domain, we began to work on his goals using the previously identified cognitive strategies. At this point it was important to work with all the people involved in his care including staff and family members. They were encouraged to use the techniques developed within therapy to provide some structure and to allow independent action. This was essential at home where his mother had provided much of his care and where he would work to achieve two of his three goals. She was encouraged to allow Donald more independence.

Case study 2: Norma

Background information

Norma was a 48-year-old Jamaican woman who came to England at the age of six with her mother to join her father, who had come over several years earlier. She had a large family but remained in touch with only one sister who visited weekly with her children. Norma lived in a 24-hour staffed group home for people with severe and enduring mental health problems. She had suffered from schizophrenia since her late teens and had never been married or lived independently. She left school at the age of 15 and then had a number of unskilled jobs, mostly as a cleaner, but these tended to be relatively shortlived.

Norma was referred for CRT by her psychiatrist, who noted that her memory was poor. She presented as a large woman who was unsteady on her feet and found it physically difficult to get around. She was extremely inactive, spent much of her afternoons asleep and rarely left the group home, although she could generally be encouraged to go on monthly leisure outings (to the seaside, for example). She participated willingly in a number of chores in the house, which she carried out in a highly routine manner. She was mostly friendly to other residents and staff but became distressed and occasionally aggressive if her routines were disrupted. She exhibited high levels of negative symptoms in the form of apathy, social withdrawal and lack of spontaneity. She spoke and acted slowly, and her speech was frequently stereotyped and perseverative. She occasionally reported hearing voices. Whilst Norma had had frequent admissions during her twenties and thirties, she had not had a psychiatric admission for at least five years. She currently received olanzapine.

Assessment

Norma's initial assessment on the WAIS-III and WTAR showed that there had been a decline in functioning. There was no significant difference between her performance and verbal skills. As she was referred for memory problems, these were tested more extensively using the Wechsler memory scale. While her long-term verbal and non-verbal memory were significantly impaired, her working memory was poor but in the normal range. She was slow to initiate responses and was slow to change to other responses but her concentration was good. She was also methodical and persistent. Her executive functioning problems were confirmed with the Verbal and Design Fluency, the Similarities subtest of the WAIS-III and Trails B. She also produced few categories (abstraction problems) and had problems set shifting on the WCST.

As staff reported that Norma took part in few activities, we assessed a baseline level of functioning by a weekly timetable of activities and went into more detail on a single day. Her activities were indeed few and these also lasted a very short time when she did take part. The majority of time was spent in bed. When Norma did carry out a task in the house it was done well, but she was not able to respond to changes in the type of task or the equipment she used. If she was faced with a change in the timing or type of task she would withdraw, become frustrated and occasionally become aggressive in response to feeling under pressure.

Although Norma had few activities she did not highlight this as a major problem. However, she was aware of memory difficulties particularly in relation to the visits by her sister. Over the course of therapy she began to identify activities that could improve her quality of life.

Formulation

Norma is a 48-year-old woman who has been involved with the psychiatric services for 29 years. She is dependent on psychiatric care in a hostel. Although she occasionally reports hearing voices, her presentation is characterised by high levels of negative symptoms, particularly poverty of action and lack of motivation. This is reflected in her performance in the cognitive assessment where although she is persistent she is slow in her actions and inflexible and difficult to engage on new tasks. She shows consistently poor executive functioning with clear difficulties in response initiation, set shifting and sustained attention. These problems make it difficult for her to adjust to changes in the environment so she regulates the environment either by only being involved in routine actions or by avoiding the situation altogether. She enjoys one-to-one relationships and uses humour in her avoidance of situations. Her long-term memory is impaired, consistent with the referral, and Norma is aware that she cannot remember things associated with her sister's life, which she finds distressing.

Norma's working memory is reasonably intact and this helps her to hold lengthy conversations. The cognitive assessments also show that her sustained attention and monitoring are unimpaired. Norma is motivated to take part in therapy and she is able to cope with an hour of therapy even from the start of treatment. Her main agreed problem is poor memory but staff also identified inactivity and lack of interests. Norma's own goal is to remember what she discusses with her sister, but with encouragement from the staff she also agreed other goals, which were developed during therapy. A summary of the formulation is given in Table 11.2.

Treatment plan

The primary goal of therapy was to improve her long-term memory. This was achieved by increasing metacognitive knowledge about effective ways to improve her memory. This included learning new strategies and how to apply them in a variety of situations, particularly in relation to her sister (metacognitive regulation). She also had problems with slow responding, flexibility and initiation of responses which affected her functioning in the home. In therapy, increases in these executive skills were achieved through reflection on the tasks themselves, particularly analogical encoding to improve abstraction.

A variety of cognitive strategies were taught but with clear structure for their use in tasks, for instance, by teaching her to evaluate the task requirements and the ways in which strategies could be used to meet these. This built on Norma's methodical approach to tasks.

It is not clear what underlay Norma's avoidance. During therapy, Norma's responses to aspects of the situation and the types of task as well as her evaluation of her own her self-efficacy were noted. As therapy was focused on

Table 11.2 Norma's formulation

CRT formulation

Name Norma   *Age (in years and months)*
                                          48 years 4 months

Pre-morbid abilities
WTAR standardised score 90

Education Left school at 15 with no qualifications

Current and previous employment Brief cleaning jobs in offices and houses

Current and previous interests Watching TV and sociable. Likes painting

Cognitive function
Current estimated full-scale IQ   78
Current estimated verbal IQ   79
Current estimated performance IQ   77

Difficulties	Strengths
1. Set shifting	1. Working memory
2. Abstraction	2. Sustained attention
3. Long-term memory	3. Monitoring
4. Response initiation	

Cognitive behavioural style

Difficulties	Strengths
1. Slow	1. Methodical
2. Rigid	2. Persistent
3. Lack of initiation	

Non-cognitive factors

Difficulties	Strengths
1. Occasional aggression	1. Humour
2. Disinterest	2. Friendliness
3. Social withdrawal	3. Enjoys one-to-one relationship

Coping and use of compensatory strategies

Problem behavioural coping	Effective coping and strategies
1. Avoidance	1. Humour
	2. Use of routine

Problems	Goals
1. Inactivity	1. To carry out a brief activity every day
2. Few interests	2. To go shopping once per week
3. Poor memory	3. To remember what she discussed with her sister and topics to discuss

her skills and beliefs it was necessary to target Norma's ability to tolerate some uncertainty about the outcome of tasks. This was helped through her use of humour.

In the second phase of therapy, which moved into the functional domain, we worked on her first goal of remembering information about her sister, using her new cognitive strategies. Both staff and her sister facilitated the transfer of strategies to new situations by prompting her and summarising what she had done. Staff also helped Norma to plan and monitor activities.

Case study 3: Stephen

Background information

Stephen was an 18-year-old Caucasian man whose first contact with psychiatric services was a year prior to referral to CRT. Following the onset of his psychosis, he reported significant deterioration in his memory and attention and had consequently dropped out of college where he was studying for exams usually taken at aged 16 in maths and English. Stephen lived in a long-stay rehabilitation unit at the time of referral for CRT but would go home to visit his parents and younger sister several times a week. He also has a brother three years older who lives nearby and with whom he keeps in regular contact. Stephen left school at the age of 16 and after a year of unemployment returned to college. He was bullied at school and frequently missed several days at a time. He had a few friends at college with whom he spent much time smoking cannabis, and this appeared to have contributed to his first psychotic episode.

Stephen has a good sense of humour and feels particularly comfortable with other men. He had a number of good friendships and could be sociable and gregarious. However, he was highly sensitive to perceived criticism which often led to apparently disinterested or aggressive behaviour. He was sometimes quite paranoid and at worst this was manifested as persecutory delusions. This often coincided with hearing abusive voices which laughed at and talked about him and called him names. On other occasions, he became quite grandiose and excitable, and would infrequently report delusions that he was the Son of God.

Stephen engaged in some occupational therapy activities in the rehabilitation unit, but also spent much time off the unit with friends, when he used alcohol or cannabis (on about a weekly basis). He was often restless and rarely completed even short tasks. He frequently failed to attend appointments.

Assessment

Both Stephen's pre-morbid and current functioning were in the borderline range and there was no significant decline indicated between these assessments (WAIS-III and WTAR). Verbal skills were better than performance skills but this was not significant. His performance on verbal and long-term memory was significantly impaired on the majority of the verbal indices on the Wechsler Memory Scale III. His visual memory was not impaired. We hypothesised that sustained attention contributed to these difficulties so we assessed this using the CPT. This showed a large decrement in his ability to sustain attention. Executive functioning was variable. Although he was poor on response inhibition (Hayling Test) he performed in the normal range on set shifting (Trails B) and strategy use (Key Search, Zoo Map, BADS). We hypothesised that this was again due to distractibility rather than specific impairment in response inhibition.

During the assessment process, Stephen commented that some of the tasks were similar to each other, suggesting that he has some ability to abstract information. His performance on the Similarities subtest of the WAIS-III was better than might be expected given his full-scale IQ. He also seemed to be using visual strategies to process information although this was often not efficient for the task.

Information on his mental state suggests that this was variable and includes the experience of grandiose ideas, paranoia and voices. Alcohol and drugs were reported to be used to reduce anxiety. Anxiety was assessed on the STAI and was high on state but not as high on trait anxiety. He also has low self-esteem (Rosenberg). Depression, however, was mild as measured on the BDI.

Formulation

Stephen is an 18-year-old man with a one-year history of psychosis, who lives in a rehabilitation unit. His social presentation is initially appropriate. He has a wide group of friends and a supportive family. His positive symptoms are only partly under control and he has exacerbations of paranoia and grandiosity and hears voices. There is some co-morbid anxiety. He is very aware of these difficulties and his recent cognitive deterioration, which contributes to his low self-esteem and perceived stigma. The most striking feature of his presentation is his defensiveness and this sometimes results in paranoia and aggression.

His performance on verbal working and long-term memory is significantly impaired and executive performance is variable. He has very poor sustained attention and this seems both to contribute to his variable performance and to accentuate memory difficulties. These problems are reflected in his difficulty in following conversations, which is detrimental to his friendships and his paranoia. His awareness of all these problems contributes to his low self-esteem and emotional withdrawal. These issues, as well as his inability to remember information which is salient for activities that are important to him, lead to a failure to generate realistic goals.

A notable strength is his ability to notice structural similarities between tasks and he seems to do this by comparing visual memories of the task. Sometimes this is not an efficient strategy and leads to performance decrements in tasks with a strong verbal component. When engaged he is very motivated and could develop a good therapeutic relationship. He has good insight into his cognitive difficulties and copes by reducing stimulation. On occasions this is helpful but it affects most of his functioning and contributes to low mood and hopelessness. This is when he is particularly vulnerable to drug and alcohol misuse. Despite these difficulties there is evidence that Stephen can make plans to achieve highly valued goals.

Stephen's problems include difficulty in following conversations, lack of activity, poor concentration, poor memory, goal generation and drug and alcohol misuse. He discussed his goals at length with his key worker as part of his care planning and available educational resources (e.g. college) were identified. His goals include going to college to study computing one day per week, to concentrate for hour-long band rehearsals and to learn and remember the words of a new song. A summary of the formulation is given in Table 11.3.

Treatment plan

The initial plan included an emphasis on engagement in therapy, developing a therapeutic relationship and increasing hopefulness. The cognitive aims were to increase sustained attention, verbal working memory and long-term memory and to reduce impulsiveness. Success on the cognitive tasks led to increased hope and self-efficacy and contributed to engagement in therapy. Initially we aimed for a few 'quick wins' – psychoeducation to improve attention generally, and mnemonic strategies. The therapy concentrated on analogical encoding, which capitalised on Stephen's ability to identify similarities between tasks, together with strategy development, relying on visualising which was more efficient than current strategies. This depended on teaching metacognitive knowledge of effective strategies and broad schemas for ease of analogical reasoning. Spontaneous strategies were reinforced and new strategies were taught when Stephen became more confident and the therapeutic alliance had strengthened. Analogical encoding allowed the introduction of some behavioural control (i.e. metacognitive regulation) by taking time to reflect on similarities between tasks. This reduced impulsivity which had resulted in poor performance.

Sustained attention was shaped gradually with reinforcement on tasks that were within Stephen's competence. As he was sensitive to perceived criticism, the tasks were initially well within this competence limit. Physical visual aids,

Table 11.3 Stephen's formulation

CRT formulation

Name Stephen

Age (in years and months)
18 years 9 months

Pre-morbid abilities WTAR standardised score IQ 85

Education Left school at 16 with no qualifications. Brief spell at college.

Current and previous employment Does odd jobs for father's friend

Current and previous interests
Spending time with friends, music—sings in a band.

Cognitive function
Current estimated full-scale IQ   79
Current estimated verbal IQ   84
Current estimated performance IQ   73

Difficulties	Strengths
1. Sustained attention	1. Visual long-term memory
2. Verbal long-term memory	2. Planning
3. Verbal working memory	3. Set shifting
4. Response inhibition	

Cognitive behavioural style

Difficulties	Strengths
1. Impulsive	1. Visualising
2. Lack of verbal behaviour	2. Noticing similarities between tasks
3. Lack of persistence	

Non-cognitive factors

Difficulties	Strengths
1. Paranoid	1. Sociable
2. Low self-esteem	2. Humour
3. Aggressive	3. Good insight into cognitive difficulties
	4. Motivated when engaged

Coping and use of compensatory strategies

Problem coping and strategies	Effective coping and strategies
1. Drug and alcohol use	1. Use of social support
2. Emotional withdrawal	2. Reduces stimulation when necessary
3. Gives up in response to perceived criticism	3. Makes plans

Problems	Goals
1. Difficulty in following conversations	1. Go to college to study computing one day a week
2. Drug and alcohol use	2. To concentrate for hour-long band rehearsal
3. Lack of activity / goals	3. To remember the words of a new song
4. Poor concentration	
5. Poor memory	

such as pictures that he drew, and visualising were helpful and visual cues were used as prompts to remember information. For example, in remembering a conversation he imagined what was discussed. These strategies were used to build metacognitive knowledge of his cognitive style and strengths.

Stephen's misuse of drugs and alcohol initially affected his engagement in therapy and cognitive performance. Psycho-education during therapy concentrated on the negative impact, and we discussed Stephen's reasons for their use. Building confidence through the therapy reduced his anxiety and this was the start of some more general anxiety management work. If drugs and alcohol had become a barrier to increasing cognitive performance then we would have considered making them a specific focus of intervention.

In the second phase of therapy, the main issues were how to use his strategies to achieve some of the minor goals, e.g. learning the words to a song. Study skills for college were also developed, using therapy homework, gradually building up his attention span and his ability to work independently.

Tackling specific problems in therapy

The case studies were presented to give a flavour of the type of therapy offered within CRT, but there are also particular difficulties that arose during therapy with each of these people. We have summarised these difficulties and some of the techniques which may be used to tackle them in the following sections.

Problems in engagement

Stephen's case illustrates a number of common problems which can lead to difficulties in engaging in psychological treatment programmes. These include:

1   *Hopelessness, low mood and depression.* These are commonly associated with apathy, lack of energy and motivation, and hopelessness in particular may result in beliefs that change is not possible or worthwhile.
2   *Previous failures within education.* This often leads to a poor sense of self-efficacy within learning environments, low self-esteem and an avoidance of situations associated with learning or education. This may be particularly problematic if combined with a mistrust of psychiatric or other public services.
3   *Paranoia, grandiosity and low self-esteem*: these factors reflect problems both with self-image and trusting other people. They are likely to be associated with high levels of sensitivity to criticism, defensiveness, avoidance or misunderstanding of the motivations of other people.
4   *Drug and alcohol misuse*: this may result in problems in attendance, lack

of motivation, as well as cognitive side effects, such as poor memory and concentration. To undertake a CRT programme, some abstinence is required (e.g. not drinking or taking drugs prior to sessions) which may also be a disincentive to engage.

There are a number of ways in which these problems can be tackled.

Making CRT personally meaningful

This will require a detailed understanding of the motivations, goals and interests of the person so that the rationale and goals for therapy are highly tailored to be personally meaningful for the participant. The therapist may need to explain to the participant how their cognitive problems seem to interfere with their attainment of certain goals. Therapy can also be framed to make it more acceptable to the client and so it may be perceived as non-stigmatising. For example, some people respond well to the idea that it is a type of education, whereas others may prefer a more illness-oriented framework. In Stephen's case, the therapist tailored the goals to his interests (music) and aims (to go to college) after identifying the importance to him of having a socially valued role, having an opportunity to meet friends and to have sufficient qualifications to apply for a job that would make him financially independent.

Removing practical obstacles to therapy

In Stephen's case, this will include psycho-education about the impact of drugs and alcohol and encouraging him to minimise his intake. If this continues to be a problem, it may need to be addressed in its own right before beginning CRT.

In addition, other pragmatic factors which are easily overlooked but which can have a marked impact on therapy include (a) the timing of sessions, to avoid difficulties in getting out of bed, drowsiness due to medication, difficulties with public transport, etc.; (b) the location of the sessions, which should be manageable for the participant to get to and which he or she finds acceptable.

Establishing a good therapeutic relationship

This should be a collaborative relationship in which the participant is given unconditional positive regard. At the beginning of therapy, this can be facilitated by a sensitive and careful assessment of both cognitive and non-cognitive factors which may influence CRT and the participant's response to treatment. This gives the therapist the opportunity to get to know the participant, to individually tailor treatment and to establish a non-judgemental and gentle therapeutic environment. Cognitive deficits can be normalised and empathy can be given for cognitive problems the participant is able to identify. Many participants respond well to being enlisted in collaborative hypothesis testing to investigate possible causes of their difficulties using behavioural experiments (see formulation in Chapter 10 for more details).

Adapting CRT tasks and their delivery

A number of techniques can be used in adapting the therapy content and its delivery to help engage participants:

1 Provide high levels of structure, so that the participant consistently has experiences of success, is not left to flounder and works well within his or her level of competence. Verbal instruction should be kept to a minimum, and where possible, tasks should be taught by modelling or by a gradual scaffolding process, so that new task elements are introduced stepwise.
2 Whilst providing high levels of structure at first, avoid being too directive and adopt a stance in which the therapist continually reflects and comments upon the participant's behaviour in a non-judgemental manner, highlighting and positively reinforcing adaptive behaviour. At this stage, building the confidence and sense of self-efficacy of the participant should be prioritised above teaching new skills. For some people, it may take many weeks before the therapist is able to suggest changes to the participant's behaviour, and so the therapist must work behaviourally, highlighting and reinforcing appropriate behaviour and ignoring non-adaptive behaviour.
3 Keep tasks varied and interesting, using a variety of modalities and engaging materials. The participant should be presented with tasks which differ in their difficulty level so as to be challenged at times, whilst at others finding tasks very easy. The therapist therefore needs to be creative and to introduce elements of humour or competition into the therapy. Many participants enjoy taking the role of therapist in monitoring the therapist's performance on tasks.
4 Choose tasks and strategies to ensure the participant makes rapid, noticeable and meaningful improvements. For example, Stephen was concerned about his memory, and the therapist may have gained considerable mileage in immediately teaching the use of memory strategies to help him learn a new song (one of his goals). Change should be frequently drawn attention to and reinforced.

Involving other people

This may include other staff, family members or friends, who may be able to encourage or remind the participant to attend, to reinforce the importance of therapy, and to help in homework assignments. Furthermore, other people may inadvertently or deliberately sabotage the therapy, for example, by arranging conflicting activities if they are not able to see the value of the therapy.

Targeting unhelpful cognitive behavioural styles

Whilst different cognitive behavioural styles can lead to widely varying presentations, their regulation relies on similar principles, regardless of whether, for example, someone is disorganised and chaotic or slow and passive. In both cases, the therapist aims to provide high levels of consistent structure by which the participant learns to regulate his or her own behaviour. This can be achieved via a number of means:

1 *Agree upon simple rules for behaviour.* For example, Donald and his therapist agreed upon a time limit for each task, which was monitored with a timer that buzzed at the end of the allotted time. During this time, Donald agreed with his therapist that he would avoid talking, but at the end of each task they spend a short period of time discussing the task or other topics that had come to his mind whilst he had been carrying it out. A similar technique could have been adopted with Norma to encourage more rapid responses with an alternative more relative reward (e.g. to have a two-minute rest after each task).

2 *Limit the task requirements.* This may include physically limiting the amount of information available (e.g. by covering up some aspects of the task) or by presenting the task a step at a time. Reducing additional attentional demands, such as limiting extraneous noise or stimulation, can also be beneficial.

3 *Limit the scope of possible responses to task instructions.* For example, until Donald was able to regulate his own speed of working, he was always asked to make only one response. When this one response had been made, he would be asked to stop and he and the therapist would reflect upon this and the task requirements. This helped to teach both his metacognitive self-regulation and inhibition of action.

4 *Use physical prompts to encourage self-regulation.* At the most basic level, the therapist may need to model the behaviour simultaneously as the participant completes the task (e.g. point to each item as it should be attended to). For Norma, the therapist consistently proceeded at a speed just slightly greater than Norma's own speed. As the participant progresses, he or she can take greater responsibility for the use of physical

Table 11.4 Common cognitive and behavioural problems and solutions

Problem	Possible solutions
Slow to initiate responses	1. Give a time limit by which the task should be completed. 2. Provide cue words which the participant can use to guide his or her own behaviour (e.g. STOP–PLAN–ACT). 3. Model the speed at which to work. 4. Suggest the participant acts on or articulates his or her thoughts first, and reflects upon them second, rather than relying solely on internal reflection. 5. Develop covert reminders for the participant to use to keep him or herself moving.
Fast and impulsive (at the extreme, chaotic)	1. Encourage reflection and planning before every task. 2. Discuss the structure of tasks with the participant before beginning. 3. Ask the participant to describe aloud each behaviour as it is carried out. 4. Divide the task into stages, and ask the participant to complete only one stage and then to stop and reflect on the next. 5. Model the task behaviour concurrently with the participant. 6. Give the task instructions a step at a time or ask the participant to work at the speed at which you are describing the required behaviour. 7. Ask the participant to describe the behaviour before it is carried out.
Adopts inefficient strategies	1. Ask the participant to monitor the effectiveness of the strategy. 2. Brainstorm to identify possible alternative strategies and then compare performance using one of these alternatives with the original inefficient strategy. 3. Discuss the pros and cons of the strategy. 4. Set up a competition to test out two alternative strategies. 5. Check the therapist's own biases about what is an efficient strategy.
Concentrates on detailed rather than global processing	1. Ask the participant to provide a variety of explanations for the problem, including both detailed and global perspectives and to switch between them. 2. Educate the participant about the differences between detailed and global processing. 3. Ask the participant to reflect on whether his or her (or another person's) response was detailed or global. 4. Ask the participant to test out using descriptions with varying levels of detail to guide behaviour.

prompts. For example, before beginning tasks Donald and his therapist would agree upon and write down a series of steps that Donald would follow in undertaking the task. He would then consult this list after completing each stage in the task.

5 *Encourage self-talk to self-regulate*. This is at first modelled by the therapist and is gradually taken over by the participant. The use of verbal instructions can help not only to guide but also to slow down behaviour.

Table 11.4 provides a quick guide to fault finding and the solutions which may be integrated into therapy.

Chapter 12

Cognitive remediation therapy in the future

There is now clearly more optimism for the development of therapies to improve cognition in schizophrenia. Both laboratory and clinical studies have shown improvements on individual cognitive tests and in some studies these have led to functional changes. Our model concentrated on this issue: What is the key change in cognition that will improve functioning? Our conclusion was that the bottom-up models that assume change will be based solely on practice of task-specific, low-level cognitive skills is unlikely to have dramatic effects. Therapy should concentrate on training cognitive skills that will lead to a flexible transfer of strategies and cognitive schemas. Therefore executive functioning and particularly metacognitive knowledge and metacognitive processing should be targets for CRT and the instructional techniques should be designed to develop these skills. Therapy is still at an early stage and we consider that further investigations of the effectiveness of types of task and instruction are essential. The usefulness of some instructional techniques from adult education for training people with some existing cognitive difficulties needs also to be tested.

It is also important not to forget how we came to discover this cognitive therapy. The importance of cognitive difficulties has never been disputed but there was a failure to investigate the likelihood of improving these problems. The historical context is one excuse – the assumption of the immutability of cognitive problems. But this immutability was derived from false conclusions from cross-sectional studies and comparisons of cohorts of patients with diagnoses of schizophrenia at different stages of illness.

In our research for this book we discovered another area of ignorance – that of the studies in the transfer of skills from one context to another. This area has expanded massively over the last ten years and has produced important findings for training and therapeutic interventions. We should overlook this no longer. Our current ignorance is also based on seeing all the trees and no wood. Schizophrenia research has been concerned with bottom-up approaches for too long with a concentration on the biological and physiological substrates and little about the co-ordination of neural activity into the general thinking behaviour of our patients. The use of the term neurocognitive has led us down a neural pathway that has made us forget that cognition is about thinking, reasoning, remembering and deciding. Neuropsychological tests merely assess behaviours and are not a microscope on the activity of lobes of the brain. Test performance is affected by thinking capacities which include strategic thinking as well as thinking dispositions which incorporate cognitive behavioural style. It is our contention that we need to consider how to improve this thinking activity, and particularly meta-cognition, as this is the thinking activity that allows flexible responding which is so necessary for everyday functioning in our social lives and work.

It is also salutary to consider how therapies would normally develop and consider how this has occurred for CRT. Figure 12.1 shows the development of therapy from small single cases through small controlled studies and eventually to effective therapy which is implemented. This assumes a positive approach, with favourable results in abundance in the literature and a halt if there are negative results which cannot be accounted for by factors that differ between participants or factors that are inherent in the design of the study. Now compare this with the way in which CRT developed which is shown in Figure 12.2. Here we can see that the studies initially were based on a different hypothesis – that cognitive difficulties were immutable so therapy would not change it. This produced the very useful studies which showed little change following therapy. But these studies were not testing the type of therapy and so were not designed to separate the elements of training or

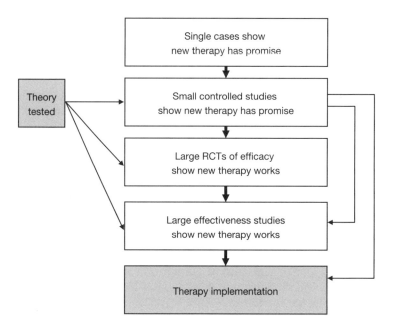

Figure 12.1 Normal history of therapy development

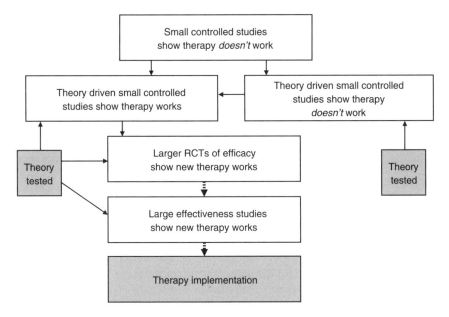

Figure 12.2 Cognitive remediation development

testing these elements in a rigorous way. We now need to continue the development of therapy and model testing through the provision of clinical services and evaluations.

Even more research?

Although we are optimistic, the effects of CRT are modest, and in order to improve the effects we do need to carry out further research. The scope of this research is wide, although several key issues need further investigation immediately. Models of cognition are essential for the development of interventions and certainly the extent and patterning of cognitive difficulties needs further exploration. This is despite the wealth of studies already in the literature. We advocate the use of a more experimental cognitive psychology approach rather than the use of neuropsychological tests for all the reasons set out in Chapter 3. This is not flying in the face of much opposition as several other authors have suggested such a change of direction (e.g. Serper and Harvey, 1994; Keefe, 1995; MacDonald and Carter, 2002). Studies also need to be large so that individual differences can be separated out and they should also cover the course of schizophrenia so that episode-linked factors can be differentiated from factors associated with a lack of complete recovery between episodes.

The role of cognitive processing in its prediction of outcome seems more muted in some rehabilitation programmes, e.g. vocational programmes. This might be accounted for by a system of compensation for cognitive difficulties. We need to know how the compensation takes place so that this can be embedded within comprehensive programmes. As part of current rehabilitation programmes, researchers have begun to tease out the specific cognitive difficulties that interfere with progress at different phases of the rehabilitation process (Kupper and Hoffman, 2000; Bryson and Bell, 2003). These studies need further development to refine the strategic skills that are necessary for success in different individuals and in different types of programme. This research may also lead to changes in the rehabilitation programmes themselves which have generally concentrated on the improvement of knowledge and specific skill but have rarely trained specifically for flexibility of transfer of that knowledge to other situations.

Our model suggests that increased efficiency of cognitive processing will lead to success or improved performance on individual tasks. However, we also identify metacognition as a key variable in the transfer of learning from one situation to another. Experimental psychopathologists now need to identify measures that assess specific aspects of metacognition. This assessment should not only evaluate performance levels but would also test hypotheses derived from our model.

If we return to the biopsychosocial model introduced in the first chapter of this book we also need to consider issues of genetic control and its relationship to cognitive outcome. Genes such as catecho-O-methyl transferase (COMT) have now been linked to cognitive performance problems. It is possible that these genes also affect the outcome from CRT in people with schizophrenia. However, it may be that the concentration of efforts on metacognitive knowledge and regulation overcome the limits placed on the cognitive system by these genetic influences.

In order to develop an efficient cognitive treatment, we need to concentrate not only on the design of specific treatments, but also on developing cognitive models of performance in schizophrenia and the continued identification of cognitive abilities linked to functional outcome. The models will then support the development of therapy and the targets will be relevant for functional outcomes. The general issues and some specific questions are listed in Table 12.1 and discussed in more detail below.

Developing cognitive models of performance in schizophrenia

Measurement issues

The change in focus from neuropsychological tests to experimental cognitive psychology heralds a new set of comparisons from brain injury to normal cognition. There is also a move towards investigating single trials in terms of

Table 12.1 Issues to consider for future research

	Developing cognitive models of performance in schizophrenia	Identifying cognitive abilities linked to functional outcome	Research on cognitive remediation
Measurement issues	1. Single trials vs. global scores 2. Variability in cognitive performance 3. Assessment of metacognition	1. Theory underlying test selection 2. Cognitive vs. neuropsychological approach 3. Increasing specificity of functional measures	1. Selection of the specific primary outcomes 2. Selection of the specific functional outcome
Design	1. Longitudinal studies	1. Identification of vulnerability factors 2. Select sample size according to statistical power	1. Model testing – accounting for possible mediating and interactional factors 2. Integrated vs. stand-alone CRT programmes
Participants		Within-group factors	

accuracy and reaction time instead of the dependence on total scores which are likely to be affected by sustained attention to the task as well as any underlying cognitive and strategic processing (e.g. Perlstein *et al.*, 1998). The simplification of tasks may produce more consistency and interpretability of the performance data. In addition, attention has recently been paid to the variability rather than level of cognitive performance within the same individual as this may be an issue for future models of schizophrenia (e.g. Spaulding *et al.*, 2003). Wexler *et al.* (2004) report that variability in reaction time rather than the reaction time itself over a large number of trials was correlated with concept formation, working memory and reasoning as well as being related to the complexity of employment and number of hours spent working.

Identifying both the specific task-related cognitive performance variables as well as variability of performance over the whole task is vital to the search for the underlying difficulties of people with schizophrenia. Whether a few cognitive variables underlie all the performance deficits or independent cognitive difficulties affect performance on specific tasks has always been a thorny issue. This is often termed the specific versus generalised deficit. Meta-analyses of neuropsychological tests do not illuminate this issue because there is a wide variability in effect sizes between different tests measuring the same construct and for different studies using the same test. This is clearly affected by a number of factors, the most potent of which is the discriminating power of the tests being observed. This is not a recent issue as it was raised 30 years ago by Chapman and Chapman (1973).

Metacognition has been highlighted in our model but there are as yet few measures to assess it, particularly in schizophrenia. One recently reported study of insight uses a paradigm devised by Koriat and Goldsmith (1996). This uses the WCST in the usual way and allows the standard measurement of the number of categories completed and perseverative errors. But after each sort the participant has to make two decisions: (a) how confident he or she is that the sort is correct; (b) whether he or she is willing to enter the response into a lottery where a correct response will be rewarded with money and an incorrect response will result in a loss. These are suggested to represent the monitoring aspect of metacognition (how confident are you) and the behavioural control aspect (choosing to put the sort in the lottery). Koren *et al.* (2004) used this method and found that there was some disparity between the executive functioning measures and the metacognition measures which were more highly related to insight. This follows the work of Danion and colleagues (2001a) who also found a disparity between general knowledge, confidence in that knowledge and the behaviour based on this knowledge in people with schizophrenia, with the link between behaviour and control being relatively poor. This study also emphasised the effect of motivation on the measures, with general knowledge scores increasing with the introduction of incentives to respond correctly. To improve everyday behaviours we need both to capitalise on the metacognitive ability to self-monitor and to ensure that this knowledge is used to guide behaviour. Further development of metacognitive measures is required to test not only our own model but to also check the effects of different variables on metacognitive aspects of task performance.

Interpretation issues

A move to an experimental paradigm also suggests that there is more control over the specific cognitive operations needed for the task. However, this may only reveal cognitive processing factors associated with good task performance. Strategic processing may vary between different tasks, within tasks carried out by the same individuals at different times, and between different individuals at the same time. For example, take a simple list learning study. It is assumed as psychological fact that items will be remembered more often if they are at the beginning (primacy effect) or end of the list (recency effect). In most studies of group data these tendencies almost inevitably emerge. However, these effects are not ubiquitous in individual data. Sometimes primacy effects occur in the absence of recency and vice versa. This does not affect the number of remembered words (span). These effects differ across time and across different tests in normal populations and are probably the result of the adoption of different mnemonic and learning strategies, for example, rehearsal (Della Sala *et al.*, 1998). So participants in memory tasks are not passive and they may evaluate the goals of a task differently from each other. The absence of the cognitive 'facts' in some individuals therefore does not automatically indicate that there is strategic deficit, particularly when the number of items recalled does not differ between groups. However, it does indicate the need for variability rather than prescription in the teaching of CRT.

Design issues

The purpose of these studies is to investigate the stability of strategic processing, and therefore there needs to be a concentration on cross-sectional studies (i.e. over a number of similar tasks) as well as longitudinal studies (the stability of processing across the same task). It may be that there is some instability which informs our model by suggesting that task-specific information can be learnt but not necessarily implemented in different contexts or over time. This then suggests support for the problems in metacognition, that metacognitive knowledge or regulation needs to be the main target of our interventions.

Participant issues

People with diagnoses of schizophrenia who remain in contact with services may be different from the people who appear to have only a single episode. Although there is evidence that cognitive difficulties seem to be related to symptom levels rather than chronicity (Greenwood *et al.*, 2000), it cannot be assumed that these difficulties are produced by the same underlying cognitive performance pattern. Future research therefore needs to explore within group factors such as length of illness and symptom expression.

Identifying cognitive abilities linked to functional outcome

Measurement issues

Generalising across studies of the relationship between cognitive skills and functional outcomes is dependent on the use of similar measures. First, cognitive skills have tended to be measured in a haphazard manner. There is little evidence of specific theory guiding many of the batteries of tests. They seem often to depend on what is in the psychological cupboard at the time. Even when there are choices based on theory, many of the tests used are suggested to measure different things in different studies. The task load is also often different between studies using the same task, e.g. the memory load in the continuous performance test. Comparing like with like is therefore problematic. In particular, cognitive tests have differing variability so that when there is a large variability in scores there is a higher likelihood of finding a relationship between test performance and a functioning outcome. For this reason it may be easier to find relationships between functional outcomes and tests with a large range of score, for example, list learning (verbal memory). Differences in such test characteristics have no relation to the constructs being measured. Hence highly significant correlations, particularly those from cross-sectional studies, may have no implication for future functioning when performance is improved. It is only possible to detect such relationships empirically in treatment studies.

Even when the same task is used, investigators may pick different elements of the test to evaluate. For instance there are several different measures of performance on the Wisconsin Card Sorting Test which assess aspects of performance and skill. It has been suggested that perseverative errors measure the difficulty of switching set, the number of attempts before achieving the first category measure the early experience of conceptual learning, large numbers of errors suggest that responses are haphazard and the number of categories acknowledges overall conceptual learning. It appears to us that the conceptual muddle surrounding the WCST confuses rather than enlightens us and that it is time to dispense with this test and the traditional neuro-psychological approach.

Similarly in the measurement of functional domains, many measures are reliable and valid but they do not necessarily measure the same items in the same domains. Some even give different weights to different aspects of the domain. For instance, the PSE counts all delusions separately whereas the BPRS gives them one category and the same weight as anxiety. Some measures only change over relatively long periods of time, for example Social Functioning Scale (Birchwood et al., 1990), and therefore are unhelpful in studies investigating some predictive relationships in short-term studies. Aspects of functioning that are relevant to consumers have rarely been tested, particularly in symptom measures. Consumers tend to emphasise distress and effects on everyday life rather than the phenomenology of the symptom (e.g. whether a voice is heard inside or outside the head). These emphases may prove to be informative specifically for measures of the severity of the symptom.

Studies can be criticised for both having too few measures of cognition and too many. When too few tests are used this produces problems in the interpretation of the relationships between cognition and functioning as they may be specific to the test and not to the underlying cognitive skill that is supposed to be measured by that test. When many tests are used the variance is often reduced by using factor analyses to extract cognitive performance factors. The factors extracted may be different across studies and few, if any, confirmatory analyses are carried out. The factors may depend on the characteristics of the sample (see below) or they may be affected by the number of tests included. Perhaps most importantly they lose some explanatory variance that may be essential in linking cognitive with functional domains because the specific items do not load highly on the first few factors that explain the majority of the variance.

Interpretation issues

It has been assumed from correlational studies that there is a direct relationship between cognition and outcome, so that if the specific cognitive function improves, then functional improvements will automatically follow. However, there is evidence from treatment studies (e.g. Spaulding *et al.*, 1999b; Reeder *et al.*, 2004) that this relationship may not be direct and that a third factor may account for the predictive relationship.

Design issues

Many studies are cross-sectional and therefore we have to rely on replications in different groups with the same measures to assess the significance of any relationships. Although these are helpful, more longitudinal studies would improve our understanding of the predictive power of cognitive variables. This is especially important as life changes may introduce natural stressors which make non-significant relationships into highly significant ones. This approach may make it possible for us to spot important vulnerability factors.

Participant characteristics

Few studies specify sufficient characteristics of the patient groups and it may be that differences that appear in an acute group are not relevant in the chronic group. Similarly there may be differences between groups of people who tend to experience different symptom patterns. Although these are represented in the data it is rare for them to be compared directly within the same study. Often this is because of small sample sizes but some of these could be overcome using meta-analytic techniques.

Analysis issues

The samples in the majority of the earlier studies were small with usually fewer than 40 people. This poses a problem for the internal variance of a study. It may be so limited that vital differences are missed. Similarly small samples pose problems for the analysis, especially as many involve exploratory regression. This technique is notorious for producing results that are never replicated. Few sophisticated statistical methods are used, such as bootstrapping, to ensure that the results truly reflect the relationships within the data. In addition, interactive relationships are rarely investigated in the data.

It may be that the cognition to outcome relationship is affected by levels of symptoms or even different types of symptoms and these have not been investigated in the studies so far.

Research in this area is improving but larger blockbuster studies are needed. When studies with large numbers are published they tend to use data that were collected for an entirely different reason and are available for secondary analyses. This means that they are less likely to contain the range of cognitive tasks, subtle functioning outcomes, patient or symptom groups that will progress theory in this area.

Research on cognitive remediation

Measurement issues

Most of the issues have been discussed in the sections above. The balance between the exploratory effects of therapeutic change and the power to detect clinically significant effect sizes is difficult. Our model of CRT requires us to measure a variety of basic cognitive processes and executive functions as well as metacognition. These are essential to develop the intervention further and to investigate the mode of its action where clear hypotheses have been generated.

We have also specified that CRT should improve other functions such as work and a social life. These therefore need to be measured over periods of time where change is likely to take place. There is also an area of self-efficacy and self-esteem which must be measured as it is likely that this is a mediating effect of the therapy as well as an important outcome in its own right.

Design issues

The effects of CRT have in the past been measured by evaluating CRT against another therapy or a control condition. But recently there has been a move to integrate it with other therapies such as supported employment (Hogarty and Flesher, 1999b; Bell et al., 2001a; Hogarty et al., 2004) or social skills training (Spaulding et al., 1999b). This leads to difficulties in the interpretation of findings particularly for the mode of action of CRT unless the additive effects of CRT and additional therapy are controlled, for instance in a third arm of the trial in which only CRT is provided.

Analysis issues

The primary outcome for any cognitive rehabilitation programme should be the cognitive elements targeted. But how these are measured differs between studies. The following are just a few of the ways of measuring effects:

- improvement in a single test score included in the training
- improvement in a generalisation test not used within the training package
- improvement in a series of scores representing different cognitive domains
- improvement in factor scores (usually derived from the baseline data)
- change in z scores derived from normative data
- change in a composite score derived from z scores in different tests
- covariance modelling of therapy and cognitive change scores.

These different ways of measuring change may produce differing results. The reasons for choosing different styles of analysis are often not clear and they rarely include any reference to theoretical concerns about the mode of action of CRT.

The effects of trials are usually measured at the end of the follow-up period. Depending on the analytic method chosen any significant effects immediately after therapy might not be clear if they disappear after a follow-up interval. Wykes and colleagues (1999) have argued that CRT has worked if there are changes following therapy. The analogy is with different kinds of medication treatments. CRT and other psychological treatments have been assumed to be like antibiotics that are provided intensively and then stopped. It is assumed that the effects of the antibiotic will continue and for some psychological therapies, e.g. for panic disorder, this has been true. But for chronic relapsing disorders, such as asthma, the medication treatment is given intensively to counteract an episode but then maintenance treatment is provided to support the increased functioning. Schizophrenia clearly fits with the asthma analogy. Therefore if improvements cannot be maintained then the treatment should not be assumed to have failed. The loss of positive effects means merely that the effects have not been maintained.

The mode of action of CRT may also be variable, particularly with reference to the effects of cognition on functioning. Cognitive and metacognitive changes might be linked directly to functioning outcomes but they might have to reach a clinically significant threshold to find significant change in functioning outcomes.

One effect that does need further consideration is that cognition may change through the specific effects of CRT on other variables (e.g. symptoms, motivation, self-efficacy and the response to reward) and not just through improvements due to its direct effects. Some non-specific aspects of therapy (e.g. the attention demand of control therapies) may also improve cognition. However, there may be interactions between cognitive change and therapy that have an effect on functioning, whereas cognitive changes following control therapy may have little impact. So the analysis of the data from controlled trials needs to take into account interactional factors and not just research the impact of therapy on a main outcome. Studies should also be designed to test theoretically driven hypotheses about the role of mediating factors. Studies of CRT need to be powered to be able to detect the effects of both interactional and mediating factors.

CRT is a psychological therapy

So far, CRT has developed as a technique to improve brain functioning and not as a complete psychological therapy. CRT should draw on a broader context. We have described a CRT programme which follows a clear therapeutic model. The process begins with an assessment and therapy is guided by the participant's personal goals and a formulation which is updated throughout treatment.

There is a vast amount of literature about the non-specific aspects of therapy which contribute to its success, but these have not been explicitly referred in descriptions of CRT to date. For instance, a good therapeutic relationship, in which warmth and empathy are provided, has consistently been found to predict a positive response to treatment. Providing the client with a model within which to understand their difficulties and instilling a sense of achievement and self-efficacy have been identified for many years as important elements in psychological therapies. Although CRT is specifically designed to achieve some of these things (e.g. improve self-efficacy), programmes have generally concentrated on brain functioning and have not considered psychological characteristics of the person and basic therapeutic tools which are known to have an impact on therapy outcome. Ironically, it may be that some of these non-specific aspects of therapy have inadvertently contributed to the positive effects of CRT and promoted engagement. Drop-out rates in studies are generally low and anecdotal evidence suggests that CRT is acceptable to patients, since its emphasis on cognitive function rather than beliefs is normative, non-stigmatising and is not associated with the distress of symptoms. CRT programmes should acknowledge this broad therapeutic context and studies should investigate the impact of non-specific factors that might affect therapeutic outcome.

Extending cognitive remediation

It is clear that we can improve cognition and, with further theory development, we may be able to improve considerably our effect sizes. But it may also be possible to use CRT as a precursor to other rehabilitation programmes so that the cognitive improvements can immediately benefit the development of other skills. We have described two phases of therapy, one in which cognition is targeted in a neutral context and one in which strategic processing skills are incorporated into activities of everyday living. Alternatively, it may be possible to embed CRT principles within other rehabilitation programmes for skills learning.

Service issues

Staff involved in the care of people with schizophrenia should receive training on the importance of cognitive difficulties in rehabilitation and outcomes. In particular, managers need to know that improving cognition increases the cost effectiveness of rehabilitation programmes as well as increasing the overall success rate. Once services have accepted that CRT is a valuable supplement, then the level of resources that need to be diverted, to maximise the cost effectiveness of a suite of rehabilitation services can be addressed. The types of issues that must be explored for CRT include:

- the level of therapist expertise for CRT
- the number of sessions per participant
- clinical supervision for therapists
- the method of generalisation between CRT and the other rehabilitation programmes.

Who can administer CRT?

In the model of therapy we have presented, our preference has been for an individual therapist who can provide tailored assessment and treatment. Other models of therapy also include therapists with varied responsibilities in presenting tasks or guiding the interaction with computerised therapy. Although individual therapists providing one-to-one treatment may appear to be the most expensive option there is a clear utility. Losses through dropout, engagement in the tasks as well as tailoring of treatment can improve the therapy outcome and make it more beneficial to the largest number of people. These gains far outweigh the increase in expenditure. To date, CRT in our group has generally been administered by assistant psychologists (recent psychology graduates who usually have no postgraduate training) who have been selected for their experience in working with people with schizophrenia and their ability to use psychological knowledge to guide their practice. Such therapists often change their role, moving to clinical psychology training, and it is therefore likely that only one year of therapy is gained from one trained therapist. The estimated UK cost of such therapy per client using this one-year training base is about £500–600 ($1200 or €900: Wykes *et al.*, 2003). This figure includes the costs of the training, supervision by a trained clinical psychologist, the costs of accommodation for therapy, etc., and the assumption that about 12 to 16 participants will have completed training in one year.

A degree in psychology is not a necessity but some understanding of cognitive psychology is helpful. In the USA, social workers have frequently run such programmes, and recently in the UK we have also begun to train psychiatric nurses, social workers, care workers and clinical psychologists.

Therapists do not need to be highly qualified or very experienced, but they do need to fulfil a number of important criteria which include:

- experience of working within mental health services, and specifically of working with people with schizophrenia
- the ability to use a theoretical model to guide their clinical work
- the ability to understand and learn psychological models of relevant areas of cognitive function (executive functioning, attention and memory)
- the ability to engage and work with difficult clients on a one-to-one basis.

We also recommend that all therapists receive weekly clinical supervision from a clinical psychologist or another experienced mental health professional who has a good understanding of the relevant psychological models and their application to clinical practice.

Number of sessions per participant

From our own clinical experience it seems clear that CRT has to be provided in several sessions each week. Our estimate is at least three per week and this concurs with the clinical experience of other groups around the world. Unless the sessions are frequent, the gains made in one session will be lost before the next one.

In our model the sessions are also lengthy, each being about one hour and with 40 sessions being provided for each trainee. It is not yet clear whether all participants require all the sessions. However, the majority are still making gains at the end of therapy. Therefore, the service needs to be organised to provide such intensive therapy. It is because of the need for frequent sessions that we suggest setting up a separate service to provide both assessment and treatment from a cognitive perspective. Training staff takes time and if they are only able to treat a few participants each year then they will never become expert in the provision of therapy. It has also been our experience that even when the management team is enthusiastic about CRT, when staff are required to carry out treatment as well as their other tasks, the frequency (and we believe the quality) of the treatment is affected. The results are fewer gains.

There is evidence that although CRT can improve cognition the gains made are often lost. We believe this is because participants have not yet become accustomed to using the cognitive strategies and have lost the metacognitive skills they have gained in therapy. It is therefore obvious that booster sessions may be needed over the months following therapy to ensure that gains made are consolidated. This is also useful as the gains need to be harnessed in the rehabilitation programmes for such things as supported employment. Bryson and Bell (2003) found that different sets of cognitive skills were predictive of different aspects of their rehabilitation programme and in particular at the first and second half of treatment. Booster sessions could also then ensure that the skills concerned are being used appropriately. These aspects of CRT are highlighted in Table 12.2.

In conclusion

Cognitive factors are essential to consider as part of recovery. We know from studies over the last century that recovery, measured by independent employment or a fulfilling social life, is poor in at least half the people with a diagnosis of schizophrenia. We need to improve these outcomes, and one of the barriers seems to be cognitive difficulties. Not only are these same difficulties directly related to outcomes but they may also have an effect on moderators such as medication adherence. For instance, Vauth *et al.* (2004) found that higher levels of conceptual flexibility were related to attributing adherence to the support of others, whereas better attention was related to the perception of the benefits of medication. These relationships suggest different approaches to therapies aimed at improving adherence. We need to consider any rehabilitation programmes for individuals in the context of their patterns of cognitive processing. The current prescription of therapies to improve social skills, employment as well as medication adherence is clearly limited by its failure to take into account cognitive problems, and will produce as much failure as success. Only through the development of more

Table 12.2 Issues to consider in developing CRT programmes

1. The broad context of psychological therapies:
   * draw on a clear therapeutic model
   * carry out an assessment
   * establish personal goals
   * develop and continuously revise a formulation.

2. Non-specific effects of therapy:
   * therapeutic relationship
   * warmth
   * empathy
   * provide client with a model
   * increase self-efficacy.

3. Integrating CRT into a comprehensive rehabilitation programme:
   * teach CRT first and then integrate skills into other programmes
   * embed CRT principles within other rehabilitation programmes.

4. Service issues:
   * staff training
   * informing managers
   * the level of therapist expertise for CRT
   * the number of sessions per participant
   * clinical supervision for therapists.

sophisticated approaches are we likely to be able to increase success and reduce the numbers of people considered to have limited recovery.

But of course the barrier set by cognitive processing is not the only problem. Consumers have described the three cornerstones of recovery as hope, willingness and responsible action, where glimmers of hope are encouraged and the person learns through their own actions. To foster these attributes is one of the fundamental aims of CRT. Hope is born out of the small personal successes in CRT. Willingness to make changes is encouraged through targeting motivation and self-efficacy. The progress through CRT is based on learning to respond flexibly and master some of the cognitive skills needed for responsible action. We hope that this will lead to their further empowerment to make choices so that they can begin to take part in their own individual recovery. We now have some evidence of recovery from dramatic improvements in personally judged quality of life from our own work with consumers and from others (e.g. Cupitt *et al.*, 2004).

But let us end on a tale of someone in our own programme. Her mental health team had run out of options in finding ways to engage her in rehabilitation programmes. When we began therapy she did not do anything around her house and rarely left it. We had to start therapy by visits to her home which were very short. After a couple of weeks she was able to go to her community mental health service but only because she was accompanied by her daughter. After a further three weeks she was not only attending regularly but also arrived early for the sessions. Her sustained attention improved and she began to plan activities for the forthcoming week and remember to attend her appointments. She was enthusiastic and looked much happier and her family commented on the difference in her demeanour. She now did not just get up on days when she had to attend CRT sessions but she got up on other days too. This was the effect of a specific therapy which provided some hope for people who have experienced much early failure and loss. It is now our task to take this method of therapy further and offer it as part of the panoply of interventions that help people recover from the disabling condition of schizophrenia.

References

Adams, H. E., Brantley, P. J., Malatesta, V. and Turkat, I. D. (1981) 'Modification of cognitive-processes – a case study of schizophrenia', *Journal of Consulting and Clinical Psychology*, 49, pp. 460–464.

Addington, J. and Addington, D. (1993) 'Premorbid functioning, cognitive functioning, symptoms and outcome in schizophrenia', *Journal of Psychiatry and Neuroscience*, 18, pp. 18–23.

—— (1998) 'Facial affect recognition and information processing in schizophrenia and bipolar disorder', *Schizophrenia Research*, 32, pp. 171–181.

—— (1999) 'Neurocognitive and social functioning in schizophrenia', *Schizophrenia Bulletin*, 25, pp. 173–182.

—— (2000) 'Neurocognitive and social functioning in schizophrenia: a 2.5 year follow-up study', *Schizophrenia Research*, 44, pp. 47–56.

Addington, J., McCleary, L. and Munroe-Blum, H. (1998) 'Relationship between cognitive and social dysfunction in schizophrenia', *Schizophrenia Research*, 34, pp. 59–66.

Addington, J., Addington, D. E. and Hutchinson, J. E. (2001) 'Neurocognition in early psychosis: a 2-year follow-up', *Schizophrenia Research*, 49, p. 128.

Albus, M., Hubmann, W., Ehrenberg, C., Forcht, U., Mohr, F., Sobizack, N., Wahlheim, C. and Hecht, S. (1996) 'Neuropsychological impairment in first-episode and chronic schizophrenic patients', *European Archives of Psychiatry and Clinical Neuroscience*, 246, pp. 249–255.

Aleman, A., Hijman, R., de Haan, E. H. F. and Kahn, R. S. (1999) 'Memory impairment in schizophrenia: a meta-analysis', *American Journal of Psychiatry*, 156, pp. 1358–1366.

Alexander, P. A. and Murphy, P. K. (1998) 'Profiling the differences in students' knowledge, interest, and strategic processing', *Journal of Educational Psychology*, 90, pp. 435–447.

—— (1999) 'Nurturing the seeds of transfer: a domain-specific perspective', *International Journal of Educational Research*, 31, pp. 561–576.

Allen, H. A. and Frith, C. D. (1983) 'Selective retrieval and free emission of category exemplars in schizophrenia', *British Journal of Psychology*, 74, pp. 481–490.

Allen, H. A., Liddle, P. F. and Frith, C. D. (1993) 'Negative features, retrieval processes and verbal fluency in schizophrenia', *British Journal of Psychiatry*, 163, pp. 769–775.

Allen, D. N., Goldstein, G. and Weiner, C. (2001) 'Differential neuropsychological patterns of frontal- and temporal-lobe dysfunction in patients with schizophrenia', *Schizophrenia Research*, 48, pp. 7–15.

Allen, D. N., Goldstein, G. and Warnick, E. (2003) 'A consideration of neuropsychologically normal schizophrenia', *Journal of the International Neuropsychological Society*, 9, pp. 56–63.

Allport, G. W. (1937) *Personality: A Psychological Interpretation*. New York: Holt.

Amabile, T. M., Hennessey, B. A. and Grossman, B. S. (1986) 'Social influences on creativity – the effects of contracted-for reward', *Journal of Personality and Social Psychology*, 50, pp. 14–23.

American Psychiatric Association (2000) *Diagnostic and Statistical Manual of Mental Disorders*, 4th edn, Washington, DC: American Psychiatric Association.

Anderson, R., Reeder, L. and Simon, H. (2004) 'Situated learning and education', *Educational Researcher*, 25, pp. 5–11.

Arieti, S. (1955) *Interpretation of Schizophrenia*. New York: Basic Books.

Arnold, S. E., Franz, B. R. and Trojanowski, J. Q. (1994) 'Elderly patients with schizophrenia exhibit infrequent neurodegenerative lesions', *Neurobiology of Aging*, 15, pp. 299–303.

Asarnow, R. F. and MacCrimmon, D. J. (1981) 'Span of apprehension deficits during the post-psychotic stages of schizophrenia – a replication and extension', *Archives of General Psychiatry*, 38, pp. 1007–1011.

Austin, M. P., Mitchell, P. and Goodwin, G. M. (2001) 'Cognitive deficits in depression – possible implications for functional neuropathology', *British Journal of Psychiatry*, 178, pp. 200–206.

Aylward, E., Walker, E. and Bettes, B. (1984) 'Intelligence in schizophrenia – meta-analysis of the research', *Schizophrenia Bulletin*, 10, pp. 430–459.

Babcock, H. (1933) *Dementia Praecox: A Psychological Study*. New York: Science Press.

Baddeley, A. (2000) 'The episodic buffer: a new component of working memory?', *Trends in Cognitive Sciences*, 4, pp. 417–423.

—— (2003) 'Working memory: looking back and looking forward', *Nature Reviews Neuroscience*, 4, pp. 829–839.

Baddeley, A. and Wilson, B. A. (1994) 'When implicit learning fails – amnesia and the problem of error elimination', *Neuropsychologia*, 32, pp. 53–68.

Baddeley, A. D. (1986) *Working Memory*. Oxford: Oxford University Press.

—— (1998) 'When long-term learning depends on short-term storage', *Journal of Memory and Language*, 27, pp. 586–595.

Baddeley, A. D. and Hitch, G. J. (1974) 'Working memory,' in G. A. Bower (ed.) *The Psychology of Learning and Motivation*. Oxford: Academic Press, pp. 47–89.

Balogh, D. W. and Merritt, R. D. (1985) 'Susceptibility to type-A backward pattern masking among hypothetically psychosis-prone college-students', *Journal of Abnormal Psychology*, 94, pp. 377–383.

Barch, D. A. (2003) 'Cognition in schizophrenia: Does working memory work?', *Current Directions in Psychological Science*, 12, pp. 146–150.

Barch, D. M. and Berenbaum, H. (1996), 'Language production and thought disorder in schizophrenia', *Journal of Abnormal Psychology*, 105(1), pp. 81–88.

Barch, D. M. and Carter, C. S. (1998) 'Selective attention in schizophrenia: relationship to verbal working memory', *Schizophrenia Research*, 33, pp. 53–61.

Barch, D. M. and Carter, C. S. (2005) 'Amphetamine improves cognitive function in medicated individuals with schizophrenia and in healthy volunteers', *Schizophrenia Research*, in press.

Barch, D. M., Carter, C. S., Braver, T. S., Sabb, F. W., Macdonald, A., Noll, D. C. and Cohen, J. D. (2001) 'Selective deficits in prefrontal cortex function in medication-naive patients with schizophrenia', *Archives of General Psychiatry*, 58, pp. 280–288.

Barch, D. M., Csernansky, J. G., Conturo, T. and Snyder, A. Z. (2002) 'Working and long-term memory deficits in schizophrenia: Is there a common prefrontal mechanism?', *Journal of Abnormal Psychology*, 111, pp. 478–494.

Bark, N., Revheim, N., Huq, F., Khalderov, V., Ganz, Z. W. and Medalia, A. (2003) 'The impact of cognitive remediation on psychiatric symptoms of schizophrenia', *Schizophrenia Research*, 63, pp. 229–235.

Baron, J. (1985), *Rationality and Intelligence*. Cambridge: Cambridge University Press.

—— (2000) *Thinking and Deciding*. Cambridge: Cambridge University Press.

Bartlett, F. C. (1932) *Remembering: An Experimental and Social Study*. Cambridge: Cambridge University Press.

Baruch, I., Hemsley, D. R. and Gray, J. A. (1988) 'Differential performance of acute and chronic-schizophrenics in a latent inhibition task', *Journal of Nervous and Mental Disease*, 176, pp. 598–606.

Basso, M. R., Nasrallah, H. A., Olson, S. C. and Bornstein, R. A. (1998) 'Neuropsychological correlates of negative, disorganized and psychotic symptoms in schizophrenia', *Schizophrenia Research*, 31, pp. 99–111.

Bauman, E. (1971a) 'Schizophrenic short-term memory – deficit in subjective organization', *Canadian Journal of Behavioural Science*, 3, pp. 55–61

—— (1971b), 'Schizophrenic short-term memory – role of organization at input', *Journal of Consulting and Clinical Psychology*, 36, pp. 1–14.

Bavin, L., Wagner, M., Cohen, R. and Rockstroh, B. (2001) 'Increased semantic and repetition priming in schizophrenic patients', *Journal of Abnormal Psychology*, 110, pp. 67–75.

Beadle-Brown, J., Murphy, G., Wing, L., Gould, J., Shah, A. and Holmes, N. (2002) 'Changes in social impairment for people with intellectual disabilities: a follow-up of the Camberwell cohort', *Journal of Autism and Developmental Disorders*, 32, pp. 195–206.

Beatty, W. W., Jocic, Z., Monson, N. and Staton, R. D. (1993) 'Memory and frontal-lobe dysfunction in schizophrenia and schizoaffective disorder', *Journal of Nervous and Mental Disease*, 181, pp. 448–453.

Bebbington, P. and Kuipers, L. (1994) 'The predictive utility of expressed emotion in schizophrenia – an aggregate analysis', *Psychological Medicine*, 24, pp. 707–718.

Beck, A. T. (1952) 'Successful outpatient psychotherapy of a chronic schizophrenic with a delusion based on borrowed guilt', *Psychiatry: Journal of the Study of Interpersonal Processes*, 15, pp. 305–312.

Becker, T., Leese, M., McCrone, P., Clarkson, P., Szmukler, G. and Thornicroft, G. (1998) 'Impact of community mental health services on users' social networks – PRiSM Psychosis Study 7', *British Journal of Psychiatry*, 173, pp. 404–408.

Beech, A., Powell, T., Mcwilliam, J. and Claridge, G. (1989) 'Evidence of reduced cognitive inhibition in schizophrenia', *British Journal of Clinical Psychology*, 28, pp. 109–116.

Bell, M. D. and Bryson, G. (2001) 'Work rehabilitation in schizophrenia: Does cognitive impairment limit improvement?', *Schizophrenia Bulletin*, 27, pp. 269–279.

Bell, M. D. and Lysaker, P. H. (1995) 'Psychiatric symptoms and work performance among persons with severe mental illness', *Psychiatric Services*, 46, pp. 508–510.

Bell, M. D., Greig, T. C., Kaplan, E. and Bryson, G. (1997) 'Wisconsin card sorting test dimensions in schizophrenia: factorial, predictive, and divergent validity', *Journal of Clinical and Experimental Neuropsychology*, 19, pp. 933–941.

Bell, M., Bryson, G., Greig, T., Corcoran, C. and Wexler, B. E. (2001a) 'Neurocognitive enhancement therapy with work therapy – effects on neuropsychological test performance', *Archives to General Psychiatry*, 58, pp. 763–768.

Bell, M. D., Greig, T. C., Bryson, G. and Kaplan, E. (2001b) 'Patterns of object relations and reality testing deficits in schizophrenia: Clusters and their symptom and personality correlates', *Journal of Clinical Psychology*, 57, pp. 1353–1367.

Bell, M., Bryson, G. and Wexler, B. E. (2003) 'Cognitive remediation of working memory deficits: durability of training effects in severely impaired and less severely impaired schizophrenia', *Acta Psychiatrica Scandinavica*, 108, pp. 101–109.

Bell, M. D., Bryson, G., Fiszdon, J. M., Greig, T. and Wexler, B. E. (2004) 'Neurocognitive enhancement therapy and work therapy in schizophrenia: work outcomes at 6 months and 12 month follow-up', *Biological Psychiatry*, 55, p. 335.

Bellack, A. S. (1992) 'Cognitive rehabilitation for schizophrenia – is it possible – is it necessary', *Schizophrenia Bulletin*, 18, pp. 43–50.

Bellack, A. S., Mueser, K. T., Morrison, R. L., Tierney, A. and Podell, K. (1990) 'Remediation of cognitive deficits in schizophrenia', *American Journal of Psychiatry*, 147, pp. 1650–1655.

Bellack, A. S., Blanchard, J. J. and Mueser, K. T. (1996) 'Cue availability and affect perception in schizophrenia', *Schizophrenia Bulletin*, 22, pp. 535–544.

Bellack, A. S., Sayers, M., Mueser, K. T. and Bennett, M. (1994) 'Evaluation of social-problem solving in schizophrenia', *Journal of Abnormal Psychology*, 103, pp. 371–378.

Bellack, A. S., Gold, J. M. and Buchanan, R. W. (1999) 'Cognitive rehabilitation for schizophrenia: problems, prospects, and strategies', *Schizophrenia Bulletin*, 25, pp. 257–274.

Bellack, A. S., Weinhardt, L. S., Gold, J. M. and Gearon, J. S. (2001) 'Generalization of training effects in schizophrenia', *Schizophrenia Research*, 48, pp. 255–262.

Bellucci, D. M., Glaberman, K. and Haslam, N. (2003) 'Computer-assisted cognitive rehabilitation reduces negative symptoms in the severely mentally ill', *Schizophrenia Research*, 59, pp. 225–232.

Benedict, R. H. B. and Harris, A. E. (1989) 'Remediation of attention deficits in chronic-schizophrenic patients – a preliminary study', *British Journal of Clinical Psychology*, 28, pp. 187–188.

Benedict, R. H. B., Harris, A. E., Markow, T., Mccormick, J. A., Nuechterlein, K. H. and Asarnow, R. F. (1994) 'Effects of attention training on information-processing in schizophrenia', *Schizophrenia Bulletin*, 20, pp. 537–546.

Bengtsson-Tops, A. and Hansson, L. (2001) 'Quantitative and qualitative aspects of the social network in schizophrenic patients living in the community. Relationship to sociodemographic characteristics and clinical factors and subjective quality of life', *International Journal of Social Psychiatry*, 47, pp. 67–77.

Bentall, R. (2003) *Madness Explained: Psychosis and Human Nature*. London: Allen Lane.

Bentall, R. P. and Slade, P. D. (1985) 'Reality testing and auditory hallucinations –

a signal detection analysis', *British Journal of Clinical Psychology*, 24, pp. 159–169.

Bentall, R. P., Lewis, S., Tarrier, N., Haddock, G., Drake, R. and Day, J. (2003) 'Relationships matter: the impact of the therapeutic alliance on outcome in schizophrenia', *Schizophrenia Research*, 60, p. 319.

Ben-Yishay, Y., Piasetsky, E. B. and Rattok, A. (1987) 'Effectiveness of an attention-training program', in M. Meier, A. Benton and L. Diller (eds), *Neuropsychological Rehabilitation*. New York: Guilford Press, pp. 165–181.

Berg, E. A. (1948) 'A simple, objective technique for measuring flexibility in thinking', *Journal of General Psychology*, 39, pp. 15–22.

Biemiller, A. and Meichenbaum, D. (1998) 'The consequences of negative scaffolding for students who learn slowly – a commentary on C. Addison Stone's "The metaphor of scaffolding: its utility for the field of learning disabilities"', *Journal of Learning Disabilities*, 31, pp. 365–369.

Bilder, R. M., Goldman, R. S., Robinson, D., Reiter, G., Bell, L., Bates, J. A., Pappadopulos, E., Willson, D. F., Alvir, J. M. J., Woerner, M. G., Geisler, S., Kane, J. M. and Lieberman, J. A. (2000) 'Neuropsychology of first-episode schizophrenia: initial characterization and clinical correlates', *American Journal of Psychiatry*, 157, pp. 549–559.

Bilder, R. M., Goldman, R. S., Volavka, J., Czobor, P., Hoptman, M., Sheitman, B., Lindenmayer, J. P., Citrome, L., McEvoy, J., Kunz, M., Chakos, M., Cooper, T. B., Horowitz, T. L. and Lieberman, J. A. (2002a), 'Neurocognitive effects of clozapine, olanzapine, risperidone, and haloperidol in patients with chronic schizophrenia or schizoaffective disorder', *American Journal of Psychiatry*, 159, pp. 1018–1028.

Bilder, R. M., Volavka, J., Czobor, P., Malhotra, A. K., Kennedy, J. L., Ni, X. Q., Goldman, R. S., Hoptman, M. J., Sheitman, B., Lindenmayer, J. P., Citrome, L., Mcevoy, J. P., Kunz, M., Chakos, M., Cooper, T. B. and Lieberman, J. A. (2002b) 'Neurocognitive correlates of the COMT Val (158) Met polymorphism in chronic schizophrenia', *Biological Psychiatry*, 52, pp. 701–707.

Binder, J., Albus, M., Hubmann, W., Scherer, J., Sobizack, N., Franz, U., Mohr, F. and Hecht, S. (1998) 'Neuropsychological impairment and psychopathology in first-episode schizophrenic patients related to the early course of illness', *European Archives of Psychiatry and Clinical Neuroscience*, 248, pp. 70–77.

Birchwood, M., Smith, J., Cochrane, R., Wetton, S. and Copestake, S. (1990) 'The social functioning scale – the development and validation of a new scale of social adjustment for use in family intervention programs with schizophrenic patients', *British Journal of Psychiatry*, 157, pp. 853–859.

Birchwood, M., Iqbal, Z., Chadwick, P. and Trower, P. (2000) 'Cognitive approach to depression and suicidal thinking in psychosis I. Ontogeny of post-psychotic depression', *British Journal of Psychiatry*, 177, pp. 516–521.

Bleuler, E. (1950) *Dementia Praecox or the Group of Schizophrenias*. New York: International Universities Press.

Bokat, C. E. and Goldberg, T. E. (2003) 'Letter and category fluency in schizophrenic patients: a meta-analysis', *Schizophrenia Research*, 64, pp. 73–78.

Borod, J. C., Alpert, M., Brozgold, A., Martin, C., Welkowitz, J., Diller, L., Peselow, E., Angrist, B. and Lieberman, A. (1989) 'A preliminary comparison of flat affect schizophrenics and brain-damaged patients on measures of affective processing', *Journal of Communication Disorders*, 22, pp. 93–104.

Bowen, L., Wallace, C. J., Glynn, S. M., Neuchterlein, K. H., Lutzker, J. R. and Kuehnel, T. G. (1994) 'Schizophrenic individuals cognitive functioning and performance in interpersonal interactions and skills training procedures', *Journal of Psychiatric Research*, 28, pp. 289–301.

Bracy, O. (1995) *CogRehab Software.* Indianapolis: Psychological Software Services.

Bradshaw, W. and Brekke, J. S. (1999) 'Subjective experience in schizophrenia: factors influencing self-esteem, satisfaction with life, and subjective distress', *American Journal of Orthopsychiatry*, 69, pp. 254–260.

Braff, D. L. (1993) 'Information processing and attention dysfunctions in schizophrenia', *Schizophrenia Bulletin*, 19, pp. 233–259.

Bransford, J. D. and Schwartz, D. L. (1999) 'Rethinking transfer: a simple proposal with multiple implications,' in A. Iran-Nejad and P. D. Pearson (eds) *Review of Research in Education*, 24th edn, Washington, DC: American Educational Research Association, pp. 61–100.

Bray, N. J., Buckland, P. R., Williams, N. M., Williams, H. J., Norton, N., Owen, M. J. and O'Donovan, M. C. (2003) 'A haplotype implicated in schizophrenia susceptibility is associated with reduced COMT expression in human brain', *American Journal of Human Genetics*, 73, pp. 152–161.

Brazo, P., Marie, R. M., Halbecq, I., Benali, K., Segard, L., Delamillieure, P., Langlois-Thery, S., Van der Elst, A., Thibaut, F., Petit, M. and Dollfus, S. (2002) 'Cognitive patterns in subtypes of schizophrenia', *European Psychiatry*, 17, pp. 155–162.

Brebion, G., Amador, X., Smith, M. J. and Gorman, J. M. (1997a) 'Mechanisms underlying memory impairment in schizophrenia', *Psychological Medicine*, 27, pp. 383–393.

Brebion, G., Smith, M. J., Amador, X., Malaspina, D. and Gorman, J. M. (1997b) 'Clinical correlates of memory in schizophrenia differential links between depression, positive and negative symptoms, and two types of memory impairment', *American Journal of Psychiatry*, 154, pp. 1538–1543.

Brebion, G., Amador, X., Smith, M. J. and Gorman, J. M. (1998) 'Memory impairment and schizophrenia: the role of processing speed', *Schizophrenia Research*, 30, pp. 31–39.

Brebion, G., Amador, X., Smith, S., Malaspina, D., Sharif, Z. and Gorman, J. M. (2000a) 'Depression, psychomotor retardation, negative symptoms, and memory in schizophrenia', *Neuropsychiatry Neuropsychology and Behavioral Neurology*, 13, pp. 177–183.

Brebion, G., Smith, M. J., Gorman, J. M., Malaspina, D., Sharif, Z. and Amador, X. (2000b) 'Memory and schizophrenia: differential link of processing speed and selective attention with two levels of encoding', *Journal of Psychiatric Research*, 34, pp. 121–127.

Brebion, G., Groman, J. M., Malaspina, D., Sharif, Z. and Amador, X. (2001) 'Clinical and cognitive factors associated with verbal memory task performance in patients with schizophrenia', *American Journal of Psychiatry*, 158, pp. 758–764.

Brenner, H. D., Hodel, B., Roder, V. and Corrigan, P. (1992) 'Treatment of cognitive dysfunctions and behavioral deficits in schizophrenia', *Schizophrenia Bulletin*, 18, pp. 21–26.

Brenner, H. D., Roder, V., Hodel, B., Kienzle, N., Reed, D. and Liberman, R. P. (1994) *Integrated Psychological Therapy for Schizophrenic Patients (IPT).* New York: Hogrefe and Huber.

Broadbent, D. E. (1958) *Perception and Communication.* London: Pergamon.

Brown, C., Harwood, K., Hays, C., Heckman, J. and Shot, J. (1993) 'Effectiveness of cognitive rehabilitation for improving attention in patients with schizophrenia', *Occupational Therapy Journal of Research*, 13, pp. 71–86.

Bryson, G. and Bell, M. D. (2001) 'Work performance improvement in schizophrenia: symptom and cognitive predictors', *Schizophrenia Research*, 49, p. 258.

—— (2003) 'Initial and final work performance in schizophrenia: cognitive and symptom predictors', *Journal of Nervous and Mental Disease*, 191, pp. 87–92.

Bryson, G., Bell, M. and Lysaker, P. (1997) 'Affect recognition in schizophrenia: a function of global impairment or a specific cognitive deficit', *Psychiatry Research*, 71, pp. 105–113.

Bryson, G., Whelahan, H. A. and Bell, M. (2001) 'Memory and executive function impairments in deficit syndrome schizophrenia', *Psychiatry Research*, 102, pp. 29–37.

Burda, P. C., Starkey, T. W. and Dominguez, F. (1991) 'Computer administered treatment of psychiatric inpatients', *Computers in Human Behavior*, 7, pp. 1–5.

Burgess, P. and Shallice, T. (1996) *The Hayling and Brixton Tests.* Bury St Edmunds: Thames Valley Test Company (TVTC).

Butler, P. D., DeSanti, L. A., Maddox, J., Harkavy-Friedman, J. M., Amador, X. F., Goetz, R. R., Javitt, D. C. and Gorman, J. M. (2003) 'Visual backward-masking deficits in schizophrenia: relationship to visual pathway function and symptomatology', *Schizophrenia Research*, 59, pp. 199–209.

Buzan, T. and Buzan, B. (1996) *The Mind Map Book: How to Use Radiant Thinking to Maximize Your Brain's Untapped Potential.* London: Plume.

Cadenhead, K. S., Serper, Y. and Braff, D. L. (1998) 'Transient versus sustained visual channels in the visual backward masking deficits of schizophrenia patients', *Biological Psychiatry*, 43, pp. 132–138.

Calev, A. (1984a) 'Recall and recognition in chronic non-demented schizophrenics – use of matched tasks', *Journal of Abnormal Psychology*, 93, pp. 172–177.

—— (1984b) 'Recall and recognition in mildly disturbed schizophrenics – the use of matched tasks', *Psychological Medicine*, 14, pp. 425–429.

Calev, A., Edelist, S., Kugelmass, S. and Lerer, B. (1991) 'Performance of long-stay schizophrenics on matched verbal and visuospatial recall tasks', *Psychological Medicine*, 21, pp. 655–660.

Campione, J. C., Shapiro, A. M. and Brown, A. L. (1995) 'Forms of transfer in a community of learners. Flexible learning and understanding', in A. E. McKeough, J. Lupart and A. Marim (eds) *Teaching for Transfer – Fostering Generalisation in Learning*, Mahwah, NJ: Lawrence Erlbaum Associates, Inc., pp. 35–68.

Cancro, R., Sutton, S., Kerr, J. and Sugerman, A. A. (1971) 'Reaction time and prognosis in acute schizophrenia', *Journal of Nervous and Mental Disease*, 153, pp. 351–359.

Cannon, M., Jones, P., Huttunen, M. O., Tanskanen, A., Huttunen, T., Rabe-Hesketh, S. and Murray, R. M. (1999) 'School performance in Finnish children and later development of schizophrenia – a population-based longitudinal study', *Archives of General Psychiatry*, 56, pp. 457–463.

Cannon, M., Walsh, E., Hollis, C., Kargin, M., Taylor, E., Murray, R. and Jones, P. (2001) 'Predictors of later schizophrenia and affective psychosis among attendees at a child psychiatry department', *British Journal of Psychiatry*, 178, pp. 420–426.

Cannon, T. D., Bearden, C. E., Hollister, J. M., Rosso, I. M., Sanchez, L. E. and Hadley, T. (2000) 'Childhood cognitive functioning in schizophrenia patients and their unaffected siblings: a prospective cohort study', *Schizophrenia Bulletin*, 26, pp. 379–393.

Cannon, M., Caspi, A., Moffitt, T. E., Harington, H., Taylor, A., Murray, R. M. and Poulton, R. (2002) 'Evidence for early-childhood, pan-developmental impairment specific to schizophreniform disorder: results from a longitudinal birth cohort', *Archives of General Psychiatry*, 59, pp. 449–456.

Carroll, A., Fattah, S., Clyde, Z., Coffey, I., Owens, D. G. C. and Johnstone, E. C. (1999) 'Correlates of insight and insight change in schizophrenia', *Schizophrenia Research*, 35, pp. 247–253.

Carstairs, K., Okocha, C. I., Hemsley, D., Toone, B. and Sivakumar, K. (1995) 'An application of Shallice's response selection model to the symptoms of schizophrenia', *Neurology Psychiatry and Brain Research*, 3, pp. 211–218.

Carter, C., Robertson, L., Nordahl, T., Chaderjian, M., Kraft, L. and OShoraCelaya, L. (1996) 'Spatial working memory deficits and their relationship to negative symptoms in unmedicated schizophrenia patients', *Biological Psychiatry*, 40, pp. 930–932.

Caspi, A., Reichenberg, A., Weiser, M., Rabinowitzc, J., Kaplan, Z., Knobler, H., Davidson-Sagi, N. and Davidson, M. (2003) 'Cognitive performance in schizophrenia patients assessed before and following the first psychotic episode', *Schizophrenia Research*, 65, pp. 87–94.

Censits, D. M., Ragland, J. D., Gur, R. C. and Gur, R. E. (1997) 'Neuropsychological evidence supporting a neurodevelopmental model of schizophrenia: a longitudinal study', *Schizophrenia Research*, 24, pp. 289–298.

Cervone, D. (1993) 'The role of self-referent cognitions in goal setting, motivation, and performance,' in M. Rabonowitz (ed.) *Cognitive Science Foundations of Instruction*. Hillsdale, NJ: Lawrence Erlbaum Associates, Inc., pp. 57–95.

Chadwick, P., Lees, S. and Birchwood, M. (2000) 'The revised beliefs about voices questionnaire (BAVQ-R)', *British Journal of Psychiatry*, 177, pp. 229–232.

Chapman, L. J. and Chapman, J. P. (1973) 'Problems in measurement of cognitive deficit', *Psychological Bulletin*, 79, pp. 380–385.

—— (1978) 'Measurement of differential deficit', *Journal of Psychiatric Research*, 14, pp. 303–311.

Chen, E. Y. H., Wilkins, A. J. and McKenna, P. J. (1994) 'Semantic memory is both impaired and anomalous in schizophrenia', *Psychological Medicine*, 24, pp. 193–202.

Chen, E. Y. H., Lam, L. C. W., Chen, R. Y. L., Nguyen, D. G. H., Chan, C. K. Y. and Wilkins, A. J. (1997) 'Neuropsychological correlates of sustained attention in schizophrenia', *Schizophrenia Research*, 24, pp. 299–310.

Chen, E. Y. H., Kwok, C. L., Chen, R. Y. L. and Kwong, P. P. K. (2001) 'Insight changes in acute psychotic episodes – a prospective study of Hong Kong Chinese patients', *Journal of Nervous and Mental Disease*, 189, pp. 24–30.

Chen, W. J. and Faraone, S. V. (2000) 'Sustained attention deficits as markers of genetic susceptibility to schizophrenia', *American Journal of Medical Genetics*, 97, pp. 52–57.

Chen, W. J., Liu, S. K., Chang, C. J., Lien, Y. J., Chang, Y. H. and Hwu, H. G. (1998) 'Sustained attention deficit and schizotypal personality features in nonpsychotic relatives of schizophrenic patients', *American Journal of Psychiatry*, 155, pp. 1214–1220.

Cicerone, K. D., Dahlberg, C., Kalmar, K., Langenbahn, D. M., Malec, J. F., Bergquist, T. F., Felicetti, T., Giacino, J. T., Harley, J. P., Harrington, D. E., Herzog, J., Kneipp, S., Laatsch, L. and Morse, P. A. (2000) 'Evidence-based cognitive rehabilitation: recommendations for clinical practice', *Archives of Physical Medicine and Rehabilitation*, 81, pp. 1596–1615.

Ciompi, L. (1980) 'The natural history of schizophrenia in the long term', *British Journal of Psychiatry*, 136, pp. 413–420.

Cirillo, M. A. and Seidman, L. J. (2003) 'Verbal declarative memory dysfunction in schizophrenia: From clinical assessment to genetics and brain mechanisms', *Neuropsychology Review*, 13, pp. 43–77.

Clare, L., McKenna, P. J., Mortimer, A. M. and Baddeley, A. D. (1992) 'Preserved procedural and implicit memory in schizophrenia: further evidence for an amnesic syndrome pattern of impairment', *Schizophrenia Research*, 6, p. 156.

—— (1993) 'Memory in schizophrenia – what is impaired and what is preserved', *Neuropsychologia*, 31, pp. 1225–1241.

Cohen, J. D. and Servan-Schreiber, D. (1992) 'Context, cortex, and dopamine – a connectionist approach to behavior and biology in schizophrenia', *Psychological Review*, 99, pp. 45–77.

Cohen, J. D., Barch, D. M., Servan-Schreiber, D. and Carter, C. S. (1996) 'Context processing disturbances in schizophrenia: Empirical test of a theoretical model', *Biological Psychiatry*, 39, p. 370.

Cohen, J. D., Barch, D. M., Carter, C. and Servan-Schreiber, D. (1999) 'Context-processing deficits in schizophrenia: converging evidence from three theoretically motivated cognitive tasks', *Journal of Abnormal Psychology*, 108, pp. 120–133.

Concise Oxford Dictionary, 10th edn. (1999) New York: Oxford University Press.

Conklin, H. M., Curtis, C. E., Katsanis, J. and Iacono, W. G. (2000) 'Verbal working memory impairment in schizophrenia patients and their first-degree relatives: evidence from the digit span task', *American Journal of Psychiatry*, 157, pp. 275–277.

Cook, J. A. and Razzano, L. (2000) 'Vocational rehabilitation for persons with schizophrenia: recent research and implications for practice', *Schizophrenia Bulletin*, 26, pp. 87–103.

Cooper, G. and Sweller, J. (1987) 'Effects of schema acquisition and rule automation on mathematical problem-solving transfer', *Journal of Educational Psychology*, 79, pp. 347–362.

Cornblatt, B. and Obuchowski, M. (1997) 'Update of high-risk research: 1987–1997', *International Review of Psychiatry*, 9, pp. 437–447.

Corrigan, P. W. and Basit, A. (1997) 'Generalization of social skills training for persons with severe mental illness', *Cognitive and Behavioral Practice*, 4, pp. 191–206.

Corrigan, P. W. and Toomey, R. (1995) 'Interpersonal problem-solving and information-processing in schizophrenia', *Schizophrenia Bulletin*, 21, pp. 395–403.

Corrigan, P. W. and Nelson, D. R. (1998) 'Factors that affect social cue recognition in schizophrenia', *Psychiatry Research*, 78, pp. 189–196.

Corrigan, P. W., Green, M. F. and Toomey, R. (1994) 'Cognitive correlates to social cue perception in schizophrenia', *Psychiatry Research.*, 53, pp. 141–151.

Corrigan, P., Hirschbeck, J. and Wolfe, M. (1995) 'Memory and vigilance training to improve social perception in schizophrenia', *Schizophrenia Research*, 17, pp. 257–265.

Cosway, R., Byrne, M., Clafferty, R., Hodges, A., Grant, E., Abukmeil, S. S., Lawrie, S. M., Miller, P. and Johnstone, E. C. (2000) 'Neuropsychological change in young people at high risk for schizophrenia: results from the first two neuropsychological assessments of the Edinburgh High Risk Study', *Psychological Medicine*, 30, pp. 1111–1121.

Cowan, N. (1988) 'Evolving conceptions of memory storage, selective attention and their mutual constrains within the human information-processing systems', *Psychological Bulletin*, 104, pp. 163–191.

Crawford, J. R., Moore, J. W. and Cameron, I. M. (1992) 'Verbal fluency – A nart-based equation for the estimation of premorbid performance', *British Journal of Clinical Psychology*, 31, pp. 327–329.

Cromwell, R. L. and Spaulding, W. (1978) *How Schizophrenics Handle Information*. New York: Spectrum.

Cuesta, M. J. and Peralta, V. (1995) 'Cognitive disorders in the positive, negative, and disorganization syndromes of schizophrenia', *Psychiatry Research*, 58, pp. 227–235.

Cuevas, H. M., Fiore, S. M. and Oser, R. L. (2002) 'Scaffolding cognitive and meta-cognitive processes in low verbal ability learners: use of diagrams in computer-based training environments', *Instructional Science*, 30, pp. 433–464.

Cuppitt, C., Byrne, L. and Tompson, N. (2004) 'Delivering cognitive remediation therapy in clinical setting', *Clinical Psychology*, 37, pp. 10–14.

Cutting, J. E. (1985) 'Perception and cognition – Heil, J', *Contemporary Psychology*, 30, pp. 186–188.

Daban, C., Amado, I., Bayle, F., Gut, A., Willard, D., Bourdel, M. C., Loo, H., Olie, J. P., Millet, B., Krebs, M. O. and Poirier, M. F. (2002) 'Correlation between clinical syndromes and neuropsychological tasks in unmedicated patients with recent onset schizophrenia', *Psychiatry Research*, 113, pp. 83–92.

Danion, J. M., Rizzo, L. and Bruant, A. (1999) 'Functional mechanisms underlying impaired recognition memory and conscious awareness in patients with schizophrenia', *Archives of General Psychiatry*, 56, pp. 639–644.

Danion, J. M., Gokalsing, E., Robert, P., Massin-Krauss, M. and Bacon, E. (2001a) 'Defective relationship between subjective experience and behavior in schizophrenia', *American Journal of Psychiatry*, 158, pp. 2064–2066.

Danion, J. M., Meulemans, T., Kauffmann-Muller, F. and Vermaat, H. (2001b) 'Intact implicit learning in schizophrenia', *American Journal of Psychiatry*, 158, pp. 944–948.

David, A. S. (1999) 'Intelligence and schizophrenia', *Acta Psychiatrica Scandinavica*, 100, pp. 1–2.

David, A., Van Os, J., Jones, P., Harvey, I., Foerster, A. and Fahy, T. (1995) 'Insight and psychotic illness – cross-sectional and longitudinal associations', *British Journal of Psychiatry*, 167, pp. 621–628.

David, A. S., Malmberg, A., Brandt, L., Allebeck, P. and Lewis, G. (1997) 'IQ and risk for schizophrenia: a population-based cohort study', *Psychological Medicine*, 27, pp. 1311–1323.

Davidson, L. (2003) *Living Outside Mental Illness: Qualitative Studies of Recovery in Schizophrenia*. New York: New York University Press.

Davidson, M., Harvey, P. D., Powchik, P., Parrella, M., White, L., Knobler, H. Y., Losonczy, M. F., Keefe, R. S. E., Katz, S. and Frecska, E. (1995) 'Severity of symptoms in chronically institutionalized geriatric schizophrenic patients', *American Journal of Psychiatry*, 152, pp. 197–207.

Davidson, M., Reichenberg, A., Rabinowitz, J., Weiser, M., Kaplan, Z. and Mark, M. (1999) 'Behavioral and intellectual markers for schizophrenia in apparently healthy male adolescents', *American Journal of Psychiatry*, 156, pp. 1328–1335.

De Corte, E. (2003) 'Transfer as the productive use of acquired knowledge, skills, and motivations', *Current Directions in Psychological Science*, 12, pp. 142–146.

Deegan, P. E. (1997) 'Recovery and empowerment for people with psychiatric disabilities', *Social Work in Health Care*, 25, pp. 11–24.

—— (1998) *The Number Sense: How the Mind Creates Mathematics*. Harmondsworth: Penguin.

Delahunty, A. and Morice, R. (1993) *A Training Programme for the Remediation of Cognitive Deficits in Schizophrenia*. Albury, NSW: Dept. of Health.

Delahunty, A., Morice, R. and Frost, B. (1993) 'Specific cognitive flexibility rehabilitation in schizophrenia', *Psychological Medicine*, 23, pp. 221–227.

Delahunty, A., Reeder, C., Wykes, T., Morice, R. and Newton, E. (2002) *Revised Cognitive Remediation Therapy Manual*. London: Institute of Psychiatry.

Deldin, P. J., Keller, J., Gergen, J. A. and Miller, G. A. (2000) 'Right-posterior face processing anomaly in depression', *Journal of Abnormal Psychology*, 109, pp. 116–121.

Della Sala, S. and Logie, R. H. (1997) 'Impairments of methodology and theory in cognitive neuropsychology: a case for rehabilitation?', *Neuropsychological Rehabilitation*, 7, pp. 367–385.

Della Sala, S., Logie, R. H., Trivelli, C., Cubelli, R. and Marchetti, C. (1998) 'Dissociation between recency and span: neuropsychological and experimental evidence', *Neuropsychology*, 12, pp. 533–545.

DeSisto, M., Harding, C. M., Mccormick, R. V., Ashikaga, T. and Brooks, G. W. (1995) 'The Maine and Vermont 3-decade studies of serious mental-illness 2. Longitudinal course comparisons', *British Journal of Psychiatry*, 167, pp. 338–342.

DeSisto, M., Harding, C. M., Mccormick, R. V., Ashikaga, T. and Brooks, G. W. (1999) 'The Maine and Vermont three-decade studies of serious mental illness: longitudinal course comparisons', in P. Chohen, C. Slomkowski *et al.* (eds) *Historical and Geographical Influences on Psychopathology*. Mahwah, NJ: Lawrence Erlbaum Associates, Inc., pp. 331–348.

De Soto, C. B. (1960) 'Learning a social structure', *Journal of Abnormal and Social Psychology*, 60, pp. 417–421.

Dewey, J. (1910) *How We Think*. Buffalo, NY: Prometheus Books.

Donohoe, G. and Robertson, I. H. (2003) 'Can specific deficits in executive function explain the negative symptoms of schizophrenia? A review', *Neurocase*, 9, pp. 97–108.

Drake, R. J. and Lewis, S. W. (2003) 'Insight and neurocognition in schizophrenia', *Schizophrenia Research*, 62, pp. 165–173.

Duffy, L. and O'Carroll, R. (1994) 'Memory impairment in schizophrenia – a comparison with that observed in the alcoholic Korsakoff syndrome', *Psychological Medicine*, 24, pp. 155–165.

Dunn, R. S. and Dunn, K. J. (1979) 'Learning styles teaching styles – should they . . . can they . . . be matched', *Educational Leadership*, 36, pp. 238–244.

Durkin, D. (1978) 'What classroom observations reveal about reading comphrehensive instruction', *Reading Research Quarterly*, 14, pp. 481–533.

Dykstra, T. (1997) 'First person account: How I cope', *Schizophrenia Bulletin*, 23, pp. 697–699.

Edwards, J., Jackson, H. J. and Pattison, P. E. (2002) 'Emotion recognition via facial expression and affective prosody in schizophrenia: a methodological review', *Clinical Psychology Review*, 22, pp. 789–832.

Efron, R. (1970a) 'Effect of stimulus duration on perceptual onset and offset latencies', *Perception and Psychophysics*, 8(4), pp. 231–234.

—— (1970b) 'The relationship between duration of a stimulus and duration of a perception', *Neuropsychologia*, 8(1), pp. 37–55.

Egan, M. F., Goldberg, T. E., Gscheidle, T., Weirich, M., Bigelow, L. B. and Weinberger, D. R. (2000) 'Relative risk of attention deficits in siblings of patients with schizophrenia', *American Journal of Psychiatry*, 157, pp. 1309–1316.

Egan, M. F., Goldberg, T. E., Kolachana, B. S., Callicott, J. H., Mazzanti, C. M., Straub, R. E., Goldman, D. and Weinberger, D. R. (2001a) 'Effect of COMT Val(108/158) Met genotype on frontal lobe function and risk for schizophrenia', *Proceedings of the National Academy of Sciences of the United States of America*, 98, pp. 6917–6922.

Egan, M. F., Hyde, T. M., Bonomo, J. B., Mattay, V. S., Bigelow, L. B., Goldberg, T. E. and Weinberger, D. R. (2001b) 'Relative risk of neurological signs in siblings of patients with schizophrenia', *American Journal of Psychiatry*, 158, pp. 1827–1834.

Ekman, P. and Friesen, W. V. (1975) *Unmasking the Face: A Guide to Recognising Emotions from Facial Clues.* Englewood Cliffs, NJ: Prentice Hall.

Elvevag, B., Duncan, J. and McKenna, P. J. (2000a) 'The use of cognitive context in schizophrenia: an investigation', *Psychological Medicine*, 30, pp. 885–897.

Elvevag, B., Weinberger, D. R., Suter, J. C. and Goldberg, T. E. (2000b) 'Continuous performance test and schizophrenia: a test of stimulus-response compatibility, working memory, response readiness, or none of the above?', *American Journal of Psychiatry*, 157, pp. 772–780.

Elvevag, B., Weinstock, D. M., Akil, M., Kleinman, J. E. and Goldberg, T. E. (2001) 'A comparison of verbal fluency tasks in schizophrenic patients and normal controls', *Schizophrenia Research*, 51, pp. 119–126.

Ericsson, K. A., Chase, W. G. and Faloon, S. (1980) 'Acquisition of a memory skill', *Science*, 208, pp. 1181–1182.

Estes, W. K. and Taylor, H. A. (1964) 'Detection method + probabilistic models for assessing information processing from brief visual displays', *Proceedings of the National Academy of Sciences of the United States of America*, 52, pp. 446–453.

Faraone, S. V., Green, A. I., Seidman, L. J. and Tsuang, M. T. (2001) ' "Schizotaxia": clinical implications and new directions for research', *Schizophrenia Bulletin*, 27, pp. 1–18.

Field, C., Galletly, C. Anderson, D. and Walker, P. (1997) 'Computer-aided cognitive rehabilitation: possible application to the attentional deficit of schizophrenia, a report of negative results.', *Perceptual and Motor Skills*, 85, pp. 995–1002.

Filion, D. L., Dawson, M. and Schell, A. (1998) 'The psychological significance of human startle eyeblink modification: a review', *Biological Psychology*, 28, pp. 187–188.

Fine, C., Lumsden, J. and Blair, R. J. R. (2001) 'Dissociation between "theory of mind" and executive functions in a patient with early left amygdala damage', *Brain*, 124, pp. 287–298.

Fiszdon, J. M., Bryson, G. J., Wexler, B. E. and Bell, M. D. (2004) 'Durability of cognitive remediation training in schizophrenia: performance on two memory tasks at 6-month and 12-month follow-up', *Psychiatry Research*, 125, pp. 1–7.

Flavell, J. H. (1979) 'Meta-cognition and cognitive monitoring – new area of cognitive-developmental inquiry', *American Psychologist*, 34, pp. 906–911.

Flavell, J. H., Miller, P. H. and Miller, S. A. (2002) *Cognitive Development*, 4th edn. Upper Saddle River, NJ: Prentice Hall.

Fleming, K., Goldberg, T. E., Gold, J. M. and Weinberger, D. R. 1995, 'Verbal working-memory dysfunction in schizophrenia – use of a Brown-Peterson paradigm', *Psychiatry Research*, 56(2), pp. 155–161.

Fleming, K., Goldberg, T. E., Binks, S., Randolph, C., Gold, J. M. and Weinberger, D. R. (1997) 'Visuospatial working memory in patients with schizophrenia', *Biological Psychiatry*, 41, pp. 43–49.

Freeman, L. C., Romney, A. K. and Freeman, S. C. (1987) 'Cognitive structure and informant accuracy', *American Anthropologist*, 89, pp. 310–325.

Friedman, J. I., Harvey, P. D., McGurk, S. R., White, L., Parrella, M., Raykov, T., Coleman, T., Adler, D. N. and Davis, K. L. (2002) 'Correlates of change in functional status of institutionalized geriatric schizophrenic patients: focus on medical comorbidity', *American Journal of Psychiatry*, 159, pp. 1388–1394.

Frith, C. D. (1979) 'Consciousness, information-processing and schizophrenia', *British Journal of Psychiatry*, 134, pp. 225–235.

—— (1987) 'The positive and negative symptoms of schizophrenia reflect impairments in the perception and initiation of action', *Psychological Medicine*, 17, pp. 631–648.

—— (1992) *The Cognitive Neuropsychology of Schizophrenia*. Hove, UK: Lawrence Erlbaum Associates.

Frith, C. D. and Corcoran, R. (1996) 'Exploring "theory of mind" in people with schizophrenia', *Psychological Medicine*, 26, pp. 521–530.

Frith, C. D. and Done, D. J. (1988) 'Towards a neuropsychology of schizophrenia', *British Journal of Psychiatry*, 153, pp. 437–443.

—— (1989) 'Experiences of alien control in schizophrenia reflect a disorder in the central monitoring of action', *Psychological Medicine*, 19, pp. 359–363.

Fucetola, R., Seidman, L. J., Kremen, W. S., Faraone, S. V., Goldstein, J. M. and Tsuang, M. T. (2000) 'Age and neuropsychological function in schizophrenia: a decline in executive abilities beyond that observed in healthy volunteers', *Biological Psychiatry*, 48, pp. 137–146.

Fuchs, L. S., Fuchs, D., Prentice, K., Burch, M., Hamlett, C. L., Owen, R., Hosp, M. and Jancek, D. (2003a) 'Explicitly teaching for transfer: effects on third-grade students' mathematical problem solving', *Journal of Educational Psychology*, 95(2), pp. 293–305.

Fuchs, L. S., Fuchs, D., Prentice, K., Burch, M., Hamlett, C. L., Owen, R. and Schroeter, K. (2003b) 'Enhancing third-grade students' mathematical problem solving with self-regulated learning strategies', *Journal of Educational Psychology*, 95, pp. 306–315.

Fujii, D. and Wylie, A. (2003) 'Neurocognition and community outcome in schizophrenia: long-term predictive validity', *Schizophrenia Research*, 59, pp. 223–279.

Furst, A. J. and Hitch, G. J. (2000) 'Separate roles for executive and phonological components of working memory in mental arithmetic', *Memory and Cognition*, 28, pp. 774–782.

Garety, P. A. and Freeman, D. (1999) 'Cognitive approaches to delusions: a critical review of theories and evidence', *British Journal of Clinical Psychology*, 38, pp. 113–154.

Garety, P. and Hemsley, D. R. (1994) *Delusions: Investigations into the Psychology of Delusional Reasoning*. Hove, UK: Psychology Press.

Garner, R. (1990) 'When children and adults do not use learning strategies – toward a theory of settings', *Review of Educational Research*, 60, pp. 517–529.

Gelman, R. and Greeno, J. (1989) 'On the nature of competence. Principles for understanding in a domain', in L. B. Resnick (ed.) *Knowing, Learning and Instruction. Essays in Honor of Robert Glaser*. Hillsdale, NJ: Lawrence Erlbaum Associates, Inc., pp. 125–186.

Gentner, D., Loewenstein, J. and Thompson, L. (2003) 'Learning and transfer: a general role for analogical encoding', *Journal of Educational Psychology*, 95, pp. 393–408.

Gick, M. L. and Holyoak, K. J. (1983) 'Schema induction and analogical transfer', *Cognitive Psychology*, 15, pp. 1–38.

Glahn, D. C., Cannon, T. D., Gur, R. E., Ragland, J. D. and Gur, R. C. (2000) 'Working memory constrains abstraction in schizophrenia', *Biological Psychiatry*, 47, pp. 34–42.

Goddard, L., Dritschel, B. and Burton, A. (2001) 'The effects of specific retrieval instruction on social problem-solving in depression', *British Journal of Clinical Psychology*, 40, pp. 297–308.

Gold, J. M., Randolph, C., Carpenter, C. J., Goldberg, T. E. and Weinberger, D. R. (1992) 'Forms of memory failure in schizophrenia', *Journal of Abnormal Psychology*, 101, pp. 487–494.

Gold, J. M., Blaxton, T. A., Hermann, B. P., Randolph, C., Fedio, P., Goldberg, T. E., Theodore, W. H. and Weinberger, D. R. (1995) 'Memory and intelligence in lateralized temporal-lobe epilepsy and schizophrenia', *Schizophrenia Research*, 17, pp. 59–65.

Gold, J. M., Carpenter, C., Randolph, C., Goldberg, T. E. and Weinberger, D. R (1997) 'Auditory working memory and Wisconsin card sorting test performance in schizophrenia', *Archives of General Psychiatry*, 54(2), pp. 159–165.

Gold, J. M., Iannone, V. N., Queern, C. and Buchanan, R. W. (1999) 'Working memory in schizophrenia: impairments in storage and processing', *Schizophrenia Research*, 36(1–3), p. 130.

Gold, J. M., Rehkemper, G., Binks, S. W., Carpenter, C. J., Fleming, K., Goldberg, T. E. and Weinberger, D. R. (2000) 'Learning and forgetting in schizophrenia', *Journal of Abnormal Psychology*, 109, pp. 534–538.

Gold, J. M., Iannone, V. N., McMahon, R. P. and Buchanan, R. W. (2001) 'Cognitive correlates of competitive employment among patients with schizophrenia', *Schizophrenia Research*, 49, p. 134.

Gold, S., Arndt, S., Nopoulos, P., O'Leary, D. S. and Andreasen, N. C. (1999) 'Longitudinal study of cognitive function in first-episode and recent-onset schizophrenia', *American Journal of Psychiatry*, 156, pp. 1342–1348.

Goldberg, T. E., Weinberger D. R., Berman, K. F., Pliskin, M. H. and Podd, M. H. (1987) 'Further evidence for dementia of the prefrontal type in schizophrenia – a controlled study of teaching the Wisconsin card sorting test', *Archives of General Psychiatry*, 44, pp. 1008–1014.

Goldberg, T. E., Weinberger, D. R., Pliskin, N. H., Berman, K. F. and Podd, M. H. (1989) 'Recall memory deficit in schizophrenia – a possible manifestation of prefrontal dysfunction', *Schizophrenia Research*, 2, pp. 251–257.

Goldberg, T. E., Torrey, E. F., Gold, J. M., Ragland, J. D., Bigelow, L. B. and Weinberger, D. R. (1993) 'Learning and memory in monozygotic twins discordant for schizophrenia', *Psychological Medicine*, 23, pp. 71–85.

Goldberg, T. E., Patterson, K. J., Taqqu, Y. and Wilder, K. (1998) 'Capacity limitations in short-term memory in schizophrenia: tests of competing hypotheses', *Psychological Medicine*, 28, pp. 665–673.

Goldman, R. S., Axelrod, B. N. and Tompkins, L. M. (1992) 'Effect of instructional cues on schizophrenic-patients performance on the Wisconsin card sorting test', *American Journal of Psychiatry*, 149(2), pp. 1718–1722.

Goldman-Rakic, P. S. (1987) 'Circuitry of primate prefrontal cortex and regulation of behavior by representational knowledge', in F. Plum and V. Mountacastle (eds) *Handbook of Physiology: The Nervous System*. Bethesda, MD: American Physiological Society, pp. 373–417.

—— (1991) 'Prefrontal cortical dysfunction in schizophrenia: the relevance of working memory,' in B. J. Carroll and J. E. Barrett (eds) *Psychopathology and the Brain*. New York: Raven Press.

—— (1992) 'Working memory and the mind', *Scientific American*, 267, pp. 111–117.

—— (1999) 'The physiological approach: functional architecture of working memory and disordered cognition in schizophrenia', *Biological Psychiatry*, 46, pp. 650–661.

Goldstein, G., Allen, D. N. and Seaton, B. E. (1998) 'A comparison of clustering solutions for cognitive heterogeneity in schizophrenia', *Journal of the International Neuropsychological Society*, 4, pp. 353–362.

Gourovitch, M. L., Goldberg, T. E. and Weinberger, D. R. (1996) 'Verbal fluency deficits in patients with schizophrenia: semantic fluency is differentially impaired as compared with phonologic fluency', *Neuropsychology*, 10, pp. 573–577.

Gouzoulis-Mayfrank, E., Voss, T. A., Morth, D., Thelen, B., Spitzer, M. and Meincke, U. (2003) 'Semantic hyperpriming in thought-disordered patients with schizophrenia: state or trait? – a longitudinal investigation', *Schizophrenia Research*, 65, pp. 65–73.

Graham, S. and Harris, K. R. (1989) 'Components analysis of cognitive strategy instruction – Effects on learning-disabled students compositions and self-efficacy', *Journal of Educational Psychology*, 81, pp. 353–361.

Granholm, E., Asarnow, R. F. and Marder, S. R. (1996) 'Display visual angle and attentional scanpaths on the span of apprehension task in schizophrenia', *Journal of Abnormal Psychology*, 105, pp. 17–24.

Grant, C., Addington, J., Addington, D. and Konnert, C. (2001) 'Social functioning in first and multiepisode schizophrenia', *Canadian Journal of Psychiatry-Revue Canadienne de Psychiatrie*, 46, pp. 746–749.

Grant, D. A. and Berg, E. A. (1948) 'A behavioral analysis of degree of reinforcement and ease of shifting to new responses in a Weigl-type card-sorting problem', *Journal of Experimental Psychology*, 38, pp. 404–411.

Gras-Vincendon, A., Danion, J. M., Grange, D., Bilik, M., Willardschroeder, D., Sichel, J. P. and Singer, L. (1994) 'Explicit memory, repetition priming and cognitive skill learning in schizophrenia', *Schizophrenia Research*, 13, pp. 117–126.

Gray, J. A., Joseph, M. H., Hemsley, D. R., Young, A. M. J., Warburton, E. C., Boulenguez, P., Grigoryan, G. A., Peters, S. L., Rawlins, J. N. P., Taib, C. T., Yee, B. K., Cassaday, H., Weiner, I., Gal, G., Gusak, O., Joel, D., Shadach, E., Shalev, U., Tarrasch, R. and Feldon, J. (1995a) 'The role of mesolimbic dopaminergic and retrohippocampal afferents to the nucleus accumbens in latent inhibition: implications for schizophrenia', *Behavioural Brain Research*, 71, pp. 19–31.

Gray, N. S., Pilowsky, L. S., Gray, J. A. and Kerwin, R. W. (1995b) 'Latent inhibition in drug-naive schizophrenics – relationship to duration of illness and dopamine D2 binding using spet', *Schizophrenia Research*, 17, pp. 95–107.

Green, M. F. (1996) 'What are the functional consequences of neurocognitive deficits in schizophrenia?', *American Journal of Psychiatry*, 153, pp. 321–330.

Green, M. F., Nuechterlein, K. H. and Breitmeyer, B. (1997) 'Backward masking performance in unaffected siblings of schizophrenic patients. Evidence for a vulnerability indicator', *Archives of General Psychiatry*, 54, pp. 465–472.

Green, M. F., Nuechterlein, K. H., Breitmeyer, B. and Mintz, J. (1999) 'Backward masking in unmedicated schizophrenic patients in psychotic remission: possible reflection of aberrant cortical oscillation', *American Journal of Psychiatry*, 156, pp. 1367–1373.

Green, M. F., Kern, R. S., Braff, D. L. and Mintz, J. (2000) 'Neurocognitive deficits and functional outcome in schizophrenia: Are we measuring the "right stuff"?', *Schizophrenia Bulletin*, 26, pp. 119–136.

Green, M. F., Marder, S. R., Glynn, S. M., McGurk, S. R., Wirshing, W. C., Wirshing, D. A., Liberman, R. P. and Mintz, J. (2002) 'The neurocognitive effects of low-dose haloperidol: a two-year comparison with risperidone', *Biological Psychiatry*, 51, pp. 972–978.

Green, M. F., Nuechterlein, K. H., Breitmeyer, B., Tsuang, J. and Mintz, J. (2003) 'Forward and backward visual masking in schizophrenia: influence of age', *Psychological Medicine*, 33, pp. 887–895.

Greenwood, K. E., Sigmundsson, T., Morris, R. G. and Wykes, T. (2000) 'A comparison of profiles of executive impairments in schizophrenia: the relationship with chronicity and symptoms', *Schizophrenia Research*, 41, p. B301.

Greenwood, K. E., Reeder, C. and Wykes, T. (2003) 'The functional outcome of executive impairments in the psychomotor poverty syndrome: verbal working memory may mediate the relationship between memory and real-life skills', *Schizophrenia Research*, 60, pp. 136–137.

Greenwood, K. E., Sigmundsson, T., Wykes, T. and Morris, R. (2004) 'Real world planning impairments in the disorganisation but not the psychomotor poverty syndrome of schizophrenia', *Schizophrenia Research*, 67, p. 271.

Greig, T. C., Bryson, G. J. and Bell, M. D. (2004) 'Theory of mind performance in schizophrenia: diagnostic, symptom, and neuropsychological correlates', *Journal of Nervous and Mental Disease*, 192, pp. 12–18.

Greve, K. W., Farrell, J. F., Besson, P. S. and Crouch, J. A. (1995) 'A psychometric analysis of the California card sorting test', *Archives of Clinical Neuropsychology*, 10, pp. 265–278.

Greve, K. W., Williams, M. C., Haas, W. G., Littell, R. R. and Reinoso, C. (1996) 'The role of attention in Wisconsin card sorting test performance', *Archives of Clinical Neuropsychology*, 11, pp. 215–222.

Greve, K. W., Ingram, F. and Bianchini, K. J. (1998) 'Latent structure of the Wisconsin card sorting test in a clinical sample', *Archives of Clinical Neuropsychology*, 13, pp. 597–609.

Grigorenko, E. L. and Sternberg, R. J. (1998) 'Dynamic testing', *Psychological Bulletin*, 124, pp. 75–111.

Gruzelier, J., Seymour, K., Wilson, L., Jolley, A. and Hirsch, S. (1988) 'Impairments on neuropsychological tests of temporo-hippocampal and fronto-hippocampal functions and word fluency in remitting schizophrenia and affective disorders', *Schizophrenia Research*, 1, pp. 191–192.

Haas, G. L., Radomsky, E. D., Montrose, D. M., Miewald, J., Keshavan, M. and Sweeney, J. A. (2003) 'Short- and long-term recovery of cognitive functioning following the first episode of schizophrenia', *Schizophrenia Research*, 60, p. 137.

Haddock, G., McCarron, J., Tarrier, N. and Faragher, E. B. (1999) 'Scales to measure dimensions of hallucinations and delusions: the psychotic symptom rating scales (PSYRATS)', *Psychological Medicine*, 29, pp. 879–889.

Hafner, H., Maurer, K., Loffler, W., An der Heiden, W., Hambrecht, M. and Schultze-Lutter, F. (2003) 'Modeling the early course of schizophrenia', *Schizophrenia Bulletin*, 29(2), pp. 325–340.

Hamera, E. and Brown, C. (2000) 'Developing a context-based performance measure for persons with schizophrenia: the test of grocery shopping skills', *American Journal of Occupation Therapy*, 54, pp. 20–25.

Hanes, K. R., Andrewes, D. G., Smith, D. J. and Pantelis, C. (1996) 'A brief assessment of executive control dysfunction: discriminant validity and homogeneity of planning, set shift, and fluency measures', *Archives of Clinical Neuropsychology*, 11, pp. 185–191.

Hans, S. L., Auerbach, J. G., Asarnow, J. R., Styr, B. and Marcus, J. (2000) 'Social adjustment of adolescents at risk for schizophrenia: the Jerusalem Infant Development Study', *Journal of the American Academy of Child and Adolescent Psychiatry*, 39, pp. 1406–1414.

Harding, C. M., Brooks, G. W., Ashikaga, T., Strauss, J. S. *et al.* (1987a) 'The Vermont longitudinal study of persons with severe mental illness: I. Methodology, study sample, and overall status 32 years later', *American Journal of Psychiatry*, 144, pp. 718–726.

Harding, C. M., Brooks, G. W., Ashikaga, T., Strauss, J. S. *et al.* (1987b) 'The Vermont longitudinal study of persons with severe mental illness: II. Long-term outcome of subjects who retrospectively met DSM-III criteria for schizophrenia', *American Journal of Psychiatry*, 144, pp. 727–735.

Harrison, G., Hopper, K., Craig, T., Laska, E., Siegel, C., Wanderling, J., Dube, K. C., Ganev, K., Giel, R., An der Heiden, W., Holmberg, S. K., Janca, A., Lee, P. W. H., Leon, C. A., Malhotra, S., Marsella, A. J., Nakane, Y., Sartorius, N., Shen, Y., Skoda, C., Thara, R., Tsirkin, S. J., Varma, V. K., Walsh, D. and Wiersma, D. (2001) 'Recovery from psychotic illness: a 15- and 25-year international follow-up study', *British Journal of Psychiatry*, 178, pp. 506–517.

Hartman, M., Steketee, M. C., Silva, S., Lanning, K. and Andersson, C. (2003) 'Wisconsin card sorting test performance in schizophrenia: the role of working memory', *Schizophrenia Research*, 63, pp. 201–217.

Harvey, P. D. (1985) 'Reality monitoring in mania and schizophrenia – the association of thought disorder and performance', *Journal of Nervous and Mental Disease*, 173, pp. 67–73.

—— (2004) 'Treatment of cognitive deficits in elderly schizophrenic patients', in R. Keefe (ed.) *Improving Cognitive Function in the Schizophrenic Patient*, 2nd edn., London: Science Press.

Harvey, P. D. and Keefe, R. S. (2001) 'Studies of cognitive change in patients with schizophrenia following novel antipsychotic treatment', *American Journal of Psychiatry*, 158, pp. 176–184.

Harvey, P. D. and Pedley, M. (1989) 'Auditory and visual distractibility in schizophrenia – clinical and medication status correlations', *Schizophrenia Research*, 2, pp. 295–300.

Harvey, P. D. and Serper, M. R. (1990) 'Linguistic and cognitive failures in schizophrenia – a multivariate analysis', *Journal of Nervous and Mental Disease*, 178, pp. 487–494.

Harvey, P. D., Davidson, M., Mueser, K. T., Parrella, M., White, L. and Powchik, P. (1997) 'Social-adaptive functioning evaluation (SAFE): a rating scale for geriatric psychiatric patients', *Schizophrenia Bulletin*, 23, pp. 131–145.

Harvey, P. D., Howanitz, E., Parrella, M., White, L., Davidson, M., Mohs, R. C., Hoblyn, J. and Davis, K. L. (1998) 'Symptoms, cognitive functioning, and adaptive skills in geriatric patients with lifelong schizophrenia: a comparison across treatment sites', *American Journal of Psychiatry*, 155, pp. 1080–1086.

Harvey, P. D., Bertisch, H. A., Friedman, J. I., Parrella, M., White, L. and Davis, K. L. (2003) 'Cognitive and functional decline in older patients with schizophrenia: evidence for threshold effects?', *Biological Psychiatry*, 53, p. 45.

Hatano, G. and Greeno, J. G. (1999) 'Commentary: alternative perspectives on transfer and transfer studies', *International Journal of Educational Research*, 31, pp. 645–654.

Hayes, R. L. and McGrath, J. J. (2001) *Cognitive Rehabilitation for People with Schizophrenia and Related Conditions (Cochrane review)*. Oxford: Update Software.

Heaton, R. K., Baade, L. E. and Johnson, K. L. (1978) 'Neuropsychological test results associated with psychiatric disorders in adults', *Psychological Bulletin*, 85, pp. 141–162.

Heaton, R., Paulsen, J. S., Mcadams, L. A., Kuck, J., Zisook, S., Braff, D., Harris, M. J. and Jeste, D. V. (1994) 'Neuropsychological deficits in schizophrenics – relationship to age, chronicity, and dementia', *Archives of General Psychiatry*, 51, pp. 469–476.

Heaton, R. K., Gladsjo, J. A., Palmer, B. W., Kuck, J., Marcotte, T. D. and Jeste, D. V. (2001) 'Stability and course of neuropsychological deficits in schizophrenia', *Archives of General Psychiatry*, 58, pp. 24–32.

Hebb, D. O. (1949) *The Organization of Behaviour.* New York: Wiley.

Hegarty, J. D., Baldessarini, R. J., Tohen, M., Waternaux, C. and Oepen, G. (1994) '100 years of schizophrenia – a metaanalysis of the outcome literature', *American Journal of Psychiatry*, 151, pp. 1409–1416.

Heilbrun, A. B. (1980) 'Impaired recognition of self-expressed thought in patients with auditory hallucinations', *Journal of Abnormal Psychology*, 89, pp. 728–736.

Heinrichs, R. W. and Zakzanis, K. K. (1998) 'Neurocognitive deficit in schizophrenia: a quantitative review of the evidence', *Neuropsychology*, 12, pp. 426–445.

Heinrichs, R. W., Ruttan, L., Zakzanis, K. K. and Case, D. (1997) 'Parsing schizophrenia with neurocognitive tests: evidence of stability and validity', *Brain and Cognition*, 35, pp. 207–224.

Hellman, S. G., Kern, R. S., Neilson, L. M. and Green, M. F. (1998) 'Monetary reinforcement and Wisconsin card sorting performance in schizophrenia: Why show me the money?', *Schizophrenia Research*, 34(1–2), pp. 67–75.

Hemsley, D. R. (1977) 'What have cognitive deficits to do with schizophrenic symptoms', *British Journal of Psychiatry*, 130, pp. 167–173.

—— (1982) 'Cognitive impairment in schizophrenia,' in A. Burton (ed.) *The Pathology and Psychology of Cognition.* London: Methuen, pp. 169–203.

—— (1987) 'An experimental psychological model for schizophrenia,' in H. Hafner, W. Gattaz and K. Janzair (eds) *Search for the Causes of Schizophrenia*, Berlin: Springer-Verlag.

—— (1993) 'A simple (or simplistic-questionable) cognitive model for schizophrenia', *Behaviour Research and Therapy*, 31, pp. 633–645.

—— 1994) 'A cognitive model for schizophrenia and its possible neural basis', *Acta Psychiatrica Scandinavica*, 90, pp. 80–86.

—— (1996) 'Schizophrenia – a cognitive model and its implications for psychological intervention', *Behavior Modification*, 20, pp. 139–169.

—— (2005) 'The schizophrenic experience: taken out of context', *Schizophrenia Bulletin*, 31, pp. 1–11.

Hepp, H. H., Maier, S., Hermle, L. and Spitzer, M. (1996) 'The Stroop effect in schizophrenic patients', *Schizophrenia Research*, 22, pp. 187–195.

Heresco-Levy, U., Ermilov, M., Giltsinsky, B., Lichtenstein, M. and Blander, D. (1999) 'Treatment-resistant schizophrenia and staff rejection', *Schizophrenia Bulletin*, 25, pp. 457–465.

Hermanutz, M. and Gestrich, J. (1991) 'Computer-assisted attention training in schizophrenics – a comparative study', *European Archives of Psychiatry and Clinical Neuroscience*, 240, pp. 282–287.

Heydebrand, G., Weiser, M., Rabinowitz, J., Hoff, A. L., Delisi, L. E. and Csernansky, J. G. (2004) 'Correlates of cognitive deficits in first episode schizophrenia', *Schizophrenia Research*, 68, pp. 1–9.

Hijman, R., Pol, H. E. H., Sitskoorn, M. M. and Kahn, R. S. (2003) 'Global intellectual impairment does not accelerate with age in patients with schizophrenia: a cross-sectional analysis', *Schizophrenia Bulletin*, 29, pp. 509–517.

Hill, S. K., Ragland, J. D., Gur, R. C. and Gur, R. E. (2002) 'Neuropsychological profiles delineate distinct profiles of schizophrenia, an interaction between memory and executive function, and uneven distribution of clinical subtypes', *Journal of Clinical and Experimental Neuropsychology*, 24, pp. 765–780.

Hirsch, S., Bowen, J., Emami, J., Cramer, P., Jolley, A., Haw, C. and Dickinson, M. (1996) 'A one year prospective study of the effect of life events and medication in the aetiology of schizophrenic relapse', *British Journal of Psychiatry*, 168, pp. 49–56.

Hodel, B. and Brenner, H. D. (1994) 'Cognitive therapy with schizophrenic patients –

conceptual basis, present state, future directions', *Acta Psychiatrica Scandinavica*, 90, pp. 108–115.

Hoff, A. L., Riordan, H., Odonnell, D. W., Morris, L. and Delisi, L. E. (1992) 'Neuropsychological functioning of 1st-episode schizophreniform patients', *American Journal of Psychiatry*, 149, pp. 898–903.

Hoff, A. L., Sakuma, M., Wieneke, M., Horon, R., Kushner, M. and Delisi, L. E. (1999) 'Longitudinal neuropsychological follow-up study of patients with first-episode schizophrenia', *American Journal of Psychiatry*, 156, pp. 1336–1341.

Hoffmann, H. and Kupper, Z. (2003) 'Predictive factors of successful vocational re-integration in patients with chronic schizophrenia', *Psychiatrische Praxis*, 30, pp. 312–317.

Hoffmann, H., Kupper, Z. and Kunz, B. (2000) 'Hopelessness and its impact on rehabilitation outcome in schizophrenia – an exploratory study', *Schizophrenia Research*, 43, pp. 147–158.

Hogarty, G. E. and Flesher, S. (1992) 'Cognitive remediation in schizophrenia – Proceed – with caution', *Schizophrenia Bulletin*, 18, pp. 51–57.

—— (1999a) 'Developmental theory for a cognitive enhancement therapy of schizophrenia', *Schizophrenia Bulletin*, 25, pp. 677–692.

—— (1999b) 'Practice principles of Cognitive Enhancement Therapy for schizophrenia', *Schizophrenia Bulletin*, 25, pp. 693–708.

Hogarty, G. E., Flesher, S., Ulrich, R., Carter, M., Greenwald, D., Pogue-Geile, M., Keshavan, M., Cooley, S., DiBarry, A. L., Garrett, A., Parapally, H. and Zoretich, R. (2004) 'Cognitive enhancement therapy for schizophrenia: effects of a 2-year randomized trial on cognitive and behaviour', *Archives of General Psychiatry*, 61, pp. 866–876.

Holthausen, E. A. E., Wiersma, D., Knegtering, R. H. and van den Bosch, R. J. (1999a) 'Psychopathology and cognition in schizophrenia spectrum disorders: the role of depressive symptoms', *Schizophrenia Research*, 39, pp. 65–71.

Holthausen, E. A. E., Wiersma, D. and van den Bosch, R. J. (1999b) 'Psychopathology and social functioning in psychotic patients with and without cognitive deficits', *Schizophrenia Research*, 36, p. 135.

Holthausen, E. A. E., Wiersma, D., Sitskoorn, M. M., Hijman, R., Dingemans, P. M., Schene, A. H. and van den Bosch, R. J. (2002) 'Schizophrenic patients without neuropsychological deficits: subgroup, disease severity or cognitive compensation?', *Psychiatry Research*, 112, pp. 1–11.

Holthausen, E. A. E., Wiersma, D., Sitskoorn, M. M., Dingemans, P. M., Schene, A. H. and van den Bosch, R. J. (2003) 'Long-term memory deficits in schizophrenia: primary or secondary dysfunction?', *Neuropsychology*, 17, pp. 539–547.

Holyoak, K. J. and Thagard, P. (1997) 'The analogical mind', *American Psychologist*, 52, pp. 35–44.

Holzman, P. and Gardner, R. (1960) 'Leveling-sharpening and memory organization', *Journal of Abnormal and Social Psychology*, 61, pp. 176–180.

Hooker, C. and Park, S. (2002) 'Emotion processing and its relationship to social functioning in schizophrenia patients', *Psychiatry Research*, 112, pp. 41–50.

Hughes, C., Kumari, V., Soni, W., Das, M., Binneman, B., Drozd, S., O'Neil, S., Mathew, V. and Sharma, T. (2003) 'Longitudinal study of symptoms and cognitive function in chronic schizophrenia', *Schizophrenia Research*, 59, pp. 137–146.

Huston, P. E. and Shakow, D. (1949) 'Learning capacity in schizophrenia – with special reference to the concept of deterioration', *American Journal of Psychiatry*, 105, pp. 881–888.

Hutton, S. B., Puri, B. K., Duncan, L. J., Robbins, T. W., Barnes, T. R. E. and Joyce, E. M. (1998) 'Executive function in first-episode schizophrenia', *Psychological Medicine*, 28, pp. 463–473.

Huxley, P. and Thornicroft, G. (2003) 'Social inclusion, social quality and mental illness', *British Journal of Psychiatry*, 182, pp. 289–290.

Iddon, J. L., McKenna, P. J., Sahakian, B. J. and Robbins, T. W. (1998) 'Impaired generation and use of strategy in schizophrenia: evidence from visuospatial and verbal tasks', *Psychological Medicine*, 28, pp. 1049–1062.

Ihnen, G. H., Penn, D. L., Corrigan, P. W. and Martin, J. (1998) 'Social perception and social skill in schizophrenia', *Psychiatry Research*, 80, pp. 275–286.

Ikebuchi, E., Nakagome, K. and Takahashi, N. (1999) 'How do early stages of information processing influence social skills in patients with schizophrenia?', *Schizophrenia Research*, 35, pp. 255–262.

Ismail, B., Cantor-Graae, E. and Mcneil, T. F. (2000) 'Minor physical anomalies in schizophrenia: cognitive, neurological and other clinical correlates', *Journal of Psychiatric Research*, 34, pp. 45–56.

Jaeger, J., Berns, S., Tigner, A. and Douglas, E. (1992) 'Remediation of neuro-psychological deficits in psychiatric populations – rationale and methodological considerations', *Psychopharmacology Bulletin*, 28, pp. 367–390.

Javitt, D. C., Strous, R. D., Grochowski, S., Ritter, W. and Cowan, N. (1997) 'Impaired precision, but normal retention, of auditory sensory ("echoic") memory information in schizophrenia', *Journal of Abnormal Psychology*, 106, pp. 315–324.

Javitt, D. C., Rabinowicz, E., Silipo, G. and Shelley, A. M. (1999) 'Electro-physiological dissection of working memory dysfunction in schizophrenia', *Schizophrenia Research*, 36, pp. 254–255.

Jeste, S. D., Patterson, T. L., Palmer, B. W., Dolder, C. R., Goldman, S. and Jeste, D. V. (2003) 'Cognitive predictors of medication adherence among middle-aged and older outpatients with schizophrenia', *Schizophrenia Research*, 63, pp. 49–58.

Johns, L. C. and McGuire, P. K. (1999) 'Verbal self-monitoring and auditory halluci-nations in schizophrenia', *Lancet*, 353, pp. 469–470.

Johns, L. C. and van Os, J. (2001) 'The continuity of psychotic experiences in the general population', *Clinical Psychology Review*, 21, pp. 1125–1141.

Johns, L. C., Nazroon, J. Y., Bebbington, P. and Kuipers, E. (2002) 'Occurrence of hallucinatory experiences in a community sample and ethnic variations', *British Journal of Psychiatry*, 180, pp. 174–178.

Johnson-Laird, P. N. (1983) *Mental Models – Towards a Cognitive Science of Language, Inference and Consciousness.* Cambridge, MA: Harvard University Press.

Johnson-Selfridge, M. and Zalewski, C. (2001) 'Moderator variables of executive functioning in schizophrenia: meta-analytic findings', *Schizophrenia Bulletin*, 27, pp. 305–316.

Jones, S. H., Gray, J. A. and Hemsley, D. R. (1992) 'Loss of the kamin blocking effect in acute but not chronic schizophrenics', *Biological Psychiatry*, 32, pp. 739–755.

Jones, W., Bellugi, U., Lai, Z., Chiles, M., Reilly, J., Lincoln, A. and Adolphs, R. (2000) 'Hypersociability in Williams syndrome', *Journal of Cognitive Neuroscience*, 12, pp. 30–46.

Joseph, P. L. A., Sturgeon, D. A. and Leff, J. (1992) 'The perception of emotion by schizophrenic patients', *British Journal of Psychiatry*, 161, pp. 603–609.

Joyce, E. M., Collinson, S. L. and Crichton, P. (1996) 'Verbal fluency in schizophrenia: relationship with executive function, semantic memory and clinical alogia', *Psychological Medicine*, 26, pp. 39–49.

Joyce, E., Hutton, S., Mutsatsa, S., Gibbins, H., Webb, E., Paul, S., Robbins, T. and Barnes, T. (2002) 'Executive dysfunction in first-episode schizophrenia and relationship to duration of untreated psychosis: the West London Study', *British Journal of Psychiatry*, 181, pp. S38–S44.

Kagan, J. (1965) 'Personality and the learning process', *Daedalus*, 94, pp. 553–563.

Kahneman, D. (1973) *Attention and Effort*. Englewood Cliffs, NJ: Prentice Hall.

—— (1968) 'Method findings and theory in studies of visual masking', *Psychological Bulletin*, 70, pp. 404–425.

Kamin, L. (1968) ' "Attention-like" processes in classical conditioning', in M. Jones (ed.) *Miami Symposium on the Prediction of Behavior*. Miami: University of Miami Press, pp. 9–33.

Kaney, S. and Bentall, R. P. (1992) 'Persecutory delusions and the self-serving bias – evidence from a contingency judgment task', *Journal of Nervous and Mental Disease*, 180, pp. 773–780.

Kanwisher, N. (2000) 'Domain specificity in face perception', *Nature Neuroscience*, 3, pp. 759–763.

Kapur, S. (2003) 'Psychosis as a state of aberrant salience: a framework linking biology, phenomenology, and pharmacology in schizophrenia', *American Journal of Psychiatry*, 160, pp. 13–23.

Katona, G. (1940) *Organizing and Memorizing*. New York: Columbia University Press.

Kazes, M., Danion, J. M., Berthet, L., Amado, I., Willard, D., Robert, P. and Poirier, M. F. (1999) 'Impairment of consciously controlled use of memory in schizophrenia', *Schizophrenia Research*, 36, p. 172.

Kee, K. S., Kern, R. S. and Green, M. F. (1998) 'Perception of emotion and neurocognitive functioning in schizophrenia: what's the link?', *Psychiatry Research*, 81, pp. 57–65.

Keefe, R. S. E. (1995) 'The contribution of neuropsychology to psychiatry', *American Journal of Psychiatry*, 152, pp. 6–15.

Keefe, R. S. and Gold, J. M. (2004) 'The effects of pharmacology on cognitive deficits in schizophrenia', in R. S. Keefe (ed.) *Improving Cognitive Function in the Schizophrenic Patient*, 2nd edn. London: Science Press.

Keefe, R. S. E., Roitman, S. E. L., Harvey, P. D., Blum, C. S., Dupre, R. L., Prieto, D. M., Davidson, M. and Davis, K. L. (1995) 'A pen-and-paper human analog of a monkey prefrontal cortex activation task – spatial working memory in patients with schizophrenia', *Schizophrenia Research*, 17, pp. 25–33.

Keefe, R. S. E., Silva, S. G., Perkins, D. O. and Lieberman, J. A. (1999) 'The effects of atypical antipsychotic drugs on neurocognitive impairment in schizophrenia: a review and meta-analysis', *Schizophrenia Bulletin*, 25, pp. 201–222.

Keitzman, M. L. (1991) 'Information processing and schizophrenia', in S. R. Steinhauer, J. Gruzelier and J. Zubin (eds) *Neuropsychology, Psychophysiology and Information Processing*. Amsterdam: Elsevier.

Kemp, R. and David, A. (1996) 'Psychological predictors of insight and compliance in psychotic patients', *British Journal of Psychiatry*, 169, pp. 444–450.

Kern, R. S., Green, M. F. and Goldstein, M. J. (1995) 'Modification of performance on the span of apprehension, a putative marker of vulnerability to schizophrenia', *Journal of Abnormal Psychology*, 104, pp. 385–389.

Kern, R. S., Wallace, C. J., Hellman, S. G., Womack, L. M. and Green, M. F. (1996) 'A training procedure for remediating WCST deficits in chronic psychotic patients: an adaptation of errorless learning principles. [erratum appears in J Psychiatr Res 1997 May-Jun; 31(3):1]', *Journal of Psychiatric Research*, 30, pp. 283–294.

Kern, R. S., Green, M. F. and Wallace, C. J. (1997) 'Declarative and procedural learning in schizophrenia: a test of the integrity of divergent memory systems', *Cognitive Neuropsychiatry*, 2, pp. 39–50.

Kerns, J. G. and Berenbaum, H. (2002) 'Cognitive impairments associated with formal thought disorder in people with schizophrenia', *Journal of Abnormal Psychology*, 111, pp. 211–224.

Kiefer, M., Apel, A. and Weisbrod, M. (2002) 'Arithmetic fact retrieval and working memory in schizophrenia', *Schizophrenia Research*, 53, pp. 219–227.

Klin, A. (2000) 'Attributing social meaning to ambiguous visual stimuli in higher-functioning autism and Asperger syndrome: the social attribution task', *Journal of Child Psychology and Psychiatry and Allied Disciplines*, 41(831), p. 846.

Kluwe, R. H. (1982) 'Cognitive knowledge and executive control: metacognition', in D. R. Griffin (ed.) *Animal Mind – Human mind*. New York: Springer-Verlag, pp. 201–224.

Koh, S. D., Kayton, L. and Berry, R. (1973) 'Mnemonic organization in young nonpsychotic schizophrenics', *Journal of Abnormal Psychology*, 81, pp. 299–310.

Koh, S. D., Kayton, L. and Peterson, R. A. (1976) 'Affective encoding and consequent remembering in schizophrenic young adults', *Journal of Abnormal Psychology*, 85, pp. 156–166.

Kolb, D. A. (1984) *Experiential Learning*. Englewood Cliffs, NJ: Prentice Hall.

Koreen, A. R., Siris, S. G., Chakos, M., Alvir, J., Mayerhoff, D. and Lieberman, J. (1993) 'Depression in 1st-episode schizophrenia', *American Journal of Psychiatry*, 150, pp. 1643–1648.

Koren, D., Seidman, L. J., Harrison, R. H., Lyons, M. J., Kremen, W. S., Caplan, B., Goldstein, J. M., Faraone, S. V. and Tsuang, M. T. (1998) 'Factor structure of the Wisconsin card sorting test: dimensions of deficit in schizophrenia', *Neuropsychology*, 12, pp. 289–302.

Koren, D., Seidman, L. J., Poyurovski, M., Goldsmith, M., Viksman, P., Zichel, S. and Klein, E. (2004) 'The neuropsychological basis of insight in first-episode schizophrenia: a pilot metacognitive study', *Schizophrenia Research*, 70, pp. 195–202.

Koriat, A. and Goldsmith, M. (1996) 'Monitoring and control processes in the strategic regulation of memory accuracy', *Psychological Review*, 103, pp. 490–517.

Krabbendam, L. and Aleman, A. (2003) 'Cognitive rehabilitation in schizophrenia: a quantitative analysis of controlled studies', *Psychopharmacology*, 169, pp. 376–382.

Kraepelin, E., Huntingdon, N. Y., Robert, E. (eds) (1971) *Dementia Praecox and Paraphreni*. Melbourne, NY: Krieger.

Kravariti, E., Morris, R. G., Rabe-Hesketh, S., Murray, R. M. and Frangou, S. (2003) 'The Maudsley early-onset schizophrenia study: cognitive function in adolescent-onset schizophrenia', *Schizophrenia Research*, 65, pp. 95–103.

Kremen, W. S., Seidman, L. J., Pepple, J., Tsuang, M. T. and Faraone, S. V. (1994)

'Neuropsychological risk indicators for schizophrenia – a review of family studies', *Schizophrenia Bulletin*, 20, pp. 103–119.

Kremen, W. S., Buka, S. L., Seidman, L. J., Goldstein, J. M., Koren, D. and Tsuang, M. T. (1998) 'IQ decline during childhood and adult psychotic symptoms in a community sample: a 19-year longitudinal study', *American Journal of Psychiatry*, 155, pp. 672–677.

Kremen, W. S., Hoff, A. L., Wieneke, I. and Delisi, L. E. (2000a) 'Individual cognitive profile analysis in schizophrenia: evidence from a new sample', *Biological Psychiatry*, 47, p. 106.

Kremen, W. S., Seidman, L. J., Faraone, S. V., Toomey, R. and Tsuang, M. T. (2000b) 'The paradox of normal neuropsychological function in schizophrenia', *Journal of Abnormal Psychology*, 109, pp. 743–752.

Kremen, W. S., Seidman, L. J., Faraone, S. V. and Tsuang, M. T. (2001) 'Intelligence quotient and neuropsychological profiles in patients with schizophrenia and in normal volunteers', *Biological Psychiatry*, 50(6), pp. 453–462.

Kupper, Z. and Hoffmann, H. (2000) 'Course patterns of psychosocial functioning in schizophrenia patients attending a vocational rehabilitation program', *Schizophrenia Bulletin*, 26, pp. 681–698.

Kurtz, M. (2005) 'Neurocognitive impairment across the lifespan in schizophrenia: an update', *Schizophrenia Research* (in press).

Kurtz, M. M., Moberg, P. J., Gur, R. C. and Gur, R. E. (2004a) 'Approaches to cognitive remediation of neuropsychological deficits in schizophrenia: a review and meta-analysis', *Neuropsychology Review*, 11, pp. 197–210.

Kurtz, M. M., Moberg, P. J., Mozley, L. H., Swanson, C. L., Gur, R. C. and Gur, R. E. (2001b) 'Effectiveness of an attention- and memory-training program on neuropsychological deficits in schizophrenia', *Neurorehabilitation and Neural Repair*, 15, pp. 75–80.

Kurtz, M. M., Wexler, B. E. and Bell, M. D. (2004) 'The Penn Conditional Exclusion Test (PCET): relationship to the Wisconsin card sorting test and work function in patients with schizophrenia', *Schizophrenia Research*, 68(1), pp. 95–102.

Lancaster, R. S., Evans, J. D., Bond, G. R. and Lysaker, P. H. (2003) 'Social cognition and neurocognitive deficits in schizophrenia', *Journal of Nervous and Mental Disease*, 191, pp. 295–299.

Langdon, R., Coltheart, M., Ward, P. B. and Catts, S. V. (2002) 'Theory-of-mind impairments in schizophrenia: an alternative account based on performance deficits in perspective-taking', *Schizophrenia Research*, 53, p. 139.

Laurent, A., Biloa-Tang, M., Bougerol, T., Duly, D., Anchisi, A. M., Bosson, J. L., Pellat, J., d'Amato, T. and Dalery, J. (2000) 'Executive/attentional performance and measures of schizotypy in patients with schizophrenia and in their nonpsychotic first-degree relatives', *Schizophrenia Research*, 46, pp. 269–283.

Laws, K. R., McKenna, P. J. and McCarthy, R. A. (1996) 'Reconsidering the gospel according to group studies: a neuropsychological case study approach to onset schizophrenia', *Cognitive Neuropsychiatry*, 1, pp. 319–343.

Leff, J. and Trieman, N. (2000) 'Long-stay patients discharged from psychiatric hospitals – social and clinical outcomes after five years in the community. The TAPS Project 46', *British Journal of Psychiatry*, 176, pp. 217–223.

Lemelin, S. and Baruch, P. (1998) 'Clinical psychomotor retardation and attention in depression', *Journal of Psychiatric Research*, 32, pp. 81–88.

Lencz, T., Bilder, R. M., Turkel, E., Goldman, R. S., Robinson, D., Kane, J. M. and Lieberman, J. A. (2003) 'Impairments in perceptual competency and maintenance on a visual delayed match-to-sample test in first-episode schizophrenia', *Archives of General Psychiatry*, 60, pp. 238–243.

Lenzenweger, M. F., Cornblatt, B. A. and Putnick, M. (1991) 'Schizotypy and sustained attention', *Journal of Abnormal Psychology*, 100, pp. 84–89.

Liddle, P. F. and Morris, D. L. (1991) 'Schizophrenic syndromes and frontal-lobe performance', *British Journal of Psychiatry*, 158, pp. 340–345.

Loeb, P. A. (1996) *Independent Living Scales Manual.* San Antonio, TX: Psychological Corporation.

Logie, R. H. (1995) *Visuo-Spatial Working Memory.* Hove, UK & Lawrence Erlbaum, Associates Ltd.

Lopez-Luengo, B. and Vazquez, C. (2003) 'Effects of attention process training on cognitive functioning of schizophrenic patients', *Psychiatry Research*, 119, pp. 41–53.

Lubow, R. E., Weiner, I., Schlossberg, A. and Baruch, I. (1987) 'Latent inhibition and schizophrenia', *Bulletin of the Psychonomic Society*, 25, pp. 464–467.

Luria, A. R. (1966) *Higher Cortical Functions in Man.* New York: Basic Books.

Lysaker, P. and Bell, M. (1994) 'Insight and cognitive impairment in schizophrenia – performance on repeated administrations of the Wisconsin card sorting test', *Journal of Nervous and Mental Disease*, 182, pp. 656–660.

—— (1995) 'Work Rehabilitation and Improvements in Insight in Schizophrenia', *Journal of Nervous and Mental Disease*, 183, pp. 103–106.

Lysaker, P., Bell, M. D., Zito, W. S. and Bioty, S. M. (1995) 'Social skills at work: deficits and predictors of improvement in schizophrenia', *Journal of Nervous and Mental Disease*, 183, pp. 688–692.

Lysaker, P. H., Clements, C. A., Wright, D. E., Evans, J. and Marks, K. A. (2001) 'Neurocognitive correlates of helplessness, hopelessness, and well-being in schizophrenia', *Journal of Nervous and Mental Disease*, 189, pp. 457–462.

MacCabe, J. H., Aldouri, E., Fahy, T. A., Sham, P. C. and Murray, R. M. (2002) 'Do schizophrenic patients who managed to get to university have a non-developmental form of illness?', *Psychological Medicine*, 32, pp. 535–544.

McClure, R. K. (2001) 'The visual backward masking deficit in schizophrenia', *Progress in Neuro-Psychopharmacology and Biological Psychiatry*, 25, pp. 301–311.

MacDonald, A. W. and Carter, C. S. (2002) 'Cognitive experimental approaches to investigating impaired cognition in schizophrenia: a paradigm shift', *Journal of Clinical and Experimental Neuropsychology*, 24, pp. 873–882.

Mcdowell, J. E. and Clementz, B. A. (1996) 'Ocular-motor delayed response task performance among schizophrenia patients', *Neuropsychobiology*, 34, pp. 67–71.

McGhie, A. and Chapman, J. (1961) 'Disorders of attention and perception in early schizophrenia', *British Journal of Medical Psychology*, 34, pp. 103–113.

McGurk, S. R. and Meltzer, H. Y. (2000) 'The role of cognition in vocational functioning in schizophrenia', *Schizophrenia Research*, 45, pp. 175–184.

McGurk, S. R. and Mueser, K. T. (2003) 'Cognitive functioning and employment in severe mental illness', *Journal of Nervous and Mental Disease*, 191(12), pp. 789–798.

—— (2004) 'Cognitive functioning, symptoms, and work in supported employment: a review and heuristic model', *Schizophrenia Research*, 70(2–3), pp. 147–173.

McGurk, S., Mueser, K., Harvey, P. D., LaPuglia, R. and Marder, S. R. (2003)

'Cognitive and symptom predictors of work outcomes for clients with schizophrenia in supported employment', *Psychiatric Services*, 54, pp. 1129–1135.

Mackworth, N. H. (1948) 'The breakdown of vigilance during prolonged visual search', *Quarterly Journal of Experimental Psychology*, 1, pp. 6–21.

Maher, B. A. (1974) 'Delusional thinking and perceptual disorder', *Journal of Individual Psychology*, 30, pp. 98–113.

Mahurin, R. K., Velligan, D. I. and Miller, A. L. (1998) 'Executive-frontal lobe cognitive dysfunction in schizophrenia: a symptom subtype analysis', *Psychiatry Research*, 79, pp. 139–149.

Malenka, R. C., Angel, R. W., Hampton, B. and Berger, P. A. (1982) 'Impaired central error-correcting behavior in schizophrenia', *Archives of General Psychiatry*, 39, pp. 101–107.

Mandal, M. K., Pandey, R. and Prasad, A. B. (1998) 'Facial expressions of emotions and schizophrenia: a review', *Schizophrenia Bulletin*, 24, pp. 399–412.

Massel, H. K., Corrigan, P. W., Liberman, R. P. and Milan, M. A. (1991) 'Conversation skills training of thought-disordered schizophrenic patients through attention focusing', *Psychiatry Research*, 38, pp. 51–61.

Mathews, A., Mogg, K., May, J. and Eysenck, M. (1989) 'Implicit and explicit memory bias in anxiety', *Journal of Abnormal Psychology*, 98, pp. 236–240.

Mayer, R. E. (1999) 'Multi-media aids to problem-solving transfer', *International Journal of Educational Research*, 31, pp. 611–623.

Mayer, R. and Wittrock, M. C. (1996) 'Problem-solving transfer', in D. C. Berliner and R. C. Calfee (eds) *Handbook of Educational Psychology*. New York: Macmillan, pp. 47–62.

Medalia, A., Aluma, M., Tryon, W. and Merriam, A. E. (1998) 'Effectiveness of attention training in schizophrenia', *Schizophrenia Bulletin*, 24, pp. 147–152.

Medalia, A., Dorn, H. and Watras-Gans, S. (2000a) 'Treating problem-solving deficits on an acute care psychiatric inpatient unit', *Psychiatry Research*, 97, pp. 79–88.

Medalia, A., Revheim, N. and Casey, M. (2000b) 'Remediation of memory disorders in schizophrenia', *Psychological Medicine*, 30, pp. 1451–1459.

Medalia, A., Revheim, N. and Casey, M. (2001) 'The remediation of problem-solving skills in schizophrenia', *Schizophrenia Bulletin*, 27, pp. 259–267.

Medalia, A., Revheim, N. and Casey, M. (2002) 'Remediation of problem-solving skills in schizophrenia: evidence of a persistent effect', *Schizophrenia Research*, 57, pp. 165–171.

Meichenbaum, D. H. (1966) 'Effects of social reinforcement on level of abstraction in schizophrenics', *Journal of Abnormal Psychology*, 71, pp. 354–362.

—— (1969) 'Effects of instructions and reinforcement on thinking and language behavior of schizophrenics', *Behaviour Research and Therapy*, 7, pp. 101–114.

Meichenbaum, D. and Cameron, R. (1973) 'Training schizophrenics to talk to themselves – means of developing attentional controls', *Behavior Therapy*, 4, pp. 515–534.

Menditto, A. A., Baldwin, L. J., Oneal, L. G. and Beck, N. C. (1991) 'Social learning procedures for increasing attention and improving basic skills in severely regressed institutionalized patients', *Journal of Behavior Therapy and Experimental Psychiatry*, 22, pp. 265–269.

Messick, S. (1976) *Individuality in Learning.* San Francisco: Jossey-Bass.

Miller, W. R. and Rollnick, S. (2002), *Motivational Interviewing: Preparing People for Change*, 2nd edn. New York: Guilford Press.

Miller, S., Saccuzzo, D. P. and Braff, D. L. (1979) 'Information processing deficit in remitted schizophrenics', *Journal of Abnormal Psychology*, 88, pp. 446–449.

Minzenberg, M. J., Ober, B. A. and Vinogradov, S. (2002) 'Semantic priming in schizophrenia: a review and synthesis', *Journal of the International Neuropsychological Society*, 8, pp. 699–720.

Mirsky, A. F. (1988) 'Research on schizophrenia in the Nimh Laboratory of Psychology and Psychopathology, 1954–1987', *Schizophrenia Bulletin*, 14, pp. 151–156.

Mirsky, A. F., Lochhead, S. J., Jones, B. P., Kugelmass, S., Walsh, D. and Kendler, K. S. (1992) 'On familial factors in the attentional deficit in schizophrenia – a review and report of 2 new subject samples', *Journal of Psychiatric Research*, 26, pp. 383–403.

Moelter, S. T., Hill, S. K., Ragland, J. D., Lunardelli, A., Gur, R. C., Gur, R. E. and Moberg, P. J. (2001) 'Controlled and automatic processing during animal word list generation in schizophrenia', *Neuropsychology*, 15, pp. 502–509.

Moritz, S., Mersmann, K., Kloss, M., Jacobsen, D. Andresen, B., Krausz, M., Pawlik, K. and Naber, D. (2001) 'Enhanced semantic priming in thought-disordered schizophrenic patients using a word pronunciation task', *Schizophrenia Research*, 48, pp. 301–305.

Morris, R. G., Rushe, T., Woodruffe, P. W. R. and Murray, R. M. (1995) 'Problem-solving in schizophrenia – a specific deficit in planning ability', *Schizophrenia Research*, 14, pp. 235–246.

Morrison, R. L., Bellack, A. S. and Mueser, K. T. (1988) 'Deficits in facial-affect recognition and schizophrenia', *Schizophrenia Bulletin*, 14, pp. 67–83.

Mueser, K. T., Bellack, A. S., Douglas, M. S. and Wade, J. H. (1991) 'Prediction of social skill acquisition in schizophrenic and major affective-disorder patients from memory and symptomatology', *Psychiatry Research*, 37, pp. 281–296.

Mueser, K. T., Kosmidis, M. H. and Sayers, M. D. (1992) 'Symptomatology and the prediction of social skills acquisition in schizophrenia', *Schizophrenia Research*, 8, pp. 59–68.

Mueser, K. T., Becker, D. R., Torrey, W. C., Xie, H. Y., Bond, G. R., Drake, R. E. and Dain, B. J. (1997) 'Work and nonvocational domains of functioning in persons with severe mental illness: a longitudinal analysis', *Journal of Nervous and Mental Disease*, 185, pp. 419–426.

Murphy, D. and Cutting, J. (1990) 'Prosodic comprehension and expression in schizophrenia', *Journal of Neurology Neurosurgery and Psychiatry*, 53, pp. 727–730.

Murray, R. M., O'Callaghan, E., Castle, D. J. and Lewis, S. W. (1992) 'A neurodevelopmental approach to the classification of schizophrenia', *Schizophrenia Bulletin*, 18, pp. 319–332.

Myin-Germeys, I., Krabbendam, L., Jolles, J., Delespaul, P. A. and van Os, J. (2002) 'Are cognitive impairments associated with sensitivity to stress in schizophrenia? An experience sampling study', *American Journal of Psychiatry*, 159, pp. 443–449.

Nathaniel-James, D. A. and Frith, C. D. (1996) 'Confabulation in schizophrenia: evidence of a new form?', *Psychological Medicine*, 26, pp. 391–399.

Nathaniel-James, D. A., Brown, R. and Ron, M. A. (1996) 'Memory impairment in schizophrenia: its relationship to executive function', *Schizophrenia Research*, 21, pp. 85–96.

Nebes, R. D., Butters, M. A., Mulsant, B. H., Pollock, B. G., Zmuda, M. D., Houck, P. R. and Reynolds, C. F. (2000) 'Decreased working memory and processing speed mediate cognitive impairment in geriatric depression', *Psychological Medicine*, 30, pp. 679–691.

Neely, J. H. (1991) 'Semantic context and word recognition – a citation-classic commentary on semantic priming and retrieval from lexical memory – evidence for facilitatory and inhibitory processes and semantic priming and retrieval from lexical memory – roles of inhibition less spreading activation and limited capacity attention by Neely, J.H', *Current Contents/Social and Behavioral Sciences*, 20, p. 10.

Neisser, U. (1968) *Cognitive Psychology*. Englewood Cliffs, NJ: Prentice Hall.

Nelson, H. E., Pantelis, C., Carruthers, K., Speller, J., Baxendale, S. and Barnes, T. R. E. (1990) 'Cognitive functioning and symptomatology in chronic schizophrenia', *Psychological Medicine*, 20, pp. 357–365.

Ngan, E. T. C. and Liddle, P. F. (2000) 'Reaction time, symptom profiles and course of illness in schizophrenia', *Schizophrenia Research*, 46(2–3), pp. 195–201.

Nietfeld, J. L. and Schraw, G. (2002) 'The effect of knowledge and strategy training on monitoring accuracy', *Journal of Educational Research*, 95, pp. 131–142.

Nieuwenstein, M. R., Aleman, A. and de Haan, E. H. F. (2001) 'Relationship between symptom dimensions and neurocognitive functioning in schizophrenia: a meta-analysis of WCST and CPT studies', *Journal of Psychiatric Research*, 35, pp. 119–125.

Nisbet, H., Siegert, R., Hunt, M. and Fairley, N. (1996) 'Improving schizophrenic in-patients' Wisconsin card-sorting performance', *British Journal of Clinical Psychology*, 35, pp. 631–633.

Nopoulos, P., Flashman, L., Flaum, M., Arndt, S. and Andreasen, N. (1994) 'Stability of cognitive functioning early in the course of schizophrenia', *Schizophrenia Research*, 14, pp. 29–37.

Norman, D. A. and Shallice, T. (1986) 'Attention and action: willed and automatic human control of behaviour,' in R. J. Davidson, G. E. Schwartz and D. Shapiro (eds) *Consciousness and Self-Regulation*, 4th edn. New York: Plenum Press, pp. 1–18.

Novic, J., Luchins, D. J. and Perline, R. (1984) 'Facial affect recognition in schizophrenia. Is there a differential deficit', *British Journal of Psychiatry*, 144, pp. 533–537.

Nuechterlein, K. H. (1983) 'Pre-emptive thinking and schizophrenia research – psychosis and schizophrenia – cerebral mechanisms, autonomic responsiveness, and attention in schizophrenia – discussion', *Nebraska Symposium on Motivation*, 31, pp. 319–344.

Nuechterlein, K. H. and Dawson, M. E. (1984) 'Information processing and attentional functioning in the developmental course of schizophrenic disorder', *Schizophrenia Bulletin*, 10, pp. 160–203.

Nuechterlein, K. H. and Green, M. F. (1991) 'Neuropsychological vulnerability or episode factors in schizophrenia', *Behavioral and Brain Sciences*, 14, p. 37.

Nuechterlein, K. H., Dawson, M. E., Gitlin, M., Ventura, J., Goldstein, M. J., Snyder, K. S., Yee, C. M. and Mintz, J. (1992) 'Developmental processes in schizophrenic disorders – longitudinal studies of vulnerability and stress', *Schizophrenia Bulletin*, 18, pp. 387–425.

Nuechterlein, K. H., Dawson, M. E. and Green, M. F. (1994) 'Information-processing abnormalities as neuropsychological vulnerability indicators for schizophrenia', *Acta Psychiatrica Scandinavica*, 90, pp. 71–79.

Oades, R. D., Muller, B. W., Bender, S. and Sartory, G. (2000) 'A conditioned blocking impairment in nonparanoid schizophrenia: onset age and illness duration', *Schizophrenia Research*, 41, p. B318.

O'Carroll, R. E., Russell, H. H., Lawrie, S. M. and Johnstone, E. C. (1999) 'Errorless learning and the cognitive rehabilitation of memory – impaired schizophrenic patients', *Psychological Medicine*, 29, pp. 105–112.

Olbrich, R. and Mussgay, L. (1990) 'Reduction of schizophrenic deficits by cognitive training – an evaluative study', *European Archives of Psychiatry and Clinical Neuroscience*, 239, pp. 366–369.

O'Leary, D. S., Flaum, M., Kesler, M. L., Flashman, L. A., Arndt, S. and Andreasen, N. C. (2000) 'Cognitive correlates of the negative, disorganized, and psychotic symptom dimensions of schizophrenia', *Journal of Neuropsychiatry and Clinical Neurosciences*, 12, pp. 4–15.

Oliver, N. and Kuipers, E. (1996) 'Stress and its relationship to expressed emotion in community mental health workers', *International Journal of Social Psychiatry*, 42, pp. 150–159.

Oltmanns, T. F., Ohayon, J. and Neale, J. M. (1978) 'Effect of anti-psychotic medication and diagnostic criteria on distractibility in schizophrenia', *Journal of Psychiatric Research*, 14, pp. 81–91.

Palmer, B. W., Heaton, R. K., Paulsen, J. S., Kuck, J., Braff, D., Harris, M. J., Zisook, S. and Jeste, D. V. (1997) 'Is it possible to be schizophrenic yet neuropsychologically normal?', *Neuropsychology*, 11, pp. 437–446.

Palmer, B. W., Heaton, R. K., Gladsjo, J. A., Evans, J. D., Patterson, T. L., Golshan, S. and Jeste, D. V. (2002) 'Heterogeneity in functional status among older outpatients with schizophrenia: employment history, living situation, and driving', *Schizophrenia Research*, 55, pp. 205–215.

Pantelis, C., Barnes, T. R. E., Nelson, H. E., Tanner, S., Weatherley, L., Owen, A. M. and Robbins, T. W. (1997) 'Frontal-striatal cognitive deficits in patients with chronic schizophrenia', *Brain*, 120, pp. 1823–1843.

Pantelis, C., Barber, F. Z., Barnes, T. R. E., Nelson, H. E., Owen, A. M. and Robbins, T. W. (1999) 'Comparison of set-shifting ability in patients with chronic schizophrenia and frontal lobe damage', *Schizophrenia Research*, 37, pp. 251–270.

Pantelis, C., Stuart, G. W., Nelson, H. E., Robbins, T. W. and Barnes, T. R. E. (2001) 'Spatial working memory deficits in schizophrenia: relationship with tardive dyskinesia and negative symptoms', *American Journal of Psychiatry*, 158, pp. 1276–1285.

Paris, S. G. and Winograd, P. (1990) 'Promoting metacognition and motivation of exceptional children', *Remedial and Special Education*, 11, pp. 7–15.

Park, S. and Holzman, P. S. (1992) 'Schizophrenics show spatial working memory deficits', *Archives of General Psychiatry*, 49, pp. 975–982.

Patel, A., Everitt, B., Knapp, M., Reeder, C. and Wykes, T. (2004) 'Schizophrenia patients with cognitive deficits: costs and factors associated with costs', *Schizophrenia Research*, 67, p. 274.

Patterson, T. L., Klapow, J. C., Eastham, J., Heaton, R. K., Evans, J. D., Koch, W. L. and Jeste, D. V. (1998) 'Correlates of functional status in older patients with schizophrenia', *Psychiatry Research*, 80, pp. 41–52.

Paulsen, J. S., Heaton, R. K. and Jeste, D. V. (1994) 'Neuropsychological impairment and in tardive dyskinesia', *Neuropsychology*, 8, pp. 227–241.

Paulsen, J. S., Heaton, R. K., Sadek, J. R., Perry, W., Dellis, D. C., Kruck, J., Zisook, S., Jeste, D. V. and Braff, D. L. (1995) 'Learning and memory in schizophrenia', *Schizophrenia Research*, 15, p. 109.

Peer, J., Rothmann, T., Penrod, R., Penn, D. and Spaulding, W. (2004) 'Social cognitive biases and neurocognitive deficits in paranoid symptoms: evidence for an interaction effect and changes during treatment', *Schizophrenia Research*, 71(2–3), pp. 463–471.

Penades, R., Boget, T., Lomena, F., Bernardo, M., Mateos, J. J., Laterza, C., Pavia, J. and Salamero, M. (2000) 'Brain perfusion and neuropsychological changes in schizophrenic patients after cognitive rehabilitation', *Psychiatry Research-Neuroimaging*, 98, pp. 127–132.

Penades, R., Boget, T., Lomena, F., Mateos, J. J., Catalan, R., Gasto, C. and Salamero, M. (2002) 'Could the hypofrontality pattern in schizophrenia be modified through neuropsychological rehabilitation?', *Acta Psychiatrica Scandinavica*, 105, pp. 202–208.

Penades, R., Boget, T., Catalan, R., Bernardo, M., Gasto, C. and Salamero, M. (2003) 'Cognitive mechanisms, psychosocial functioning, and neurocognitive rehabilitation in schizophrenia', *Schizophrenia Research*, 63, pp. 219–227.

Penn, D. L., Mueser, K. T., Spaulding, W., Hope, D. A. and Reed, D. (1995) 'Information processing and social competence in chronic schizophrenia', *Schizophrenia Bulletin*, 21, pp. 269–281.

Penn, D. L., Corrigan, P. W., Bentall, R. P., Racenstein, J. M. and Newman, L. (1997a) 'Social cognition in schizophrenia', *Psychological Bulletin*, 121, pp. 114–132.

Penn, D. L., Spaulding, W., Reed, D., Sullivan, M., Mueser, K. T. and Hope, D. A. (1997b) 'Cognition and social functioning in schizophrenia', *Psychiatry – Interpersonal and Biological Processes*, 60, pp. 281–291.

Penn, D. L., Ritchie, M., Francis, J., Combs, D. and Martin, J. (2002) 'Social perception in schizophrenia: the role of context', *Psychiatry Research*, 109, pp. 149–159.

Perlstein, W. M., Carter, C. S., Barch, D. M. and Baird, J. W. (1998) 'The Stroop task and attention deficits in schizophrenia: a critical evaluation of card and single-trial Stroop methodologies', *Neuropsychology*, 12(3), pp. 414–425.

Perry, W., Heaton, R. K., Potterat, E., Roebuck, T., Minassian, A. and Braff, D. L. (2001a) 'Working memory in schizophrenia: transient "online" storage versus executive functioning', *Schizophrenia Bulletin*, 27, pp. 157–176.

Perry, W., Potterat, E. G. and Braff, D. L. (2001b) 'Self-monitoring enhances Wisconsin card sorting test performance in patients with schizophrenia: performance is improved by simply asking patients to verbalize their sorting strategy', *Journal of the International Neuropsychological Society*, 7, pp. 344–352.

Phillips, W. and Silverstein, S. (2003) 'Convergence of biological and psychological perspectives on cognitive co-ordination in schizophrenia', *Behavioural and Brain Sciences*, 26, pp. 65–138.

Pickup, G. J. and Frith, C. D. (2001) 'Theory of mind impairments in schizophrenia: symptomatology, severity and specificity', *Psychological Medicine*, 31, pp. 207–220.

Pilling, S., Bebbington, P., Kuipers, E., Garety, P., Geddes, J., Orbach, G. and Morgan, C. (2002a) 'Psychological treatments in schizophrenia: I. Meta-analysis of family intervention and cognitive behaviour therapy', *Psychological Medicine*, 32, pp. 763–782.

Pilling, S., Bebbington, P., Kuipers, E., Garety, P., Geddes, J., Martindale, B., Orbach, G. and Morgan, C. (2002b) 'Psychological treatments in schizophrenia: II. Meta-analyses of randomized controlled trials of social skills training and cognitive remediation', *Psychological Medicine*, 32, pp. 783–791.

Pinkham, A. E., Penn, D. L., Perkins, D. O. and Lieberman, J. (2003) 'Implications for the neural basis of social cognition for the study of schizophrenia', *American Journal of Psychiatry*, 160, pp. 815–824.

Poole, J. H., Ober, B. A., Shenaut, G. K. and Vinogradov, S. (1999) 'Independent frontal-system deficits in schizophrenia: cognitive, clinical, and adaptive implications', *Psychiatry Research*, 85, pp. 161–176.

Posner, M. I. and Boies, S. J. (1971) 'Components of attention', *Psychological Review*, 78, pp. 391–408.

Pukrop, R., Matuschek, E., Ruhrmann, S., Brockhaus-Dumke, A., Tendolkar, I., Bertsch, A. and Klosterkotter, J. (2003) 'Dimensions of working memory dysfunction in schizophrenia', *Schizophrenia Research*, 62, pp. 259–268.

Rabinowicz, E. F., Opler, L. A., Owen, D. R. and Knight, R. A. (1996) 'Dot enumeration perceptual organization task (DEPOT): evidence for a short-term visual memory deficit in schizophrenia', *Journal of Abnormal Psychology*, 105, pp. 336–348.

Rabinowicz, E. F., Silipo, G., Goldman, R. and Javitt, D. C. (2000) 'Auditory sensory dysfunction in schizophrenia – imprecision or distractibility?', *Archives of General Psychiatry*, 57, pp. 1149–1155.

Ragland, J. D., Moelter, S. T., McGrath, C., Hill, S. K., Gur, R. E., Bilker, W. B., Siegel, S. J. and Gur, R. C. (2003) 'Levels-of-processing effect on word recognition in schizophrenia', *Biological Psychiatry*, 54, pp. 1154–1161.

Reber, A. S. (1967) 'Implicit learning of artificial grammars', *Journal of Verbal Learning and Verbal Behavior*, 6, pp. 855–863.

Reed, R. A., Harrow, M., Herbener, E. S. and Martin, E. M. (2002) 'Executive function in schizophrenia: is it linked to psychosis and poor life functioning?', *Journal of Nervous and Mental Disease*, 190, pp. 725–732.

Reeder, C., Newton, E., Frangou, S. and Wykes, T. (2004) 'Which executive skills should we target to affect social functioning and symptom change? A study of a cognitive remediation therapy program', *Schizophrenia Bulletin*, 30, pp. 87–100.

Reitan, R. (1958) 'Validity of the trail making test as an indicator of organic brain damage', *Perceptual and Motor Skills*, 8, pp. 271–276.

Rempfer, M., Hamera, E., Brown, C. and Cromwell, R. (2003) 'The relations between cognition and the independent living skill of shopping in people with schizophrenia', *Psychiatry Research*, 117, pp. 103–112.

Revheim, N., Kamintzer, D., Casey, M. and Medalia, A. (2001) 'Implementation of a cognitive rehabilitation program in an IPRT setting', *Psychiatric Rehabiliation Skills*, 5, pp. 403–425.

Riding, R. J. and Buckle, C. F. (1990) *Learning Styles and Training Performance*. Sheffield: Training Agency.

Riding, R. and Cheema, I. (1991) 'Cognitive styles: an overview and integration', *Educational Psychology* 11, pp. 193–215.

Riding, R. J., Glass, A. and Douglas, G. (1993) 'Individual differences in thinking:

cognitive and neurophysiological perspectives. Special issues: Thinking', *Educational Psychology*, 13, pp. 267–279.

Robertson I. T. (1985) 'Human information-processing strategies and syle', *Behaviour and Information Technology*, 4, pp. 19–29.

Rojas-Drummond, S., Mercer, N. and Dabrowski, E. (2001) 'Collaboration, scaffolding and the promotion of problem solving strategies in Mexican pre-schoolers', *European Journal of Psychology of Education*, 16, pp. 179–196.

Rosenbaum, G., Mackavey, W. R. and Grisell, J. L. (1957) 'Effects of biological and social motivation on schizophrenic reaction time', *Journal of Abnormal and Social Psychology*, 54, pp. 364–368.

Rosenfarb, I. S., Nuechterlein, K. H., Goldstein, M. J. and Subotnik, K. L. (2000) 'Neurocognitive vulnerability, interpersonal criticism, and the emergence of unusual thinking by schizophrenic patients during family transactions', *Archives of General Psychiatry*, 57, pp. 1174–1179.

Ross, R. G., Harris, J. G., Olincy, A. and Radant, A. (2000) 'Eye movement task measures inhibition and spatial working memory in adults with schizophrenia, ADHD, and a normal comparison group', *Psychiatry Research*, 95, pp. 35–42.

Rossell, S. L. and David, A. S. (1997) 'Improving performance on the WCST: variations on the original procedure', *Schizophrenia Research*, 28, pp. 63–76.

Rund, B. R. (1998) 'A review of longitudinal studies of cognitive functions in schizophrenia patients', *Schizophrenia Bulletin*, 24, pp. 425–435.

Rund, B. R., Melle, I., Friis, S., Larsen, T. K., Midboe, L. J., Opjordsmoen, S., Simonsen, E., Vaglum, P. and McGlashan, T. (2004) 'Neurocognitive dysfunction in first-episode psychosis: correlates with symptoms, premorbid adjustment, and duration of untreated psychosis', *American Journal of Psychiatry*, 161, pp. 466–472.

Rushe, T. M., Morris, R. G., Miotto, E. C., Feigenbaum, J. D., Woodruff, P. W. R. and Murray, R. M. (1999) 'Problem-solving and spatial working memory in patients with schizophrenia and with focal frontal and temporal lobe lesions', *Schizophrenia Research*, 37, pp. 21–33.

Russell, A. J., Munro, J. C., Jones, P. B., Hemsley, D. R. and Murray, R. M. (1997) 'Schizophrenia and the myth of intellectual decline', *American Journal of Psychiatry*, 154, pp. 635–639.

Rutschmann, J., Cornblatt, B. and Erlenmeyerkimling, L. (1986) 'Sustained attention in children at risk for schizophrenia – findings with 2 visual continuous performance tests in a new sample', *Journal of Abnormal Child Psychology*, 14, pp. 365–385.

Salamé, P., Danion, J. M., Peretti, S. and Cuervo, C. (1998) 'The state of functioning of working memory in schizophrenia', *Schizophrenia Research*, 30, pp. 11–29.

Salokangas, R. K. R. (1983) 'Prognostic implications of the sex of schizophrenic patients', *British Journal of Psychiatry*, 142, pp. 145–151.

Sandford, J. A. and Browne, R. J. (2004) *Captain's Log [CD-ROM]: Cognitive Training System. Version 1.0.* Indianapolis: Psychological Software Services.

Sawyer, R. J., Graham, S. and Harris, K. R. (1992) 'Direct teaching, strategy instruction, and strategy instruction with explicit self-regulation – effects on the composition skills and self-efficacy of students with learning disabilities', *Journal of Educational Psychology*, 84, pp. 340–352.

Sayers, S. L., Bellack, A. S., Mueser, K. T., Tierney, A. M., Wade, J. H. and Morrison,

R. L. (1995) 'Family interactions of schizophrenic and schizoaffective patients – determinants of relatives' negativity', *Psychiatry Research*, 56, pp. 121–134.

Saykin, A. J., Gur, R. C., Gur, R. E., Mozley, P. D., Mozley, L. H., Resnick, S. M., Kester, D. B. and Stafiniak, P. (1991) 'Neuropsychological function in schizophrenia – selective impairment in memory and learning', *Archives of General Psychiatry*, 48, pp. 618–624.

Saykin, A. J., Shtasel, D. L., Gur, R. E., Kester, D. B., Mozley, L. H., Stafiniak, P. and Gur, R. C. (1994) 'Neuropsychological deficits in neuroleptic naive patients with first-episode schizophrenia', *Archives of General Psychiatry*, 51, pp. 124–131.

Schacter, D. L. (1987) 'Implicit memory – history and current status', *Journal of Experimental Psychology – Learning Memory and Cognition*, 13, pp. 501–518.

Schank, R. C. (1977) *Scripts, Plans, Goals, and Understanding*. Hillsdale, NY: Lawrence Erlbaum Associates, Inc.

Schmand, B., Brand, N. and Kuipers, T. (1992) 'Procedural learning of cognitive and motor skills in psychotic patients', *Schizophrenia Research*, 8, pp. 157–170.

Schneider, F., Heimann, H., Himer, W., Huss, D., Mattes, R. and Adam, B. (1990) 'Computer-based analysis of facial action in schizophrenic and depressed patients', *European Archives of Psychiatry and Clinical Neuroscience*, 240, pp. 67–76.

Schuepbach, D., Keshavan, M. S., Kmiec, J. A. and Sweeney, J. A. (2002) 'Negative symptom resolution and improvements in specific cognitive deficits after acute treatment in first-episode schizophrenia', *Schizophrenia Research*, 53, pp. 249–261.

Schunk, D. H. (1986) 'Vicarious influences on self-efficacy for cognitive skill learning', *Journal of Social and Clinical Psychology*, 4, pp. 316–327.

—— (1996) 'Goal and self-evaluative influences during children's cognitive skill learning', *American Educational Research Journal*, 33(2), pp. 359–382.

Seidman, L. J., Lanca, M., Kremen, W. S., Faraone, S. V. and Tsuang, M. T. (2003) 'Organizational and visual memory deficits in schizophrenia and bipolar psychoses using the Rey-Osterrieth complex figure: effects of duration of illness', *Journal of Clinical and Experimental Neuropsychology*, 25, pp. 949–964.

Sergi, M. J. and Green, M. F. (2003) 'Social perception and early visual processing in schizophrenia', *Schizophrenia Research*, 59, pp. 233–241.

Serper, M. R. and Harvey, P. D. (1994) 'The need to integrate neuropsychological and experimental schizophrenia research', *Schizophrenia Bulletin*, 20, pp. 1–11.

Servan-Schreiber, D., Cohen, J. D. and Steingard, S. (1996) 'Schizophrenic deficits in the processing of context – a test of a theoretical model', *Archives of General Psychiatry*, 53, pp. 1105–1112.

Shallice, T. (1982) 'Specific impairments of planning', *Philosophical Transactions of the Royal Society of London Series B – Biological Sciences*, 298, pp. 199–209.

—— (1988) *From Neuropsychology to Mental Structure*. Cambridge: Cambridge University Press.

Shallice, T. and Burgess, P. (1990) 'The frontal lobes and failures of supervisory control', *Quarterly Journal of Experimental Psychology Section A – Human Experimental Psychology*, 42, pp. 201–202.

—— (1996) 'The domain of supervisory processes and temporal organization of behaviour', *Philosophical Transactions of the Royal Society of London Series B – Biological Sciences*, 351, pp. 1405–1411.

Shallice, T. and Warrington, E. K. (1970) 'Independent functioning of verbal memory stores – a neuropsychological study', *Quarterly Journal of Experimental Psychology*, 22, pp. 261–273.

Shallice, T., Burgess, P. W. and Frith, C. D. (1991) 'Can the neuropsychological case study approach be applied to schizophrenia', *Psychological Medicine*, 21, pp. 661–673.

Shapiro, M. B. and Nelson, E. H. (1955) 'An investigation of the nature of cognitive impairment in co-operative psychiatric patients', *British Journal of Medical Psychology*, 28, pp. 239–256.

Shapiro, M. B. and Ravenette, A. T. (1959) 'A preliminary experiment on paranoid delusions', *Journal of Mental Science*, 105, pp. 295–312.

Shepherd, M., Watt, D., Falloon, I. and Smeeton, N. (1989) 'The natural history of schizophrenia – a 5-year follow-up study of outcome and prediction in a representative sample of schizophrenics', *Psychological Medicine*, 15(46).

Shute, V. J. and Gawlick, L. A. (1995) 'Practice effects on skill acquisition, learning outcome, retention, and sensitivity to relearning', *Human Factors*, 37, pp. 781–803.

Silver, H., Feldman, P., Bilker, W. and Gur, R. C. (2003) 'Working memory deficit as a core neuropsychological dysfunction in schizophrenia', *American Journal of Psychiatry*, 160, pp. 1809–1816.

Silverstein, S. M., Menditto, A. A. and Stuve, P. (1999) 'Shaping procedures as cognitive retraining techniques in individuals with severe and persistent mental illness', *Psychiatric Rehabilitation Skills*, 3, pp. 59–76.

Silverstein, S. M., Menditto, A. A. and Stuve, P. (2001) 'Shaping attention span: an operant conditioning procedure to improve neurocognition and functioning in schizophrenia', *Schizophrenia Bulletin*, 27, pp. 247–257.

Singely, M. and Anderson, J. (1989) *The Transfer of Cognitive Skills*. Cambridge, MA: Harvard University Press.

Smith, T. E., Hull, J. W., Huppert, J. D. *et al.* (2002) 'Recovery from psychosis in schizophrenia and schizoaffective disorder: symptoms and neurocognitive rate-limiters for the development of social behavior skills', *Schizophrenia Research*, 55, pp. 229–237.

Snitz, B. E., Curtis, C. E., Zald, D. H., Katsanis, J. and Iacono, W. G. (1999) 'Neuro-psychological and oculomotor correlates of spatial working memory performance in schizophrenia patients and controls', *Schizophrenia Research*, 38, pp. 37–50.

Sohlberg, M. and Mateer, C. (1987) 'Effectiveness of an attention-training program', *Journal of Clinical and Experimental Neuropsychology*, 9, pp. 117–130.

Sonnier, I. L. (1991) 'Hemisphericity: a key to understanding individual differences among teachers and learners', *Journal of Instructional Psychology*, 18, pp. 17–22.

Spaulding, D. M. (2003) 'Reflections: back from remission', *American Journal of Nursing*, 103, p. 31.

Spaulding, W. and Sullivan, M. (1992) 'From laboratory to clinic: psychological methods and principles in psychiatric rehabilitation', in R. P. Liberman (ed.) *Handbook of Psychiatric Rehabilitation*. New York: Macmillan, pp. 30–55.

Spaulding, W., Huntzinger, R. S., Lecompte, P. and Cromwell, R. L. (1984) 'Clinical and etiological implications of a specific attention deficit in schizophrenia', *Journal of Nervous and Mental Disease*, 172, pp. 279–286.

Spaulding, W. D., Storms, L., Goodrich, V. and Sullivan, M. (1986) 'Applications of experimental psychopathology in psychiatric rehabilitation', *Schizophrenia Bulletin*, 12, pp. 560–577.

Spaulding, W., Reed, D., Storzbach, D., Sullivan, M. and Weiler, M. (1998) 'The effects of a remediational approach to cognitive therapy for schizophrenia 3826', in T. Wykes, N. Tarrier *et al.* (eds) *Outcome and Innovation in Psychological Treatment of Schizophrenia*. Chichester: Wiley, pp. 145–160.

Spaulding, W. D., Fleming, S. K., Reed, D., Sullivan, M., Storzbach, D. and Lam, M. (1999a) 'Cognitive functioning in schizophrenia: implications for psychiatric rehabilitation', *Schizophrenia Bulletin*, 25, pp. 275–289.

Spaulding, W. D., Reed, D., Sullivan, M., Richardson, C. and Weiler, M. (1999) 'Effects of cognitive treatment in psychiatric rehabilitation', *Schizophrenia Bulletin*, 25, pp. 657–676.

Spaulding, W. D., Sullivan, M. E. and Poland, J. S. (2003) *Treatment and Rehabilitation of Severe Mental Illness.* New York: Guilford Press.

Sperling, G. (1960) 'The information avaliable in brief visual presentation', *Psychological Monographs*, 74, p. 29.

Spitzer, M., Braun, U., Maier, S., Hermle, L. and Maher, B. A. (1993) 'Indirect semantic priming in schizophrenic patients', *Schizophrenia Research*, 11, pp. 71–80.

Squire, L. R. and Cohen, N. (1979) 'Memory and amnesia – resistance to disruption develops for years after learning', *Behavioral and Neural Biology*, 25, pp. 115–125.

Staal, W. G., Hijman, R., Pol, H. E. H. and Kahn, R. S. (2000) 'Neuropsychological dysfunctions in siblings discordant for schizophrenia', *Psychiatry Research*, 95, pp. 227–235.

Stark, R., Mandl, H., Gruber, H. and Renkl, A. (1999). 'Instructional means to overcome transfer problems in the domain of economics: empirical studies', *International Journal of Educational Research*, 3, pp. 591–609.

Startup, M. (1996) 'Insight and cognitive deficits in schizophrenia: evidence for a curvilinear relationship', *Psychological Medicine*, 26, pp. 1277–1281.

Steffy, R. A. and Galbraith, K. J. (1980) 'Relation between latency and redundancy-associated deficit in schizophrenic reaction-time performance', *Journal of Abnormal Psychology*, 89, pp. 419–427.

Steinhauer, S. R., Condray, R., Zubin, J. and Dougherty, G. (1991) 'Schizotypal symptoms and information-processing deficits in families of schizophrenic patients', *Schizophrenia Research*, 4, p. 393.

Sternberg, R. J., Wagner, R. K., Williams, W. M. and Horvath, J. A. (1995) 'Testing common-sense', *American Psychologist*, 50, pp. 912–927.

Stratta, P., Mancini, F., Mattei, P., Casacchia, M. and Rossi, A. (1994) 'Information-processing strategy to remediate Wisconsin card sorting test performance in schizophrenia – a pilot study', *American Journal of Psychiatry*, 151, pp. 915–918.

Stratta, P., Daneluzzo, E., Prosperini, P., Bustini, M., Mattei, P. and Rossi, A. (1997a) 'Is Wisconsin card sorting test performance related to "working memory" capacity?', *Schizophrenia Research*, 27, pp. 11–19.

Stratta, P., Mancini, F., Mattei, P., Daneluzzo, E., Bustini, M., Casacchia, M. and Rossi, A. (1997b) 'Remediation of Wisconsin card sorting test performance in schizophrenia – a controlled study', *Psychopathology*, 30, pp. 59–66.

Stratta, P., Daneluzzo, E., Bustini, M., Prosperini, P. and Rossi, A. (2000) 'Processing of context information in schizophrenia: relation to clinical symptoms and WCST performance', *Schizophrenia Research*, 44, pp. 57–67.

Stratta, P., Prosperini, P., Daneluzzo, E., Bustini, M. and Rossi, A. (2001) 'Educational level and age influence spatial working memory and Wisconsin card sorting test performance differently: a controlled study in schizophrenic patients', *Psychiatry Research*, 102, pp. 39–48.

Surguladze, S., Rossell, S., Rabe-Hesketh, S. and David, A. S. (2002) 'Cross-modal semantic priming in schizophrenia', *Journal of the International Neuropsychological Society*, 8(7), pp. 884–892.

Suslow, T., Schonauer, K. and Arolt, V. (2001) 'Attention training in the cognitive rehabilitation of schizophrenic patients: a review of efficacy studies', *Acta Psychiatrica Scandinavica*, 103, pp. 15–23.

Tamlyn, D., McKenna, P. J., Mortimer, A. M., Lund, C. E., Hammond, S. and Baddeley, A. D. (1992) 'Memory impairment in schizophrenia – its extent, affiliations and neuropsychological character', *Psychological Medicine*, 22, pp. 101–115.

Tek, C., Kirkpatrick, B. and Buchanan, R. W. (2001) 'A five-year followup study of deficit and nondeficit schizophrenia', *Schizophrenia Research*, 49, pp. 253–260.

Tek, C., Gold, J., Blaxton, T., Wilk, C., McMahon, R. P. and Buchanan, R. W. (2002) 'Visual perceptual and working memory impairments in schizophrenia', *Archives of General Psychiatry*, 59, pp. 146–153.

Tenyi, T., Herold, R., Szili, I. M. and Trixler, M. (2002) 'Schizophrenics show a failure in the decoding of violations of conversational implicatures', *Psychopathology*, 35, pp. 25–27.

Teuber, H. L. (1950) 'Recent advances in diagnostic psychological testing', in M. R. E. Harrower (ed.) *Neuropsychology.* Springfield, IL: Charles C. Thomas, pp. 85–102.

Thorndike, E. L. and Woodworth, R. R. (1901) 'The influences of improvement in one mental function upon the efficiency of other functions', *Psychology Review*, 8, pp. 247–261.

Thornley, B. and Adams, C. (1998) 'Content and quality of 2000 controlled trials in schizophrenia over 50 years', *British Medical Journal*, 317, pp. 1181–1184.

Tienari, P. (1991) 'Interaction between genetic vulnerability and family environment – the Finnish adoptive family study of schizophrenia', *Acta Psychiatrica Scandinavica*, 84, pp. 460–465.

Toulopoulou, T., Rabe-Hesketh, S., King, H., Murray, R. M. and Morris, R. G. (2003) 'Episodic memory in schizophrenic patients and their relatives', *Schizophrenia Research*, 63, pp. 261–271.

Tracy, J. I., Mattson, R., King, C., Bundick, T., Celenza, M. A. and Glosser, G. (2001) 'A comparison of memory for verbal and non-verbal material in schizophrenia', *Schizophrenia Research*, 50, pp. 199–211.

Trenerry, M., Crosson, B., DeBoe, J. and Leber, W. (1989) *Stroop Neuropsychological Screening Test.* New York: Psychological Assessment Resources.

Tulving, E. and Markowitsch, H. J. (1998) 'Episodic and declarative memory: role of the hippocampus', *Hippocampus*, 8, pp. 198–204.

Turken, U., Vuilleumier, P., Mathalon, D. H., Swick, D. and Ford, J. M. (2003) 'Are impairments of action monitoring and executive control true dissociative dysfunctions in patients with schizophrenia?', *American Journal of Psychiatry*, 160, pp. 1881–1883.

Turner, D., Luke, C., Pomarol-Clotet, E., McKenna, P., Robbins, T. and Shakian, B. (2004) 'Modafinil improves cognition and attentional shifting in patients with chronic schizophrenia', *Neuropsychopharmacology Review*, 29, pp. 1363–1373.

Turvey, M. T. (1973) 'Peripheral and central processes in vision – inferences from an information-processing analysis of masking with patterned stimuli', *Psychological Review*, 80, pp. 1–52.

Twamley, E. W., Doshi, R., Nayak, G. V., Palmer, B. W., Golshan, S., Heaton, R., Patterson, T. L. and Jeste, D. (2002) 'Generalized cognitive impairments, ability to perform everyday tasks, and level of independence in community living situations of older patients with psychosis', *American Journal of Psychiatry*, 159, pp. 2013–2020.

Twamley, E. W., Jeste, D. V. and Bellack, A. S. (2003) 'A review of cognitive training in schizophrenia', *Schizophrenia Bulletin*, 29, pp. 359–382.

Ueland, T. and Rund, B. R. (2004) 'A controlled randomized treatment study: the effects of a cognitive remediation program on adolescents with early onset psychosis', *Acta Psychiatrica Scandinavica*, 109, pp. 70–74.

Vallar, G. and Papagno, C. (2002) 'Neuropsychological impairments of verbal short-term memory,' in A. D. Baddeley, M. D. Kopelman, and B. Wilson (eds) *Handbook of Memory Disorders*, 2nd edn. Chichester: Wiley, pp. 249–270.

Van der Does, A. J. W., Dingemans, P. M. A. J., Linszen, D. H. and Nugter, M. A. (1996) 'Symptoms, cognitive and social functioning in recent-onset schizophrenia: A longitudinal study', *Schizophrenia Research*, 19, pp. 61–71.

van der Gaag, M. (1992) *The Results of Cognitive Training in Schizophrenic Patients*. Delft: Eburon.

van der Gaag, M., Kern, R. S., van den Bosch, R. J. and Liberman, R. P. (2002) 'A controlled trial of cognitive remediation in schizophrenia', *Schizophrenia Bulletin*, 28, pp. 167–176.

van Os, J., Wright, P. and Murray, R. M. (1997) 'Follow-up studies of schizophrenia I: natural history and non-psychopathological predictors of outcome', *European Psychiatry*, 12, pp. 327–341.

Vauth, R., Loschmann, C., Rusch, N. and Corrigan, P. W. (2004) 'Understanding adherence to neuroleptic treatment in schizophrenia', *Psychiatry Research*, 126(1), pp. 43–49.

Velligan, D. I., Mahurin, R. K., Diamond, P. L., Hazleton, B. C., Eckert, S. L. and Miller, A. L. (1997) 'The functional significance of symptomatology and cognitive function in schizophrenia', *Schizophrenia Research*, 25, pp. 21–31.

Velligan, D. I., Bow-Thomas, C. C., Mahurin, R. K., Miller, A. L. and Halgunseth, L. C. (2000) 'Do specific neurocognitive deficits predict specific domains of community function in schizophrenia?', *Journal of Nervous and Mental Disease*, 188, pp. 518–524.

Velligan, D. I., Prihoda, T. J., Sui, D., Ritch, J. L., Maples, N. and Miller, A. L. (2003) 'The effectiveness of quetiapine versus conventional antipsychotics in improving cognitive and functional outcomes in standard treatment settings', *Journal of Clinical Psychiatry*, 64, pp. 524–531.

Vendrell, P., Junque, C., Pujol, J., Jurado, M. A., Molet, J. and Grafman, J. (1995) 'The role of prefrontal regions in the Stroop task', *Neuropsychologia*, 33, pp. 341–352.

Ventura, J., Nuechterlein, K. H., Subotnik, K. L. and Hwang, S. S. (2003) 'Coping behavior and symptom outcome in recent-onset schizophrenia', *Schizophrenia Research*, 60, p. 28.

Vinogradov, S., WillisShore, J., Poole, J. H., Marten, E., Ober, B. A. and Shenaut,

G. K. (1997) 'Clinical and neurocognitive aspects of source monitoring errors in schizophrenia', *American Journal of Psychiatry*, 154, pp. 1530–1537.

Vinogradov, S., Kirkland, J., Poole, J. H., Drexler, M., Ober, B. A. and Shenaut, G. K. (2003) 'Both processing speed and semantic memory organization predict verbal fluency in schizophrenia', *Schizophrenia Research*, 59, pp. 269–275.

Vollema, M. G., Geurtsen, G. J. and Vanvoorst, A. J. P. (1995) 'Durable improvements in Wisconsin card sorting test performance in schizophrenic patients', *Schizophrenia Research*, 16, pp. 209–215.

Vygotsky, L. S. (1962) *Thought and Language*. Cambridge, MA: MIT Press.

Wagner, B. R. (1968) 'The training of attending and abstracting responses in chronic schizophrenia', *Journal of Experimental Research in Personality*, 3, pp. 77–88.

Wapner, S. and Krus, D. M. (1960) 'Effects of lysergic-acid diethylamide, and differences between normals and schizophrenics on the Stroop color–word test', *Journal of Neuropsychiatry*, 2, pp. 76–81.

Warner, R. (2003) 'Fact vs fantasy. A reply to Bentall and Morrison', *Journal of Mental Health*, 12, pp. 351–359.

—— (2004) *Recovery from Schizophrenia: Psychiatry and Political Economy*. London: Brunner-Routledge.

Warrington, E. K. and Weiskran, L. (1974) 'Effect of prior learning on subsequent retention in amnesic patients', *Neuropsychologia*, 12, pp. 419–428.

Waters, F. A. V., Badcock, J. C., Maybery, M. T. and Michie, P. T. (2003) 'Inhibition in schizophrenia: association with auditory hallucinations', *Schizophrenia Research*, 62, pp. 275–280.

Watson, C. G., Thomas, R. W., Andersen, D. and Felling, J. (1968) 'Differentiation of organics from schizophrenics at two chronicity levels by use of Reitan-Halstead organic test battery', *Journal of Consulting and Clinical Psychology*, 32, pp. 679–684.

Weickert, T. W., Goldberg, T. E., Gold, J. M., Bigelow, L. B., Egan, M. F. and Weinberger, D. R. (2000) 'Cognitive impairments in patients with schizophrenia displaying preserved and compromised intellect', *Archives of General Psychiatry*, 57, pp. 907–913.

Weinberger, D. R. (1988) 'Schizophrenia and the frontal lobe', *Trends in Neurosciences*, 11(8), pp. 367–370.

Weiss, K. M., Vrtunski, P. B. and Simpson, D. M. (1988) 'Information overload disrupts digit recall performance in schizophrenics', *Schizophrenia Research*, 1, pp. 299–303.

Wertheimer, M. (1945) *Productive Thinking*. New York: Harper and Row.

Wetherell, J. L., Palmer, B. W., Thorp, S. R., Patterson, T. L., Golshan, S. and Jeste, D. V. (2003) 'Anxiety symptoms and quality of life in middle-aged and older outpatients with schizophrenia and schizoaffective disorder', *Journal of Clinical Psychiatry*, 64, pp. 1476–1482.

Wexler, B. E., Anderson, M., Fulbright, R. K. and Gore, J. C. (2000) 'Preliminary evidence of improved verbal working memory performance and normalization of task-related frontal lobe activation in schizophrenia following cognitive exercises', *American Journal of Psychiatry*, 157, pp. 1694–1697.

Wexler, B.E., Nicholls, S. S. and Bell, M. D. (2004) 'Instability of cognitive processing systems in schizophrenia', *Schizophrenia Research*, 71(2–3), pp. 513–514.

White, C., Farley, J. and Charles, P. (1987) 'Chronic-schizophrenic disorder. 2.

Reaction time, social performance and arousal', *British Journal of Psychiatry*, 150, pp. 374–379.

Whittaker, J. F., Deakin, J. F. W. and Tomenson, B. (2001) 'Face processing in schizophrenia: defining the deficit', *Psychological Medicine*, 31, pp. 499–507.

Wiedl, K. H. (1999) 'Cognitive modifiability as a measure of readiness for rehabilitation', *Psychiatric Services*, 50, pp. 1411–1413.

Wiedl, K. H. and Wienobst, J. (1999) 'Interindividual differences in cognitive remediation research with schizophrenic patients – indicators of rehabilitation potential?', *International Journal of Rehabilitation Research*, 22, pp. 55–59.

Wiersma, D., Wanderling, J., Dragomirecka, E., Ganev, K., Harrison, G., An der Heiden, W., Nienhuis, F. J. and Walsh, D. (2000) 'Social disability in schizophrenia: its development and prediction over 15 years in incidence cohorts in six European centres', *Psychological Medicine*, 30, pp. 1155–1167.

Wilder-Willis, K. E., Shear, P. K., Steffen, J. J. and Borkin, J. (2002) 'The relationship between cognitive dysfunction and coping abilities in schizophrenia', *Schizophrenia Research*, 55, pp. 259–267.

Wilson, B., Alderman, N., Burgess, P., Emslie, H. and Evans, J. (1996) *Behavioural Assessment of the Dysexecutive Syndrome (BADS)*. Bury St Edmunds: Thames Valley Test Company (TVTC).

Wing, J. K. (1978) *Reasoning about Madness*. Oxford: Oxford University Press.

Witkin, H. A. (1961) 'Cognitive-development and the growth of personality', *Acta Psychologica*, 18, pp. 245–257.

Wohlberg, G. W. and Kornetsky, C. (1973) 'Sustained attention in remitted schizophrenics', *Archives of General Psychiatry*, 28, pp. 533–537.

Wood, D. (1998) *How Children Think and Learn: The Social Context of Cognitive Development*, 2nd edn. Oxford: Blackwell.

Wood, D., Bruner, J. S. and Ross, G. (1976) 'Role of tutoring in problem-solving', *Journal of Child Psychology and Psychiatry and Allied Disciplines*, 17, pp. 89–100.

Woodward, N., Purdon, S., Meltzer, H. and Zald, D. (2004) A meta-analysis of neuropsychological change to clozapine, olanzapine, quetiapine, and risperidone in schizophrenia', *International Journal of Psychopharmacology*, in press.

Woodward, T. S., Weinstein, S., Takane, Y., Hunter, M. A. and Ngan, E. T. C. (2004) 'Extent and lateralization of linguistic processing in schizophrenia I: Assessment of effective connectivity using Constrained Principal Component Analysis (CPCA)', *Schizophrenia Research*, 67(1), p. 266.

Woonings, F. M. J., Appelo, M. T., Kluiter, H., Slooff, C. J. and van den Bosch, R. J. (2003) 'Learning (potential) and social functioning in schizophrenia', *Schizophrenia Research*, 59(2–3), pp. 287–296.

Wykes, T. (1994) 'Predicting symptomatic and behavioural outcomes of community care', *British Journal of Psychiatry*, 165, pp. 486–492.

—— (1998) 'What are we changing with neurocognitive rehabilitation? Illustrations from two single cases of changes in neuropsychological performance and brain systems as measured by SPECT', *Schizophrenia Research*, 34, pp. 77–86.

—— (2000) 'Cognitive rehabilitation and remediation in schizophrenia', in T. Sharma and P. Harvey (eds) *Cognition and Schizophrenia: Impairments, Importance and Treatment Strategies*. Oxford: Oxford University Press, pp. 332–351.

Wykes, T. and Dunn, G. (1992) 'Cognitive deficit and the prediction of rehabilitation success in a chronic psychiatric group', *Psychological Medicine*, 22, pp. 389–398.

Wykes, T. and Hurry, J. (1991) 'Social behavior and psychiatric disorders', in P. Bebbington (ed.) *Social Psychiatry: Theory, Methodology, and Practice*. New Brunswick: Transaction Publishers, pp. 183–208.

Wykes, T. and Sturt, E. (1986) 'The measurement of social behaviour in psychiatric patients: an assessment of the reliability and validity of the SBS schedule', *British Journal of Psychiatry*, 148, pp. 1–11.

Wykes, T. and Van der Gaag, M. (2001) 'Is it time to develop a new cognitive therapy for psychosis – cognitive remediation therapy (CRT)?', *Clinical Psychology Review*, 21, pp. 1227–1256.

Wykes, T., Sturt, E. and Katz, R. (1990) 'The prediction of rehabilitative success after three years. The use of social, symptom and cognitive variables', *British Journal of Psychiatry*, 157, pp. 865–870.

Wykes, T., Katz, R., Sturt, E. and Hemsley, D. (1992) 'Abnormalities of response processing in a chronic psychiatric group. A possible predictor of failure in rehabilitation programmes?', *British Journal of Psychiatry*, 160, pp. 244–252.

Wykes, T., Reeder, C. and Corner, J. (2000) 'The prevalence and stability of an executive processing deficit, response inhibition, in people with chronic schizophrenia', *Schizophrenia Research*, 46, pp. 241–253.

Wykes, T., Brammer, M., Mellers, J., Bray, P., Reeder, C., Williams, C. and Corner, J. (2002) 'Effects on the brain of a psychological treatment: cognitive remediation therapy: functional magnetic resonance imaging in schizophrenia', *British Journal of Psychiatry*, 181, pp. 144–152.

Wykes, T., Reeder, C., Williams, C., Corner, J., Rice, C. and Everitt, B. (2003) 'Are the effects of cognitive remediation therapy (CRT) durable? Results from an exploratory trial in schizophrenia', *Schizophrenia Research*, 61, pp. 163–174.

Wykes, T., Tarrier, N. and Everitt, B. (2004) 'Cognitive behaviour therapy (CBT) for schizophrenia: the effect of clinical models and methodological rigour', *Schizophrenia Research*, 67, pp. 203–204.

Wykes, T., Reeder, C., Corner, J., Williams, C. and Everitt, B. (1999) 'The effects of neurocognitive remediation on executive processing in patients with schizophrenia', *Schizophrenia Bulletin*, 25, pp. 291–307.

Young, D. and Freyslinger, M. (1995) 'Scaffolded instruction and the remediation of Wisconsin card sorting test deficits in chronic schizophrenia', *Schizophrenia Research*, 16(3), pp. 199–207.

Young, D. A., Zakzanis, K. K., Campbell, Z., Freyslinger, M. G. and Meichenbaum, D. H. (2002) 'Scaffolded instruction remediates Wisconsin card sorting test deficits in schizophrenia: a comparison to other techniques', *Neuropsychological Rehabilitation*, 12, pp. 257–287.

Zahn, T. P. and Carpenter, W. T. (1978) 'Effects of short-term outcome and clinical improvement on reaction-time in acute schizophrenia', *Journal of Psychiatric Research*, 14, pp. 59–68.

Zimmerman, B. J. (1995) 'Self-regulation involves more than metacognition – a social cognitive perspective', *Educational Psychologist*, 30, pp. 217–221.

Zubin, J. (1975) 'Problems of attention in schizophrenia', in M. L. Kietzman, S. Sutton, and J. Zubin (eds) *Experimental Approaches to Psychopathology*. New York: Academic Press.

Zubin, J. and Spring, B. (1977) 'Vulnerability – new view of schizophrenia', *Journal of Abnormal Psychology*, 86, pp. 103–126.

Index

Page entries in **bold** refer to tables. Page entries in *italic* refer to figures